Rescues, Rants, and Researches:
A Re-View of Jay Miller's Writings on Northwest Indien Cultures

by Jay Miller

edited by Darby C. Stapp and Kara N. Powers

Memoir 9

Journal of Northwest Anthropology

Richland, WA

2014

JOURNAL OF NORTHWEST ANTHROPOLOGY
FORMERLY NORTHWEST ANTHROPOLOGICAL RESEARCH NOTES

EDITORS

Darby C. Stapp
Richland, WA

Deward E. Walker, Jr.
University of Colorado

ASSOCIATE EDITORS

C. Melvin Aikens (University of Oregon), Haruo Aoki (University of California), Virginia Beavert (Yakama Tribe), Don E. Dumond (University of Oregon), Don D. Fowler (University of Nevada), Raymond D. Fogelson (University of Chicago), Rodney Frey (University of Idaho), Ronald Halfmoon (Lapwai), Tom F. S. McFeat (University of Toronto), and Jay Miller (Lushootseed Research).

Julia G. Longenecker Operations Manager
Kara N. Powers   Editorial Assistant

Composed by Northwest Anthropology LLC, Richland, WA; Printed by Create Space, On Demand Publishing LLC. Missing issue claim limit 18 months. For back issues and catalogue of prices contact Coyote Press, P O Box 3377, Salinas, CA 93912. <http://www.californiaprehistory.com>.

POLICY

Journal of Northwest Anthropology, published semiannually by Northwest Anthropology LLC in Richland, Washington, is a refereed journal and welcomes contributions of professional quality dealing with anthropological research in northwestern North America. Regular issues are published semiannually with additional memoirs issued as funds are available. Theoretical and interpretive studies and bibliographic works are preferred, although highly descriptive studies will be considered if they are theoretically significant. The primary criterion guiding selection of papers will be how much new research they can be expected to stimulate or facilitate.

SUBSCRIPTIONS

The subscription price is $45.00 U.S. per annum for individuals and small firms, payable in advance, $60.00 for institutional subscriptions, and $30.00 for students with proof of student status. Remittance should be made payable to *Northwest Anthropology LLC.* Subscriptions, manuscripts, change of address, and all other correspondence should be addressed to:

Darby C. Stapp
Journal of Northwest Anthropology
P.O. Box 1721
Richland, WA 99352-1721

telephone (509) 554-0441
e-mail   dstapp@pocketinet.com
website   www.northwestanthropology.com

MANUSCRIPTS

Manuscripts can be submitted in an electronic file in Microsoft Word sent via e-mail or on a CD to the Richland, WA, office. An abstract must accompany each manuscript. Footnotes will be avoided and if used at all will be assembled at the end of the text. Questions of reference and style can be answered by referring to the style guide found on the website or to *Journal of Northwest Anthropology*, 47(1):109–118. Other problems of style can be normally solved through reference to *The Manual of Style,* University of Chicago Press. All illustrative materials (drawings, maps, diagrams, charts, and plates) will be designated "Figures" in a single, numbered series and will not exceed 6 x 9 inches. All tabular material will be part of a separately numbered series of "Tables." Authors will receive one free reprint of articles, memoirs, or full-issue monographs. Additional reprints may be produced by the author; however, they must be exact duplicates of the original and are not to be sold for profit.

Contents

Preferred Reference Style:

Miller, Jay

   2014 Rescues, Rants, and Researches: A Re-View of Jay Miller's Writings on Northwest Indien Cultures. Edited by Darby C. Stapp and Kara N. Powers. *Journal of Northwest Anthropology, Memoir* 9.

PREFACE

We are pleased to bring this collection of Jay Miller's work to our readership. Jay has been contributing to the *Journal of Northwest Anthropology* (*JONA*) and its predecessor, *Northwest Anthropological Research Notes* (*NARN*), for over three decades. His first publication in *NARN* appeared in 1975 and since that time, he has published 18 additional articles. In 2000, Jay became an Associate Editor of the journal.

When we decided in 2012 to begin publishing more *JONA Memoirs*, we proposed the idea of a Jay Miller collection of Northwest research articles. Jay responded with interest and suggested including a number of his new manuscripts. We then worked together over the next year to select the articles and design the memoir, *Rescues, Rants, and Researches: A Re-View of Jay Miller's Writings on Northwest Indien Cultures*.

Jay Miller

Jay's long-term aim has been "to make sense of native North America" in the grand Americanist tradition of synthesizing details into coherent wholes, especially beliefs about inherent intelligence (mind) and life force (*powah*) embodied in the key rituals of their varied universes. Along the way, particular features in immediate danger of loss or, as we more politely say now, "going to sleep," are rescued and shared. In the explosive destruction that accompanied European invasions, pieces became so scattered that only wide-ranging research and reading can locate and piece them back together. The well-known French anthropologist Claude Levi-Strauss, who just died at his century mark, noted that this same technique is used by geologists to analyze and understand cataclysmic events that are eons old and much erased by subsequent erosion and intrusions.

Since living in the Northwest, an additional goal of Jay's has been to reintegrate the study of the Pacific Northwest into the understanding of Native America, using the Redeeming (Spirit Canoe) Rite of Puget Sound Salish to draw out these comparisons. Ironically, while this region is said to rest on the shoulders of comparativists of the stature of Franz Boas and Levi-Strauss, local practitioners have looked either inward or to Asia for context and understanding. Abounding in language families and isolates unique to the region, suggesting origins in the coastal migration rather than the intermountain route during the Ice Age, Edward Sapir and others did propose links to major language stocks of great time depth that can be pursued.

Avoiding alienating academic fads, such as the denial of "tribe" or "culture" as valid social categories or deconstruction of cherished beliefs, Jay has relished being a "throwback" to the original ideals of Boasian anthropology. Generally, after five years of being involved with an elder and community, he begins to publish "stepping stones" based on locally specialized information to lead to an eventual generalized synthesis of that culture. First drafts usually had a bemused or wry tone that occasionally survived to print.

Beginning as an archaeologist on the Anasazi Origins Project (AOP) of Cynthia Irwin-Williams, Jay early on came to realize that ethnographers and linguists had the advantage of asking living humans for answers and interpretations. Thus, beginning as an undergraduate, Jay began the reading of the vast Puebloan literature that led to his doctorate at Rutgers (abetted by Tewa scholar Alfonso Ortiz at Princeton) synthesizing 7000 years of Keresan Pueblo identity, including their likely cultural reinforcement as the lords of Chaco Canyon in the center of their homeland. Intending to stay with the Pueblos, he instead ended up in the Northwest during the school year; with summers in Oklahoma, first among the last of the Lenape or Delaware speakers, especially with the extraordinary Nora Thompson Dean. Time was also spent with Lillie Hoag Whitehorn, which required sorting out her mother's Delaware language and influences from her father's Caddoan ones. Jay was briefly employed by Nevada tribes which took Jay to the Great Basin, where he was drawn to their vital essentials of water and community gatherings (fandangoes). Most recently, Jay has spent his summers among Creek ritualists continuing mound building, with a focus on this oldest of Americanist intellectual concerns: the meaning and purpose of mounds across the Americas, as well as the world.

In the Northwest, women led the way, guided by their devoted training and inspiration from Boas. Viola Garfield and Amelia Susman Schultz oriented Jay to the Tsimshians, where colleagues welcomed him into modern communities in spite of the common remark among departmental "hot shots" that Indianology was no longer fashionable. Erna Gunther introduced Jay to Salishans, but it was the formidable Vi Anderson Hilbert, who was both a state and national treasure, who insisted he help with the recording and preserving of Lushootseed language, culture, and rituals—indigenous to Puget Sound. Jay has continued to finish their projects as a memorial to her efforts.

At Colville, Washington, in the 1980s, Isabel Friedlander Arcasa, who also lived a century, was Jay's guide and mentor on a project supervised by Roderick 'Rick' Sprague. Arcasa also was the first to mention to Jay about a classmate at Fort Spokane named Christine Quintasket, the sister of another of Jay's teachers, Charlie Quintasket. Christine wrote under the pseudonym Mourning Dove, so when Jay was handed the unfinished and unpublished manuscript of what became Christine's autobiography, Jay already had insider information, and two ready advisors to help with editing.

Footnoting *Mourning Dove: A Salishan Autobiography* (Miller 1990) provided a fellowship to the Newberry Library, in Chicago, Illinois, where Jay later joined the staff for five years. While there, after regular trips to Colville, Jay published Christine's Salishan auto-biography, as well as the specific and comparative study of the Redeeming Rite. Following this publication, Jay published a Tsimshian overview (1997b) while teaching grammar to Haida and Tsimshian teachers in training, and then a second book contextualizing the Redeeming within Lushootseed worldview (1999b). Encouraged by Rick Sprague's shared interest in the history of anthropology, Miller began preparing ethnographic papers to "put in the hopper" for publication in *NARN* and later *JONA*, as space became available. Amazingly, this collection does not completely empty the hopper because a few papers remain in development for future issues.

Rescues, Rants, and Researches

Rescues, Rants, and Researches is organized into seven major parts, along with references cited and an index. **Part I, Native Worlds**, contains four articles about cosmology, mythology, and religion. **Part II, Kinship and Society**, has six articles related to social organization, community structure, and individual status. **Part III, Biographies**, contains four articles tracing the lives of individuals important in the Northwest. **Part IV, Food Factors**, has three articles on traditional resources and their use. **Part V, Knowledge Quest**, contains eight articles about the study of Northwest peoples, largely by anthropologists, but others as well. **Part VI, Summing Up**, provides Jay's summary of *Rescues, Rants, and Researche*s. **Part VII, Appendixes**, contains three appendixes of supplementary material. Appendix A is one of Jay's on-going ~ working lists, this one being a preliminary inventory of names, places, and researches useful for research and cultural resource management in Seattle and native Puget Sound; the list is being shared here with the hope that others can and will add to it. Appendix B addresses a frequent frustration of Jay's when seeking a chronology of local archaeological research; drawing on the tribal concept of "the winter count," Jay has compiled this *Arky Epitaph* ("memorial memory") of people, places, and archaeological projects. Appendix C is a listing of Jay's various publications dealing with Native tribes and ideas all across North America, mostly in the Northwest, Northeast and Southwest.

Readers will note the atypical spelling of *Indien* in the title and text. The decision by Jay to use this spelling for the natives of the Americas was inspired by several overlapping experiences, reinforced by working extensively with elders of many tribes, all of whom insisted on being called "Indiens." In particular, teaching in bilingual Canada, the advantages of the French spelling of Indien, for both the noun and the adjective, became readily apparent to Jay. On top of that, grappling with the wonderful book on Creek culture, *A Sacred Path: The Way of the Muscogee Creeks*, by the late Jean Hill Chandhuri, edited by her husband, Joytotpaul Chaudhuri, PhD, a native of India, immediately showed Jay the advantages of changed final vowel to distinguish source from editor (Chandhuri and Chandhuri 2001). Once the spelling was accepted within the title of one of Jay's papers by an academic journal, the way was cleared for its utility.

Readers will also note that native words for indigenous concepts, categories, and things have been italicized. Native words for proper nouns such as individuals, groups, and places have not been italicized, however, to respect the integrity of these native languages and avoid interference with English grammatical rules.

The Future

Our goal at the *Journal of Northwest Anthropology* is to publish material that will stimulate or facilitate new anthropological and ethnohistoric research. We have easily met this goal in producing *Memoir 9, Rescues, Rants, and Researches: A Re-View of Jay Miller's Writings on Northwest Indien Cultures*. We know our readers will agree, and we look forward to the future research that will be generated and the manuscripts that will be submitted to us for publication.

Darby C. Stapp and Kara N. Powers
Journal of Northwest Anthropology
December 2013

ACKNOWLEDGMENTS

The author Jay Miller wishes to thank the following people and institutions for their aid and support throughout the years in making this memoir and Northwest research possible.

For aid with Salish research, it is a pleasure to thank Vi and Don Hilbert for all their help and encouragement, along with their family of Lois, Ron, Jay, Bedelia, Jill, John, and all the grandchildren. Within the larger Lushootseed family, thanks goes to Peggy Dunn, Alf Shepard, Robbie Rudine, Janet Yoder, Pam Cahn (*wiw'su*), Carolyn Marr, Brad Burns, Carolyn Michael, Barbara Iliff Brotherton, Dean Reiman, and many more.

Among other degreed members, appreciation goes to Drs. Thom Hess, Pam Amoss, Dale Kinkade, Laurel Sercombe, William Seaburg, Dawn (łup) Bates, Andie Palmer, Robin Wright, Bill Holm, Greg Watson, Bob and Laura Dassow Walls, Mary Laya, John Adams, Sally Anderson, Astrida Blukis Onat, Ann Bates, Carol Eastman, Fr. Patrick Twohy, Viola Garfield, and Erna Gunther.

Among the native community, while they cannot all be named, or wish to be, I can single out the late Isadore Tom, Ed Davis, Lawrence Webster, Martin Sampson, Susie Sampson Peter, Morris Dan, Theresa Willup, Helen Ross, Lottie Sam, Walter Sam, and Dewey Mitchell. Younger members include Lona Wilbur, Dobie Tom, and the families of Andy Fernando and Jack and Deborah Fiander. Blue, Sherry, and Sanger Clark provided strong support.

Many people have helped me to understand the complexities of Tsimshian culture. In particular, at Hartley Bay, these were Chief John and Helen Clifton; Ernest, Lynne, Cameron and Jodie Hill; Ernest and Margie Hill, Sr.; and Mildred Wilson. At Klemtu, my teachers were Violet and Peter Neasloss, Chief Tom Brown, and others. Other colleagues include John and Luceen Dunn, Susan Marsden, Marjorie Halpin, Margaret Seguin, Carol Sheehan, Bill Holm, Robin Wright, Viola Garfield, Amelia Susman Schultz, Jean Mulder, Marie-Lucie Tarpent, Bruce Rigsby, Dale Kinkade, Jay Powell, Vickie Jensen, Guy Gibeau, and the late Stanley Newman.

Students in the Simon Fraser University, Native Language Teacher Program at Prince Rupert clarified and expanded my thinking: Cameron and Eva-Ann Hill, Nadine Robinson, Mel Tait, Maureen Yeltatzie, Beatrice Skog, Isabelle Hill, Pansy Collison, Deborah Schmakeit, Marilyn Bryant, Karla Gamble, and Shani Heal. Mary Tomlinson, Mercedes de la Nuez, and Thomas Perry helped me smooth out complications with Canadian bureaucracy.

At the beginning, support came from James and Charlotte Toulouse, Carmie Lynn, Laura Lee, Charlotte Mary, Jeremy Alan, Tamaya Lynn, Trent, Marie, Ella Mae, and others. As an undergraduate at the University of New Mexico, Stanley Newman, W.W. "Nibs" Hill, Philip Bock, Bruce Rigsby, and, especially, Florence Hawley Ellis and Mary Elizabeth Smith set my academic course. Outside the classroom, Cynthia Irwin-Williams and the Anasazi Origins Project gave me first-hand experience as an archaeologist on Sia Pueblo Land. Later, as an advisor at Salmon Ruin, I was introduced to Chaco outliers and reoccupations.

As a graduate student at Rutgers and Princeton, my teachers were Robin Fox, Yehudi Cohen, Warren Shapiro, and Mark Leone. Margaret Bacon, Jane Lancaster, and Martin Silverman gave encouragement. Alfonso Ortiz, Esther Goldfrank and Karl Wittfogel, Elizabeth Brandt, Wick Miller, Tom Windes, Anna Sofaer, and John Stein provided insights.

My parents and siblings aided as needed, as did fellow students Janet Pollak, Michele Teitelbaum, Cheryl Wase, Edward Deal, Nina Versaggi, Nancy Trembley, Ken and Mark Wilkie, Corinne Black, Karen and Tom Reynolds, John and Luceen Dunn and family, Glenn and Dorothy Williams and family, Andrew and Nancy Core and family, and Roland Wildman.

Support also came from Marilyn Richen, Ann Schuh, Bob and Christine Keyes-Back, Tom and Donna Steinburn, Nancy Griffin, and, especially, Monday Nite. At the *Journal of Northwest Anthropology*, Darby Stapp, Kara Powers, and Julie Longenecker have brought it all to fruition.

Darby Stapp and Kara Powers, editors of this memoir, would like to thank Julie Longenecker, Dave Payson, James Knobbs, Kimberly Sutherland, Laura Hanses, and Deward E. Walker, Jr., for their assistance in putting this volume together.

DEDICATION

To the Grand Dames ~ Amelia, Erna, Esther, Isabel, Ruth, Viola, and Vi.

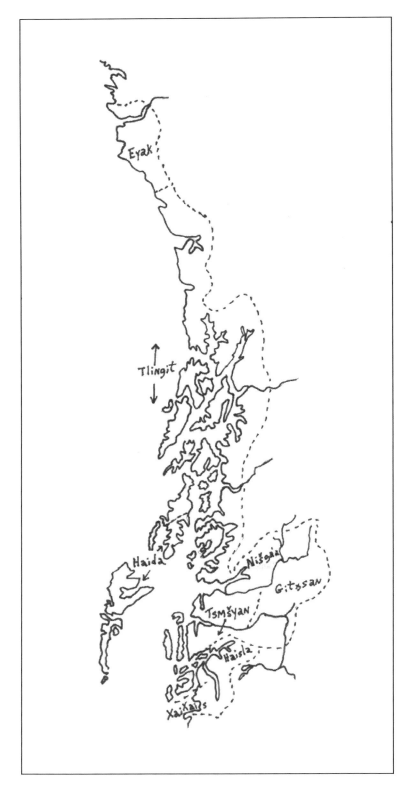

Map 1. Map of northern portion of Northwest Coast, showing general locations of native groups mentioned in text (drawn by Jay Miller).

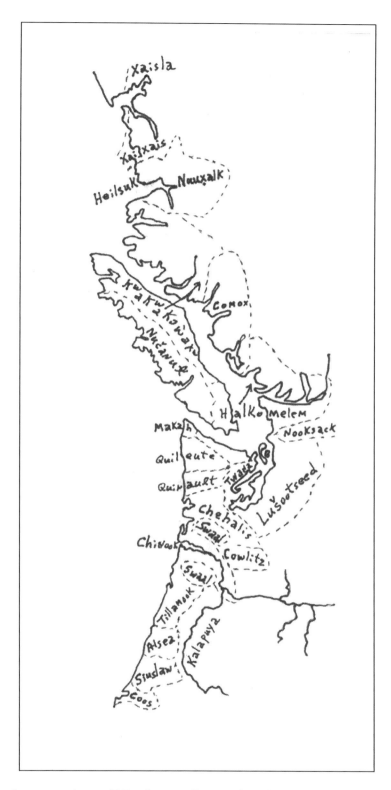

Map 2. Map of southern portion of Northwest Coast, showing general locations of native groups mentioned in text (drawn by Jay Miller).

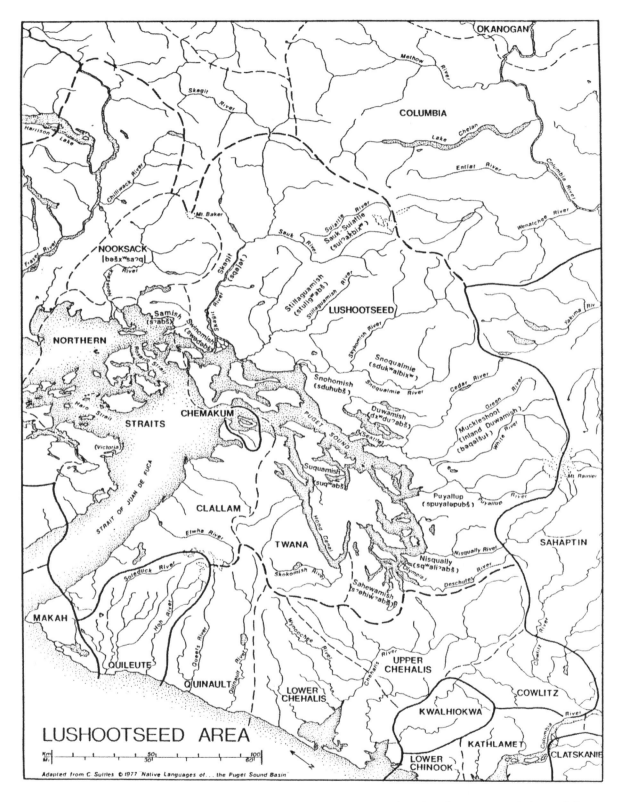

Map 3. Map of Lushootseed area showing general locations of native languages (adapted from Suttles 1977 by Laura Dassow Walls).

PART I. NATIVE WORLDS

Together with its sheer arrogance, the phrase "The New World" resonates with bitter irony because American natives had to regather and remake their worlds in the aftermath of both willing and unwilling destructions. What happened to Native America was more than a decimated shattering; it was a massive explosion, sending bits, pieces, and peoples across the continent. To make coherent deductions about native systems, themes, and variations, therefore, requires finding and reassembling best cases or reports covering the entire area. To fill in gaps, judicious use can be made by comparisons to global examples illustrative of typical human solutions or responses. Our overall intent is more than a flat jigsaw puzzle. Rather it is something like a whole pot that forcefully exploded into bits, pieces, and contents. From telling fragments such as bits of its rims, curves, and bottoms; its designs, shape, and function can be determined with likely probability.

For the Pacific Northwest, moreover, that reassembling is complicated by long-range influences from China as contrasted with influences from Mexico for the rest of the continent. Thus, Raven as transformer, split animal images, ranked classes, and Heaven as deity are transPacific. Yet Northwest trade networks crossed the Rockies to reach across the continent, spreading dentalia and salmon flour. In recent centuries, nothing better represents these transcontinental routes than the spread of the horse, together with its name *kiutan* in Chinuk Wawa, derived from Spanish.

Indeed, it is ideas, best expressed in native languages, which survive longest in the onslaught of commercialization. Mythology gives them coherence, and so this collection begins with my summary of that of the Northwest, followed by filling a gap among academics with regard to the significance of the transformer Misp[h] and his twin. The blendings of old and new worlds are featured in the next articles concerned with interpreting an eclipse seen at Makah. Lastly, my present understanding of the Redeeming Rite is reviewed. Distinctive of Puget Sound, it unified Lushootseeds and allowed them to hold their own in terms of intertribal prestige. Wherever possible, all of the other sections will also end with an article set at or near Seattle.

An Overview of Northwest Coast Mythology

Recognizing a lynch pin within a greater World system is especially rewarding. For example, this overview of Northwest mythology was long a working, on-going research project. I actually began my book on the Tsimshian (Miller 1997b) by writing out the crucial epics (*adaaxw*) at the heart of this culture; then I wrote the study around them. The eventual spur to pull this overview together was a request from Wayne Suttles to provide the chapter on mythology for the Northwest Coast (Volume 7) of the *Handbook of North American Indians*. My chapter was in review when Wayne called to say Claude Levi-Strauss wanted to do the chapter so mine was superseded and I put it away. Levi-Strauss never did the chapter, and Dell Hymes took it over, providing a useful review of his own specialized work on native ethnopoetics. When my chapter was eventually published in *NARN*, Dell complimented me on it, but I never told him the back-story.

Missing Misp[h]: Restor(y)ing the Transformer of Tsamosans of Coastal Washington

Already "in the hopper" for eventual *JONA* publication, the overlooked Transformer ~ Changer known as Misp[h] finally gets his due here, along with his twin brother. Had Thelma Adamson not been institutionalized for her long life, he would have long since been as well known as Moon, Raven, Coyote, Mink, Bluejay, and other local culture heroes.

James Swan and Makah Cosmology: A Clarification

Reconnecting the "teachable moment" by James Swan at Makah's Neah Bay during the lunar eclipse was predictably my first foray into Northwest ethnography. As I was leaving New Jersey to move to Seattle, my landlord's son introduced me to "an Indian woman" from Washington State who went to his church. He was an Italian Presbyterian, but stranger things happened in Jersey (long before the Sopranos). I phoned and made arrangements to visit her; I already had a distant family connection to Yakama, and thought that it might build into local research interests. My original intention was to concentrate on Tsimshian on the northern coast because I had studied the language with faculty at New Mexico, and became friends with married graduate students who undertook dissertation research on its language loss, at a nadir before its enthusiastic rebound under the Sm'algyax Language Authority. I also knew that Viola Garfield, who had long studied their kinship and clan system, was retired from the University of Washington and living in Seattle, where she could advise me. Having already worked with Keresan Pueblos in the Southwest and Delawares in Oklahoma (after they were visiting homelands in New Jersey), I was drawn to matrilineal peoples.

In New Jersey, over cake and coffee at her dining room table, "the Indien woman" explained that she was a Makah, from the far northwest tip of the U.S. She mentioned Makah Days as a public event I should attend once I got to Seattle, expecting a five-hour drive to the coast. As we talked, her stern husband stood by and listened. She was welcoming and he was not. As the conversation went on, it came out that he was then a Jersey State Trooper, but they had met when he was an MP at the tiny Air Force station on the Makah Reservation. They were among the first modern-day interracial couples to marry, though local resentment accounted for their move back to his family in Jersey.

Intrigued to know more about the Makah, I began reading all I could find, and quickly made the connection between the two quotes that are the basis for this article. Once I found *NARN*, co-editor Rick Sprague accepted the paper quickly. James Swan and his diaries at the University of Washington were then receiving considerable attention (McDonald 1972), which peaked with the publication of *Winter Brothers* by Ivan Doig (1980).

I did attend Makah Days within weeks of my arrival in Seattle, and, since I had just met Erna Gunther, I brought her greetings to several of the elders. She had spent years there collecting what we would now call traditional ecological knowledge (TEK) and genealogies. During later trips to Neah Bay, I met the woman from Jersey and learned that her husband had taken the job of chief of police and a son had a scholarship to Dartmouth. The Ozette site was being "dug" (with water hoses), which eventually resulted in the museum and cultural center in Neah Bay. Young Doctor is highlighted there as the man who first made a distinction between ceremonial art for the Makah community and secular art for sale, particularly to tourists, visitors, and collectors. He carved and did woodwork, as women maintained a strong tradition of basketry. A featured form was the *wabet*, a wide round basket to carry family dishes and cutlery to feasts.

Native Healing in Puget Sound

More personally, near Seattle, while Vi Hilbert (see Part III) and I were visiting elders, we met Ed Davis, who was then in his eighties, a strong Shaker, and a moral force in the troubled Snoqualmie Tribe. After we heard him describe being an errand runner as a boy during preparations for a Redeeming Canoe Rite at Lake Sammamish, I was motivated to assemble all known accounts of this distinctive Puget Sound rite. Long after he died, I learned from other academics who had interviewed him later that as a young man Ed was himself the patient at the very last of these healings in 1908. This article summarizes what is currently known of this rite.

AN OVERVIEW OF NORTHWEST COAST MYTHOLOGY[a]

ABSTRACT

Past and present research on the oral literature, particularly mythology, of the Pacific Northwest or Northwest Coast is reviewed in terms of significant features of style, content, and social context, and particular series of protagonists such as tricksters like Raven and the various transformers. A bibliographic essay is included.

Native peoples of the Northwest Coast (NWC) have a rich and varied oral literature, as suggested by separate words for 'myths' as distinct from 'stories' in these languages (Boas 1916b:565; Ballard 1929:142; de Laguna 1972:839).[1] Boas (1916b:565) noted that a myth pertained "to a period when the world was different from what it is now," and purported to detail how an already-existing world was modified during the Myth Age. There was little if any interest in how this world was itself created. The Myth Age has been described as prehistoric (Boas 1929:407) and as chaotic and precultural (Jacobs 1959a). However, the Myth Age world can be better described as inchoate, exaggerated, and undifferentiated into current categories and forms.

Spatially the world of myth and the world of the present are the same because events mentioned in the myths permanently altered the terrain in ways that account for existing features. For the northern tribes and some Oregon Athapascans, the primordeal world was in twilight or darkness until daylight was found, stolen, or simply dawned. Among the more northerly tribes the protagonist called Raven arranged to steal and scatter the luminaries and other existing features. Further south, other protagonists, generally called Transformers or Changers, modified the Myth Age world. For example, along the Washington coast, Transformers found people walking upside-down and set them upright. As Boas (1929:409–410) noted, Raven as a character altered the world in his selfishness and greediness, benefiting people only inadvertently, incidentally, or accidentally. The Transformers, however, recognized the existence of people and often accomplished their feats in order to spite or thwart people.

Another feature of the undifferentiated Myth Age was the lack of any clear distinctions between humans, animals, and supernaturals. All of these intermarried and had basically shimmering human forms, although some wear animal or bird skins over these. While the myths involve beings called Beaver, Raven, Ice, Southwind, and so forth; these should be viewed as anthropomorphized characters having animal or climatic names and attributes. Animals as such did not exist until the Myth Age was transformed into the contemporary era. This transformation might be gradual, as in the Raven series, or instantaneous, as among the Twana Salish who described the world as 'capsizing' (by analogy to a canoe, Elmendorf 1960:536), sometime after the Transformer had turned the anthropomorphized prototypes into representations of modem animal species. We will consider these myth series or cycles in more detail below, after we treat some of the more important aspects of the style and content of NWC mythology.

---

[a] This article was previously published in *Northwest Anthropological Research Notes*, 23(2):125–141 (1989).

Style

Any discussion of NWC mythology must keep in mind that our myth collections are richer and fuller for the northern, matrilineal Tlingit, Haida, and Tsimshian; less so for the central Wakashan (Nootka and Kwakiutl) and Salishan tribes; and meager for the southern Penutian and Athapascan Oregon tribes. There is a slight possibility that the entire published record represents an unintentionally selective range for a tribe, kin unit, or ethnic group.

While the myths were presented as separate or discrete events or episodes, it is important to remember that they were drawn from a common fund retained by the members, or more especially the elite, of a society. The characters, events, and places in different myths actually represent only pieces of an integrated mythic fabric. For example, Boas (1916a) was able to present an overview of traditional Tsimshian world view by analyzing a large collection of myths recorded by Henry Tate, a Tsimshian. While Marius Barbeau (1917) criticized the collection because Tate's status as a commoner (and thereby not entitled to the sacred histories *[adaawx]* of noble houses) meant that these myths had to be unjustly vague as to ownership and social context, and Maud (1989) argued that the texts were recorded first in English; the data on world view nevertheless speak for themselves.

Accordingly, the earth is a flat disk supported on a pole resting on the chest of *Am'ala'* ('smokehole'), who replaced a previous supernatural. In the Myth Age, all of the future people and animals lived together at Prairie Town on the upper Skeena River. After a flood, everyone left Prairie Town and settled in separate towns or houses on the earth. The animals retained their human forms in their own settlements. When a male bear had his fishing line break or a female bear had her tumpline snap, it meant that they had been killed by a human hunter; only to return to Bear Town a few days later provided that they had been treated with proper ritual by the hunter and his kin. On the edge of the earth, Pestilence Chief, his daughter, and maimed people lived together. The ocean surrounded the earth and in it lived fish and sea mammals. The killer-whales divided into the same four semi-moieties (phratries) as the Tsimshian themselves and displayed their crest membership by the form of their dorsal fins. Across the ocean are different worlds inhabited by anthropomorphic beings such as dwarfs, ghosts, and salmon. In the Salmon Country, each species has its own town, with the Spring Salmon farthest away and the Silver, Steelhead, Humpback, Coho, and Trout successively closer to the ocean and the earth. Over-arching this terrestrial realm is the Sky World, from which various supernaturals, generally called 'shining youths,' have descended to the accompaniment of four flashes of lightning and four claps of thunder in order to help or to marry a mortal.

The populations of all of these Tsimshian worlds mirrored NWC concerns with rank in that distinctions between nobles, commoners, and slaves were either specified or implied. The various details or descriptions of these characters, places, attributes, and events were embodied in different myths; yet it was only in the context of the entire mythology that these pieces made sense. The mythic totality was more than the sum of its parts because it could constantly generate new variants of the mythology. The separate myths were especially important, however, for providing stylistic content, and social information.

Stylistic features of NWC mythology included conventional beginnings and endings, pattern numbers, performance styles, and metaphorical usages and themes. In the instances where researchers have thought to ask, conventionalizations have been recorded. Jacobs (1972) was an especially important source for stylistics in native Washington and Oregon. Not every myth necessarily included them; however, they were generally understood by implication. A common beginning immediately introduced the protagonist of a myth and/or other participants. Endings usually conveyed a sense of finality unless it was a long myth occupying several evening recitations, in which case only a halt was indicated each evening before the last one. Our best examples are drawn from the Clackamas Chinook (Jacobs 1949:221) for whom the usual beginning specified that an individual or group lived together in a house or village and the common ending was the reduplication story, story or the indication "the people are coming soon."

Four was the pattern number for the reoccurrence of events or individuals among the northern tribes and five was the pattern number among the southern ones. The Tillamook, however, used four repetitions for female characters and five for males, while three was sometimes used in northwestern Washington (Jacobs 1972).

Performance styles were seldom recorded. One Yakutat Tlingit told Raven myths with "the most energetic sound effects: tappings, slurps, belches, explosive pows, and dramatic dialogue" (de Laguna 1972:841). The animal character called Raven by the Lushootseed of Puget Sound speaks with an intense nasal quality when mimicked by narrators. Recitations were punctuated by a distinctive sound or response which indicated the continued interest of the audience. Some myths include brief songs which belonged to specific characters. Robert Miller (1952) for the Makah and McClellan (1970) for the Tlingit and others have discussed the effect which the life circumstances of a narrator can have on the order and the performance of stories.

Metaphors were not frequent but were exemplified by the ravenous gluttony of Raven for the northern tribes and by the equation of long hair with beauty and of baldness or pendulous breasts with ugliness among southern tribes. One Coquille Athapascan speaker used metaphors such as the "deer ran like thunder" (Jacobs 1972).

An important literary device was reversal (Miller 1988). The seasonal and diurnal cycles were reversed for the land of the living and that of the dead. Animals appeared as humans in their own villages, but as animals around people. In the example of the Salmon Country given above, reversal was important. The Spring Salmon sent scouts up the Skeena River to see if what they called their salmon were spawning. At an affirmative report, the Springs started out announcing the good news in the other Salmon towns as they passed them. The Silvers, Humpbacks, and Dogs said they would follow shortly; the Cohos that they would wait until fall; the Trout asked to accompany the Springs; and these two together continue on to meet the Steelhead who were already returning from the Skeena. What the Salmon called their salmon, humans called cottonwood leaves which have fallen into the river (1916b:454).

Content

The content of these myths expressed vital NWC social and environmental concerns. Among the former were rank and wealth, and among the latter were the sea, the forest, and the weather.

Slaves and commoners, if they appeared at all, were superficial in the mythology. The very performance of various exploits served to indicate that someone was wiser, stronger, and wealthier than other stock characters. A protagonist might appear poor, orphaned, and dirty; but he, or rarely she, was eventually revealed as wise and/or wealthy: a member of the elite and as such the worthy recipient of supernatural aid, gifts, and power. Only the Chinook character called Bluejay constantly showed presumption by trying to outdo people of higher status. Under-pinning the elite status was the concept of wealth as it was reiterated in material terms. Copper, dentalia, and abalone had great value along the entire coast. Among northern tribes were found such wealth-conferring supernaturals as a Beaver with copper eyes, claws, ears, and teeth. The power of such metaphors was indicated by the fact the Tlingitized Tagish attributed the famous Klondike Gold Rush of 1898 to an Indian's encounter with Wealth Woman, who had gold fingernails and wore martin skins, dentalia, and copper (McClellan 1963).

The great concern of all coastal peoples with the sea was exemplified by visits to the Undersea World for the purpose of acquiring supernatural aid or a spouse. In the process, the shore terrain was described and listeners were assured that the beings below the sea recognized the same social ranks and economic values as do humans. Among the noble spouses of humans were Sea Otter, Frog, Seal, Salmon, and so forth. The human married to them generally arranged for her or his kin to receive sea products, such as fish and whales, in fulfillment of expected marital exchanges.

The dangers of the sea and also of the impenetrable forest bramble were represented by various monsters forming an interlinked series from the Land Otter People of the north to the Sasquatch or Wild Man of the central area. For the Tlingit, Haida, and Tsimshian, Land Otter Men captured drowned humans and metamorphosed them into Land Otters with human fingernails. Land Otters were especially feared because of their ability to mimic the appearance of someone that a human alone in the woods happened to think about or long for. The Kwakiutl recognized a Wild Man called Bukwus, who captured people by offering them food and who was associated with a crew of Land Otters who appeared as the victim's relatives, minks who appeared as paddles, and a skate who appeared as the canoe itself (Boas 1935:146). The Fraser River Salish have a similar being called Sasquatch, who stole women and food.

Concern with the weather, sometimes life-threatening on the coast, was represented by such personifications as Fog Woman, the Four Winds, and the Thunderbirds. Some myths also implied that the native life-style could not be sustained or successful if fair weather had not been introduced during the Myth Age.

Many of the motif distributions on the North Pacific Coast have been worked out by Thompson (1966) in conjunction with his more general concern with North American folklore. The NWC shared with the rest of North America such motifs as the origin of death (Thompson 1966:284 #151), the deluge (286 #51), misplaced genitalia (288 #57), bungling host (301 #103), vagina dentata (309 #115), star husband (330 #193), Orpheus (337 #215), and the rolling head (342 #238). Particular motifs of more limited distribution which the NWC shared with other culture areas included a person swallowed by a monster becoming bald—shared with Siberia (322 #166a); a woman stolen by killerwhales—shared with the Plateau (342 #235); a dog husband—shared with the Arctic, Subarctic, Plateau, and Plains (347 #247); and the princess who rejected her cousin—shared with the Plains and Southwest (349 #256). Motifs or motif versions specifically localized in the NWC included the variants of the heat test motif of a burning food test for the Haida and of the swallowing of red-hot rocks for the Haida and Comox (312 #120a, b); miraculous creation motif variants of birth from tears along the northern coast or from body secretions among the Haida and Kwakiutl (323 #166a, b); the motif of the marooned hunter on the northern coast (326 #175); and the motif of the death of Pitch by exposure to the sun, specifically localized on the north and central coast (356 #285). Randall (1949) has also compared the Cinderella theme as it occurred on the NWC and in central Europe. The distinctive NWC series dealing with Raven, Mink, and Bluejay will be treated separately below.

Social Context

Much of the vitality of these myths can also be attributed to their social context. A full command of the myth traditions of a town, social group, household, or tribe was the mark of a properly educated member of the elite. Boys destined to be chiefs, social leaders, or advisors were carefully instructed in the myths associated with their group. These were generally conveyed at what Jacobs (1972) called "predawn pedagogic sessions." For a native perspective on the instructive value of legends and stories, Hilbert's (1985a) preface is superb.

While myths could be casually discussed at any time, their telling was closely circumscribed. Winter was the proper season, the elderly the proper raconteurs, and during the evening when the people were weather bound, the proper time. Among the Tlingit, myths were not recited during social events such as potlatches. The educated already knew them, asserting their shared nobility through oratorical allusions, songs, dramatic dances, art works, witty remarks, moral admonitions, and apt proverbs derived from the myths (de Laguna 1972:839). Myths, or rather particular myth versions, were considered social property, at least in the north. Garfield (1953) noted that the story of the man called Kats, the hunter who married a Bear woman, belonged to the Tlingit Teqeodi clan and to certain Nishka Tsimshian and Haida lineages who claimed Kats as an ancestor. An exemplary collection of Tlingit house stories [*at.oow* owned art form, Tlingit crest], presented in ethnopoetic format, comprise the first volume of Tlingit oral literature published by the Dauenhauers (1987).

It is now appropriate to return to the great mythic series so closely associated with the NWC, although they are not exclusive to this region. These were generally called the Raven series and the Transformer series, with the Trickster series either forming a part of the Raven series in the north or a separate series involving Mink or Bluejay in the central area.

The Raven Series

The wide appeal of the protagonist called Raven was bound up with the complexity of his character, allowing an audience the possibility of both identity and catharsis with Raven. Some of his important characteristics were superhuman powers and abilities, social license, and entertaining incongruities. Raven accomplished the gross distinctions of the modern world by skill, cunning, and incredible feats. Humans could identify with his omnipotence and craftiness. In this guise, Raven was a Transformer. However, Raven was also a Trickster when he was a bumbling host, an amorous interloper, and a devious glutton. Then Raven had complete license, as did the raconteur, to say the unsayable, plot the unthinkable, exalt the lowly, and defame the mighty. This was the cathartic ability of Raven. Further, Raven myths included some delightful paradoxes, as when he convinced Bear that a stone had insulted it, or when Raven was swallowed by a whale and lived inside it by stripping off meat and cooking it. In a rather full discussion of the Raven series, Boas (1916b:567-723) indicated that "Raven was really an umbrella term for many different names associated with a protagonist shared on both shores of the North Pacific."

There was some disagreement as to the proper sequence of episodes in the Raven series. They did not seem to be free-floating. Boas (1916b:562) believed that a sequence could be established by a comparative study of the relative frequency, and thus popularity, of the episodes as found in published collections. Louis Shotridge, a Tlingit, said that the serious or Transformer episodes should occur in a logical order, while the humorous or Trickster myths could occur anywhere that a narrator felt his audience would appreciate them (Boas 1916b:582, footnote 1). Garfield (1953) made the point that Raven's own life cycle established a chronology for the series. An additional complication was that, while the outline of the entire series may have been generally known, the particular details and episodes were the property of particular social groups, who distinguished their privilege by varying the incidents.

Raven was born in the sky of an incestuous or an unfaithful mother. He descended to earth as a Shining Youth, but became humanized both by a ritual adoption as well as by eating scabs. The overall effect of this was to make him voracious, which set the tenor and motivation for his subsequent adventures. Oblivious of humans, his greed led him to differentiate the world by tricking various owners into releasing the Sun, Moon, and Stars, Fresh Water, Candlefish, the Tides, Fair Weather, Fire, Death, Salmon, and Land. He gave many animals their present attributes, painting colors on birds and cutting out the tongue of Cormorant. In still other episodes,

Raven was humiliated, teased, and maligned. Always, he sought food. Finally, Raven moved out to sea, invited the sea monsters to the first potlatch, feasted and entertained them, and either received their promise not to harm humans or turned them and himself into stone.

The Transformer Series

As the Raven series presented the gross differentiations of the world, so the Transformer series presented a concern with details and particulars. While Raven usually worked alone, there were usually multiple Transformers, whom Melville Jacobs (1959b:196, 232–236) preferred to call Announcers, although only one was named and the others were ancillary twins or team brothers (Boas 1916b:586).

The Transformers might simply appear on earth, descend from the sky, or be the offspring of marriages between animals and humans. Transformer myths ranged from the Straits of Georgia to the Oregon coast. Throughout this area, the Trickster myths formed a distinct series featuring Mink toward the north and Bluejay toward the south. The Trickster series concentrated on the amorous adventures and improprieties of these protagonists.

In contrast, the Transformer traveled around meeting the ancestors of humans and animals, interacting with them, tricking them, and leaving them permanently changed in preparation for the advent of the present world. The Transformers created features of the contemporary landscape, legitimized the ancestry of names and privileges, invented useful tools, and gave animals their present forms and attributes. For example, the Transformers met people sharpening weapons, intent on killing those who were changing the world, and used the same weapons to transform the people into animals. The rectal insertion of a spear created mink or otter, while that of a knife or paddle created beaver.

Finally, the Transformers left, replacement teams of Transformers no longer arrived, or, according to the Quinault and Quileute, the Transformers turned to stone near the mouth of the Columbia River.

Conclusions

In addition to the major myth series, NWC mythology abounds in various incidents of the Myth Age which testify to the importance of interpersonal behaviors and processes, such as marriage, sex, aggression, altruism, and exchange. In general, the mythology as a whole can be said to reinforce traditional concern with wealth, rank, and prestige; to codify the knowledge of the world and the larger cosmology; to suggest alternative solutions, whether negatively or positively valued, to cultural concerns and paradoxes; to educate youngsters of the elite in the proper names, crests, privileges, and etiquette of their station; to entertain people when they were weather bound; and to permit an emotional outlet for both narrators and audience. In a majority of cases, moreover, these stories teach by negative example. As de Laguna remarked:

> Narrative, rather than exposition or abstract explanation, was the form in which the conceptual schema and the values of the social and moral order were verbally expressed. (de Laguna 1972:838)

Essay on Sources

The interpretation of Northwest Coast literature displays the heavy stamp of four scholars: Franz Boas, Melville Jacobs, Claude Levi-Strauss, and Dell Hymes.

Relying on Native folklore collectors like Henry Tate and William Beynon for the Tsimshian and George Hunt for the Kwagyuł ~ Kwakwaka'wakw, Boas amassed a great store of myths and stories. Around the turn of this century, mythology became a central concern of the Boas research strategy because it was distinctive of different cultural backgrounds, readily acquired in linguistic transcription and English translation, and provided a strongly empirical means for tracing the historical movements of traits and motifs. Boas held the opinion that Culture was "reflected" in mythology both in terms of detailed ethnographic information encapsulated within the content of myths and in terms of the secondary explanations which the myths themselves provided to integrate traits from disparate historical sources into the coherent patterns of a culture (Spier 1931). In his classic account of Tsimshian mythology, Boas was able to draw from the myths valid ethnographic information on house construction and occupation, social structure, kinship, prestige system, rituals, religion, supernaturals and cosmology, while at the same time suggesting an interior origin for the Tsimshian which more recent research has discounted. Most recently, the careful ethnopoetic translations of stories by John Dunn (1988) has revitalized Tsimshian research, which has been further encouraged by the publication of Marius Barbeau and William Beynon materials (Cove 1985; MacDonald and Cove 1987).

In the mid-twentieth century, Melville Jacobs used the fine linguistic texts he had previously collected to probe deeply into the psychological dimensions of mythology. Using myths and, most particularly, myth characters, he drew inferences about the anxiety-provoking conflicts inherent in Clackamas Chinook and other cultures. He strongly argued for the equation of mythology not with poetry or narrative but with drama—laconic characterizations rich in aesthetic and emotional complexity. Jacobs was a student of Boas and provided the finest evaluation of Boas' work in folklore (Jacobs 1959c). Moreover, he wrote, late in life, two articles for a popular audience which are must reading for anyone seeking an overview of Native mythologies from Washington state and Oregon (Jacobs 1967, 1972). William Seaburg is publishing remaining manuscripts by the Jacobses.

By the late 1960s, Levi-Strauss had refined and focused his methods of structural analysis to produce four massive volumes (mythologiques, mytho-logics) devoted to myths from Native South and North America, beginning with an Amazonian myth about a marooned egg-gatherer and ending with a volume considering myths from the Northwest Coast (Levi-Strauss 1971, 1981). Throughout, he showed that mythologies represent rational attempts to consider alternative cultural strategies, to intellectually solve paradoxes inherent between real and ideal behaviors, and to work out elaborate affirmations that the world is logical. He attributed to this "mytho-logic" the full canonical power that is reserved for "science" by the industrial nations.

The current leading figure is Dell Hymes (1965, 1968, 1975a, 1975b, 1976, 1981), who has concentrated his attention on Chinookan mythology to provide reinterpretations and insights into performance and ethnopoetic measures overlooked by earlier researchers.

Building upon his insights have been the work of Dale Kinkade (1983) for Salish texts and John Dunn (1988) for Tsimshian ones. Publications by the Dauenhauers (1987), the husband is a poet and the wife a native speaker of Tlingit, set a new standard. Further, the book by Hilbert (1985b) combines careful translations, some in measured verse, with the insights of a cultural insider.

The majority of Northwest Coast oral literature collections have been published in periodical series founded by Franz Boas and his students. Thus, *Columbia University Publications in Anthropology* include important text collections by Frachtenberg from Coos (1913) and Lower Umpqua (1914), by Andrade on Quileute (1931), and by Boas from Kwakiutl (1910, 1935a, 1935b, 1943) and Bella Bella (1928) and on Kwakiutl religion (1930). This series is notable for close-translations of native language texts on the same or adjoining pages, but the texts lack abstracts and performance annotations.

Bureau of American Ethnology, Bulletins include folklore from the Chinook and Kathlamet Chinook (Boas 1894, 1901), Tsimshian (Boas 1902), Skidegate Haida (Swanton 1905a, b), Tlingit at Sitka and Wrangel (Swanton 1909), Alsea (Frachtenberg 1920), and some Nootkan and Quileute material (Densmore 1939). The series is characterized by generally close English translations from native texts, which are usually provided together with short abstracts. There are no details on performance. Among the *Annual Reports of the Bureau of American Ethnology,* the 31st includes the classic Boas (1916b) study of Tsimshian and comparative NWC mythology.

The *University of Washington Publications in Anthropology* contain fairly close English translations by Ballard (1927, 1929) for Puget Sound Salish myths, by Gunther (1927) for Klallam, by Jacobs for Coos (1940), Kalapuya (1949), and Clackamas Chinook (1960), and by Spier and Sapir (1930) for Wishram and Wasco. These volumes generally include some performance and life history material on the narrators.

The *Anthropological Papers of the American Museum of Natural History* published mythology compiled by Boas from the Bella Coola (1898b) and by Boas and George Hunt (Boas 1905, 1906) for the Kwagyuł ~ Kwakwaka'wakw. The Swanton (1905a) summary of Haida ethnography includes abstracts of his Skidegate, Masset, and Kaigani Haida texts.

The *Memoirs of the American Folklore Society* include an uneven volume on Coast Salish myths (Adamson 1934), one on the Bella Coola (Boas 1932), and the final statement on the Kwakiutl by Boas (1935a): *Kwakiutl Culture as Reflected in Mythology.* These memoirs are limited to English translations of varying quality, which depend on the abilities of the collector; abstracts are often included.

The many issues of the *Journal of American Folklore* are the best source for short collections of myths published in English. After about 1950, the authors have included more psychological, performance, stylistic, theoretical, and cultural information (Miller 1952; Hymes 1985).

Important other treatments are those of Melville Jacobs (1959c) analyzing the content, style, and psychological tensions in Clackamas mythology as dramas, the Nehalem Tillamook collection by Elizabeth Jacobs (1959), and the careful discussions by Viola Garfield (1953, 1961, 1966) tracing the cultural import of mythology among the matrilineal tribes. Readers should be especially warned, however, that the popular collections by Clark (1953) and by Reagan and Walters (1933) were expurgated and/or cast in European molds so they do not reflect true Pacific Northwest literature.

Further, the meager Haida corpus (Swanton 1905a) has grown thanks to the efforts of John Enrico on the language, Wendy Bross Stuart on songs, reworking of Marius Barbeau texts, and poetic rephrasings by Robert Bringhurst of Swanton stories.

NOTE

[1] Some terms for "myth" as distinct from "story" are:

Bella Coola	*smaiusta*	(McIlwraith 1948:293)
Tlingit	*tłagu*	(de Laguna 1972:839)
Tsimshian	*ada'ox*	(Boas 1916b:565) [*adaawx*]
Kwakiutl	*nu'yam*	(Boas 1916b:565)

| Chinook | *ik!anam* | (Boas 1916b:565) |
| Puget | *sXwiya'b* | (Ballard 1929:142) [*sx̱ʷiyʔab, syəhub*] |

According to Boas (1916b:584) the designations for Raven include:

Tlingit	*yeł*	
Haida	*nAnkilsłas*	'He Whose Voice Is Obeyed'
Tsimshian	*tXamsEn*	'Giant' or 'Raven'
Bella Bella	*he'mask.as*	'Real Chief'
Nootka	*qo'icinimit'*	

With regard to the Transformers, Boas (1916b:586ff) reported that among the Kwakiutl, Nootka, Quinault, and Chinook, they were twins. Some names for the Transformers are:

Comox	*Kumsno'oc*	(Boas 1916b:586)
Nitinath	*alis*	(Boas 1916b:586)
Nootka	*Mucus Bay*	(Boas 1916b:586)
Puget	*Dokweboł*	'Moon' (Ballard 1929:69ff)
Katzie	*Swaneset, Khaals*	(Jenness 1955:10ff)

11

Journal of Northwest Anthropology, Memoir 9:12–18   2014

MISSING MISP[h]: RESTOR(Y)ING THE TRANSFORMER OF TSAMOSANS OF COASTAL WASHINGTON

ABSTRACT

Virtually unknown among Northwest Changer ~ Transformers is Misp[h] (and his twin) of the Tsamosans in southwest Washington. As twins born miraculously to a murderous mother, they destroyed her ogress sisters, saved nebulously-formed children, and decreed skills, foods, and customs at specific places and times. Their living embodiment is a duck—once call old squaw (old squawk), now longtail—with appropriately complex changes in bright plumage according to seasons and gender.

Introduction

The major loss, academically, from the life-long institutionalization of Thelma Adamson after her fieldwork among Tsamosan Salishan speakers of Southwestern Washington has been the continuing failure to recognize Misp[h] as a major transformer in the oral literature of these Coast Salish of Southwestern Washington. As a graduate student, Adamson spent 1926 collecting folklore among the Upper Chehalis at Oakville, followed by a turn to ethnography in 1927, when her mentor Franz Boas joined her to conduct linguistic research at the same community. Her dissertation—completed, approved, but never filed in May of 1929—was a study of transformers and tricksters among Coast Salish. Her supporting folklore collection was published, through the efforts of Ruth Benedict, in 1934 and reissued in 2009 (Adamson 1934, 2009). Yet the regional and folkloric significance of Misp[h] and his duck avatar was overlooked until now.

Ironically, Salish oral literature is particularly well known because of the sustained efforts of linguists and storytellers willing to record in these natives languages, as well as the interest of internationally known scholars and folklorists, such as Franz Boas; Melville Jacobs (1959b, 1960); Del Hymes; Dale Kinkade (1963a,b; 1964a,b; 1966; 1967; 1983; 1987; 1991; 1992a,b); Arthur Ballard; June Collins; and Vi Hilbert (Miller and Hilbert 1993, 1996, 2004); as well as popular collections (Matson 1968, 1972); culminating in a recent Salish compendium (Thompson and Egesdal 2008) along with reprintings of Thelma Adamson (2009) and Katherine Palmer and George Sanders (2012). These and other sources appear with annotations in the standard reference (Walls 1987), but Misp[h] remains missing.

The Adamson reissue, especially, makes more available the epic of Misp[h] and his brother Kumol told by Lucy Heck (Adamson 2009:329–432), a noblewoman from the Lower Chehalis of Grays Harbor. Earlier, Livingston Farrand heard versions of Misp[h] from Quinault-speaking Bob Pope in 1902. Ronald Olson learned it again from Bob Pope, John Dixon, and Jonah Cole in 1926 among Quinaults.

The earliest reference found so far appears in a letter, dated 20 July 1855, from James Swan at Shoalwater to George Gibbs, who asked for word lists of various native languages of the Northwest (Swan 1855). Swan's source seems to have been Old Toke, a Chinook leader living at Tokeland on Willapa Bay, now the location of the tiny Shoalwater Bay reservation. The six-page letter includes stories of Thunderbird, the Smisspee (duck), the winds, and customs and religious beliefs of Indians from Columbia River to Nisqually. Smisspee is obviously Misp[h], as explained in this extracted quote from the letter's page 2:

> The Smisspee is a small duck of the Sheldrake species and the only tradition about it that I have heard is that it was formerly a man or as the Indians express it they were "ankartz Tillikums" [ahnkutty tilakums, past people]. This bird came to the ?ema? [Nemah] River in this bay when a great many Indians lived and seeing the river full of salmon asked why they did not catch them. The Indians replied they did not know what salmon were, and were afraid of them. The Smisspee then showed them how to make nets and spears and they took immense quantities of fish. And from this bird all Indians learned to catch fish. (Swan 1855)

Quinault creation, according to a cultural and economic overview by Justine James and Leilani Chubby (2002:99), involved three distinct epochs, each with its own reformer. At the beginning was Xwani Xwani [X^wani X^wani], then came the protean Animal People, and third, setting the stage for the time of human people, was Misp[h]—the culture hero ~ transformer ~ reformer ~ adjuster.

Misp[h] and his twin, in particular, did much to form present Grays Harbor, and coastal Washington State. He was a key ancestral figure for Tsamosans. While other regional reformers are well known, such as Kw'ati of the Quileute and Makah, Misp[h] is not. In part this is a consequence of the life-long institutionalization of Thelma Adamson. Thus, Misp[h] has remained unheralded for seventy-five years.

Such great epics of Native America can easily be misunderstood by mainstream readers because they teach by negative examples, rather than extolling the rewards of virtue or financial success. Further, presenting these stories in English voids many of their nuances. The idioms used in the native language explicitly indicate what is real and what is not, what is worthwhile and what is greedy, or what is good for everyone and what is selfish. By the end of these epics, morality, decency, and community values are instituted, not always in the easiest or safest manner.

Only at the end of each epic are Misp[h] and his brother identified with their duck avatar— the immature male in winter plumage most like a "long-tail," once also known (among 20 local names)[1] as "old squaw," though "old squawk" is more appropriate since its species Latin name *Clangula hyemalis* refers to its noisy clanging in winter (*clangula* = clang, noise; *hyemalis* = of winter). Though attributed to the female, it is the male that is the noisiest. This species is remarkably apt for a transformer since it is so visibly changeable, going through two complete annual bright plumage changes, unlike the bright breeding to dull coloration of most birds, as well as gestational ones as it ages. Its diet is also human-like, relying on mollusks, crustaceans, insects, and aquatic plants. It can also dive to a depth of 200 feet.

To aid in following the longer epic versions, a generalized condensation follows:

> An industrious young man (Wildcat) camps alone, either drying fish or making a canoe. He soon becomes backlogged, while continuing to gain more basic materials. One day, while he is away, his work is finished for him. After several days of this unknown help, he hides to see who is doing it. A young woman appears who then marries him. They live together until the fishing season or canoe is done and then go back to his home town. Before they get there, she lets down her hair to hide her face and, once inside, sits backward looking at the wall. She lives quietly in the house, tormented by Bluejay who wants to see her face and hear her laugh. When she can endure no more, she hides her husband, pulls back her hair to

reveal a frightful face and laughs five times, killing more people each time until everyone is dead, even her disobedient husband. She eats all of them, but saves her husband's genitals in a basket above her bed. She becomes pregnant and has twins. The oldest one is Misp[h], the other Kəmol.

The twins grow quickly and precociously. When their mother leaves for the day, they do everything she had forbidden them to do, finding their father's parts in the basket and his former town littered with gnawed bones. Alarmed, they go home to burn down their own house and flee. The mother sees the smoke and ash, including a bit retaining the design on the side of her cherished basket. Angry, she rushes home, finds the smoldering ruins, and chases after her sons.

They trick and kill her, then move on. Along the way they meet and kill her four sisters (their aunts), each of whom kills children (unformed souls/spirits) in a special way before eating them. Each aunt is gutted and the more recently dead children are revived and given professions that are thereafter passed down family lines. They go from town to town around the Olympic Peninsula, decreeing livelihoods and abilities specific to each community. Near the end, the brother is killed and revived as a duck, while Misp[h] becomes a duck-shaped stone at the mouth of the Columbia River. Ever after, their spirits return as ducks in the late summer.

Since the motivation of Misp[h] and his twin is to make the world ready for today, the epic by Lucy Heyden Heck is summarized next because it is the most detailed one known and would have been the basis for Adamson to properly highlight the importance of Misp[h]'s role among the Coast Salish.

The Reformer Twins
Paraphrase of Lucy Heck to Thelma Adamson

Chief Woodpecker lived in a town of twelve houses at present Humptulips City. He was a skilled carpenter who built all the houses and many of the canoes. His son worked with him, so as to master woodworking. When it came time, the son was sent alone into the forest to make his first canoe, and his father insisted that no one was to help the boy. He had to succeed on his own.

The boy selected a cedar tree, felled it, and began shaping it until dusk when he returned to his remote camp for the night. The next day he shaped the inside. When he came back on the third day, he found a big camas bulb inside the canoe form. It was tied with a long black hair. Surprised and suspicious, he hid the bulb in nearby brush. The fourth day, two bulbs were in the canoe, each tied with a long hair. On the fifth day, there were three bulbs, and on the sixth, four camas and elk marrow used for a protective greasing (sun block) of the face. When he returned the seventh day to rough out the canoe, nothing was there. Instead, he worked for a while until he became sleepy and took a nap inside the canoe.

He dreamed a pretty girl with very long hair was sitting beside him, asking why he did not eat the camas she brought to him. She pledged her love to this boy of royal blood. When he awoke, she was actually sitting there and they agreed to marry. She said she lived upriver, but would move to his town as long as it was after dark because she was very bashful.

Just outside the town, the girl unbraided her hair so it hung over her face. Inside the house, she sat with her face to the wall. At bed time, she slept beside her husband in the chief's section. The next morning, she again sat facing the wall with her hair down, weaving a basket. She ate her meal of camas in the same position. Ever nosey, Bluejay began to mutter about this overly modest behavior. When he got no response, he kept insisting to see her face and hear her laughter. He kept this up for five long days.

The fifth morning, the wife asked her husband to go with her far beyond the prairie while she dug camas. Instead, when they got there, she dug a very deep hole and told her husband to hide inside it. She stuffed his ears and nose with fine cedar bark, covered him with a box, and left him in supposed safety. Too curious, the husband raised the edge of the box, waiting to hear her laugh.

Back at the house, the girl began to dress up, braid her hair, and grease and paint her face. Then she went to Bluejay and said they would now laugh. She clapped her hands together and shouted. Bluejay fell over dead. As she continued laughing out loud, everyone in the house died, their eyes bulging out and tongues lolling. She went house to house in the town, shouting and killing. Then she started at one end and ate everyone up.

When she went to find her husband, he was dead. She wept. Then she took his torso, put it in a basket, and hung it over their bed at home. During the night, the basket shook. The next morning, the girl was pregnant with twins, who were born five days later. The elder was Misp[h] and the younger was Kmol. Two days after birth, they were walking and using bows and arrows She favored Misp[h] and always threatened to eat Kmol if he cried. After five days, they were men Each day their mother left to dig camas, warning them not to look in her basket nor go downriver.

They became suspicious and looked in the basket, identifying their father's remains. They went downriver and found his village, littered with skeletons. They knew the worst and decided to flee from home. They burned up their house and walked away—with Misp[h] behind his brother in front. Their mother sensed something was wrong, then saw ashes in the air. One cinder showed the design pattern of her basket, and she suddenly realized her home had burned up. She raced after her sons, singing a song to weaken them. They prepared for her attack by climbing to the top of a tree covered in loose bark, praying to the tree to hold on tightly to its own bark. The tree gave them special words (*dicta*) to grip onto its trunk. When their mother saw them in the tree, she spoke softly and nicely to lure them down. Instead they suggested she climb up, telling her the special words. She did not always remember them so she only got up slowly. Near the top, Misp[h] pushed the bark with his foot and it fell off and crushed their mother.

They climbed down and went on, knowing they had four aunts who were cannibals like their mother. A prairie, named Seated Children, near Humptulip City had a stepped slope filled with children, who were known as "Always Tears" because they were crying, dirty, and fearful. At the bottom were two trees leaning together with a swing between them. Further out was a huge bloody rock. Those children warned the twins that the woman who lived on the prairie would eat them.

They greeted their aunt, and she asked after their mother. They said she was slowed by a heavy pack and would be along soon. Their aunt tried to get Kmol to swing, but Misp[h] took his place, teaching the children instead to chorus "Go and Come Back." Misp[h] jumped off the swing beyond the rock and survived. He told his aunt it was her turn to swing, urging the children to sing "Go and Never Come Back." She hit the rock and died as her belly burst open. The twins revived the most recently dead children, but those longest dead stayed dead. The uneaten children were washed, dressed, and painted. They were told they would live there to become very old. Those who revived would live to middle age, while those (presouls) who stayed dead became stillborns.

The twins went on until they came to a prairie where they saw a pile of dirt covered in clam shells, shaped like a seated child. Five wide seats behind this figure were filled with children. The men greeted their aunt, and she asked after their mother. They said she would be along. The children explained that each was sent to fetch a stick standing near the figure without laughing, but he or she always failed, was dashed against the rock, and eaten. Misp[h] fetched the stick soberly, then said it was the aunt's turn. She laughed, so he grabbed her by the heels and dashed her against the rock so that she burst open and children's bodies tumbled out. The most recent victims revived fully after they were washed and cleaned, but those longer dead were slower to recover. Some never did. These children founded royal-blooded families.

At the next prairie, children were speared as each came to sit on a large fungus. Misp[h] sat but was not harmed, so it was the third aunt's turn. He speared her heart and threw her against a rock so her belly burst open. Again, the most recent meals were revived, but those longer dead were less lucky. These children became spirit helpers for hunting (Hunt power).

The twins went on to the prairie at Carlyle, where they met the fifth aunt, who killed children with a boy's game of see-saw that had a flat rock at either end. The aunt and Misp[h] got on the teeter-totter. He jumped off when she was on the high end and she burst on the rock below. Victims spilling out were cleaned up and revived, founding a community of hunters, both men and skilled women.

At the mouth of the Humptulips, where they decreed the building of fish traps, the twins resolved to right the wrongs of the world. They went westward, coming to a house where people were shooting arrows inside. It was raining and no one there knew how to fix leaks in the roof. Instead, they shot arrows at the drips to try to stop them, as Bluejay explained. The twins went up on the roof and saw that the shingles were placed the wrong way, so they set them right and the leaking stopped. All subsequent roofs were built this way.

They went toward the shore and came upon a house where Bluejay and his wife were cohabitating on the roof, so the Twins decreed modesty in the future. Further up the beach, clams were stuck on sticks to cook in the sunlight. Instead, the twins taught people there to cut out the clams from the shell and cook them on sticks over an open fire.

They went on and, at the surf, met a man walking upside-down carrying firewood between his legs. They set him upright and instructed everyone to carry firewood on the right shoulder. Farther up the coast they came to a house where they heard groaning, "Ouch, my head; Ouch, my hand." A man was splitting wood by driving the wedge into the log with his head. Instead, Misp[h] made him a stone mallet and gave instructions, still followed, to split wood by hammering onto a wedge. People there tried to cook their food by dancing on it. The brothers told them to get their nets to catch salmon, but the people instead got digging sticks for clamming.

At Corner Creek, they met a man sharpening the edges of three big clam shells and singing about how he would deal with the reformers. Instead, Misp^h stuck the shells in his head and butt, turning him into a deer to be hunted to feed people. At Copalis, they met a man being dragged into the sea by his own head lice. The twins washed his hair in urine and rinsed it in fresh water, killing the lice. Then they carved him a comb that was made of wood, and taught him to comb, oil, and braid his hair. Finally, they called for people to bring out their salmon nets, but instead they got their clamming sticks. Ever after, they have clammed there.

At the Rocks, Wolves were eating raw crabs. Misp^h tried to reform them into proper people who cooked their food, but they asked to remain as they were and so became five brothers consisting of four Wolves and a Dog. At Moclips, they taught proper sex technique to the people (especially modesty and respect by girls). At Rock Creek, they found a deeply sleeping man and attached clam shells to his front teeth. He became X^{w}ani X^{w}ani [active in a later age]. At Taholah, they called for people to bring out their fish gear and they did. As a reward, the twins taught them to make tight basket traps. Farther on they found empty houses, and following the stream [Raft Creek] they came to a suspicious whirlpool. They heated rocks in a fire and dropped them into the water until it began to boil. A huge black being with an enormous mouth floated up and they cut it open, finding whole families, canoes, and houses. Those most recently killed could be revived. Among them were Bluejay and X^{w}ani X^{w}ani, who decided to repopulate that locale using skin rubbed off Misp^h and himself. They blew on the exfoliate pellets and they became people, gifted with a special fish trap.

They went on and shouted for people to build fish traps because they already had fire, good houses, and tools. But they were dirty, so the twins taught them to bathe and groom. At Quileute, they shouted for fish traps but instead people launched canoes and ran out trolling lines, as they still do. Feeling threatened, the twins ran away and decreed the Quileutes would be mean. At Ozette, they also called for fishtraps, but some went into the hills to hunt and others went out to troll. They did everything properly.

They went on, calling for fish traps at each town, but some just went out to sea, others embraced warfare, and some developed other skills. At one town, they cleared away rocks, creating a whirlpool, and so killed a monster.

When they reached the Columbia River, at Clatsop, they called for fish traps but instead people caught crabs. Clatsops were confirmed in their royal blood. At Astoria, people came out with their nets and received runs of huge Chinook salmon. Across the river, people were drying sturgeon heads on warm rocks, but the twins instead taught them to smoke sturgeon. Farther on they met people who did not know how to eat, putting food into every body orifice but the mouth. They were taught to chew and swallow, as well as drink. They then had to teach them how to sleep and to use a net.

At the next town, people packed everything they had and then went to sleep, thinking that was how things could be moved. Instead, the twins taught them to pack things up and move them by canoe. At Fort Columbia, everyone had a huge snake as a pet. If they did not feed these serpents enough, they ate children. Misp^h, instead, arranged to kill all the snakes and burn them up on a high hill, where the place where he sat to rest is now marked by a rock shaped like a duck.

At Chinook City, the town was infested with wood rats, which ate people alive. The twins set fire to the area, killing all the rats and enabling people to set out their nets. At Ilwako, people had their nets and used them well. At Nasell, they called for nets, but instead people went out to hunt or to hook sturgeon. They had no fires and had to be taught to use fire sticks and to cook. At Nemah, people went out to hunt or built small salmon traps. At Bay Center, people brought out herring traps. Then the twins went across the bay and met people spearing salmon.

At Westport, people got crabs and clams, and the twins decreed "A whale will always wash ashore here; you are good people [and deserve it]." Further on, people at Ts'e'tc hunted elk and were decreed to have royal blood to establish the chiefly families of the Harbor people. At Mulla, people hooked sturgeon. At Hoquiam, people hooked sturgeon and set out herring traps. At James Rock, people had herring traps and boxy canoes. Instead they were taught to make proper canoes. At Owl, people ate gophers and changed into these night birds. At Chinoose Creek, people kept their herring traps and sturgeon hooks. At Cold Water, people caught only silver salmon.

Finally, the twins returned to the Humptulips, where they started and decided that they would finish by becoming a kind of duck that arrived in the middle of the fishing season. Before they came, salmon had to be prepared in a very strict manner, using a sharpened clam shell to gut the fish and separate head and tails from the body. After these ducks arrived, people could prepare fish in whatever manner was convenient. These are river ducks that are always in pairs, like the twins, that go north in the spring and arrive back in the fall. (Paraphrased by Jay Miller based on text in Adamson 1934:329–342)

Conclusions

Restored to the scholarly record, Misp[h] and his twin transformed the Tsamosan world to be as it is today. Their living embodiment is the long-tail [old swawk] duck, which breeds in the high arctic, and visits coastal waters. Its very changeability makes it an apt representative of Transformers ~ Changers ~ Adjusters who prepared the world for the humans who were "coming soon."

NOTE

[1] Roster of Old Squawk Duck Names (Terres 1980:197):

Calloo	John Connelly	Old Wife	Scoldenore	Swallow-tailed duck
Cockawee	Long-tailed	Old Molly	Scolder	Uncle Huldy
Coween	Old Billy	Old Injun**	South Southerly	Winter Duck
Hound*	Old Granny	Quandy	Squeaking Duck	

*Hound references its baying cry
**Old Injun for its travel single file

JAMES SWAN AND MAKAH COSMOLOGY:
A CLARIFICATION[a]

ABSTRACT

The world view of the Makah Indians of Neah Bay as described by Frances Densmore in the 1920s is shown to have been directly influenced by the early Indian agent James Swan. Young Doctor, Makah artist and pragmatic traditionalist, provides the link.

Several years ago, George Quimby (1970) discussed the influence of the New Englander James Swan upon the art forms of the Makah Indians at Neah Bay. This brief article returns to the influence of Swan in another sector of Makah culture. Many years of anthropological research among Native Americans has prepared the professional audience to expect and even seek differences between the world view of white America and the many world views of Native America. For the Native American Indian the world is generally animate and the abode of mythical and mystical supernaturals. The world is viewed as alive and populated by beings that include the loved, the respected, the hated, the feared, the particular, and the omnipotent.

Anthropologists are prepared to record and respect the unexpected in Native American cosmologies. Yet traditionally these cosmologies conform to the above outline. For this reason, when a world view is learned which is close to that of white America, outside influence is suspected, but only occasionally conclusively proven.

I know of no description of the aboriginal Makah world view. The description that occurs in the anthropological literature has distinctly American prototypes. It was recorded at Neah Bay by the early American female anthropologist, Frances Densmore. This hearty woman from Minnesota devoted her life to the recording and study of Native American music (Lurie 1966). During her stay among the Makah in 1926, she not only witnessed one of the first Makah Day Ceremonies, she also recorded the Makah world view from a man named Young Doctor. The account appears this way in Densmore's report:

> According to Young Doctor, the people in oldest times believed that the world was a round, flat disk, balanced on a pillar and revolving once a day. It was surrounded by water and, in revolving, one edge tipped and went under water, causing the high tide. . . . The sun did not move but the revolution of this disk caused the day and night. Thus the influence of a forgotten white man affected tribal beliefs. (Densmore 1939:32)

Notice that this account violates the expectation of an animate world populated by supernaturals. Densmore rightly recognized the white influence behind the description. Yet Densmore failed to identify the probable American source. Densmore was not unaware of the importance of Swan among the Makah, in fact she quotes from his monograph on the Makah on several occasions in her own analysis of Makah music.

---

[a] This article was previously published in *Northwest Anthropological Research Notes*, 10(2):125–141 (1976).

Since Densmore did not link Swan with this influence, there was the possibility that she was unable to prove the link. Since the Densmore book serves as one of the primary sources on the Makah it is important to establish the original stimulus for the recorded world view. Fortunately, Swan himself specifies his involvement and suggests why it has had lasting influence. This is detailed in Swan's 1870 report:

> Of the revolutions of the heavenly bodies they know nothing more than that the sun in summer is higher in the heavens than during the winter, and that its receding or approach causes the difference of cold and heat of the seasons. The stars are believed to be the spirits of Indians and representatives of every animal that had existed on earth, whether beast, bird, or fish. . . . The moon they believe is composed of a jelly-like substance, such as fish eat. They believe that eclipses are occasioned by a fish like the "cultus" cod, or *toosh-kow*, which attempts to eat the sun or moon, and which they strive to drive away by shouting, firing guns, and pounding with sticks upon the tops of their house. On the 5th of December, 1862, I witnessed the total eclipse of the moon, and had an opportunity of observing their operations. There was a large party gathered that evening at the house of a chief who was giving a feast. I had informed some of the Indians during the day that there would be an eclipse that evening, but they paid no regard to what I said, and kept on with their feasting and dancing till nearly ten o' clock, at which time the eclipse had commenced. Some of them coming out of the lodge at the time, observed it and set up a howl, which soon called out all the rest, who commenced in fearful din. . . . *I tried* to *explain* the cause *of the eclipse,* but could gain no converts to the new belief, except one or two who had heard me explain and predict the eclipse during the previous day, and who thought as I could foretell so correctly what was going to take place, I could also account for the cause. (Swan 1870:90, emphasis added)

Despite Swan's thoughts to the contrary, his discussion of astronomy had an impact. The conditions were such that his influence probably had maximum impact on the Makah. Swan had told them the eclipse would happen, the Makah were all together at a feast, and all of them were greatly affected by the event. Swan seems to have spoken uninterrupted and while his audience did not express immediate conviction, his words were not unheeded.

According to Swan's account, the Makah world view he learned was that of an animate universe inhabited by spirits of the dead and mythological animals, such as the celestial cod. By the time that Densmore arrived 64 years later, a Makah could describe a mechanized world that was not entirely that of the white man and not entirely that of the aboriginal Makah. Rather, a blend had been achieved which served to characterize the new world that the Makah had entered.

Journal of Northwest Anthropology, Memoir 9:21–28 2014

NATIVE HEALING IN PUGET SOUND

ABSTRACT

An updated overall description and contextualization is provided of the lapsed Redeeming Rite, formerly known as Spirit Canoe ~ Soul Recovery, among Lushootseeds of Puget Sound, based on three decades of literature reviews and interviews.

The region around Puget Sound (the Sound), Washington, with Seattle near its center, is the home of the Lushootseed Salish. The Sound itself is a basin for numerous rivers falling from the mountain ranges that rim the area. Each of these rivers was occupied by the winter towns and seasonal camping resorts of a tribal community (Haeberlin and Gunther 1930).

Running north to south along the east side of the Sound, these rivers named for their resident tribes are the Skagit, Stillaguamish, Snohomish, Snoqualmie, Duwamish, Puyallup, and Nisqually. On the west side of the Sound, along the Kitsap peninsula, are the Suquamish and Sahewamish, without major rivers. Closely related, but linguistically distinct, neighbors were the Nooksack to the north, the Twana and Chehalis to the west, and the Straits of Juan de Fuca Salishan tribes to the north, such as the Samish, Lummi, and Klallam.

In terms of the overall Puget Basin, Marian Smith (1940:7), after fieldwork with Puyallup and Nisqually, outlined a comprehensive spatial model with expanding components for each watershed, the maximum extent of allegiance and loyalty for most Lushootseeds. These units, cross-referenced with the Lushootseed Dictionary (Bates, Hess, and Hilbert 1994, hereafter LD) were (a) hearth mates (*hudali* LD:312) eating together; (b) within a cedar plank household (*al'al, altx^w* LD:320); (c) among houses (*al'al'al* LD:320) of all local residents; (d) of birthright (*g^wəɖ'ali* LD:98) locals—those born there in contrast to inlaws, visitors, and foreigners; (e) including all seasonal settlements, towns, and resorts (*dx^wuq'əlb* LD:183, 296); (f) inter-community networks of close kin (*q'ušəd* LD:197 = "feet together") and people (*iišəd* LD345 = "feet apart"); (g) along creeks (*ɖəlix^w* LD:90, 302) of tributary drainages; (h) within the entire drainage of a watershed (*stulək* LD:346).

The major nodes in this overall system were cedar plank houses located along the shore near spots rich in local resources. Often these included a salmon stream, berry patch, and hunting territory.

The mountains are coated with thick stands of evergreen trees, including the Western red cedar, whose straight grain made it ideal for woodworking. Most of the technology derived from this tree, including planks for houses, tools for labor, boxes for cooking and storing, and canoes that were the primary means of transportation because an impenetrable undergrowth covered most of the land.

The native people had a very complicated social life, comparable to complex farmers in other areas, yet they lived by harvesting what nature provided. They did not plant crops or tend fields and they did not have to stay in one place. While women did encourage the growth of certain wild plants, they did this unobtrusively. They moved with the seasons to camps where natural foods were available. The climate was mild, due to the offshore Japanese Current, and rainy, so the region teemed with plants and animals. Chief among these were five species of salmon, "who" spawned and died in the rivers each year, although some years the runs were more abundant than others. By working hard for a few weeks, a household could catch and dry enough fish to last the winter. After the summer fish runs, families went into the uplands to collect dozens of kinds of berries, which were also stored for winter use. Men hunted a variety of mammals, both sea and land, during the fall and winter. In the spring, fresh greens and early fish runs improved the diet.

The dense vegetation and the rugged terrain limited the number of places where people could live so every house in every town had about fifty occupants. Positions in the house reflected rank in society. Thus, the owner of the house and his family had the best location in the rear, away from the drafts at the doorway. This family constituted a nobility and provided the leaders of the community. Along the sides were common folks, who contributed food and upkeep to the household in return for the prestige of living with wealthy relatives. Just inside the door, exposed to the weather and enemy attack, were slaves, either themselves captured in raids or descended from captives. Each family had its own fire along the center of the house, since eating together as a commensal unit was what defined close relations. Nobles usually had more than one wife, but each seems to have had her own fireplace to feed her own and any other children she invited to share a meal.

On important occasions, particularly during winter, the head of the house would host public events. Then, most resident families would move out to other accommodations, either nearby homes or tents, to make room for guests, and two or three large fires would be lit in the middle of the house. Huge amounts of food, gathered by slaves and members of the house and prepared by the wives under the direction of the senior wife of the chief, would be served throughout the festivities. Changes in status—such as the assumption of names and stages in life such as puberty, marriage, and death—would provide the occasions for inviting in guests. The more prominent the family, the more people would be invited from farthest away. Important families had far-flung networks of friends and kin, linked by marriage, trade, and social obligations.

The crux of the entire system and the basic reason for gathering people together was the display of bonds with particular spirit powers. No one could be successful in this society without help from supernaturals. Invariably, for centuries, the leading families had bonded with the most powerful spirits in their locales. Lesser family members, some commoners, and even a few slaves would also have spirit partners, but these were less powerful than those of the leaders.

Every career, from woodworking and canoe making to berry picking and midwifery, was enabled by a spirit power. Leaders had spirits that empowered them to give wise council and acquire wealth, as well as hunt the most dangerous of animals. Most chiefs had inherited power from Thunder and passed it along to their heirs for generations. Leaders also had wealth or property power to enable them to be generous.

Most spirits, however, only visited their human partner in the winter months, when economic activities were over and people lived quietly in their towns. During the long rainy winters, people gathered to welcome back their spirits by singing and dancing a mime of how they had first met a spirit in some remote spot in the land or sea. The rest of the year, the spirits lived in villages of their own "on the other side" of the human dimension, traveling during the winter in a great spiral though the Salish country from the east to the north, west, and south before returning home. Towns knew their route from centuries of experience and began to prepare to host their own power displays once they had been invited to the celebrations of the town that preceded them on the circuit.

For most people in most places, these public displays set the pattern for traffic with the supernatural. In every community, however, there were and are specialists who maintain personal and permanent relations with another kind of spirit power. While the Lushootseed word for spirits derives from the word for "dream," it has two related meanings. First, it means spirit immortals generally, and, second, it means the major subset of these spirits, those that confer powers to be successful at ordinary, mundane things. The other subset of these spirits are, quite literally, the doctors of the universe.

Though usually known as shamans, both the spirits and their human allies are named by the same word, which derives from the term for "name" or "call" because in the native system of medicine, to correctly identify the cause of an illness is to diagnose the cure. Only these doctors and their powers were and are in continuous contact in all times and places.

The head of a household and the leader of a town, who would also be the head of the most distinguished house, either had to acquire such a doctoring spirit or have a close relative or colleague who was a shaman. Just as European noble families sent sons into the church and the military to widen their power base, so too did Lushootseed nobles try to have members in all positions of authority.

Moreover, modern Salish families extend this strategy to include many contemporary options, particularly religious ones (Amoss 1978; Jilek 1982). Thus, while families continue to attend winter ceremonials to welcome the return of spirit partners, on Sunday they will devotedly attend Protestant and Catholic services. In addition, for the past century, natives of Puget Sound and beyond have belonged to a religion, incorporated in Washington state, uniquely their own. Known as the Indian Shaker Church, it was founded by a local man, John Slocum, and his wife Mary. John died and went to heaven but God sent him back to preach a new religion. While many of the overt actions are like details of Catholic worship, such as candles and repeatedly making the Sign of the Cross, the use of hand bells to accompany hymns during circular processions are creative touches. When natives join the Shaker Church, furthermore, their spirit powers convert with them, thus continuing the ancestral religious tradition. The primary role of Shakers in the modern native community is curing, but unlike the ancient shamanic traditions that also continues, Shaker curing is much more democratic in the sense that it is performed by all believers free of charge.

Shamanism continues to be the career of aloof individuals who mostly work alone. Traditionally, shamans are feared for this reason, and are often described as mean and selfish, but they are nevertheless respected for the good that they do or can do. Today, when a shaman enters a room or a native gathering, quiet quickly falls over the people. Since his spirits come with him or her and cannot be seen, everyone has to be especially careful not to give offense to them. Among the Salish, sexual equality was well developed. With proper supernatural sanction, any man or woman could perform any task. Gender roles, therefore, existed only in the statistical sense that men tended to do some things and women to do others.

When someone falls ill, the character and duration of the disease will determine who is called to provide treatment. If it is a European-derived case of measles or a problem that requires surgery, then a university-trained physician will be consulted or the patient will visit a hospital. But natives are subject to many more diseases than allopathic medicine can account for in its treatments. Bad relations with the cosmos, the community, the family, and the self are often manifest in particular diseases. Though psychologically-derived (according to Western categories), these problems are nonetheless real and sometimes fatal.

To improve community sentiment and general wellbeing, Shakers will generally be called in because they cure communally and never accept money for their treatments, although they are given donations to pay for gas and lodging as they travel.

For instances of cosmic disharmony and spiritual disaffection, a shaman will be called, loudly and repeatedly so that his spirits will also know that they are needed. He or she will be expensive, although fees will be returned to the family if the cure is unsuccessful or the patient dies.

If a shaman loses too many cases, however, he or she will be killed by their own relatives because of a belief that the powers have turned malevolent and will henceforth only kill and not cure. Then a shaman becomes a liability to the community. The execution is performed by a family member to prevent the murder from becoming a blood feud between hostile families. Sometimes, however, the family of a dead patient will not wait and kill the shaman themselves. Then a blood feud will begin in earnest unless the avenging family gives lots of goods to the shaman's mourners.

Illnesses cured by shamans can have either external or internal causes. Sometimes, another shaman will become jealous or envious of someone or be hired by an enemy to make that someone sick. Often, the onset of this illness was caused by magically "shooting" a sharp object into the patient's body. The victim can be attacked at three levels: the mind, the spirit, and the breath. A shaman relied on his spirit helpers to tell him or her what was wrong and how to cure it. Lushootseed shamans had a characteristic gesture for making a diagnosis. They placed the wrist against the forehead, presumably because the double pulses aided their trance state.

For the Salish, as for other Native Americans, the mind is located in the heart at the center of the body (Miller 1980). The brain serves only as an organ for the storage of remembered thoughts and emotions. Therefore, sorcery applied to the heart will confuse and weaken someone, leaving them susceptible to worse illness. The shaman will have to suck out whatever probing object was magically shot into the body. Often, he will place loose fists on top of each other to form a sucking tube. Modesty required that the shaman avoid touching the patient's body as much as possible. Once the problem was gathered inside the fists, it was either sent away, if not too dangerous, or, on rare occasions, it was drowned in a basket filled with water.

The second instance, spirit illness, was a common phenomenon of winter. Spirit powers were acquired in youth, before puberty in the old days and by initiation today, but they did not begin visiting their human partners annually until middle age, when a successful career and healthy family were taken as proof that there was indeed a spirit ally. Everything had a spirit, and every human success was attributed to some greater connection with the forces of the universe.

Every winter, when the spirit returns to its human, that mortal becomes ill. The first time this happens, a shaman is called to "draw out" the song that has lodged in the throat of the man or woman. The shaman will then sing the song of the initiate so everyone in the house can hear it and remember it because, thereafter, whenever that human becomes ill, people will have to gather with drums and sing while the invalid dances to become attuned again with his or her spirit power.

Today, at large weekend gatherings all winter long, everyone sings and dances an evocation of their encounter with a spirit. The kind of song each sings and the gestures used suggests to what general category that spirit belongs, but the name of the power and its specific details can never be revealed without the human forfeiting his or her life.

Sometimes, in this second kind of illness, a shaman will find one of these spirit allies attractive and will steal it from its human, who then becomes ill. If a more powerful shaman cannot retrieve the spirit, than the person will die, unless he or she can acquire another power, which is virtually impossible.

Thirdly, a spirit, shaman, or deceased loved-one might steal the breath of someone. Since the word for life derives from the word for breath, such a theft leads to death, either quickly if that is what the perpetrator wants or lingeringly if revenge or suffering is the intention. Breath is somehow linked with the soul, so the delay in death seems to relate to the time allowed for the soul to wander to the land of the dead, where it becomes a ghost. When someone dies, everything they owned is given away because any memento might make a relative fixate on the deceased and thus become a prime candidate for being killed by an ancestor. The dead cannot help that they kill their descendants because they are believed to be lonely in the land of the dead and have very little else to do.

Indeed, the dead are more significant in the lives of the Lushootseed people than anything else except the spirits. Living in close and caring communities, the bonds of the flesh, like those of the spirit, continue beyond the grave. In the same way that only shamans can remain in contact with their powers, so too can they make contact with the dead. To do so, they engaged in one of the most impressive and meaningful ceremonies of Native North America and the world. Though it has been called the Spirit Canoe Ceremony in the academic literature of fifty years ago, it more correctly was intended for "soul recovery" and "redeeming of lost vitalities." Last held in the winter of 1900 [as I published based on all my sources, but actually 1908 according to the last patient], it is only vaguely known to present Lushootseed elders. Yet, at various times over the past century, missionaries, scholars, and visitors have provided glimpses of the rite, which have been recently assembled and analyzed (Miller 1988a).

Redeeming Rite

What is unique about this enactment is that, while shamans almost always work alone, here several shamans worked in conjunction to mime a journey to the land of the dead, a confrontation to regain a soul, and a hasty return to put the lost essence back into the patient. Only the Midewiwin (Shamans Academy) of the Great Lakes tribes involves a comparable cooperation among shamans, and its modern procedures can only be traced to a religious revival in A.D. 1700 (Hickerson 1970).

During the Redeeming, the main features of Lushootseed culture were epitomized and validated in a community setting. Weeks of preparation were required during the coldest months of the year. For balance, an even number of shamans, usually four or six, co-officiated during the rite. Only shamans with a special power could safely go to the afterworld and almost all of them were men. They went at midwinter because everything in the afterworld was the reverse of their own. When the snow covered the ground here, there it was summer, the trails were lined with flowers, and the climate was warm. Similarly, our day was their night, our high tide was their low one, and objects broken here were whole there.

Everyone in the community was involved in the preparations. Women cooked food and cleaned the house, men hunted and helped out as needed. Children ran errands for everyone. Meanwhile, the shamans, or the shaman associated with the house, went into the woods and selected a large cedar tree, which was taken to a convenient location near the community. There it was split into planks, each shaped into a particular form, either with a rounded top, a snout, or a disk. Every drainage had its own style of plank. For example, the Snohomish cut out the shape of the snout because they traced descent from a legendary cetacean.

Each plank was coated with a chalky white layer of paint to provide a background before thick black outlines were drawn along the edges. The day before the ceremony, each shaman was assigned a plank and painted an image of his power in the very center, colored in combinations of red, white, and black. Sometimes, dots in red or black surrounded the figure. These represented the song that linked shaman and spirit. Since humans were alien in the afterworld, they felt as though they were traveling through an engulfing viscosity. Whenever they sang or talked, their breath escaped as bubbles moving through the thickness.

Poles were also made for or by the shamans since these had multiple purposes during the rite, variously serving as bows, punt probes, spears, or paddles.

Every shaman kept with him a carved humanoid figure about a yard high representing his special power. Before a Redeeming ceremony, this figure was repainted and dressed, as appropriate, to look its best. These figures represented beings called Little Earths, primordial spirits who lived in the forest. When they heard the shamans singing as they departed for the afterworld, these spirits came running into the house to go along to the land of the dead and help out.

When all was prepared, the spectators sat quietly along the walls of the house. The shamans and their helpers lined up outside, ready to march in and set up the paraphernalia so they could start their odyssey.

To the sound of drumming and singing, the procession entered the house. The shamans were wearing special cedar bark headbands and painted faces. Each carried his Little Earth, with an assistant carrying the painted plank. Sometimes, the planks were held so that they appeared to peek inside the door before entering. Each shaman placed his figurine in a line down the center of the house and sat down on the sides. The helpers arranged the planks along the sides so that each shaman faced the image of his centrally painted spirit power. The boards at the ends were painted on only one side, while those in the middle were painted on both sides. In this manner, the images looked at each other and provided protection for the shaman both front and back. When the schematic vehicle had been constructed in the middle, the shamans returned to stand in the cubical space between each board. Then they were off.

They had to hurry because, in Lushootseed belief, any illness was a prelude to death, not a temporary disability. Their patient was wasting away without any clear problem because the dead were sapping his or her vitality. During the entire ritual, the victim rested on a cedar mat at the rear of the house.

Along the way, the voyagers made routine stops to gather power, learn the future, and collect information. These places appear here with capital letters since they are spiritual rather than ordinary experiences.

At the first stop, shamans visited a land filled with artifacts, each of which sang a song. The shamans moved among them, learning and repeating the songs since knowing them would help people to use tools more efficiently. Artifacts themselves represented the full cooperation of natural products, human resourcefulness, and spiritual inspiration. The manufacture of good and useful items required supernatural assistance. Since this was the initial encounter with the "other side," everyone was reminded that it was the spiritual aspects of existence which were most important. It was a logical beginning place for such a journey, and for life in general.

After some time, the trip continued until they got to a berry thicket. It too was supernatural because the berries were the size of birds, hopping about in the shape of human babies. Since everything was believed to have an essential human form under the cloak of its species or appearance, this visit was a reminder of the common humanity of life. The shamans tried to pluck a berry or two with their poles. Their clumsy antics created much humor for the audience. If they managed to get even one, there would be a plentiful berry harvest the next fall.

Continuing on, they next came to a lake where their vehicle was reconfigured into a flat canoe. Since deep lakes were and are the abodes of powerful spirits, another source of power was encountered. Indeed, the shaman with a lake spirit like Otter called out its name to speed the canoe across the water. In addition, lakes and marshes provide a wide variety of foods, which were also celebrated. Next, they came to a wide prairie where the shamans used their poles as bows and pretended to hunt meat. If they were successful, then there would be plenty of game in the fall.

Fifth, they came to Mosquito Place where they were attacked by insects the size of birds. They fought these off with their poles and were careful not to be stung for that would be fatal. Since mosquitos were shamans in the spirit world because their ability to suck blood was useful in curing, the encounter was a test of shamanic ability.

Moving on, they came to a Beaver den, where they hunted using their poles as spears. If they killed a beaver, the furs would be of high quality the next year.

Afterwards, the shamans went on to meet the Dawn as they had been traveling most of the night. The appearance of light added to the heaviness of their thick surroundings so the doctors had to pause to "lift the daylight" with their pole over their heads. Because dawn had different intensities, they had to lift five times, the sacred pattern number, to safely pass underneath the light.

After this exertion, they rested all day long, since it was night in the land of the dead, preparing to resume the next evening.

After they picked up their journey, the next difficulty was a raging river with collapsing banks and rushing boulders. The shamans held a quick conference and decided to tip up one end of a plain cedar plank so each of them could walk up it and jump across the river, using their poles to vault. A shaman was most vulnerable at that moment because a weak spirit or a lingering grudge might unbalance him. If a shaman slipped or fell, he died within a year. In at least one case, this actually happened.

Now the party was close to the town of the dead, whose physical surroundings looked like the location of the nearest human graveyard. Sometimes the encounter with the ghosts was actually staged among the graves.

The vehicle was beached nearby. While a few shamans reversed the planks and figures so they could head back home, the rest went along the trail to the town. There they sometimes encountered a ghost, played by a member of the audience, out picking berries. They knew he was a ghost because he or she walked crossing and recrossing the feet. Pretending that they too were ghosts, they asked for news and learned the quality and name of the newest occupant and where it dwelled.

Then the shamans killed the ghost and buried it in a shallow grave. This was possible because there were at least two lands of the dead. The first, where they were, was inhabited by people who were still remembered by the living. When all memory of them was gone, they died again and passed to the second land of the dead. From there, according to some shamans, they could be reborn into a descendant and start living again. The cycle was endless.

By learning from the ghost what they were after (a soul, spirit, or mind) the shamans planned their strategy for when they got to the town. Acting like a ghost, the most powerful shaman went ahead and entered the house where the patient's vitality was, quietly leading it away. The other shamans joined them and rushed to the vehicle. Once they had pushed off, a shaman "threw his meanness" at the ghosts, who swarmed from the houses. Apparently, by successfully fighting for the lost spirit, the shamans were able to keep it. If they merely lured it away, the ghosts could take it back.

In some towns, this battle was enacted with long flaming splinters shot at the shamans by youngsters acting the part of the ghosts. If a shaman were hit or burned, he died within the year. Since the enactment took place at night, often inside a house, it was both dramatic and fraught with danger because of the hazard of fire in old wooden buildings.

The shamans paddled hard and the Little Earths provided protective powers as they sped home. Sometimes, they took a short cut that brought them back in a few hours instead of two days.

The patient was still lying quietly on a mat in the back of the house when the shamans arrived quivering with power. The most powerful of them came forward with the missing vitality and acted as though he were pouring it into the head of the invalid. Slowly at first, then with renewed vigor, the victim began to sing his or her power song and recover.

Sometimes, shamans saw the souls of other people, seeming well but soon to sicken, in the land of the dead and these too were brought back and restored. These patients liberally compensated their healer.

Everyone in the house then heard about future conditions. Any berries, meat, or artifacts brought back were given out to families who might need them. Usually, berries went to a woman since picking was her job. At least once, a baby was brought back to a childless woman, who gave birth nine months later. Other predictions were also made, both to delight or to warn the participants.

Though they might rest briefly, the paraphernalia had to be dismantled to close the route to the afterworld. The planks were taken into a remote area of the woods to rot and return to their elements. Only in the most dire of circumstances could boards be reused for an immediate return to the land of the dead and only when accompanied by special songs. Having made the journey once, they were then contaminated and unsafe. The poles may have also been abandoned, but some seem to have been reused in later rites. The figurines were carefully washed, losing much of their paint, and hidden in special places in the woods, often a hollow tree. There they awaited the next ceremonial use by the shaman. Only when he or she died was the Little Earth left to rot in the forest.

Summary

Among the traditions of shamanism, world religions, and comparative medicine, the Redeeming ceremony has a special place. Not only was it a community-wide and dramatic cure, but it also featured several shamans working together for the greater good.

Over the past two centuries other American tribes have developed similar religious means for their shamans to cooperate for the benefit of the community. The Indian Shaker Church is one example from the Northwest, but other regions have their own solutions.

Yet the Redeeming ceremony is clearly ancient in some form so the region must somehow account for its existence. Clues as to contributing factors can be seen when the Northwest is compared to other sections of Native North America during historic times. For example, tribes who were refugees from the East coast developed other integrative rituals where shamans cooperated together. After European colonies uprooted these natives and threw them together to fight for their own survival, communal shamanism became one consequence of their new cohesion. Such intensified intertribal contacts led to solutions similar to those that were ancient in the Northwest.

In Puget Sound, moreover, exactly these intertribal contacts had long been an aspect of local social, political, and religious interactions. Important leaders fostered these interchanges at their feasts, namings, marriages, funerals, and winter dances. These activities in turn had repercussions throughout the larger environment and enabled spiritual connections to be made that facilitated the elaboration of the Redeeming rite. In sum, this and similar rites became major contributors to tribal survival.

> The virtue of the Northwest in terms of the rest of Native America, therefore, is that its mechanisms for coping with diversity previewed what was to come when tribes, particularly in the East and Plains, were thrown together and had to arrange their own mutual survival. Its dense vegetation, reliable surplus [foods], and extensive network of waterways fostered the kind of hospitable exchanges that have enabled other native cultures to survive in the most oppressive circumstances. It shared a common ancestry with the rest of Native America, but then differentially emphasized some features to develop its own pattern. After contact, similar configurations emphasizing sharing and cooperative rituals also proved helpful elsewhere in Native America. (Miller 1988a:195)

PART II. KINSHIP AND SOCIETY

The pivotal importance of hereditary names is distinctive of the Northwest, fueling systems of rank, crest, clan, or kindred along the entire coast. Among its aspects and variants, upholding the universal "that knowledge is power," were academies ~ guilds whose members progressed through graded degrees of various sorts, as reviewed in the first article below. Following it are general and specific attempts to understand the fourfold semi-moiety system of the Tsimshian. The remaining articles deal with Salishans: strategic fortifications built by named war lords, claims to a dynastic "house" as a unique privilege of a Salishan great name, and key features of some exemplary names.

Native Academics: Coastal Ranks and Degrees

When I was asked to lecture at the new University of Northern British Columbia, I decided to put together a paper on educational ranks, grades, degrees, and guilds of the Pacific Northwest Coast, especially for Tsimshian and Salish, with parallels across the Americas. Four systems were recognized. The Natural, relying on all-pervasive spirits, spans the Americas; Tribal focuses on ancestral beings; Regional involves intertribal guilds; and Noble, particularly Northwestern, has graded degrees and ranks of elevated privileges, especially indicated by head-gear. Some inspiration came from Australia where elaborate initiation, totem, and increase ceremonies were directed by "men of high degree."

Tsimshian Moieties and Other Clarifications / Moiety Birth

These two moiety articles represent the first and last of an informal trilogy sorting out a better understanding of the fit of Tsimshian within the northern Northwest Coast. A study showing how these three societies (Tsimshian, Tlingit, Haida) also share a Macro-Crow kinship system added further support (Dunn 1984). At the time, the international gaze of Claude Levi-Strauss contributed to the excitement of Northwest research. Renewed fieldwork, especially in the southern or island villages, revealed a fourth dialect of Sm'algyax spoken by a handful of elderly speakers. After this fervor, a more pragmatic and community-based focus emerged.

During the 1970s, exciting work provided a better understanding of the complexities of Australian kinship systems. In particular, the term "semi-moiety" for a subgroup within one half of a dual division was gaining popularity. Comparison of the Tsimshian system of four phratries with the obvious moieties of neighboring Tlingit and Haida suggested a similar solution. Ethnographic work in Southern Tsimshian communities bore this out since Orca Killerwhales do indeed equate with Wolves as social carnivores, while semi-moiety Ravens equate with Eagles. Matri-membership determines the context for which one is Owner and which one is Other (side) in any situation or event. The formation of separate moieties from separate tribes by a process of deliberate "forgetting" (known as "erasure" in post-modern theory) underscores the importance of duality for these cultures, past and present.

While I was teaching at Prince Rupert, our class wrote a description of the culture in both languages, which exemplifies unique aspects both "emic" and succinct.

> Dzoga Tsm'syeen a ḵala ksyeen ada 'na gyiyaaks. Gaba da hoon dił helda wil liks gyigyeda wüünaya. ḵ'piil di gupl wil büs baasxga galtsiiptsap. A 'na 'na ganoonakit. Saigat txaalpxa p'deex wil ksi wit 'waat ga gyet Gispwudwada, Ganhada, Laxsgiik, Laxgibuu. 'Na smhawksa da naxnox ada halaayt. Nagoga dmt dit wilaays ga smoogit

29

ga laxaga´a. Dat ama doo wila waalm smoogyit, smgyigyet, liikagyigyet, ada łałuungyit. Gyaawin ła dzoga Tsm´syeen a´na gwa´a dił´naka boson.

The Tsimshian live along the Skeena river and sea coast, eating salmon and many other foods. They are divided into a dozen tribes ~ towns. Through their mothers, people belong to four crests named Orca ~ Blackfish, Raven, Eagle, Wolf. They believe in naxnox ~ wonders and halaayt ~ privileges and became Christians. They are organized into chiefs, councilors, ordinaries, and slaves. Now Tsimshian live in Canada and Alaska.

The most recent scholarly excitement for Tsimshian research has been the publication (Brock 2011) of the first book-length study of the fifty-year diary kept by Clah, a key figure in tribal economy, kinship, and politics. He was both the father of Henry Tate, the source for Boas's massive *Tsimshian Mythology* (1916b) and the grandfather of William Beynon, who worked on his own and with other major scholars, producing thousands of pages of material still largely in manuscript though some are being edited for print.

First Nations Forts, Refuges, and War Lord Champions around the Salish Sea

The association of war lords with famous names and strategic forts derived from my friendship with Ron Hilbert Coy, an artist who illustrated the early publications of his mother Vi Anderson Hilbert. His famous native name was linked with a fort atop a hill at the bend of the Samish River. Knowing the history of his name, complete with the taking of trophy heads of its father and son holders by Canadians, led me to look comparatively and amass these many examples from the Salish Sea. On a wider human scale, of course, this is the stuff of Arthur and Camelot—and of expanding empire. Around the world, national conquests advanced via forts, intended to defend acquired lands, as Russia advanced *ostrog* by wooden *ostrog* into Siberia and Arabs *casbah* by massive *casbah* into the Middle East.

Since publication, I have noted the association of such recent forts with large fields of potatoes, an important historic trade item that also provided ready food for those inside. Mention of the fort at Snag Cove also appears in random notes by Arthur Ballard, whose major ethnography has been suppressed by his family. He died while it was in press, and they removed it from the public.

The House of Salish ~ Noble Pedigrees, Privileges, and Names along the Skagit River between Logjam and Rock

By working comparatively and reading widely, I readily understood linguistic and cultural subtleties of claims to a "House" as a bid for prestige among the high-ranking holders of great names among Coast Salish. I also knew that these were not fundamental units of the matrilineal nations of the north coast. Yet all participate in an overall system where items of privilege and prestige are shared, rejected, or modified across cultural borders. The persistent denial of "the house" by those working only among Salish communities indicates a narrowness of understanding.

Naming Culture among Lushootseeds of Puget Sound

Focusing directly on a Salish mainstay, it is famous hereditary *names*, today and in the past, that integrate Lushootseeds of Puget Sound. Because they are eternal and international, they crosscut town, culture history, gender, age, rank, descent, kinship, pedigree, residence, territory, and waterway. On the basis of such name, at the nexus of "blood" and "mud" (kinship and landscape), basic societal institutions expand from *person* to *place*, *intersept*, and *power*, derived from immortal spirits. Building on a lifetime of living among Salish, my model illustrates their persistence.

NATIVE ACADEMICS:
COASTAL RANKS AND DEGREES

ABSTRACT

Like universities, towns of the Northwest had various institutions based on formal ranks that had internal degrees, which were earned by intensive study and initiation within a select membership determined by age and nobility. Advanced graduates held degrees at various levels within an overall system. Four native religious systems—natural, tribal, regional, and noble—are reviewed, each comparing an instance of the Pacific Northwest Coast, especially Tsimshian and Salish, with parallels across the Americas. Natural relies on all-pervasive spirits; Tribal on ancestral beings; Regional on intertribal guilds; and Noble on elevated privileges, especially indicated by head gear.

For some time now, my challenge has been to bring the study of the Northwest Coast back into the Americanist tradition by relating the Northwest to the rest of the Americas. This study has not been as easy as one might think, because the regional specialists, who abound throughout the Americas, are much more concerned with North American differences than similarities. For example, the very mention of words like "potlatch" and "crest" are enough to close off dialog and debate among other Americanists, even though these are just Northwest coastal variants of feasting and clanship emblems.

Such distinctions are nowhere more apparent than in the study of the most important institution of all, both for First Nations and for scholars, religion. Certainly, native religion has undergone profound changes since Christianity arrived in the new world, but native perspectives have nevertheless asserted themselves after conversion, particularly when Christian forms have been rendered into native languages (Shaul 1982). By tracing the origins and distributions of such native words, the ebb and flow of both native and European influences become all the more apparent and the tendency to simplify or homogenize distinct native traditions can be avoided or, at least, counterbalanced.

It is just this lumping and jumbling that I would like to address by looking at the four types or degrees of religious systems along the Northwest Coast of North America, particularly in terms of the Coast Tsimshian. Indeed, it seems fitting in the context of this new university (University of Northern British Columbia) for me to address the systems of "higher education" pursued by First Nations in this region since "the beginning of time."

In addition, I will draw comparisons between each of these systems and similar patterns in Native North America (Miller 1988a). In the process, some age-area speculations will be made, based on the theory that the more widely distributed a pattern, the more ancient it is likely to be. A particular note, however, will be paid to border overlap in the distributions of these four systems. Supporting data will be drawn from various Americanist publications and from my own research with Tsimshian in the North Coast and with Salishans to the south, along with other First Nations throughout North America.

These four systems, for now, are called Natural, Tribal, Regional, and Noble. Arranged in this way, these four systems range from most universal (the natural) to most specialized (the noble). Each is discussed and characterized in turn.

Natural

The all-pervasive belief throughout the Americas is that everything has an inherent spirit, whether or not it is known to humans. Each spirit has the potential of contacting one or more humans and teaching him or her, a particular skill or ability that will enable his or her life to be successful. Ruth Benedict's doctoral dissertation dealt with this system, which she called the guardian spirit complex.

According to this belief, each spirit has the shape of a human when living in its "holy home" at a particular place, such as inside a hill, waterfall, rapids, cave, or spring. Humans who visit such locales see only humans living in a house like their own. When these spirits leave home, however, they put on the cloak or covering of their species. Famous examples of this among the Tsimshian are the Salmon towns beyond the horizon where these fish people live and the Bear town where the princess who married the Bear went to live, thinking she was among fellow humans until Mouse woman told her otherwise.

As the spirit (in human form) left the first encounter with its human partner, it briefly shimmered into the shape of its animal counterpart, allowing it's human to know which species the spirit belonged to. During this transformation, the spirit sang a song which became fixed in the mind of the visionary and, ever after, was used to summon the spirit whenever the human was in need.

In some cases, different humans met the same spirit and accordingly sang the same tune with different words. In the eastern U.S., people who shared the same spirit often formed an association that met together to honor their spirit patron. For example, Winnebagos with a Bear spirit feasted together every year, and, like the Bear, ate with their left hand. Other spirits had similar injunctions that had to be followed for the partnership to continue, often to prevent over-identification with the spirit and a resulting dangerous vortex of power. Thus, those linked with Spider could not play a stringed instrument because these were too much like webbing.

In keeping with First Nations beliefs about the inter-connectedness of all things, each spirit has a differential amount of power to transmit. The source and summary of all this energy flow was and is a Creator being at the center of a weblike network where power flow was concentrated. While most of these creators were male, Ocean Woman brought the Great Basin into being and the Shawnee acknowledge Grandmother as their highest deity.

While Tsimshian have such a high god—heaven *laxha* "on high"—the actual releaser of this power was Raven, who came to earth as a *naxnox* (a shining youth called Txamsen) but, through the ill will of a slave, became the glutton Wigyet (Giant).

Tsimshian now use the term *naxnox* for a kind of dangerous spirit, but available evidence suggests that Tsimshian religion shared with the rest of the Americas a system of guardian spirits they called *naxnox* and represented by an elaborate series of masks. Elsewhere in the Americas, paint and gestures served to represent the spirit each human was bonded with, but the availability of red cedar and a tradition of carving encouraged these masked portrayals.

The only other two regions, both of them matrilineal, where masking was elaborated were the Northeast among Iroquois and the Southwest among Pueblos. Of interest, both Iroquois and Pueblos say their masks portray only one group of spirits, those who farmed, rather than a sample of all spirits available in the landscape.

Another ramification of this natural system, first taught me by the Lushootseed Salish, has to do with the duration and accessibility of this spirit and power. Throughout North America, summer was the time of economic pursuits and winter the time of religious ones. Thus, while someone could only be a success with one or more spirits to help and advise, innate ability being insufficient by itself; human and spirit were directly linked only during the depth of winter when full time could be devoted to this bond. Thus, throughout the Americas there were Winter Dances when people sang their power songs and impersonated their spirit guardian.

Yet, another kind of human, vital to the wellbeing of each community, maintained a constant link with his or her spirits. This was the native doctor or shaman, whose spirit was constantly nearby and ready to help cure human maladies. Among the Salish, where shamans still cure, no one should walk behind a doctor because his or her spirit hovers above and behind him or her and might injure an unprotected human who ventured behind a shaman at anytime. Thus, among the Salish, the world is populated by two different kinds of spirits: ordinary ones, who enhance a career, and special curing ones, who benefit only shamans. Moreover, shamans, have not only more direct links to their spirit, but many more of these spirits than other humans. Each encounter with a different kind of spirit conferred another song and the ability to cure or deal with another kind of malady or situation.

As much of the *naxnox* system has faded from modern Tsimshian belief, so too has native shamanism, although several terms for different kinds of shamans have been recorded. More important, however, than the traditional system of shamanism, called *halaayt* by Tsimshian, was the influence such beliefs had on the development of the other religious systems that spread along the Pacific Coast.

Tribal

Though no clear evidence has yet been found for a tribal system among the Tsimshian towns, its wide distribution along the coast suggests that it may have once been a part of Tsimshian religion. Based in a special reverence for place, the tribal system is predicated on the belief that a group, either kinship or residential, descended from a legendary ancestor who lived at that place until permanently limited to human shape by a Transformer. In this way, along the Fraser River or the outer coast of Vancouver Island, a being—simultaneously shimmering or shape-shifting as a human, species, spirit, or space—became permanently fixed in the form of a human ancestor. Many of the Nuchanuulth came from Wolves, still reverenced during mid-winter Wolf rituals. Nimpkish began when a Halibut spirit came out of the sea and removed its outer cloak to become fully human. The most famous example of this, of course, is the Bella Coola belief that the creator sent ancestors, often as pairs, to particular mountain peaks in their territory. After sending back to heaven the bird or animal skin they wore in their descent, these beings took human form and founded particular Bella Coola towns. During winter ceremonials, some of these ancestors were represented by masks worn by human descendants. Sometimes this transformation was more complicated, as when the first ancestor of the Katzie changed his daughter into the first sturgeon and sent her to live in Pitt Lake (Jenness 1955:10).

Also, along the Central coast, the earliest Kwakwaka'wakw ancestors "had no cannibal ceremonies in their winter ceremonial . . . They merely inherited the "crests" or "privileges" of the animal from which they descended" (Boas 1966:258).

Tsimshian has a perfect context for such a transformation, but there is no evidence it was ever so developed. After Raven stole the light in a box from the Head of the Nass, he tried to exchange it with people fishing for some candlefish (eulachons) but was refused. At the blinding moment when time and space began for the Tsimshian, all of the spirits who had been living in twilight took on their present shapes. Only Frogs, who were close to shamans, retained much of their primordial shape. By associating particular spirit fishers with particular places, the Tsimshian might have attributed a particular ancestor to a particular locale or town, but this remains speculation.

Among the Salish of Puget Sound where such evidence for a tribal ancestor is slim, there is artifactual evidence in the standard outline shape of the spirit planks used during Snoqualmi Soul Redeeming ceremonies. Each board was cut to represent the shape of a porpoise-like animal which was changed into the first ancestor of a downriver village according to one fragment of a legend.

Elsewhere in the Americas, aside from certain South American origin sagas about the human inhabitants of a river being delivered by a gigantic anaconda canoe, or North American Plains traditions of Stars founding communities, the only other area where totemic tribal ancestors are mentioned is the Maritimes where northeastern Algonquians each used the picture of a certain kind of animal or fish as a means of national identity.

Among the Wabanaki, these tribal emblems were scaled in terms of the intensity of the self-identification with them, with the Passamaquoddy most explicit since their tribal name literally translates as "those who pursue the pollock," a fish. Others serve as tribal badges of Malecite (Malaseet) = muskrat, Micmac = deer, and Penobscot = otter (Speck 1917:13). More communal images represent tribes members in a canoe.

Regional

Often regarded as distinctive of the Northwest Coast is the system of sects, cults, guilds, or degrees that were spreading during recent centuries from the Bella Bella to the north and to the south. Tsimshian call these grades *wihalaayt* (great *halaayt*), and each degree represented greater knowledge of esoteric lore, and greater access to power and prestige. What is fascinating about this system is that it effectively blends personal and social features into an overall system that involved the freeborn members of a town and of the larger society.

The most detailed series was at Bella Bella where survivors of six Heiltsuk towns settled together (Olson 1955; Harkin 1988). Like other Wakashans, Bella Bella had a double series of degrees, either inspired or frenzied (possessed). The inspired series (*dlu'elaxa*) was unmarked in that chiefs appeared in their usual guise with a variety of insignia. For example, a member of an inspired degree often wore a frontlet or masks painted in a variety of colors, particularly red. The frenzied series (*tseqa*) was marked as the insignia were highly specific and included masks painted black, along with violent shamanic states of ecstasy. Now, when button blankets are worn, the red side decorated with crest emblems is worn for the inspired series, but, for the frenzied displays, the blanket is worn inside out with the black side showing.

A child of an important family began his or her progression through the series at ten months with a first naming potlatch. Since human gestation was believed to take ten months, this naming marked the social birth of the child. Only those eligible for the position of high or town chief (*galaxa* = first off) went through the full series and spent four years in the first rank, often called the "cannibal," but "consumer" is a better translation.

In all, about 16 degrees or dancing societies existed and everyone was expected to be initiated into at least one. The lower grades, from 16 to 6, were open to those of good family, while those from 5 to 1 were open only to the elite. The dance and song of the lowest group was the most gentle and placid, but that of the highest was the most violent and feared. Each group owned insignia, particular cedar bark rings of appropriate color and design, and names, that is, winter holy names as distinct from summer secular names. Whistles, the breath of the spirits, were in particular concealed from non-members' sight.

Members expected to move up through the degrees to achieve the highest rank possible, very much like the cargo system that motivates political authority in Spanish America.

The first degree of the frenzied or highest series was that of *tanis* (consumer), and it was held by only six people, presumably from each of the chiefly families of the six original towns. Initiation depended not on gender but on family rank so some women became *tanis*, although most were men. One remained *tanis* for only four years, when the office was passed from mother's brother to eldest sister's eldest son.

It was this highest degree of Consumer that spread furthest along the coast as the personal privilege of the most prominent chiefs, creating a ritual network among the same elite that was most likely to intermarry. While Boas and others introduced the translation "cannibal" to refer to this grade, careful linguistic work by Susanne Hilton and John Rath (1982) revealed that because "you are what you eat" the dramatic consumption of flesh symbolized the increasing perfection of the human state.

Tsimshian call the Heiltsuk the *wədsda* or "enchanters" and recognized their superior reserves of power. Indeed, some William Beynon texts make it clear that the greatest of Tsimshian shamans went to Bella Bella to be "finished."

Tsimshian had five degrees of *halaayt*, two social and three personal. The two groups, with large memberships, were the dancers (*mila*, which means "to miss" in Heiltsuk, as in a missing person) and the dog-eaters (*nuɫm*), while the personal privileges, limited to special individuals, were those of fire throwers, destroyers, and consumers (*xgyet*). Each degree was distinguished by particular whistles, songs, gear, and gestures.

In comparison with their neighbors to the south, these Tsimshian coastal degrees show the influence of both the Bella Bella and the Owikeno, for whom only fire throwers made up the council that supervised the annual frenzied series, while the destroyers ranked highest in the inspired series and indicated readiness to become a Consumer, with a winter name that made reference to the sky or heaven, *laxha*, the most remote and powerful of Tsimshian beings.

Membership was not just a matter of initiation, however. So important were these degrees that there were at least four ways to acquire this status. The greatest chiefs and traders gave membership as a gift to each other. Others with great wealth could purchase the goodwill that "insured" initiation. In certain circumstances, the insignia, particularly whistles, were captured, forcing membership. Sometimes, members of other tribes were killed and their membership taken along with other possessions. In a famous example, a Kitimat chief had an affair with the wife of a Bella Bella chief so he could steal a whistle and force initiation.

While only the southern Tlingit chief Shakes at Wrangel was a member, if Europeans had not come, other Tlingit chiefs to the north would have been initiated eventually (Kan 1989).

The Haida (Swanton 1905a), whose degrees came from both the Tsimshian and the Bella Bella, may have had as many as a dozen degrees, with members described as "inspired" or "insured," but, there too, the consumers ranked first.

At the southern end of the distribution along the coast of Washington, some interesting overlaps can be observed. Dog-eaters, under the guise of Wolves or warriors, occurred under their Nootkan name (*lokwa.li*) among the Quileute, a language isolate. As the largest membership, its foreign origin contributed to its prestige. In fact, four of the five Quileute degrees originated elsewhere. The Fishers (*ca.yiq*) recall the Wakashan name for the frenzied winter dance grouping. The Whalers ("oily voiced") came from the Makah, and the Weather Workers ("south voiced") from the Quinault. Only the hunters were indigenous, and appropriately conferred the power to hunt elk upriver in the Olympic Mountains. In each case, membership could either be inherited through rank or purchased through wealth and bearing.

Among the Coast Salish, only some of them (Straits) had a single degree (*xədxədəb*) called the Growlers and involving death and rebirth symbolism like other shamanic systems. Hosted at one town, teenagers, both boys and girls, from several tribes were initiated to provide them with a power source before they began more serious individualized questing for spirits. By virtue of this initiation, these children shared the same spirit, a giant bloody baby that migrated with ducks.

The nearest parallel to this system of graded and diverse memberships occurs in the Great Lakes and Southwest.

Growing out of older shamanic groupings of related powers, about 1700 at Chequamegon on a Lake Superior peninsula in Wisconsin, amalgamated Ojibwa shamans forged the Midewiwin or shamans academy. In full form, it has nine degrees, four of the Earth, four of the Sky, and one for Ghost members. Each grade has an animal skin pouch appropriate to that level, such as a mammal for lower grades and bird for higher ones.

In the Southwest, for over one thousand years as indicated by the building of kiva chambers, specialized priesthoods have evolved from shamanic concerns. Among the Keresan Pueblos, whose priesthoods had precedence over those of other Pueblos, a complex hierarchy distinguished man or woman diseases, caused respectively by angry animals or witches, cured by appropriate priests, all male—although aided by male or female spirit doctors. Each priesthood was divided into the grades of novice, adept, and high priest—distinguished by their degree of knowledge and ability. In turn, the priesthoods were ranked with those treating minor complaints less powerful than those curing major diseases and, yearly, exorcising the entire town. The leader of the most powerful priesthood, as part of his responsibilities, was also initiated into all of the other orders and, possessed of complete knowledge, also served as the priestly leader of his town. In this capacity, however, he was equated with the Keres Creator, Thought Woman, and was ceremonially regarded as a woman, though he was a husband and father in ordinary life.

Noble

Privilege was the basis for the fourth system among the Tsimshian and other coastal nations. Membership was limited to leading families in various communities and signaled their elite status. Since only members of the highest class could belong, this system, called *smhalaayt* (real *halaayt*) by the Tsimshian, was truly international in scope. Its insignia were the frontlet (*amhalaayt*), woven robe and apron, and raven rattle. Tradition says it originated among the Nisga'a and spread to other First Nations. Indeed, for over a century Tlingit chiefs have lain in state wearing not the hat of their crest, as previously, but instead the *shakee.at* (frontlet) that indicated their elite status to everyone along the coast.

While I am not certain, a likely context for the creation and spread of these chiefly insignia was the displacement of the Tongass Tlingit from the lower Nass river by Nisga'a moving downstream to control the eulachon fishery. The name of the Nass derives from the Tlingit word (*naas(i)*) for "intestines" because it was the "food belly" of the North Coast in the spring (Emmons 1991:8). The Tsimshian term for the Nass River is *klusms*.

To find a similar elite system in the Americas, however, we must look into the archaeological record of the Mississippians, who led the North American heartland for a thousand years before the Spanish arrived. There, among the trappings of the Southern Cult, were copper and other emblems that signaled membership in a set of interlaced chiefdoms much like that of the historic northwest.

Perhaps a remnant of these Mississippian chiefdoms, the League of the Iroquois has a parallel to the frontlet in the *gastowe* or chief's cap of the royaner (league chief). In ancient times, from both the archaeological and linguistic record, such chiefs wore deer antlers as a badge of office. After the 50 chiefly titles of the original Five Nations were enshrined by Deganawidah at the founding of the league, five tribal versions of this feathered cap became the featured insignia.

Another possible parallel was the eagle feather headdress with full length tail, symbolizing a comet among its Pawnee originators, as a badge of high chiefship among Plains peoples, whose founding ancestors were Stars (Flaming Arrows) come to earth.

Summary

Motivations for initiates joining these four systems were variously personal, familial, and communal, but all were concerned with acquiring prestige and power to safeguard one's self, family, kin, and community. Different experiences formed the basis for particular bonds between humans and spirits. In cases where more than one human shared the same spirit, this association was celebrated by solidarities with common attributes, injunctions, and feastings. In more elaborate instances, these groupings acted as priesthoods devoted to particular cures or concerns.

With this general American pattern as backdrop, other distinctions were developed into the Tribal, Regional, and Noble degrees of ranking. The common tribal totem provided a means for ritual unity lacking in the political realm, while the regional system of graded groupings functioned much like clans memberships to distinguish internal divisions but interrelate them to those elsewhere. Only the noble system seems to be more distinctive of the Northwest, although so many chiefdoms of the East and South were devastated by European epidemics that the Bella Bella dance series may provide a glimpse into Mississippian or other archeological network of international elites.

In each case, the system was based on a type of knowledge that could be partitioned, taught by degrees and examples, through a series of one or more initiations. In this way, as with all groupings, the distinction was made between those who were "out" and those who were "in," along with the factor of "in-tensity." It was not enough for these systems to just be "in," one also had to progress deeper into the knowledge to add power and prestige.

In the process of sustaining a vision, with or without formal degrees, a general equation was enhanced that knowledge = power = long life. But the ultimate source of this knowledge was not other humans, but the spirits themselves, the immortal owners of the landscape. Yet, while human and spirit were bonded for a lifetime, the spirit, except in the case of a shaman, was not continuously present. Therefore a key is needed to reopen this bond at every instance and that key is the song provided by the spirit at the initial vision that created that partnership.

In all, therefore, though expressed by at least four modalities or systems of ranked degrees among the Tsimshian and other First Nations, American native religions express a belief in an underlying equation such that transfers of life-giving wisdom from spirits to humans is mediated by song:

Knowledge (*wilaay*) = Power = Life (*diduuls*)
↕ Song (*limi*)
Spirits (*naxnox*)

TSIMSHIAN MOIETIES
AND OTHER CLARIFICATIONS[a]

ABSTRACT

Renewed interest and research among the Tsimshian of the North Pacific Coast has led to the clarification of several important aspects of this society, dealing with social classes, focal figures, and periodicity. Also among these has been the recognition that those villages which have not relocated to modern intertribal towns continue to preserve a moiety pattern that has become obscured by the fourfold groupings of more recent date. This indicates that the Tsimshian can best be described in terms of asymmetrical Blackfish/Raven moieties in which the first one is Owner on the coast and the second has diffused into the interior to become Owner there. The opposite moiety, therefore, functions as Other in a broad, inclusive enough sense to incorporate new members into the community and society.

Despite their considerable linguistic differences, the Tsimshian, Haida, and Tlingit have long been recognized as sharing a matrilineal descent system that meshes together complex patterns of crest inheritance, social class, and resource ownership for which the Northwest Coast is justly famous. While many of these commonalities now appear to derive from a Tsimshian source, especially in terms of the crests (inherited art forms), full comparisons have been hampered because, while the Haida and Tlingit have clear moieties, the Tsimshian have been described as having four phratries. Although these four crest groups do exist, it is becoming more apparent from observations in the unrelocated southern and upriver villages that these four actually function among the Tsimshian as semi-moieties or sections of the aboriginal moiety pattern. Traditionally, each village seems to have had an Owner and Other Moiety, in addition to some resident aliens sometimes. When people congregated at the trading and missionary settlement, this Owner/Other distinction became threatened and became resolved by the pooling of the crest groups into the semi-moieties, which were already inherent in the system, but now became separated out. To strengthen this argument, I will also attempt to clarify other aspects of Tsimshian culture and society that have also been overlooked or misunderstood, especially as these relate to focal figures like the house, the chief, and the deity.

Among the factors explaining the renewed interest in the Tsimshian are the attention given to their myth of Asdiwal by Claude Levi-Strauss (1967); the skillful work of William Duncan in setting up the Christian utopia at the towns of Metlakatla and New Metlakatla (Garfield 1939; Usher 1974); and the rediscovery of the fieldnotes of William Beynon (1927), a Tsimshian who parleyed his fluency in the language, his hereditary claims to a chiefship, and his work as an ethnographer for Marius Barbeau, Franz Boas, Viola Garfield, Amelia Susman, and others into an enviable position as an informed elder (Halpin 1978). Unfortunately, Barbeau then used much of the Beynon data to develop some unacceptable interpretations of Northwest prehistory (Duff 1961, 1964).

---

[a] This article was previously published in *Northwest Anthropological Research Notes*, 16(2):148–164 (1982).

Further stimulation has been provided by the linguistic research of John Dunn (1979b), especially his description of an unreported fourth Tsimshian language among the southern most villages. Since 1976, I have been visiting these villages of Hartley Bay and Klemtu where a closer version of the aboriginal culture can still be said to function, complete with moieties.

In the following pages, an overview of Tsimshian society as presently known will be provided, arguing for moieties congruent with those of the Haida and Tlingit and looking at social, economic, and political organizations in terms of focal features like the house, fall festival, chief (as apex of the class and production systems), and the deity.

Tsimshian Revised

Usually, the Tsimshian are divided into three groups speaking two languages, Coast and Interior. The Coast Tsimshian occupied nine winter villages between the mouth and the canyon of the Skeena River (Dorsey 1897; Garfield 1939). Historically, these were the villages that clustered into discrete neighborhoods around the Hudson's Bay Company trading post moved to Port Simpson in 1834, and that were involved in an efflorescence of competitive or rivalry potlatching as a means of sorting out the relative ranks of the assembled chiefs who now had daily or routine contact (Garfield 1939). It was also these villages that supplied converts to Metlakatla after Duncan moved his followers there (Barnett 1942; Usher 1971, 1974).

As a result of this transient, furious, and unusual potlatching; the Coast Tsimshian emerged as a chiefdom under the leadership of a matriline of Eagle chiefs each bearing the hereditary name-title of Ligeex (possibly meaning Sheer Cliff), which had come to the Tsimshian from the Bella Bella through the Kitimat by virtue of the marriage of a chief to a Haisla (Northern Kwakiutlan) woman (Boas 1916b:570; Garfield 1939:184, note 3). This exalted position was achieved because the Eagle chiefs of the town-tribe of Gispaxlo'ots had a double reason for aggressive potlatching; they needed to validate the use of the Ligeex name as a replacement for the earlier name-title of Dzabesa, that was shamed when its last holder was beheaded in battle, and second, they were asserting an exclusive claim to the Skeena River trade with the Gitksan Tsimshian and the Carrier Athapaskans above the canyon. Eventually, both of these claims became publicly recognized and were taken so seriously that when the Hudson's Bay Company built a trading post at Lake Babine among the Athapaskans, endangering the need for an upriver trade by providing a local supply of goods, Ligeex mobilized a force of Tsimshian warriors sufficient to utterly destroy the post. The Hudson's Bay officials were only able to secure the right to trade up the Skeena by buying out the rights of Ligeex.

In contrast to the coastal elaboration, the Interior speech grouping consists of the Gitksan and the Niska. The Gitksan live above the canyon of the Skeena and give indications that they were once Athapaskans who became Tsimshianized to coastal patterns of kinship, crests, and cremation over the past couple centuries (Adams 1973; MacDonald 1979). The Niska occupy the valley of the Nass River, underwent a political reorganization (similar to that of the Coast Tsimshian) resulting in the name Sagewan (Mountain) becoming head chief and became early converts to Christianity of such vehemence that they hacked down their own totem poles and abandoned levels of social organization greater than the household (Usher 1974).

Among all the Tsimshian, the House is the basic unit of the social organization, encompassing three features. In the past, the House was, first, a rectangular building made of cedar planks and totemicly-carved support posts for which the Northwest Coast is famous; second, a membership of matrilineally-related males, their spouses and children, and their avunculocally-residing heirs under the leadership of the person holding the highest ranking hereditary name entitling him (rarely her) to the position of House Master; and, third, a repository of crests (songs, dances, designs, anecdotes, and more) kept behind an elaborate wooden partition at the rear of the house. All of these were legitimated by a corpus of myths that itemized the names, resource locations, wanderings, privileges, and constructions to which the House Master and his retainers were entitled through recognized claims. The essence of the household was these myths and it is them, rather than their superficial representation in art, that substantiate membership in the higher classes of chief and commoner (Barbeau 1928, 1929; Duff 1959; Halpin 1973). The lowest class of slaves lacked any claims to life or status at all.

For this reason, mythology is the key to the complexity of Northwest cultures. For example, after severe depopulation, the Owekeno Kwakiutl, just to the south, began a black market in crest privileges by selling the validating myths rather than the contingent objects to other coastal people (Olson 1950, 1954).

Thus, while gabled plank houses are no longer used by the Tsimshian and many of their crests reside in museums, the essence of the household, its myths and members, continue in stable form. At present, most Tsimshian have neolocal residences and nuclear families, but people continue to inherit names and with them receive a place in a non-residential house led by the holder of the ranking name. These House Masters have male names, but there are a few cases where there was no qualified male to inherit the master's name and, to prevent its loss, it was given to a proper kinswoman until a man became available. Myths validate names, but the fortunes of any particular name rise and fall with the prestige of its holders; as one potlatches and earns respect by being generous, the name will prosper, but as another ignores obligations to retainers and the wider community, the fame of the name will suffer accordingly (Miller 1976, 1978).

Similarly, the success or failure of a household or a kin group depends on demographic factors. As long as a woman gives birth to numerous healthy and responsible descendants, the prestige of her matriline is assured. As a household grows with such successes, minor crests are transferred to daughter households as each splinters off. If these dependent households become successful in their own right, they can negotiate to borrow the more important crests from the lineage head until such time as they themselves are able to establish an independent line. Ultimately, each of these matrilineages of linked households traces membership in one of the four crest groups *(ptəx)* known as Blackfish, Raven, Eagle, or Wolf. At the widest level, as Boas (1916b:520) and Garfield (1939:231) have already noted, when a Tsimshian married into the Tlingit or the Haida, these four "phratries" merge into moieties with the Tsimshian Blackfish-Wolf equated with the Tlingit Eagle-Wolf and Haida Raven, while the Tsimshian Raven-Eagle is equivalent to the Raven of the Tlingit and the Eagle of the Haida.

This, apparently, is the received understanding of the Tsimshian as of a few years ago. We now have, courtesy of renewed fieldwork and the Beynon (1927) manuscripts, more pieces to the Tsimshian puzzle and with them a fuller picture emerges, one that indicates a Tsimshian society that was even more complex than previously acknowledged, to the extent of dwarfing Tlingit and Haida sophistication.

On linguistic grounds, we need to recognize four Tsimshian divisions: Nass-Gitksan and Coast-Southern. Southern refers to those communities that used Southern Tsimshian (called *sküüxks* by its speakers) until a century ago when the Christian texts prepared by William Duncan and Thomas Crosby in Coast Tsimshian gave the coastal variant the necessary prestige for it to replace Southern. At present, Southern Tsimshian tenuously survives as an heirloom privilege of a Klemtu chiefly family, with about six elderly speakers (Miller 1979, n.d.).

This fourfold language division is paralleled by a four class system that differs in complexity from the three class system of chiefs, commoners, and slaves reported for the rest of the coast. Halpin (1973:100) used the Beynon-Barbeau papers to suggest that these four classes are (1) chiefs (*smgyigyet*, in the Dunn dictionary (1978:90, No. 1731): *smgyigyet*—chiefs, nobility, literally "real people," *sm'oogyit* in the singular (Dunn 1978:91, No. 1742) when in their summer, economic guise and *wutahalaayt* "great shamanic dancer" in their winter, religious aspect), (2) councilors (lekagiget, Dunn (1978:66, No. 1278) lists lagyigyet—olden times, old people, tradition) who were elite advisors to the chief and who included experts like the *gyamgyempk* (astronomer) who watched the skies, winds, and tides; (3) the commoners (*wa'ayin*), (listed by Dunn (1978:107, No. 2047) as *wah'a'ayin*—an unforgiveable offense, a commoner) who made up the membership of households subject to resource availability, demographic pressures, personality conflicts, and the public recognition of their shifts in residence by serving as helpers or guests at the potlatch of a house master (Miller n.d.; Adams 1973); and (4) both last and least, the slaves (*lelongit*), (*liluungit*—slave (Dunn 1978:66; No. 1287), by inference and folk etymology; a Tlingit) who were war captives, criminals who forfeited their freedom, and their descendents.

While all of the classes except slaves were entitled to lay claim to crest animals, chiefs were distinguished from everyone else because their crest animals were highly specific, e.g., Prince of Grizzly rather than just grizzly, and artistic versions of the crest are usually decorated with abalone (Halpin 1973:133). Moreover, chiefs had two types of artists working for them. Ordinary crest art was produced by artists and their assistants working with only mild precautions taken to see that the piece was first publicly viewed at its potlatch dedication. This art included paintings of crest figures and designs on clothing, headdress frontlets, house posts, fronts, screens, canoes, drums, feast dishes, and free-standing poles.

Each chief was also a priest, however, with responsibility for bestowing ~ throwing guardian spirit power into the children of his crest group. This power *(naxnox)* was also contained in hereditary names held by the nobility, especially councilors, and displayed during winter ceremonials. The power of each name was intimately associated with certain art objects, most especially masks, produced by fearsome *naxnox* artists called the *gitsontk* "people secluded" who worked in great secrecy, punishing with death any unqualified person unfortunate enough to stumble on their workshops hidden in the forest (Barbeau 1950; Halpin n.d.). These *naxnox* artists have all of the appearances of a secret esoteric priesthood analogous to those of the Southwestern Pueblos, where they serve to reinforce the authority of the priestly leadership clique. I have begun to suspect that the *gitsontk* performed a similar function among the Tsimshian, helping to account for the social complexity and the shift to a chiefdom level recognized since the European intrusion. Like the developed art work, however, the *naxnox* artists, slaves, and counselors have not continued into the present. This is a pity because the accounts we have of *naxnox* performances indicate that they were full of magical marvels that equaled or surpassed similar illusions reported for the Pawnee Big Doctor Performance (Weltfish 1971:329). Ligeex had some especially impressive *naxnox* name performances, which included two enormous hands that reached down from the roof of a house and took a man up into heaven (Barnett 1940, Book 2:2), or a mask called Crack of Heaven with the ability to have the house split into two, separate, and come back together as spectators sat in their seats (Boas 1916b:556). Other, more plausible feats involving masks or a 7 ft. mountain are also mentioned.

Only recently has attention focused on notions of periodicity among the Tsimshian, serving to organize and to regulate the flow of time. Congruent with the inheritance of crests and names within households, or, as the Tsimshian themselves say, "the giving of people to names," the Tsimshian maintain this static world view via a systematic belief in reincarnation through matrilines in alternating generations. The Gitksan are quite explicit on this, "young mothers frequently call their babies 'granny' or 'gramps' . . . recognized by a characteristic scar or mark on his body, or because his mother dreamed about a particular person just before his birth" (Adams 1973:30). These reincarnations never cross the sexes, although they do shift from humans to other mammals such as killer whales, contrary to the reports of Stevenson (1975) for the Haida who share with the Tsimshian this belief in soul transmutation.

Similarly, seasonal residence patterns among the Tsimshian are only now being articulated. The previous model recognized that large plank-house winter villages were occupied during the ceremonial feasting and potlatching season before the arrival of spring encouraged the townspeople to move into family camps. Each village was a corporate unit with a dominant crest group and resident affines, together with a group of specialists that included the men who cremated high ranking dead at the specific site always used by the village.

Lastly, we need to revise our understanding of chiefship among the Tsimshian. In the past, the chiefs were regarded as the titular heads of crest groups with little if any coercive power. Yet the presence of the *naxnox* artists, who we re once called "thugs" as well as "artists" in front of me, suggests otherwise. Among the Gitksan, a chief receives $20.00 at feasts because he is complete (has ten fingers and ten toes), while lesser men receive lesser monies (Adams 1973:68). The term for chiefs means "real people," reinforcing the attitude that only chiefs were fully human. Another term for chief, *miyaani* "base, trunk" further suggests that chiefs were also the basis of society, if not also the class heirarchy.

Chiefs are said to be steady and reliable, staying in one place like the houses and villages they control. Commoners, on the other hand, are considered shiftless, unreliable, and highly mobile, changing their allegiances to other households of the crest depending on the availability of more food, a kinder master, a needy relative, or more spectacular doings. While this is less true now than it was in the past, feasts and potlatches continue to be the mechanism by which people signal their shifts in allegiances by acting with the hosts or the guests at these public events (Miller n.d.).

Among the Southern Tsimshian, I was specifically told of chiefs with extremely strong personalities who had "the hobby of killing people just like Idi Amin did." Sometimes, other chiefs brought pressure to bear on such a murderer so that he and his supporters left the village or camp to settle elsewhere. At Kitkatla, however, the story is told of a murderous chief who had the people completely cowed until one day his slave, while fishing from a canoe, took matters into his own hands, literally, and managed to drown both the chief and himself. Thereafter, the name of the slave was assumed by a noble in homage and was potlatched through generous giving into a very prestigious name.

Thus, these indications suggest that Tsimshian chiefs could be very autocratic if possessed of a strong personality, but their tenure was not unlimited, especially if they persisted in many antisocial acts.

A corollary of this chiefly prominence is the Tsimshian belief in a high god. Several early missionaries and traders called attention to a belief in a vague sky god who became assimilated with the image of the Christian God after European arrival, but there is an even more fascinating belief, repressed by their convert zeal, associated with a high god simply called *gal*. Unlike the so-called Chief Above or Heaven (Boas 1916b:543), *gal* has complex and very non-Christian associations suggesting that he has some antiquity. His name has survived into the present as part of the ritual held when a bear is killed. The bear's tongue is cut into four pieces, each of which is offered to "a corner of the Universe" while thanks is given to *gal*. These "corners" relate to the Tsimshian belief, shared with other Pacific coastal cultures, that the world is a large house resting on a pole held on the chest of a supernatural whose movements cause earthquakes, so common along the Pacific rim that they have a mythological explanation.

The term *gal* has two related etymologies. The first is a particle meaning "empty" (Dunn 1978:26, No. 474), as in the word for the nose ring once worn only by the nobility (Dunn 1978:20, No. 359), which seems to mean "something that passes through an empty space." In this sense, then, *gal* is the unknown, the void, the outside of the Universe, the primal mystery; and, therefore, evokes the unimaginable, awesome powers of a chief in his full form. Similarly, Barbeau (1961:43) says "gaul" is the loon, which Dunn (1978:26, No. 477) renders as *gool*, with a long vowel. This is also plausible as a meaning since the loon is an appropriate vehicle for representing such an abstract concept because it is an acquatic bird of great abilities, able to fly high and dive deeply, at home in air, land, and water. It can go anywhere and probably has the resilience to break through the edges of the cosmic house and enter the void beyond, much as nearby Athapaskans believe swans are able to do (Ridington 1978). In all, the existence of such a belief in an omnipresent abstract divinity of unfathomable abilities seems to provide further support for the power of chiefs among the Tsimshian; *gal* may represent a forceful projection of awesome strength into the cosmos and beyond. If only as wishful thinking on the part of the chiefs, *gal* still provides a prototype of boundless authority, nonetheless.

In summary, we have up-dated our model of the Tsimshian in general, particularly for economic, social, and political institutions. We will now turn to the more specific problem of moieties among the Tsimshian, relative to the previous reassessment. To do this, we shift from a general discussion of all the Tsimshian and focus directly on the Southern Tsimshian at Kitkatla, Hartley Bay, and Klemtu, with whom I have been working at their invitation since 1976.

The Southern Tsimshian

The attraction of the Southern Tsimshian is that, unlike their coast relatives, they continue to reside on or very near their aboriginal winter village sites. This means that they have not relocated to trade or to profess a pan-Tsimshian Christianity; have internally handled the reorganization forced on them by epidemics, depopulation, and a money economy; and have been less subject to continual, daily interference from Eurocanadian agents of the industrial world. True, industry has had its effects in terms of the adoption of a money economy, diesel fishing boats, New England frame houses, compulsory education, and spoken English; but these villages have been left, by and large, to their own devices for coping with and modifying these external influences so as to better fit them into traditional patterns. For example, in these villages, the town chief plays the organ at the church services, quite literally, orchestrating the proceedings without taking formal charge of them, although this does sometimes happen when they lead a prayer service. Also, the heirs to important chiefly names are strongly encouraged to work for college degrees, thereby giving them prestige and authority in the Tsimshian and the Canadian worlds. Wherever possible, traditional forms have been preserved and adapted to modern contingencies, and it is such solutions that make these villages such rewarding places for research. Of the three villages, Kitkatla seems the most conservative, Hartley Bay the best adapted, and Klemtu the least successful because it is inhabited by both Tsimshian and XaiXais Kwakiutlans, who were enemies aboriginally and who continue their differences as intertribal, interpersonal, and domestic violence and mayhem (Olson 1955; Miller 1981a). Yet because a large cannery operated in the town until about 1960, bringing in many Oriental and Canadian workers, the town gained some internal cohesion by reformulating these tribal differences as one of exogamous moieties, the better to present a more united front to the outsiders working at the cannery (Miller 1979). At one time, I assumed that Klemtu "invented" moieties to cope with their situation, but it is now clear to me that the moieties were inherent in their system all along.

The baseline ethnography for the Southern Tsimshian includes the notebooks of William Beynon (1927) and the publications of Ronald Olson (1955) and Philip Drucker (1940). These works, however, were directed specifically toward reconstructing the past situation, paying little if any attention to the contemporary scene in these villages. Therefore, they report four phratries and intertribal differences (especially for Klemtu) that satisfied the previous model of the Tsimshian, but had little to do with how these communities actually functioned internally at the time of the visit.

During my initial experiences in Hartley Bay, I was told about Killerwhale, Eagle, and Raven crest memberships in the village. Later, during the winter feast season, I attended dinners prepared by the women of each of the crest groups as a preamble to the assumption of names and other status changes by members of the crest. All of this served to confirm the existence and functions of the crests within the village context. Therefore, it was startling to meet a woman who claimed Wolf membership at a time when I had no other criteria for evaluating her claim. When I later asked the Blackfish town chief how this could be the case, I was told "Wolves go with Blackfish," indicating that they had no independent place in the town. In other words, the Wolf is included as a grouping within the Blackfish. As it happened this woman had moved with her parents from Port Essington about the time it was abandoned and she and her children, despite decades of residence or birth in the village, continue to be reminded that they are foreigners in the community.

This equation of Blackfish and Wolf makes good sense because Northwest Coast mythology abounds in references to the common identity of Blackfish and Wolves. Both are recognized to be social carnivores and native tradition has elaborated this observation into a belief that particular supernaturals assume the form of a Blackfish pod or a Wolf pack, depending upon whether they wish to travel in water or on land. As individuals, Blackfish are also said to belong to one of the four phratries, with their membership indicated by their body color and the shape of the dorsal fin (Boas 1916b:45).

The next year I visited Klemtu and there found a full moiety system in operation, despite ethnographic reports from the 1940s describing four matri-phratries among the resident Gitisdzu Tsimshian and three quasi-matrilineal groups among the Xaixais (Olson 1949). As a strategy for presenting a united front toward outsiders temporarily working in the cannery, everyone with a Gitisdzu mother took a Blackfish affiliation and those with Xaixais mothers became Ravens. Previous Wolf or Eagle titles became assimilated into the appropriate tribal moiety. In this way, I discovered that important Eagle names reported by previous anthropologists are now held by self-identified Ravens, while Wolf titles had always been negligible in Klemtu. In short, Klemtu had completed the moiety symmetry by equating Raven and Eagle, much as Hartley Bay assimilated Wolf to Blackfish.

While there is a firm mythological basis for treating Blackfish and Wolf alike, there is no ready mythological solution for the Raven-Eagle equation, aside from the fact that they are both birds. If one were necessary, my guess is that people would cite the example of the ubiquitous Raven cycle, where Raven as culture hero assumed any number of shapes and disguises to gain access to food or women. Hence, it would be easy to argue that Raven as a classic shape-shifter could readily assume the form and role of Eagle, making them interchangeable.

The equation of Tsimshian with Blackfish at Klemtu has another important mythological ramification. According to published ethnography, all Tsimshian traced their ancestry to a place called Prairie Town (Temlaxham), a specific location on the Skeena River, two miles from modern Hazelton, British Columbia. There the chiefs, classes, and crests particularly Grizzly Bear, were said to have been instituted. After a series of catastrophes and rebuildings, the Tsimshian diaspora began from there (Barbeau 1928). Yet a few accounts make note of the anomalous datum that when the Grizzly people came down the Skeena from the interior and reached the coast, they met people who claimed Blackfish as their crest and pointed to a place called In-gwin-aks as the source of their identify (Garfield and Wingert 1950). The modern Klemtu town chief, a Blackfish, validates his position by claiming a saga in which his ancestor visited the undersea home of the

Blackfish chief, a supernatural, at a place in the Moore Islands called In-gwin-aks. Checking in the other villages, I learned that all Southern Tsimshian town chiefs are Blackfish, also claiming the In-gwin-aks story as their legitimation.

What this means is that all Southern Tsimshian towns "belong" to the Blackfish, who have come to share them with other crest groups through time, although the foreign origins of these other crests is always kept in mind.

At Hartley Bay, the Wolf group became submerged within Blackfish. The Raven group consists of older members who trace their ancestry elsewhere and uses speakers from Kitkatla, whose dialect differs from the local one, and sets them apart at feasts. The resident Eagles have an account of their origin that includes events told in greater detail by the Haida, suggesting their ultimate origin or that of their crests on the Queen Charlotte Islands (Duff 1964). In this concern, Hartley Bay can be regarded as focused on a Blackfish/Eagle moiety division since these are the dominant crests in the town, holding the ranking name-titles. The other crests are either foreign or too small to function on their own.

At Kitkatla, the Blackfish and Raven crests vie for control, with the other two phratries taking secondary roles.

In sum, then, the pattern for the Southern Tsimshian consists of villages occupied by the Blackfish and at least one other crest group. Throughout, the moiety functions on two levels. Within each village, there is a Blackfish/Other distinction; while at the intervillage level there is an equation of Blackfish with Wolf and Raven to Eagle. For this reason, the fourfold crests should not be called phratries because this implies that they are independent of each other. Rather, based on accepted terminology, especially for the analogous Australian groups, we should speak of the four crests as semi-moieties.

Of these semi-moieties, the Blackfish and Raven do seem to have prominence over the others from a linguistic perspective (Boas 1916b:480). The terms for the Blackfish and Raven crests have no ready etymologies, differing considerably from even the ordinary words for blackfish-killerwhale *(lpun)* and raven *(gaax)*. The terms for the other two crests, however, are transparent, meaning "on the Eagle" and "on the Wolf," using the ordinary terms for these animals. On this basis, it is tempting to argue that Eagle and Wolf are recent introductions, while Blackfish and Raven have been part of Tsimshian society for so long that their original names have become contracted and distorted through time. While this does indeed seem likely, we must nonetheless withhold final judgment until it is clear that these untranslatable terms were not borrowed from some other group, as the Haida have borrowed Tsimshian terms for their moieties.

Nevertheless, the Blackfish and Raven semi-moieties require a further reconsideration of the moiety pattern on the entire northern coast, especially when it is realized that the Tsimshian, Tlingit, and Haida were so intensely inter-related, for example through chiefly intermarriage, that Dunn (1979a) has been able to argue for something like a Macro-Crow terminology system shared among the three tribes. In addition, the Tlingit and Haida acknowledge the Tsimshian as the source for some of their most important crests, if not as the stimulus for their entire crest systems. This is plausible because the Tsimshian unquestionably had the most elaborate of all the crest systems, incorporating not only differences between the crest groups found among the other two tribes, but also drawing internal differences of rank among the crests or designs within each group (Halpin 1973).

Moieties in the North Pacific and Elsewhere

As a general rule, then, the *in situ* villages suggest that these moieties were organized in terms of a discrete, exclusive crest group of Owners who founded the community and then shared it with at least one Other crest group that was more diverse and inclusive. Among the Southern Tsimshian, the Owners were the Blackfish and the Other is variously the Raven, Eagle, or potentially Wolf. Among the Gitksan, where the communities are also largely intact, Adams (1973:23) found the same pattern, with the Frog crest occupying the role of Owners. This is curious because the Frog of the interior equates with the Coast Tsimshian Raven. Yet it is the Fireweed crest with its Grizzly emblem that equates with the Coast Blackfish and plays the role of Other. According to legend, when the people left Prairie Town with the Grizzly Bear crest and met the coastal people with the Blackfish one, they exchanged crests and became a single group. Actually, they did more than simply equate emblems, they revised them to fit local ecology. Thus, the Grizzly and the Blackfish become transformed into Grizzly of the Sea (complete with dorsal fin) and into Blackfish of the Lake, so it could live inland (Halpin 1973).

The modern supremacy of Frog suggests that another, later dynamic occurred in the villages above the Skeena canyon. An insight into which comes from the work of Oberg (1973:44) among the Tlingit, where he found that the Ravens had a unity lacked by the Eagle-Wolf moiety because the former were closely identified with the mythological Raven. Yet this lack of Eagle-Wolf cohesion enabled them to incorporate all of the Tlingitized Athapaskans during the historic period. Although unstated, it seems likely that the Eagles established ownership over these new areas, much as the Ravens own Tlingit coastal territory but trace the source of their crests to the mouth of the Skeena, where Tsimshian have been for several thousand years (Duff 1961, 1964). Comparing the international equations, however, shows that Tlingit Eagle-Wolf links with Tsimshian Blackfish, not the Tlingit Raven Owners as some might expect. This makes sense because Raven is the central figure of north coast mythology and the joint occupation of the mainland by Tsimshian and Tlingit encouraged them to consistently equate all of the Raven crests. Further, the Wolf crest may have come to the Tsimshian through high ranking Tlingit wives who would have needed Blackfish husbands of equal rank and ownership.

The Ravens were also the Haida Owners, with Eagle being the Other. While the crests of the Tsimshian Blackfish and the Haida Raven were largely the same, they emphasized different primary crests. Tsimshian and Haida Eagles were almost identical, and the Hartley Bay situation suggests that their myths originated through the intermarriage of Haida wives to Blackfish men.

At a more abstract level, these three nations, while sharing most crests and the intermoiety equations, have categorized the same moieties differently. The Tsimshian seem to divide them as sky (birds)/earth (mammals), the Tlingit as forager (Raven)/predator (Eagle-Wolf), and the Haida as land (Raven)/water (Eagle), both as a fisher and as descended from Foam Woman.

Returning to the intra-Tsimshian case, recalling the previous discussion, we can hypothesize that the Tsimshian Blackfish as Owners were contrasted with the Raven as Other in the distant past. When Tsimshian people and influence began to move up the Skeena to the Athapaskans and kinship bonds were formed, the earliest Gitksan hybrids would have been Raven-Frog in order for them to legally marry high-prestige coastal Blackfish and set up trading alliance. In time, the other semi-moieties would have been adopted for the purpose of continuing to arrange proper exogamous marriages. Initially, it seems plausible that coastal Blackfish traders would have married newly-made Raven-Frog women to claim and to solidify their advantages with the interior. Given this as the first step, everything else logically follows to derive the pattern of semi-moiety distribution among the Tsimshian villages.

Nor is this contrast between exclusive Owner and inclusive other moieties limited to the Northwest Coast. John Swanton (1905a; 1928:725), who had the privilege of working both in the Northwest and the Southeast of Native America, wisely noted similarities between the two areas based on "widespread commercialism." What he did not notice in his own data, however, was the analogy between Creek and Tlingit moieties, where the Creek Red moiety was considered warlike as were the Tlingit Wolves while the Creek White and Tlingit Raven were more pacific. In the words of Oberg (1973:47–48), Wolf people were considered "warlike, quick-tempered, restless wanderers" with the crests of animal killers, while the Raven people were "wise, cautious, and the real founders of Tlingit society," possessing non-predatory crests such as raven, frog, woodworm, and mountain goat. While the Tlingit Eagle-Wolf took in foreigners, however, the Creek White (not Red) moiety adopted in aliens. Rather than confusing the comparison, this difference can be shown to correlate with differences in Tlingit and Creek social organization.

Among the Creek, the White leader *(mikko)* was civil head of a town, while the Red head was military leader. The civil leader was responsible for all the townspeople, while the Red one directed only the men. Hence, White was inclusive and diverse, but Red was exclusive. As shown above, the inclusive moiety adopts outsiders; so the Creek pattern is consistent with the model, also indicating the incredible strength that proprietary rights play in the Northwest since neither the White or Red group is specifically called Owners. Furthermore, the relative position of White or Red chief depended in practice upon whether the town as a whole was considered White or Red, peaceful or warlike, by virtue of precedent or a series of competitive ball games. By contrast, the Tlingit town affiliations were much less subject to manipulation or change, save from demographic fluctuations.

Tewa data on moieties from the Southwest Culture Area provide insight into the complexity of such demographic fluctuations. As described by Ortiz (1969), himself a Tewa, the moieties are balanced along a temporal dimension into Summer and Winter memberships, with the appropriate moiety chief governing the pueblo during the respective season. Mediating between the moieties are various priesthoods who function "at the middle of the structure." Yet this balance becomes deceptive upon a closer inspection: the Winter moiety is associated with men, hunting, and a seven month season; while the Summer moiety is linked with women, farming, and a five month period. Further, the sexes are asymmetrical since "the qualities of both sexes are believed present in men, while women are only women /thus/ the Summer moiety represents sexual specificity" (Ortiz 1969:36). In terms of the previous discussion, then, Winter is inclusive and Summer is exclusive. A ramification of this asymmetry was revealed when the pueblo of San Ildefonso rearranged its social organization after a severe population loss. While Ortiz (1969:146) noted some of the consequences of population increase for the Tewa villages, those for depopulation have not been considered.

When the Winter moiety was reduced to two families, the San Ildefonso Summer moiety disbanded into North and South moieties like those used for ritual games and the Winter survivors joined the North side. According to Ortiz (1969:146), "the lesson . . . to derive from this . . . is that the people of San Ildefonso regarded the dual organization as the only way they could operate meaningfully in social relations, and the only way they could impose order on their world."

More than that, however, it indicates that the inherent asymmetry determined the possible range of solutions. Since it was the inclusive moiety that suffered demographic reverses, the whole society was reorganized. If it had been the Summer one, then the Winter members, possessed of both qualities, could have justifiably sent members into the Summer group to make it viable. Instead, the Summer moiety was dissolved and in its place the universal equation of winter and north (or north wind) and of south with summer was used to restructure this society, maintaining the exclusive association of summer-south and the inclusivity of winter-north. "North and east belong exclusively to the Winter moiety, west is shared, and only south belongs exclusively to the Summer moiety" (Ortiz 1969:149).

In a similar situation, however, the Tsimshian would have corrected the imbalance probably by adopting people into the depopulated semi-moiety by conferring appropriate name-titles upon them. The power of these names is such that when a person is given to a name, it has the social force and integrity to make them over. On a smaller scale, I have seen this strategy work in cases of psychological illness and alcoholism, where the transmission of a sufficiently important name was awesome enough to cure, reform, or strengthen someone.

While I intended a reconsideration of Tsimshian social organization in the light of new data and analysis, doing so had required a discussion that has ranged widely over the North Pacific, the arid Southwest, and the southern coast of the Atlantic to indicate that we have been dealing with a very general phenomena. Along the way, we have discussed a revised understanding of Tsimshian languages, classes, seasonality, and the focal figures of chief and Unknown, before considering the ethnography of the current semi-moieties of Blackfish-Wolf and of Raven-Eagle. Lastly, the Tsimshian moieties were treated in terms of diachronic and inter-cultural processes involving the Tlingit and Haida to establish the characteristics of exclusive Owner and inclusive Other before extending the analysis with a comparison with Creek and Tewa moieties.

In sum, all of this evidence indicated that moieties are asymmetrical, with the inclusive member having an expansive dimension that enables the entire society to take in new members and to adapt and grow.

ACKNOWLEDGMENTS

My appreciation and comprehension of Tsimshian culture has been the result of the concerned help of Chiefs Johnny Clifton and Tommy Brown, together with the Hill and Neasloss families. I particularly wish to thank the members of my Blackfish house in Hartley Bay for their support and encouragement, helping me to grasp socially and emotionally the value of crest membership. For intellectual stimulation, I would like to thank Viola Garfield, Amelia Susman Schultz, John Dunn, Jean Muldur, Marjorie Halpin, and the host of other Tsimshianists.

MOIETY BIRTH[a]

ABSTRACT

In the course of collecting data on a newly discovered language now being called Southern Tsimshian, information was acquired relating to the formation of moieties from the remnants of two different tribes by a process of selective forgetting on the part of the members of elite families.

Levi-Strauss (1969:298) wrote of two Nambikwara groups who met and joined together and he saw in this event their future intermarriage and the birth of exogamous moieties. I was recently introduced to another strategy of moiety birth on the coast of British Columbia, Canada.

Klemtu is a village bending around the shore of Trout Bay on Swindle Island somewhat east of the southern tip of the Queen Charlotte Islands. The approximately 230 Indian inhabitants identify their ancestry as either Gitidzu (Kitasoo) Tsimshian or as the Xaixais division of Bella Bella Northern Kwakiutl.

I was drawn to Klemtu in July of 1977 to record more data on Southern Tsimshian. In September of 1976, John Dunn and I had met and worked with a Southern Tsimshian speaker visiting in Hartley Bay, British Columbia. In the Tsimshian view, Southern Tsimshian is a distinct language with its own name, related more closely to Coast Tsimshian than to the Nass and Gitksan dialects of Interior Tsimshian. Currently in Klemtu there are five speakers of Southern Tsimshian, all over 60, so its survival is in grave doubt. Its existence, however, has gone unnoticed and requires a serious reconsideration of our previous models of Tsimshian society.

I mention this new language to explain my interest in visiting Klemtu. Once I had arrived, however, I began to realize that Klemtu had two claims to anthropological fame: an unreported Tsimshian speech community and recently developed moieties. The new language will be fully treated elsewhere (Dunn 1979b is a start), but the moieties will now be discussed here.

Klemtu is an important boundary on the Pacific Northwest Coast because it is the southern terminus of matrilineal descent. I had gone to Klemtu with the expectation that the Tsimshian would have four so-called phratries or crests (Blackfish, Raven, Eagle, and Wolf) and matrilineal descent. Olson (1955) had reported that the Xaixais had the same four descent groups but were weakly matrilineal (under Tsimshian influence) because of their own mythological traditions of brother-sister incest in the face of tribal extinction.

I hasten to point out that for some years now John Dunn and I have considered the four Tsimshian phratries to actually be more semi-moieties. The four crests were a historical development fostered by the abandonments of nine Coast Tsimshian villages on the Skeena River and their concentration around the Hudson's Bay Company fort at Port Simpson. The Gitksan Tsimshian beyond the Skeena River canyon have remained in their villages and Adams (1973:23) reports that each village has a Raven (there called Frog) moiety and one of the other three as its mate. The Kitqa'at tribe at Hartley Bay left its location for about a year to join other Tsimshian at Metlakatla, British Columbia under the aegis of the popular missionary William Duncan. Since

---

[a] This article was previously published in *Northwest Anthropological Research Notes*, 13(1):45–50 (1979).

their return to Hartley Bay very near their former village, they have equated Wolf and Blackfish as one moiety, but still regard Eagle and Raven as distinct. In this light, the Klemtu moieties represent either the next logical stage or the aboriginal pattern.

I did not immediately recognize the existence of the exogamous moieties in Klemtu, much less their significance. I collected genealogies of the known speakers of Southern Tsimshian and began to plot their phratries. I had also made two very soggy trips to the overgrown cemetery in hopes of getting some birth and death dates. The cemetery was old enough that some of the standing headstones were topped with carved totemic figures. I specifically saw a carved killerwhale fin, a grizzly bear, and an eagle. As a general rule, grizzlies are subsumed under Blackfish among the Tsimshian. I also collected some chiefly names, one of which had reference to the blackness of the raven and another of which Olson reported to be held by an Eagle as the paramount Xaixais name. The present holder of this Eagle name "could not remember" his crest. Several people told me that other names had been "forgotten." I had no reason to doubt their sincerity, since many place names had also lapsed from memory. But the place names began to return by a series of stages. My original map had no less than six places named by the same word referring to spruce trees growing there. Later I learned that this was a generic term for all former habitation sites as people began to recall specific names for specific places which indicated what animal, fish, or plant resources could be foraged there.

It was only after I began specifically asking people for their crests that I began to realize what had happened. The first recognition came when a very reliable source told me "all Tsimshian are Blackfish." He said he was a Xaixais and a Raven. I asked a Tsimshian who told me "all Xaixais are Ravens but I'm a Tsimshian so I'm a Blackfish." Rechecking my limited genealogies showed that both tribe and moiety followed matrilineal descent; for Tsimshian as expected, but also for Xaixais in a manner considerably stronger than I had anticipated from Olson's statement.

In this way, Xaixais married Tsimshian because Ravens married Blackfish. Most of the elder, noble people I spoke to had had marriages of this sort arranged for them. They were also quadrilingual in English, Chinook Jargon, Southern Tsimshian, Coast Tsimshian, or Bella Bella Kwakiutl. Yet the tensions in the community were such that people could say with more than a little truth, "we marry our enemies."

To expand my understanding of these moieties, I began to remind people of a woman three generations ago who was an Eagle married into Hartley Bay. I also mentioned the gravestone topped with the eagle. People admitted that in "the old days" there were other crests, but now there were only Blackfish and Ravens.

I was told that the community came to the brink of disaster in the fall of 1976 when the new community hall opened. The White contractor had wanted to protect one inside wall and so asked a local artist to paint a large design on the wall; in fact, a blackfish. The artist was a Raven, but that had slight effect when local people visited the hall the day before the opening celebration was to be held and visitors would begin to arrive from far and near. The Xaixais Ravens were outraged, a band council meeting was convened immediately in the hall, and the town chief bearing the highest ranked Tsimshian name was able to defuse their anger. Although it has not yet happened, the Raven leaders insist they will paint a Raven in the hall. However, I could not help but notice that none of the other walls seem quite appropriate for a totemic emblem.

The final proof of the moieties came for me in the Cooperative Band Store, where only sweatshirts with Blackfish or with Ravens on them were available for sale. I was also impressed by the care that my Tsimshian host took to make sure I got a sweatshirt with a Blackfish design.

The leaders told me that Klemtu was founded so that the men could earn first vouchers and then money by supplying wood to steamships plying the coast. The Hudson's Bay Company trading steamship *Beaver* began operation in 1832. However, Olson sets the date for the settlement of Klemtu about 1875. By accepting his date, a very plausible chronology emerges.

Like the Nambikwara groups, the Xaixais and Gitidzu were decimated and weakened peoples. Their own traditions blame each other and the Haida, but smallpox was probably more grimly involved. The Gitidzu and Xaixais were adapted for seasonal movements to available resources. The steamships provided a rather stable resource and so these two tribes were able to establish a permanent town—whether or not they were demographically balanced, they very soon established a conceptual balance.

For every traditional Gitidzu or Xaixais site, there is a name in both languages. In traditional Northwest Coast societies, terrain was minutely described in myth and from such myths came the ranked names which conferred access and privileges to property and resources. Because there are place names in both languages, each group can invoke a myth to establish their own prior claims. This has not happened, in large part because of a tacit agreement based on the shallow time span from the founding of Klemtu, that the Gitidzu are the rightful owners of at least four village sites and many use areas especially along Loredo Inlet, while the Xaixais rightfully own sites at Kynoch Inlet and Poison Cove. In practice, everyone in Klemtu can use both areas.

This brings us to an equally fascinating point. Traditionally each crest had its own myth of origin. In Klemtu, however, only two myth sagas are singled out for special importance. One is the ubiquitous Raven as trickster-transformer cycle and the other is the story of four men in a canoe taken beneath the sea near Moore Island where they were feasted and honored by the Killerwhale chief. Because this myth is so specific to the Gitidzu locale, it may well be the source for all Blackfish totems among the Tsimshian (Boas 1916b:483). In any event, the Raven saga establishes the Xaixais and the Killerwhale visit does the same for the Tsimshian.

It was at the end of my visit in Klemtu that someone admitted that chiefly names were being deliberately forgotten so that "those others" would not find some way to claim them. In other words, names were being deliberately withdrawn from use and knowledge in the hope they would disappear. It was then that I realized that the Klemtu exogamous moieties developed from the joining of two tribes and eight phratries by a process of the suppression of information. This could only have been done by the high ranked families who dispensed these crests, names, and data over the past two generations. This brings us to a consideration of their motivation and a return to a point made earlier.

One might be tempted to argue that the Klemtu leaders decided to reduce their differences to their least common denominator, namely a tribal one. But doing so does not explain why Xaixais become Ravens and Gitidzu become Blackfish, especially because the Tsimshian names for both of these phratries are untranslatable and thus suggestive of considerable antiquity. The other two phratries readily translate as "on the Eagle" and "on the Wolf." There is also my suspicion of earlier semi-moieties. I have already mentioned that in Hartley Bay, Wolf is subsumed by Blackfish. Based on limited geneological evidence and the Xaixais Eagle chiefly name, it would appear that in Klemtu Eagle was subsumed under Raven. Hence, the crest system had inherent within it the possibility of creating moieties.

There is also the evidence, or the lack of it, for traumatic historical interference at Klemtu. The Xaixais and Gitidzu voluntarily moved to Klemtu and voluntarily embraced Christianity. But even this was less destructive then it might have been. Many objects of art and authority were destroyed at the order of the missionary Thomas Crosby, but the traditional leaders, even now, play prominent roles in the Klemtu church. Added to this is the fact that Klemtu almost always had native Tsimshian ministers from James W. Robinson to George Edgar to the present William Robinson. Such men were more sympathetic to Tsimshian social mores than a white minister would have been.

In short, given the lack of European domination and the strong possibility that while the Gitidzu and Xaixais may have recognized four phratries each, they functioned with moieties; then the presence of moieties in Klemtu at present represents an accommodation of their tribal differences to aboriginal moieties rather than the reverse. In the process, matrilineality was strengthened among the Xaixais. For the generation under 30, who speak only English, the tribal differences have lost any meaning and been almost wholly absorbed into the moieties. At least they wear sweatshirts that identify their moiety and ex *post facto* their tribe, but not the reverse. The mechanism adopted by their elders was the simple expedient of judiciously forgetting almost everything that was not congruent with matrilineal moieties. The inter-moiety antagonism and tension was already there. Thus we may speak not so much of the creation of moieties as of the stripping away to moieties. It is birth in the sense of renewal and reviving rather than of generation or production.

One final point remains: how could the language and moieties of Klemtu have gone unreported for so long? Certainly, anthropologists were visiting the village while the process was going on.

Several answers occur to me. The most obvious is that Ronald Olson visiting in 1935 and 1949 and Philip Drucker visiting in 1937 were specifically interested in Xaixais data. I suspect the aura of Franz Boas and his Kwakiutl research was influencing their own interests. What Gitidzu material reached them was filtered through Xaixais sources. They collected Tsimshian data from homogeneous Tsimshian villages like Hartley Bay and, most especially, Port Simpson. Thus the Gitidzu themselves were overlooked in favor of the Xaixais.

In the case of field workers visiting Klemtu since the 1960s, they too have been drawn to the Xaixais out of personal interests but also out of attraction to a very remarkable native intellectual, William Freeman, who has always lived in Klemtu and collected data since he watched Franz Boas collecting information for Bella Bella in 1923. At this stage he is a superb professional informant, charging a fixed fee, and providing very tidy, pre-analyzed data about traditional culture. But like all professionals, he has a bias, and that is to slant things most favorably for the Xaixais.

Added to these intellectual factors are the more physical ones that while Klemtu is on a major shipping lane, whites are always transients given to some amazing insensitivities and discourtesies, so people are justifiably reserved. Klemtu also has a reputation as a "tough" village. When I left, someone told me to mention what a difficult time I had in Klemtu. To some extent the reputation of Klemtu is deserved, but such reinforcing statements are clearly intended to minimize outside interference. Certainly caution is advised.

Researchers interested in the "old days" have overlooked a fascinating social process coinciding with their own field work in Klemtu. Hence, Drucker (1950:161) could write of Klemtu, once known as China Hat; "China Hat culture has been only a memory for many year (sic)," without realizing that it was changing by a process of forgetting and not of memorizing.

In all, an original statement Boas (1916b:482) learned from the Tsimshian Henry Tate at Port Simpson best captures the picture for his tribe number six, the Gitesdzu, at Klemtu, "these are considered *half* Bellabella [emphasis added]."

ACKNOWLEDGMENTS

This research was made possible by a grant from the Melville and Elizabeth Jacobs Research Fund. I would also like to thank Ms. Smith, Principal, and the staff of the Klemtu Day School for their friendship and cooperation.

FIRST NATIONS FORTS, REFUGES, AND WAR LORD CHAMPIONS AROUND THE SALISH SEA[a]

ABSTRACT

Prehistoric and early historic fortifications "manned" by feared war-lord-type individuals dot the Salish Sea, as well as extend from the present-day Oregon Coast to the central reaches of the British Columbia Coast. Combating the current politically correct suppression of military aspects of Coast Salish traditions, this article summarizes ethnographic and ethnohistoric information, especially for Puget Sound Lushootseeds, to supplement the mute archaeological inventory of such sites in hopes of later filling in blanks. A list provides comparative material, integrating existing information such as location, size, place name, engineered features, and associated historical events. While archaeologists have long been listing and debating such sites, the all-important mobilization by a named leader or champion ("war lord") is ethnographically highlighted here for the first time.

Introduction

Military aspects of the Coast Salish have long been disparaged and are currently being suppressed in public contexts. Often viewed as marginal victims and unprepared fighters, Coast Salish instead relied on famous warriors (war lords) and their forts to provide safety from raids and slaving. On occasion, a charismatic war lord forged an inter-Salish alliance to attack enemy positions, often in what became coastal British Columbia. Today, the Canadian side of the Salish Sea is receiving more scholarly attention, so this article will add materials from Lushootseeds of Puget Sound where some families retain knowledge of martial ancestors, though they are less likely to have shared subsequent fates, which often ended with the head of the war lord carried off by gloating enemies. Chief Seattle is one of the few known war lords to die peacefully in old age.

Careful to note the official endorsement of the Sto:lō Nation and their elders for this sensitive topic, David Schaepe (2006:674, 701) documents a complex of stone "fortifications" (from the Latin "make strong")—including freestanding walls, terrace faces, platforms, and boulder alignments—with line-of-sight defense for the entire Fraser Canyon. Arguing that such coordinated effort must have relied on the corporate family group, rather than individual headmen, he notes, "Fortifications of this scale act as overt signs of power, prestige, and authority.[1] They are of an inherently political nature. They serve multiple purposes beyond defense, acting constantly to define territory, ownership and rights." Citing Wayne Suttles' concern with researching traditional Salish concepts with authority and conflict (Suttles 1989:251), he concludes, "I would argue for the extension of this claim to the broader Northwest Coast. Data and hypotheses derived

---

[a] This article was previously published in the *Journal of Northwest Anthropology*, 45(1):71–87 (2011).

from this study permit the introduction of archaeology as a discipline, however cautiously, to the ongoing inter-disciplinary debate over traditional Coast Salish political organization" (Schaepe 2006:701). Of consequence, however, while he mentions the hereditary names of five local leaders, he makes no attempt to link them with these forts. Such a bond is vital to understanding the situation in Puget Sound, where important names are still placed on the land and identified with specific forts.

William Angelbeck (2007:264, 2009) has generalized materials from archaeology, ethnohistory, and ethnography to reconsider Coast Salish warfare, duly noting the importance of professional warriors and fortifications, including distinctive Gulf of Georgia trench embankment and Fraser Canyon rock-walled longhouses. While Angelbeck recognized the tactically role of surprise, he overlooked significant diachronic aspects and limiting factors of ownership:

> Fear of a well-armed enemy is warranted. Prior to contact, the weapons of war— stone and wooden clubs, spears, stone knives, bows and arrows—would have been equally available to all groups. Hence the importance of the element of surprise in Northwest Coast tactics, with raids occurring during the night and early morning. (Angelbeck 2007:269)

In short, unlike prior scholars, he does not correlate the spread of forts with the adoption of bow and arrow, nor does he specify that few men owned the characteristic clubs and spears because their ownership depended on sanction from 'mean' spirits.

For the Northwest Coast as a whole, Angelbeck named famous warriors such as Tsimshians Tsi'basaa and Nekt, but not Salishan Leschi, young Si'alth (Seattle), and Kitsap. Instead he mentions a raid by Old Snatlem (2007:276), without following up with the importance of this Sneatlum trading family from Whidbey Island. In Puget Sound, warrior bravado was also enhanced by initiation into the Growlers, when bystanders often floated in canoes offshore to watch the proceedings out of harms way from a "berserk" member.

Like Camelot and Arthur, Salish forts were associated with named warriors, though only a few instances of this link have been preserved, mostly in native communities where these names are still passed on during ceremonies with speeches that trace their history, pedigree, and locale (Hilbert, Miller, and Zahir 2001). Instead, we are mostly left with the mute archaeological record, provided here in a list with the hope that a few more empty cells can be filled in while attention can still return to this military institution (Table 1). Comparative data from neighboring tribes is also introduced to round out contexts. In China and elsewhere, such war lords were stages in the formation of the state, but for Salish these champions were more independent and family-based to facilitate trade and diplomacy rather than outright political expansion.

Around the Salish Sea, native communities were composed of class-ranked societies with specialist leadership roles that included that of a haughty warrior with a fortified settlement.[2] George Gibbs, the nineteenth century lawyer and ever-keen observer, indicated that Indian forts were generally known to early settlers and politicians for western Washington State, Tualatin Plains of the Willamette River in Oregon, and the Sacramento River (Gibbs 1877).[3] Over a century ago, many regarded them in terms of the international interest in the Moundbuilders, whose enormous earthworks along the Ohio River had gained intellectual and popular interest in the nineteenth century. Gibbs added his own general observation:

> Near the house of Mr. Cameron, at [Dunn's Nook] Esquimalt, Vancouver Island, I noticed a trench, cutting off a small point of rock near the shore, which seems to have been about six feet deep and eight wide. Governor Douglas informed me that

these are not unfrequent on the island; that they generally surrounded some defensible place; and that often an escarpment was constructed facing the sea, but that the earth was thrown indiscriminately on either side of the ditch (Gibbs 1877:223)

The documentary record, supported by new information collected about the war lords associated with different forts, confirms that Coast Salish peoples built a variety of such defensive works for centuries.[4] Dwellings along the saltwater were often clustered together within a palisade for defense, while inland towns were scattered along a waterway with neighborhoods composed of one or more houses. A few locations represent specialized concerns with suspicious visitors. Natives (probably Nooksacks) around Bellingham Bay under assault by Straits Salish, who absorbed them through intermarriage, are now only known by the term Stockaders. The Swinomish fort hidden within Sullivan Slough did not withstand a smallpox epidemic which only Lahelbid, a prophet, and his family survived by his spiritual protections. The Upper Skagit town upriver at modern Concrete, Washington, was palisaded because these people had frequent downriver contacts as a result of their making and selling of saltwater canoes carved from huge local trees. As holdouts from United States policy, the late 1800s Samish house on Guemes Island had defenses.

Overviews of such fortifications include Ames and Maschner (1999), Moss and Erlandson (1992), Thompson (1990), Carlson (1997, 2001:52), and, especially, Keddie (2006), who found 19 defensive sites among 100 shoreline shell middens around Victoria, BC. While it is clear that these forts spread successively southward with the adoption of the bow during the warmer "medieval climatic optimum," Keddie[5] also suggests the localized defense of emerging reef netting locations. Others have placed forts to defend intertribal boundaries. The spread of potlatching, with increased slavery to add to production, is also implicated. These forts discouraged slaving along the coast, forcing such raids to advance upriver into the less defended interior.

The oldest forts began over 1500 years ago as bow-and-arrow technology spread south along the Pacific Coast (Ames and Maschner 1999:210–18).[6] The arrow's lethal, long-range capabilities and ready availability encouraged such protections. War leaders, especially before AD 1800, often with the haughty arrogance of Chinese war lords,[7] organized the building, stocking, and "manning" of these structures. The earliest forms appear archaeologically as semicircular trenches atop steep bluffs overlooking beaches. These occur at strategically defensive points along the borders of tribal territories, but their importance increased dramatically in the aftermath of epidemics, dislocations, and slave raiding. More exposed but delimited locations, such as peninsulas, were heavily fortified. A drawing of a fortifying palisade seen in 1841 on Whidbey Island is provided in Fig. 1.

In sum, the purpose of this article is to assemble the existing information about known fortifications and supplement the record with new information about known "named" leaders collected from ethnohistoric sources and interviews with descendents.[8] The article starts with a discussion of Salish leadership to provide insight into the types of individuals who managed the forts and other strategic settlements. Coast Salish did not usually fight as soldiers or armies but rather as champions, which has confused many scholars, especially materialist archaeologists. Examples of known forts in various regions around the Salish Sea are then presented to document fortified locales, relying on early work that aggregated these sites. While there has been subsequent work at various of these sites, their precedent was set by surveys done decades ago. Table 1, describing these known fortified settlements, is provided at the end of the article, listing information about the associated named warrior, location, size, place name, engineered features, and historical events.

Fig. 1. Fortification on Whidbey Island drawn in 1841 by Joseph Drayton of the Wilkes Expedition (see endnote 9).

Protective Warrior, Champion, and War Lord

A decade ago, I carefully summarized relevant past and present Coast Salish ethnography, but now take the opportunity to ground its abstractions on the ground (Miller 1999b:29, 58, 84, 85, 94, 120). Every Salish village had a headman, ideally from the same family "blood line" over generations. The headman was typically male, but occasionally female. The headman had first say on everything, but, afterward, all could speak their mind. During warfare, the headman decided which warrior would lead in battle. Sexual continence or chastity was required for hunters before a hunt, shamans before a cure, and warriors before a battle. While the husband was engaged in this task, the wife prayed and sang to help him, as did his sisters, lying inert to similarly incapacitate the prey.

Saltwater villages were the only communities expected to include a resident with warrior powers and also to receive frequent unknown visitors. A few men from these downriver areas might marry into upriver settlements, but they were seldom called upon to defend their in-laws. Spirit powers gifted to warriors include monsters, Loon, a man covered in red paint, and a birdman who gifted fierce men and strong women; warriors also cured their own wounds with the aid of Raccoon, Grizzly, Black Bear, Cougar, and Wild Cat. Warrior spirit power itself was known by a term that means "manliness."

A warrior flaunted a hot temper, stamina, indifference to physical risk, and a willingness to be mean by inflicting pain. His dagger and club were so closely associated with the killing of men that displaying such unsheathed weapons at a public event was tantamount to a declaration of war. A warrior was forceful and aggressive, dominant, imperious, quick-tempered, implacable, and tended toward the despotic. Puget tribes engaged in four kinds of warfare, including an organized offense during battle, raids to take booty and slaves, assaults to settle a grievance, and attacks to take revenge.

In a few cases, a war lord led several communities. All Suquamish, for example, were under a single war lord in times of trouble. Before Chief Seattle, there was Kitsap, a man famous for his bravery powers. Seattle himself was chief of both the Suquamish and the Duwamish because these were the tribes of his father and of his mother. He was a great war captain in his youth, but, in maturity, he became a kind and generous chief and diplomat.

At Quartermaster Harbor, a fortified village was built by Sadoəhebix (brother of gəlai'a [Goliah at Penn Cove on Whidbey Island[9]]), who married wives from neighboring groups, especially from Puyallup. At least one of the villagers later brought in a Skagit wife. Because of his slaving activities against the Duwamish, they were in constant danger of retaliation and, consequently, when Sadoəhebix became too old, this village was moved to Gig Harbor, just before the 1855 treaty (Marian Smith 1940a:11; #14; fieldnotes, House p. 26). A named Suquamish warrior (sxʷəlaxʷtəd) married to a Duhlelap Twana woman had a palisaded home on the south arm of Hood Canal in the present (ironically named) Robin Hood Cove (Elmendorf 1960:169).

In Oregon, a well-described, comparable instance involved Chinooks:

> One of their [Clatsop] chiefs, kati•di, was a particular offender and much disliked. He was constantly sending one or another of his ten sons (agents were always used in property appropriations) to seize goods from some commoner, the penalty of resistance being death. The Chinook on the opposite side of the river became incensed at the treatment their relatives were receiving and met together at the instance of their chief to decide upon a plan of action. The Clatsop chief was in constant fear of his life and seldom left his barricaded semi-underground house They laid siege for 5 days but he never came out so they left. (Ray 1938:56)

Documented Fortifications along the Salish Sea

Prehistoric and early historic settlements characterized as defensive-type fortifications are found throughout the Salish Sea, mostly in the mute archaeological record. Classic fortifications include lookouts at high points and peninsular settlements with palisades, moats, sharpened stakes, and secret or trick entrances. Settlements with escape tunnels, treasure vaults, and underground hideouts have also been identified as refuges, which were secluded and protected, but not bolstered by defensive features.

In terms of geographic distribution, Donald and Mitchell indicate that:

> fortified sites . . . are located in the area of Coast Salish/Wakashan boundaries, while there are very few in the central [Salishan] area. . . . On the other hand, in Southern Kwakiutl territory defensive sites are distributed throughout the area. (Donald and Mitchell 1974:342)

Fortifications were typically placed in areas that limited or complicated access. Some fortified settlements have been documented on rocky headlands impregnable on three sides and protected on the fourth by a ditch and an artificial rampart of earth. Archibald Menzies, who sailed with Captain Vancouver in the 1790s, described a fortified Coast Salish village near Homfray Channel, on the mainland side of the Strait of Georgia near Toba Inlet, as follows:

> At the farther end of these Islands we came to a small cove in the bottom of which the picturesque ruins of a deserted village placed on the summit of an elevated projecting Rock excited our curiosity and induced us to land close to it to view the structure.

This Rock was inaccessible on every side except a narrow pass from the Land by means of steps that admitted only one person to ascend at a time and which seemed to be well guarded in case of an attack, for right over it a large maple tree diffused its spreading branches in such an advantageous manner as to afford an easy and ready access from the summit of the Rock to a concealed place amongst its branches, where a small party could watch unobserved and defend the Pass with great ease. We found the top of the Rock nearly level and wholly occupied with the skeletons of Houses—irregularly arranged and very crouded [crowded]; in some places the space was enlarged by strong scaffolds projecting over the Rock and supporting Houses apparently well secured. These also acted as a defence [defense] by increasing the natural strength of the place and rendering it still more secure and inaccessible. (Menzies 1923:66)

Many fortified settlements were distinguished by palisades. For neighboring Makah, in 1850 at Neah Bay, for example, George Gibbs noted that "One of the [town] blocks is partly surrounded with a stockade of puncheons twelve or fifteen feet high, strengthened by very large posts, into which a tie-beam is mortised" (Gibbs 1877:174–175). Gibbs added that palisades could be as tall as 20–30 ft. high.

Some settlements featured a rampart, defined as a broad elevation or mound of earth raised as a fortification around a place and usually capped with a stone or earth parapet. Traces of such ramparts, originally surmounted by wooden palisades, are still visible in certain places, including Beacon Hill within the city limits of Victoria. Most ramparts date from prehistoric times, but one at Khenipsom, near Duncan, was constructed as late as the middle of the 19th century in the face of Kwakiutlan advances (Keddie 2006).

Another description of a fortification comes from the Klallam, Straits Salish. The nineteenth-century artist Paul Kane visited a fort with a named leader on 9 May 1847, writing:

. . . evening reached I-eh-nus, a Clallum village or fort . . . composed of a double row of strong pickets, the outer ones about twenty ft. high, and the inner row about five feet, enclosing a space of 150 ft. square. The whole of this inner space is roofed in, and divided into small compartments, or pens, for the use of each separate family. There were 200 of the tribe in the fort at the time of my arrival. Their chief, Yates-sut-soot, received me with great cordiality. (Harper 1971:104)

Klallam forts were also known to guard their colonies (and potato patches) at Sehome and Toanichum (Ebey's Prairie),[10] as well as home turf at Dungeness.

At Hadlock Bay, fed by Chimacum Creek, on the western side of the Quimper Peninsula, neighboring Chemakum (a language isolate which called themselves *axoqulo*) occupied a palisaded village (called *ćićabus*) above the mouth of Hood Canal. Located in the rain shadow of the Olympics, their territory was more arid than surrounding areas, which accounts for their local persistence. Known as belligerent and likely slavers, they were attacked by Snoqualmies and later "some seven years since [1855] were attacked and their fort destroyed by the Sukwamish [Suquamish], under Seahtl [Seattle]," who lost a son in this battle (Gibbs 1877:191).

The most detailed descriptions of occupied Salish forts are from notes by Nils Bruseth (1977:11–12) and Marian Smith in the early twentieth century from the Stillaguamish and Puyallup areas. In northern Puget Sound, the Stillaguamish Treasure (or Strong) House southeast of Stanwood was constructed of "big logs set on end, a roof of heavy cedar slabs." A deep trench (moat) filled with sharp stakes surrounded the house, covered by thin branches and turf. A hidden route over solid ground led inside. Any attackers would fall into the ditch and be impaled. Both sturdy and safe, the house provided many Stillaguamish families with haven and storage for their most prized items. For many years, the keeper of this fortification was Tsalbiɬt, until he grew too old and he and his wife retired to Warm Beach. Another huge house, at Trafton, welcomed guests to potlatches and other events. The inside was decorated with carved and painted wood panels, while long fires ran down the middle for heat and cooking feast foods (Bruseth 1977).

Conclusion

Coast Salish combat relied not on soldiers nor armies but rather on champions who took on war lord status when they mobilized labor to build and maintain fortified locations or forts to protect their community. Following the adoption of the available and accessible bow and lethal, long-range arrow, the oldest forts on the Pacific Coast began over 1500 years ago. War leaders (especially before AD 1800), often as arrogant champions, organized the building, stocking, and "manning" of these structures. They early appear archaeologically as semicircular trenches atop steep bluffs overlooking beaches. Often they are located at strategically defensive points along the borders of tribal territories, but conflict there increased dramatically in the aftermath of epidemics, dislocations, and slave raiding a few hundred years ago. More defendable locations, such as peninsulas, were heavily fortified.

In sum, relying on the precedent sources assembling sites by early surveys, we have assembled data about known fortifications and, more to the point, supplemented this record with new information about "named" champions collected from ethnohistoric sources and interviews with descendants. Fort examples in various regions around the Salish Sea are provided in Table 1, with cells for the associated named warrior, location, size, place name, engineered features, and historical events. These examples document fortified locales, relying on scholarly aggregation of these sites, setting precedent. Subsequent work has been piecemeal and the recent public climate has downplayed, ignored, or misrepresented Coast Salish militarism. Yet among important families of Coast Salish communities, honored names continue to be passed on, confirmed by stories of personal reckless bravery and military strategy—long an aspect of the human condition, replete with cruelty, torture, and savagery that many would prefer forgotten, except that these deeds have left marks on the land that still stir emotions in terms of family and historical drama and heroism.

Listing of Fortifications

A detailed though incomplete listing of many of fortification locations is presented in Table 1, arranged roughly north to south along the Salish Sea (Fig. 2). Sites follow their Smithsonian designations (by county, hyphen, and number, such as IS-16), following the serial order in which they were recorded on official forms.

Unless otherwise attributed, fortifications are cited in Bryan (1963), abbreviated as B63 and page number. Some ethnographic information and champion ("war lord") names have been provided by local elders, who, because of family ownerships and sensitivities, prefer to remain anonymous. Lushootseed, in contrast to Straits (Lummi, Samish, Klallam), underwent systematic sound shifts from M to B and N to D so personal names and places have been recorded in both forms (such as Sneatlum in Straits, Sdeetlub in Lushootseed, Angelbeck's Old Snatlem).

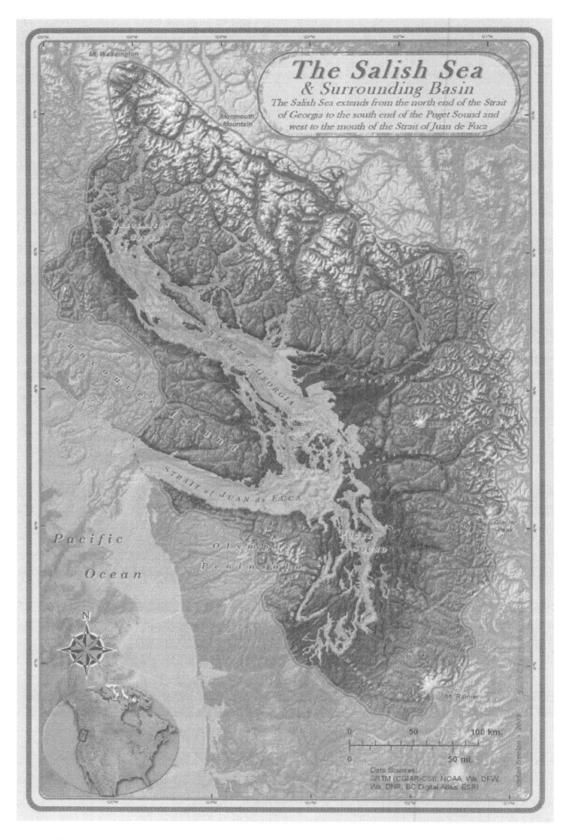

Fig. 2. Map of the Salish Sea, with Columbia River at bottom of map (Freelan 2009).

TABLE 1. FORTIFICATIONS DOCUMENTED IN THE SALISH SEA AND COLUMBIA RIVER.

Puget Sound

FORTIFICATION	ID[1]	SIZE[2]	DETAILS	WARRIOR LORD	CITATION[3]
Gooseberry Point (Lummi) Blaine (Semiahmoo) Guemes (Samish)	SK-13		Samish one had poisoned stakes	all 3 built by same Lummi man	Suttles 1951:322
Marietta 4D			mouth of Nooksack River		B63:74
Samish River			mouth near Edison, Butler Hill at a bend	čadəskadəb = Duxwaha form ~ Samish form = čanəskanəm	Sampson 1972
Pleasant Ridge			reached by a meandering slough that made access difficult		Sampson 1972
Sullivan Slough			family of lone survivors of smallpox	Lahelbid, a prophet	Sampson 1972
Quilceda Creek mouth			"at the old Snohomish fort on Kwultsehda Creek, they made external ditches, which were filled with pointed stakes and covered over." Name refers to sturgeon in this slough.		George Gibbs 1877, 223
East Stanwood	SN-1		at Trafton	Tsalbilht	Bruseth 1977
Kitsap peninsula, hočbale	#46		in marsh, fir pole palisade with peepholes cutout, mat houses inside (west of Point Bolin)		Warren Snyder 1968
Battery Pt, kextu	#76		Bainbridge Island, stockade with mat houses; ka-tyo = shell midden, graves, fort		Johnny Adams (Suquamish Docket # 133, 96, B-4 fort; Warren Snyder 1952:76, 1968:135)
Quartermaster Harbor			Maury Island	Sadoəhebix (brother was gəlai'a ~ Goliah) from Penn Cove on Whidbey Island	Marian Smith 1940:11
Snag Point	#2		palisaded house near Colby	Seattle's son Sakwalth	Warren Snyder 1952, 1968:130
Arrow Fort			Renton	Kwiashten	Tollefson 1992:226
Sand Hill			Carnation (formerly Tolt)	Patkanim	Tollefson 1996

TABLE 1 (cont'd.)   FORTIFICATIONS DOCUMENTED IN THE SALISH SEA AND
COLUMBIA RIVER.

Whidbey Island, east side, sheltered

FORTIFICATION	ID[1]	SIZE[2]	DETAILS	WARRIOR LORD	CITATION[3]
Greenbank	IS-16	85 x 10 x 3	West Holmes Harbor, across from Rocky Point		B63:73
Blower's Bluff	IS-47	120 x 6 x 3	Goliah's famous potlatch		B63:73
Penn Cove Manor	IS-52	145 x 9 x 1½			B63:73
Fort Nugent Lookout	IS-03				B63:73
Snatelum Point	IS-13		Trench lined with 4 ft. stakes	Sneatlum ~ Sdeetlub	B63:73,76
Rocky Point			Holmes Harbor, facing Hackney (Baby) Island & Greenbank		B63:73

Whidbey Island, west side, exposed

FORTIFICATION	ID[1]	SIZE[2]	DETAILS	WARRIOR LORD	CITATION[3]
Fort Nugent	IS-93				B63:73
Ebey's Landing	IS-88		Toanichum Klallam fort painted by Paul Kane 1845-1848	Lok-hi-num	Harper 1971:106, 250
Double Bluff	IS-25	270 x 8 x 4			B63:73

Camano Island

FORTIFICATION	ID[1]	SIZE[2]	DETAILS	WARRIOR LORD	CITATION[3]
Madrona Beach	IS-10	230 x 15 x 3			B63:73

Olympic Peninsula

FORTIFICATION	ID[1]	SIZE[2]	DETAILS	WARRIOR LORD	CITATION[3]
Hadlock Bay			Palisaded village		Gibbs 1877:191
Sequim Bay, I-eh-nus			Painted by Paul Kane 1845-8 showing it under attack	Yates-sut-soot	Harper 1971:250
Neah Bay			Palisaded block of houses		Gibbs 1877:174
Cannonball Island			Near Ozette, dated 200 BC–AD 200		Ames and Maschner 1999:211
James Island			Off Quileute River Mouth		B63:77

TABLE 1 (cont'd.)   FORTIFICATIONS DOCUMENTED IN THE SALISH SEA AND COLUMBIA RIVER.

Columbia River

FORTIFICATION	ID[1]	SIZE[2]	DETAILS	WARRIOR LORD	CITATION[3]
Clatsop			Barricaded semi-underground house	kati•di	Ray 1938:56

Gulf Islands

FORTIFICATION	ID[1]	SIZE[2]	DETAILS	WARRIOR LORD	CITATION[3]
Lopez Island	SJ-215	90 x 12 x 3½ with rock wall	3 trenches = Hunter's Bay		B63:74
Mackaye Harbor	SJ-205	70 yrds x 12 x 4			B63:74
facing Cattle Pt		100 yrds x 6 x 3			B63:74
Garrison Bay			San Juan Island		B63:74

Vancouver Island

FORTIFICATION	ID[1]	SIZE[2]	DETAILS	WARRIOR LORD	CITATION[3]
Beacon Hill		100 high, 300 ft. projecting trench = 6D			James Deans in Keddie 2006
		12 x 15	Oval b/t Esquimault & Victoria		Keddie 2006
Esquimault		? x 8 x 6			Gibbs 1877:22; 1855:409
Cadboro Bay			trench around houses		Keddie 2006
Baines Sound Deep Bay		two - 20D, 10D	enclosing thick shells heaps, mounds, depressions		Keddie 2006
Comox			double arc enclosing 2 houses		Keddie 2006

TABLE 1 (cont'd.)   FORTIFICATIONS DOCUMENTED IN THE SALISH SEA AND COLUMBIA RIVER.

Hideouts on BC Mainland

FORTIFICATION	ID[1]	SIZE[2]	DETAILS	WARRIOR LORD	CITATION[3]
Burrardview				Wac'aqw, with Orca power	Kennedy 2000:142
Klahuse			Toba Inlet		Kennedy & Bouchard 1983:70, 158
Sliamun			Powell River		Same

[1] Washington State counties included here are Island (IS), San Juan (SJ), Skagit (SK), Snohomish (SN).

[2] Wherever possible dimensions are given after an equal sign (=) separated (by x) for L(ength) x W(idth) x D(epth) or H(eight).

[3] Unless otherwise attributed, fortifications are cited in Bryan (1963), abbreviated as B63 and page number.

NOTES

[1] Symbolically, the fort also serves to contain the dangerous power of the champion, further protecting his community and motivating its contributing labor. Keith Carlson is currently pursuing these more complex aspects of Sto:lō forts.

[2] Ron Hilbert Coy, Lushootseed artist and son of Vi Hilbert held the name of the warrior associated with the fort on Granny's (Butler) Hill overlooking the bend of the Samish River (Sampson 1938, 1972). I made the connection between the name and fort because I already was aware of the impressive reengineered hilltop fort (named Ta'awdzep) at Kitwanga on the Skeena River associated with Nekt, a berserker lord whose Raven~Frog mother escaped from a forced Haida marriage, while her son kept quiet in the canoe bow by sucking on the tongue protruding from his father's severed head (MacDonald 1984). Fearsome intimidation, recklessness, and fierce command increased as he aged until he controlled upriver trade and social networks from his fort.

[3] A few small mounds were noted as "camas ovens," and Gibbs mentioned the likelihood that the Sacramento River mounds were built to raise native houses above flood stages. Today, British Columbia cairn and mound burials are gaining new attention among Northwest scholars as novel expressions of social ranking (Mathews 2006).

For the Plateau, Gibbs (1855:409) remarked on "a couple of modern fortifications erected by the Yakimas upon the Simkwe [Simcoe] fork" led by "Skloo" in 1847 as defense against Cayuses. Skloom was a brother of Kamaiakin, Yakama war leader. At the forks, on a ridge "some two hundred yards long, and thirty feet in height, and ... about twenty-five yards apart" were a thirty-foot square with rounded corners "formed by an [three-foot high] earthen embankment capped with stones, the interstices between which serve for loop-holes.... The other is built of adobes in the form of a rectangle, twenty by thirty-four feet, the walls three feet high and twelve to eighteen inches thick, with loop-holes six feet apart … We did not learn whether they were successfully maintained, accounts varying greatly on this subject."

[4] Comparatively, these fortified dwellings are associated with expansion into new territory, as well as defense of a homeland. Among Celts, a fortified place is a *dunon*, appearing as *dun* in place names (such as Brigadoon), which "made its way through the Germanic languages and arrived in English as the word town" (Ellis 1990:42). In the Northwest, rock enclosures, smaller in size, marked questing sites and other religious uses (Thompson 1990). Among Coast Tsimshian, lineage-owned volcanic cones (*t'oo'tsip*) served as forts that later included bountiful potato gardens in this rich soil (Miller 1997b:135).

[5] Sites around Victoria studied and dated by Grant Keddie include Pender Bay (DcRu 1, AD 400), Finlayson Point (DcRu 23, AD 800), Lime Bay Peninsula Defensive Site (DcRu 123, AD 800), and Flemming Beach, near Esquimalt (DcRu 20, DcRu 21, AD 800 to 1000), though the huge shell midden between these defensives has a basal date of over 4,000 years ago (Ames and Maschner 1999:211).

[6] Russians conquered Siberia by building *ostrogs* (forts) at each secured riverbank, administering control via taxes and converting through Orthodox missionaries, then advancing onward to build the next *ostrog*. The Normans advanced through England as nobles built *keeps* in their newly-acquired fiefdom. The land-based fur trade in North America advanced by fortified posts, and the US army marched west building forts.

[7] From BCE 632 to 226, warring states fought for supremacy over the heartland of China. From fortified positions, each lord (*pa*) struggled to become a king (*wang*) and ultimately the singular Son of Heaven (*t'ien-tzu* or *Ti*). Commoners served the purposes of noble factions, locked in strife until the militaristic Ch'in triumphed over what had begun as two dozen small states (Harrison 1972:48).

[8] In Lushootseed, the language of Puget Sound, two terms applying to such barriers vary in meanings. One is *λ̕alax̌ad*, which derives from *λ̕əl*, meaning "silent, still, stop, avoid," emphasizing its ability to block, bar, or stop. With the prefix s- added, it means a trap for game animals. The other word is *q̓əlax̌ad*, where the suffix *−ax̌ad* refers to "edge, side, perimeter, edging." It is related to the word *q̓əltəd* (with the implement suffix *−təd*, meaning something used to do something with, as a tool or instrument) translating into "clout, diaper, sanitary napkin [tampon]," with the implication that the root *q̓əl* means "blockage." A related and fascinating derivation is a term for a variety of lichen that means "frog diaper" (Gibbs 1970; Bates, Hess, and Hilbert 1994:153, 183, 311).

[9] Joseph Drayton on the circumnavigating Wilkes US expedition sketched a "Sachel fort" on Whidbey Island (Fig. 1). This was most likely the Skagit community at Penn Cove Manor (IS-52) in Table 1.

[10] Kane (1925:158) made a sketch of this Toanichum fort (Harper 1971:250; Easton and Urbanek 1995:106;), where Lok-hi-num was chief, after their landing party dodged warning shots. Two days later, 9 May 1847, they crossed to I-eh-nus on Dungeness Spit, where the leader was Yates-sut-soot.

Journal of Northwest Anthropology, Memoir 9:66–75   2014

THE HOUSE OF SALISH ~ NOBLE PEDIGREES, PRIVILEGES, AND NAMES ALONG THE SKAGIT RIVER BETWEEN LOGJAM AND ROCK

ABSTRACT

The linguistic and cultural subtleties of claims to a "House" as a prestige factor among the high-ranking holders of great names among Coast Salish are reviewed and confirmed, denying counterclaims of some Salishanists that there is either "nothing there" or analytical contamination from the "House" as an all-important basic unit of the matrilineal North Pacific Coast.

Recurrent criticism, if not outright blanket rejection, has denied any significance to the "House" (as House of Windsor, House of David) as a key unit of Salish kinship and society, especially as comparable to the all-important houses of the matrilineal cultures of the North Pacific Coast such as Tlingit, Haida, and Tsimshian. While this charge has usually been made by strict Salishanists, those of us who work comparatively along the Northwest Coast see merit in the occasional but very prestigious assertions of "House" among Coast Salishans of rank. Somewhat analogous are claims by families of modest means to "fancy names" for their town homes or rural cabins, such as "Briarwood" or "Royal Estate." The chief difference in this case, however, is that while matriHouses hold names in the north, it is great names that hold Houses in the Salish south.

In the collected papers from the most recent gathering of Northwest scholars in Paris, the editors note that [Levi-Strauss] "has also disagreed with Jay Miller's application of the notion of the 'house' to the Salish." Yet, instead of an implied blanket rejection, in that book's first chapter, Levi-Strauss himself lauds "Reading a recent book by Jay Miller on the culture we refer to as Lushootseed, I found it gratifying that in order to characterize certain traits of the social organization, the author referred several times to aristocratic European houses"(Mauze, Harkin, and Kan 2004:xx; 3). The key phrase, therefore, is "certain traits" and in that we can agree.

My stance here is that while not integrated into the whole of Salish society to the degree of the matrilineal north coast (Levi-Straus 1982; Miller 1997), such a claim to a House was and is a key element of the prestige system. It enabled important families to assert a dynastic status based on their transgenerational inheritance of great names. Moreover, the Lushootseed language confirms its importance by the use of the suffix $-al'tx^w$ to indicate such a perpetual house ($si'alal'x^w$ House of Seattle), sometimes linked with the root $g^w \partial c$- / $g^w \partial \mathcal{t}$- "be born (for), originate" (Bates, Hess, and Hilbert 1994:98, 293). As such, this "house" is metaphoric and eternal, rather than physical. Indeed, the named House-holders may seasonally occupy a variety of other built homes at strategic resource locations, easing the harvesting, preparation, and storage of that particular resource by residents of the household and their guests.

Further, scholarly understanding of the features of this Salish House suffers from a lack of published data, much of it existing only in fieldnotes and, of course, alive within Salish communities. This article relies on the dense materials assembled in the early 1950s by Sally Snyder among the Swinomish and other Skagit River native communities, and until recently under restricted access within the Melville Jacobs Collection at the University of Washington main library. The Saanich fieldnotes of Diamond Jenness (1935) also discuss the importance of the "House" for Canadian Salish. In part, disregard or suppression of these fieldnote data helps to more sharply phrase distinctions between the northern and southern coasts. Yet, as elsewhere, prestige comes from without, and First Nations along the coast intermarried and interacted within overlapping systems. Actions and events associated with successive holders of the same name are well chronicled in fieldnotes, much as are the deeds of European or Chinese nobility.

The most vivid published account of the direct link between a great name and its house, here physical as well as metaphoric, involves John Fornsby's encounter with his great grandfather, kʷəskadəb, while picking blackberries with other boys. "There were lots of berries. We crawled around and got to the middle back of the [abandoned] house. The body of my [great] grandfather kʷəskadəb was right there. We got scared. We went home. We never picked berries. I laughed [with relief] when we got back into the canoe" (Collins 1949:295–296).

This kʷəskadəb was a famous Skagit leader based on Whidbey Island around modern Coupeville on Penn Cove, still famous for its oysters. Sneatlum Point is its southern end, and the earthly landfall of founding ancestors (below). In time a namesake of an ancestral founder named x̌kəkadəb married, among others, a Samish wife named tsi ʔagʷaɬ, and one of their middle sons first received the name-title of kʷəskadəb. This historic human holder of that name had commissioned half a dozen Lower Skagit carpenters to build him a potlatch house,[1] with two painted posts holding up either end of the gable, at what briefly became Skagit City (Collins 1949:295–296), the site of a prime salmon fishery that was the key resource that justified the building of a house frame there (below).

Later, the body of this kʷəskadəb was reburied behind his potlatch house, which eventually was washed away in a flood. By then, however, kʷəskadəb had again been reburied, with proper ceremony, at the Swinomish tribal cemetery. One of his house posts, 3 ft. wide, 4 ft. thick, and 8 ft. long, landed in the back of the bay at La Conner. Johnny Fornsby hired Lummi to help him move and set up this housepost at a potlatch when the dead were gathered up from a gravehouse on Deadman's Island and buried in the same community cemetery.

kʷəskadəb was father of the equally famous Sneatlam [sniƛəb], and uncle to Goliah, the spokesman drafted to be a prominent signer for the northern Lushootseed tribes at the 1855 Treaty of Port Elliot—Mukilteo. One of his daughters married among the Chehalis, to the south.

Sneatlam became renowned throughout the Northwest as an early Catholic prayer leader and an important broker in the fur trade at Fort Nisqually. At least one of his wives was a Makah from Neah Bay. Yet one of his brothers flaunted the rules by being involved with a slave girl, who thereby became known as "mistake" (dʲaƛəb).

After his death on 16 December 1852, a carved wooden effigy of Sneatlam stood on a high bank on the eastern side of Whidbey Island, "dressed in his usual costume, and wearing the articles of which he was fond" (Gibbs 1877:203). To this day, his family has remained important in intertribal and international trading, now brokering as far away as China, especially for fireworks sold at tribal stands before the 4th of July.

A granddaughter of kʷəskadəb by the name of ba'da'yɬ (in Lushootseed, ma'na'yɬ in Straits) was captured by raiding Klallams from Dungeness, who instead quickly married her, receiving ten slaves, a seagoing canoe, and many blankets from her grandfather in exchange for twenty slaves, a canoe, and other goods from these Klallams. At the wedding, the groom appeared in an enormous rawhide mask. Elmendorf (1993:108–100), their recorder, dates these events to 1780–1810.

Extending their range of dynastic marriages, both Sneatlam, as Neetlum, and kʷəskadəb, as Wheskienum, appear in the journal of Fort Langley for June, July, and August of 1830 (Maclachlan 1998:150, 155–6). This time, Sneatlum's son was marrying the daughter of a

Cowichan leader, a chief variously known as Shashia, Joshua, Josia, or Old Joe. By luck, portraits of him and his son Cul-chil-hum were painted by Paul Kane in 1847. A brief biography, though, mentions only two sons, leaving uncertain the fate of this daughter married among Skagits when Shashia died blind and heirless in 1870 (Maclachlan 1998:228–230).

While negotiations had been decided in the spring of 1830, the formal marital exchange took place in late summer after the Vancouver Islanders had moved across to their Fraser fishery. "This afternoon [June 17, Thursday] the two Scadchats Chiefs—Neetlum and Wheskienum accompanied by a half dozen of others and Sinaughten the Sinnahomes Came here—They have about 20 Skins Lar[ge] and Small. . . ."

On June 29, Tuesday, Nanaimos and Cowichans arrived at the mouth of the Fraser, only to be attacked by Lekwiltok [southern-most Kwakiutlans] about 4 July, before the Nanaimo settled into their summer village on Friday the 16th. On 10 July 10, the Cowichan named Shashia demanded 2 guns and 10 blankets for a dozen skins, but he left empty handed "for we have hardly so much property in the Fort." His concern was, of course, not the fur trade but his upcoming wedding responsibilities.

Neetlum himself visited the fort on 7th of August, Tuesday; the Cowichan Shashia on the 8th, then on the 9th "In the evening two very large & three Small Canoes full of Scadchads made their appearance at our wharf—Their Chief (Needlum) was already in the Fort—he immediately embarked with them and pushed over to Joe's [Cowichan] camp—All the great men of the river are now assembled there—Our night watch is doubled and every thing in readiness in Case of the worst."

On Friday, 10th of August came the culminating exchange in "A great Ceremony—going on the other Side solemnising a marriage that took place last Spring between a Boy of Needlum's and a little Girl of Joe's—Canoes—Guns—Blankets—Slaves etc. etc. are exchanged on the occasion.

On Saturday, the Skagit came across to propose trading, "for which they would have nothing but Blkts [blankets]" but were soon rebuffed. "They returned to the Cawitchin Camp in the evening and Spoiled Children they are." On Sunday afternoon, 12th August, the Skagits left for home.

Clearly, through pedigree and alliances, kʷəskadəb and his family held and hold high rank, meeting the criteria by having a wealth spirit power (below) and by inviting (to at least four potlatches) (Snyder 1950s: Box 108 Folder 2 page 17 Joe Joe). Accordingly they kept affirming it with generosity, as indicated by the specially built potlatch house where he was entombed.

This location just above Skagit City served to remind everyone of a major source of his bounty, namely the dense fishery at the lower end of a logjam, two miles long, which blocked the Skagit River from above Mount Vernon to Hamilton. Spawning salmon clumped there before managing to weave their way upriver. They were so abundant that harpoons and gaffhooks could be used productively along with nets.

Until the jam was dynamited away in 1878, peoples along the Skagit had extensive contacts with their neighbors because voyagers either had to drag a canoe through the brush around the jam, or, more readily, portage over to the lower Samish or the Stillaguamish rivers to reach salt water (Collins 1974:39, cf. 1950a and b, 1952a and b).

This great name, fishery, potlatch house, and generous leader, therefore, account for the logjam in my title. They also, by tracing ultimate origins, account for the rock since, according to notes from Alice Campbell:

Long ago there were people who turned into rocks [because of the Flood]. This kʷəskadəb was the name of one [of them] way up on the Skagit. It is the name of one of Andrew Joe's relatives. They came up to ask the people there for a name (certain people used to go to certain places to obtain a name). If they had known, they could have asked the sbalix [natives around Concrete] here for a name. (Snyder 1950s: Box 108 folder 5 page 58 AC)

Thus, even before the Flood, with the founding of human society, the holders of these great name-titles were not limited to one place because these ancestors married widely and dynastically.

Ancestors

These few ancestors of the great names were the primary founders for this region, the first strictly human generation of the Skagit world. Their names indeed were and remain mighty, passed through families to new holders (Haeberlin and Gunther 1930; Wike 1952; Snyder 1964, 1975; Kennedy 1993).

While most native people lived common, uneventful lives, those with what June Collins (1966) called "renowned names"—which acted more like titles—formed a set of famous chiefly leaders who owned several big cedar-plank houses located at various richly endowed locales. That he (or they) could coordinate the building of more than one large home further spoke to his (their) leadership abilities. Indeed, in Lushootseed, such a person or family is called hikᵂ siʔab, in the sense of a grandee who is "big, great, high, most, many, very" (Bates, Hess, and Hilbert 1994:109) in terms of authority, respect, ability, and, above all, presence.

Pedigrees are carefully recalled. According to Lower Skagits, kəkadəb, the first (Lower) Skagit man, was sent down to čubaʼałšəd (*note bene*: Sneatlum Point) by the Creator to found three ancestral families who each first lived in one of the three compartments within one huge plank longhouse set inside a stockade, with those highest in rank in the middle and those who eventually colonized up the Skagit River at the one furthest back (Snyder 1950s: Box 108 folder 10 page 33 AJ).

Once this first family was established, they found themselves lured into adopting a new member with vast consequences. Taking the shape of a young man, the Underwater Wealth Spirit (tiułəbaxad), who was usually both ugly and pitiful to humans, mentally compelled (using power words or *dicta*) the family of kəkadəb to adopt him after he made himself look presentable as a baby. A daughter took him to raise, then became pregnant by him. Since he appeared handsome and hard working, to avoid scandal, they were quickly married, before their son was born. The husband fixed it so his own family could live underwater and took them back home. But this son was never happy there, and the family came back when he was old enough to quest for a spirit power.

Accordingly, he quested for a year. Times became hard and famine loomed when the son went to Sneatlam Point and to the bottomless lake across from Greenbanks. There he got power from the sea and a pair of powerful cedar shields. On his return, he told his cousin, who was also "pure" from fasting, to have his own parent's home cleaned up and renewed within four days in time for his return. Everyone worked hard and all was ready when he came into the house with the shields and sang the middle part of his song, which immediately filled the beach with food. From then on, aided by all these spirit powers, the Skagits grew mighty (Snyder 1950s: Box 109 folder 2 page 12–13 AJ, Cf). Wealth spirit married daughter of kəkadəb I (Snyder 1950s: Box 109 folder 2 page 39–40 AJ).

Eventually, trade up and down the Skagit River was managed by kəkadəb at Coupeville for everyone on Penn Cove and by a daxalxᵂəd—a sbalixᵂ near Concrete on Lake Shannon at present Baker River—for those above (Snyder 1950s: Box 109 folder 1 page 42 AD).

Later, one of those also named xkəkadəb married both a Swinomish wife and the Samish wife named tsi ʔagᵂał, having four boys and three girls. The next oldest son was the first kᵂəskadəb, who had two daughters by one wife, and a son by another—who became a 1855 treaty signer and father of a chief, while another son, who had a daughter and a son, also signed the treaty. His second wife left no descendants (cf. Snyder 1950s: Box 108 folder 10 page 71 AJ, Box 109 folder 2 page 2 AJ).

One kʷəskadəb also had a famous warrior son tax̌taɬ who was an endurance runner and athlete. He would test himself by spitting on a rock and running around Sneatlam Point and back before it dried. He could outrun deer, elk, cranes, and eagles, killing them with his bare hands (Snyder 1950s: Box 108 folder 2 page 97 AJ). Later young warriors trained by running from Sneatlum Point to Coupeville and on to Fort Casey, a strategic lookout (Snyder 1950s: Box 108, Folder 2, page 10) now marked by a U.S. defense bunker.

The half-Swinomish namesake son x̌kəkadəb, in turn, had 5–6 wives, with many descendants. The children of an Oak Harbor women included Goliah, designated a head chief in the 1855 treaty. From a half-brother there descended the woman who married Johnny Fornsby, who as a boy saw the body of his great grandfather lying in state (Snyder 1950s: Box 109 folder 2 page 31 AJ; sons of x̌kəkadəb III, Snyder 1950s: Box 108 folder 10 page 43 AJ; Box 109, folder 2, page 3 AJ).

Overall, the name of kəkadəb seems to first occur shortly after the very beginning, going even "deeper, really, from the Flood. That's why it was hard to tell the history, because the Indian only had one name [repeated over generations]" (Snyder 1950s: Box 109 folder 2 page 57 AJ).

Other ancestral founders were sent by the Creator to specific locations, either at the founding of the world or to repopulate it after the Flood. For the Swadabsh proper who were living along Swinomish slough, the important founder, who lived a third generation after the Flood, was the son of Robe Boy known by the great name of ləx̌albid.

ləx̌albid

Gender equality permeates Salish culture, as shown by the pedigree of the name of the mother of kʷəskadəb. The family of the woman named tsiʔ əgʷaɬ came into their own after the Flood (Sampson 1938:14–16; Matson 1968:29–38), and thereby came to "own" the story about a man who sensed that the Flood was coming, and so tied four seagoing canoes to the top of a mountain with four long ropes that stretched out as the waters rose ever higher. When the waters receded, the stretched mooring ropes forced the high top of the mountain to pop-off, and three canoes drifted away, some say to China. From the fourth, a man, his wife, son, and daughter landed safely. They quickly built cattail mat houses for use as a dwelling and storage out of the rain.

Slowly, life returned. Little fish came into Swinomish slough and the girl went to play with them, until, one day, a great fish took her away. Saddened, her brother and his dog wandered apart. He began to shoot small animals, prepare their pelts, and eventually sewed them into a blanket robe. When he finally came home, he thought everyone else had died. Instead, his parents were gone to Coupeville and the mat houses burned down as a sign of mourning because they too thought both their children were dead.

In great despair, the boy wept until a voice told him to gather up and match all the animal bones he could find, lay them out, and wave his robe over them four times. Immediately, all these bones became people, but they were chilled. The voice also said to gather charcoal from the burned houses, wave the robe over them, and thus fire was recreated.

Next he waded into the slough, where herring swarmed as soon as the hem of his robe touched the surface of the water. These fed the people. A mountain goat appeared to give everyone wool blankets as fine clothing to keep them warmer. These reformed people had no sense, however, so the boy made brains for them from the very soil of that place (Snyder n.d.: Tale 68, Andrew Span Joe).

Eventually, his own human kin returned and these impromptu beings wandered away. Ever after known as Robe Boy (x̌uyalič̓a, "made from a robe"), he married a human woman and had two sons, tux̌ʷiqədəb (first daylight) and ləx̌albid (daybreak), both of whom, withstanding snide criticism like their father, seemed to refuse to quest and had a hard time in the community until they proved to have had successful quests and founded several houses and villages near prime resource locations and fisheries, celebrated with appropriate rituals.

ləx̌albid had at least four houses around Fidalgo Island, located in modern terms: on the east side near the Swinomish tribal police station, further east at the fort on Sullivan Slough, on the southwest near Martha's Bay and Pull and Be Damned Road, and on the northwest at Snee-oosh (sdiʔus) Point.

Among the Lushootseed, importantly, socio-cultural institutions were arranged as concentric circles, from the most restricted of food economics to the most expansive of religious expressions in what I have called an "anchored radiance," with everything situated with the drainage of a major river draining into Puget Sound (Miller 1999b).

Drainages

In terms of the overall Puget Basin, Marian Smith, after fieldwork with Puyallup and Nisqually, outlined a comprehensive spatial model with expanding components for each watershed, the maximum extent of allegiance and loyalty for most Lushootseeds (see p. 21, this volume, for native terms). These units were (a) hearth mates eating together; (b) within a cedar plank household; (c) among houses of all neighboring residents; (d) of birthright locals—those born there in contrast to inlaws, visitors, and foreigners; including (e) all seasonal houses, settlements, towns, camps, and resorts; (f) inter-community networks; (g) tributary drainages; of (h) the entire drainage of a watershed or basin.

Membership within each unit was based on well informed understandings, both subtle and discerning, of local customs such that insiders, in contrast to outsiders, fully appreciated the complexities of "the feud, the snub, the verbal innuendo" and accordingly "were appropriate guests for a ceremonial feast" (Roberts 1975:79). To be involved in Lushootseed culture required formal training in and experience with the complexities of oratory, rank, and proper public expressions. Those of great prestige could also claim diffuse membership in a named House.

Every drainage had customs that set it apart, made obvious by dialect subtleties and by different styles of making fire, carving canoes, or using nets, for example, as well as in venerating certain spirit powers and abilities. The most complex example, for the entire length of the Skagit River, involved net use.

Throughout the Northwest, nets—placed underwater, on land, in the air, or hand held in canoes—were used to capture fish, fowl, and other foods. Three major types of fish nets were once used along the Skagit, each instituted by the decree of a Changer ~ Transformer preparing the world for human arrival. Out in the saltwater, the reef net (sx̌ʷalo, literally "willow" using its twisted bark for cords), developed by Straits Salish speakers, was deployed. In the lower river, the weir net (qʷəlʔits) was developed, and used by Swinomish and others. Upriver, the trawl net (šəbəd) was featured, made of a special mountain grass. The success of the net, however, relied on special *dicta* (formula, spells, power words) closely guarded by the leaders of a family and household because they guaranteed an abundant food supply.

Lushootseed Ethno-Chronology

Based on this background and comparisons, then, a Lushootseed chronology must start with the Creator high god (xaʔxa) who empowers (often mentally) other immortal spirits (*sqelalitut*) who dwell in the sky, on and in the earth, and under the water. Foremost among these spirits were four brothers who traveled up the Skagit River, placing a paired man and woman at various locations to create future generations there (Collins 1974:158–59; Snyder n.d.: Tale 73; Amoss 1978:66–70; Miller 1999b:60–62). These brothers, oldest to youngest, were Shield (sgʷədiləč), Knife, Fire, and Baby, each with sustaining powers and abilities appropriate to their names. Shield protected and foretold. Knife taught the proper ways to butcher and prepare game. Fire showed how to cook it. Baby told these couples how to fix all-important family talents, skills, and abilities on their children, as well as providing limiting access to *dicta* to one member in each generation.

The others went away upriver, and Knife may have stopped at the ancient Hozomeen Quarry in the Cascades, but Shield became a rock in the upper Skagit near Portage where he can be heard singing about 3:00 a.m. by those who had fasted and prepared to learn his song so as to be able to hunt and fish successfully.

This era ended with the time of Starchild and Diaper boy, begat by Stars married to human women. After they had rescued their mother from slavery and themselves married industrious wives, they gathered up everything useful on the earth and burned it in a great conflagration, then scattered these ashes everywhere so the essence of these materials, resources, and abilities could be more easily found by future generations.

Their children became the chiefly families throughout Puget Sound, each leader learning and guarding the special *dicta* to benefit his family and community. Powerful *dicta* were specifically given in compensation for the renewal of the world at the time when mortals and immortals were moving away from the bodily contact of marriage toward the immateriality of moral adoption (as Wealthman appeared to the Sneatlum family).

The land repopulated and thrived until people failed to respect the proper rules, regulations, and avoidances needed for proper living, so a Flood set things right again. The few survivors included Robe Boy, his son ləxalbid, and their many descendants at Swadabsh, as other ancestors refounded communities in other locales. Though unstated, the host of dead from the Flood must have provided the incentive for the Ghost system, still important today and propitiated by periodic burnings of food, since the deluge obviously left behind more bulky refuse and remains than did Fire's ashes.

The occasional references to those few who "drifted away" during the Flood also suggests that one of these Flood casualties was one of the kʷəskadəb who ended up a petrified rock far up the Skagit. Thus, resolving the conflicting attributes and locations of this name, the Lower Skagit who went upriver to ask for this name were actually showing respect for the people among whom this kʷəskadəb first lodged. That is why they did not ask more important tribes around Concrete and elsewhere for a name. Presumably, that kʷəskadəb revealed his location to a descendant in a dream that was followed up by the visit of this delegation.

Most recently, the Creator has again asserted his priority by empowering John and Mary Slocum to establish the 1882 Indian Shaker Church, legally incorporated in Washington state in 1910, and still thriving. As Martin Sampson, Swinomish leader, noted, the advantage of Shakers was "worshipping God direct, they increased their healing over much greater distances." Unlike shamans, whose spirits remained localized, Shaker spirits could expand into the world as far as needed since they were affiliated with a universal God. Moreover, though a shaman's spirits deserted him or her at death, the Shaker Spirit led a member "home."

Simultaneously, immortal spirits remain active among initiates of modern Siyowin, the so-called winter Smokehouse Religion that allows modern members to "inherit" family spirit powers in the context of this organization.

In modern Lushootseed beliefs about immortals or guardian spirits, such a power attaches itself to a person at birth, but only reveals its presence at puberty through at least two aspects, a being and a song, along with a personifying of the vision itself. Some or all of these aspects "travel" during the year and only join together during the winter when the person becomes "sick to sing" with the return of his or her spirit partner. For a woman, her spirit power was regarded as a personal friend, while for a man it was an impersonal force that infused his entire body when it returned (Amoss 1978:51).

The song, at least, came from the east in the fall, moved slowly south and westward during the winter, and, in late April or so, headed east again. As a group, spirits came to the Nooksak on Mt. Baker before they reached Vancouver Island, where they lingered until spring.

In contrast to these lay or career powers, shamanic curing powers were available at all times. According to Joyce Wike (1941), while the song traveled, the spirit itself stayed close to the human partner. Fierce black paint spirits traveled more widely than did those of calm red paint, who stayed nearby and could be used to cure or help others.

During the day, spirits also move around, hovering in the air (rather than treading on the ground), lower in the early morning then higher in the afternoon. They are constantly aware of human actions and leave if their partner becomes ritually impure or disrespectful. Then the spirit was said to "lift off" until it could be coaxed back by a shaman. Spirits liked daylight but, lacking form or substance, were truly ethereal. Marian Smith (1940a) reported that spirits had the most nebulous of existences, with their appetites and pleasures supplied vicariously through their links with humans, especially relatives who were kind enough to remember them and send food and treats through an open fire.

Comparisons

The role of the "House" among Coast Salish has been denied and debated by academics, with some dismissing it entirely. Physically, this cedar-plank building served as "food processing and storage, workshop, recreation center, temple, theatre, and fortress" (Suttles 1991:214; Kennedy 2000:76). Among the matrilineal northern tribes, the house is the pervasive unit, and its influence was long felt in the south, where some communities strove to assert claims to a similar but unique house as an aspiration rather than a routine feature. Thus, standout examples include the Whale House (sałułtxw) comprised of five high ranking Comox communities near Cape Mudge (Kennedy 2000:52, based on Barnett 1955:25), and Painted House of the Snoqualmies east of Seattle.

Salish houses, more recently and repeatedly, have been called similar in many ways to a "House" in the sense of European nobility [holding] property, tangible and intangible, names of heaven-born First Ancestors, confidential knowledge (sniw'), ritual property (ts'uxwten), legends, songs, dances, secret words (dicta), medicinal remedies, and ceremonial prerogatives (Jenness 1935:52; Barnett 1955:141, 191; Thom 2005:85). All of these are place-based, as inalienable patrimony, such that "senses of place focus attention on the connections and interrelations between myth, legend, ancestor, spirit, song, identity, language, property, territory, boundary and title" (Thom 2005:409).

In his unpublished notes, Jenness (1935), closely attending to his elder interviews, carefully distinguished between corporate ownership and the commons:

The real political unit was therefore not the village, but the big house occupied by a number of kinsfolk—an enlarged or genealogical "family" to which the Saanich applied the term *hunit's'lakum*, and we in speaking of the similar European nobility use the term House. Each Saanich House, as we many call it then, possessed its own long shed-roofed dwelling,[2] its own camas beds on Galiano and neighboring islands, its own set of ancestral names or titles, and its own stock of legends, songs, and medicinal remedies. (Jenness 1935:29)

The accompanying footnote expands on such privileged property:

1. Almost any departure from established custom might become the privilege of a House, heritable by later generations, and by them alone, provided the public had ratified it; and the public ratified it when during some potlatch it heard the statement of claim without demur and accepted the gift that followed the statement. All such privileges or rights, however, hinged upon proof of lineal descent, and the most obvious indication of such descent was the possession of an ancestral title. (Jenness 1935:29)

At Duncan, Cowichan Houses owned nearby weir sites along the river, but

On the other hand, the sea near the villages, the hunting grounds and berry patches round about, were common property; any villager, whatever his station in life, might fish and hunt wherever he wished within the village territory. (Jenness 1935:29)

Elite families owned property that included several houses occupied throughout a year at seasonal resource sites, famous art works, and claims to epics, songs, displays, and rituals. They also perpetuated great name titles, some of whom added to their prestige by naming a House in perpetuity. Senior members, both men and women, of elite families doubled as religious and political leaders, depending on the season. Summer was devoted to economy, and winter to religion (cf. Kennedy 2000:7, 160, 326). The lowest class was largely immobile and marked by an intensely strict provincialism (Kennedy 2000:125, from Smith 1940b:410).

Among neighbors, an apt comparison from Nuchahnulth or Nootkan distinguishes between kinship and noble descent:

The situation among the people of the West Coast is not unlike that of medieval Europe (a comparison suggested to me [a Welsh national] by a Toquaht chief) where the descent principle was fully utilized only by the elite of society and where the common people neglected to trace their genealogies the further they were removed from aristocratic rank. . . . In addition, both principles need not be of equal importance for all members of the group. (Kenyon 1980:85–86)

Emphasizing ramages traced through first-borns, Nuchahnulth differed from Salish bilaterality, yet high families in both made occasional claims to great names with hereditary Houses.

In all, Northwest natives, more so than academics, understand each other's prestige systems and so are willing to broaden their own claims by giving special regard for something as routinely important as a House within a broadened understanding of elite statuses.

Buried in rare fieldnotes but publicly proclaimed at frequent native gatherings, Coast Salishan holding great names do indeed claim named Houses as one of the "certain traits" that both marks them as unique and as participants in a greater system of prestige.

NOTES

1 Potlatch is a charged term in the Northwest Coast literature, derived from the local trade jargon (*Chinuk WaWa*) word simply meaning "to give." Among Lushootseed, the equivalent word is *sg^{w}ig^{w}i*, merely meaning "to invite" but there are also three other words that can be applied (Miller 1999b, 147 #5).

2 The best descriptions of Salishan worlds (Miller 1999) represent those of the Nuxalk (Bella Coola) (McIlwraith 1948), Katzie (Jenness 1955), and Twana (Elmendorf 1960).

Journal of Northwest Anthropology, Memoir 9:76–86   2014

NAMING CULTURE AMONG LUSHOOTSEEDS
OF PUGET SOUND

ABSTRACT

Hereditary *names*, today as in the past, bind together the Lushootseeds of Puget Sound, crosscuting considerations of culture history, gender, age, rank, descent, kinship, pedigree, residence, territory, and waterway. They are the focus of the basic units of *person, place, intersept,* and *power* from immortal spirits. They are at the heart of the crucial factors of "blood" and of "mud"—kinship and landscape. By good fortune, examples of the renowned names who "begat" the present day world can be retrieved from fieldnotes and documents, and confirmed by living holders of these names. In sum, these data allow the fuller integration of the Salish into wider patterns and traditions so typical of the rest of the Northwest Coast.

Introduction

For the Lushootseeds of Puget Sound, names, above all, provide the nexus (lynchpin) intersecting their concepts of kinship, pedigree, territory, and culture history. Full understanding of this ethnohistory of naming, however, has been obscured by a lack of available data, especially in publications. In fact, most of the supporting information occurs only in fieldnotes provided by fluent speakers of high rank, who were themselves holders of crucial ancestral names.[1] Once these data were assembled, moreover, the relationship between these Coast Salish and other cultures of the North Pacific becomes much clearer. Salish is a language family distinctive of the Northwest, divided into Coast and Interior branches.[2]

Like the "begats" of the Judeo-Christian Bible, a sequence of names establishes family lines of descent which standout distinctly within these bilateral societies. Over time, these names are successively embodied in a person within a household which is anchored to a series of locales specifically keyed to needed resources. Today that household is conceptual, but until a century ago, it was physical and multiple.

Unlike the Tsimshian with over a dozen chronological episodes in their ethno-ethnohistory (Miller 1997b), Lushootseeds recognize fewer eras.[3] Little is said about creation *de novo* of the world. Instead, successive re-creations mark distinct eras, each following a global destruction caused by human arrogance, overcrowding, and disrespect for the world.

Elders, who have now passed on, hinted there was a local genesis which was known only to shamans, while the re-creations were largely common knowledge. Key members of chiefly families, however, had much more detailed versions of these changes that included *dicta*—special words, spells, and formulae that profoundly affected all other beings in the world, and could be used to help or harm. Invoking the Creator in these *dicta* and prayers also suggests an original creation.[4] Though now mostly known as *shaq si'ab* "above lord" under missionary influence, the persistent use of *xa'xa* "taboo, sacred, godly, forbidden" indicates great antiquity for this deification.

Because important names are eternal, all fieldworkers in the Northwest have disconcerting moments when it is unclear if an elder is speaking of a mythological person from the dawn of time, a protohistoric figure, or one of their current relatives—all with the same name.

The reformers, by convention, are known as Changers, sometimes Transformers ~ Adjustors, who set the world right and prepare the way for modern humans. In the past century, as natives have stopped speaking Lushootseed in favor of English, what seem to have been teams of siblings have now been individuated as a single named person. In Puget Sound, the major Changer has become identified with the Moon, while his less powerful brother became the Sun.

All of the standard cataclysms seem to be reported, firmly based in local geology, including destruction by Flood (with canoes as escape arks), quake (viewed as the world capsizing), fire (easily correlated with volcanic eruptions like that of Mount St. Helens), and plague (with survivors protected by special rituals envisioned by named prophets). Among Lushootseeds, at least one renowned name is associated with each of these destructions, as well as systems of power provided in compensation for the lost lives. In a later section, the famous name of Lehalbid provides an example of this close association with a crisis.

Institutions

Native Lushootseed society in Puget Sound involved concepts of territory, kinship, pedigree, and culture history. It was and is organized around practical considerations of gender, age, rank, descent, residence, and waterway. In more general terms, these are concerned with *person*, *place*, and *intersept*, a kinship grouping traced through both maternal and paternal lines over at least four generations. Over all of these was and is the all-important fourth factor of religion, namely *power* from immortal spirits. Subsets conferring power focus on the high god (*xa'xa*), immortals (guardian spirits), ghosts, and *dicta* (special words). As appropriate for this rainy coastal climate, the basic symbolic opposition underlying these factors is that of "blood" and of "mud"—kinship and landscape.

Culturally, the building blocks of this society, increasing in size, included notions of the individual person (composed of a gendered aging body, a mind, and souls with spirit allies), of the house (including hearthers, locals, and distant kin), of the canoe (transport across time and space, distinguished by habitat as forest, prairie, river, or sea), and of the world (the entire drainage, linked both to resident immortals through rituals and to more remote peoples and places through marriage, ritual, and trade).

Person ~ "blood"

Personhood was characterized by gender—as male or female, by age—as older or younger, and by ranking—as freeborn or slave. The leaders of households and communities constituted the elite, "owning" (in the sense of holding and hosting) famous names and resource locations. Other members of the freeborn rank were commoners, valuable for their labor and support but otherwise undistinguished.

Lushootseeds along the coast emphasized rank and class, while those inland, upriver, and in the south Puget Sound held more Plateau ideals of a kin-based society. "Southern Puget Sound culture emphasized spirit quests and had a lesser emphasis on inherited privileges than the Northerners" (Roberts 1975:32, 35, 77), and hence provided the birthplace for the more democratic beliefs known as the Indian Shaker Church, recognizing a universal, omnipotent God.

Two primary genders are recognized. A few transgendered individuals are known from fieldnotes, but these did not constitute a "third gender." Instead each was identified by external anatomy since natives once wore few if any clothes beyond rain gear when necessary. Since memory of transgenders lasts over generations, reports of only four examples, all from the fieldnotes of Sally Snyder, suggests infrequency. Though there are no known specific anatomical cases, actual hermaphrodites were said to be due to the mother eating the wrong food. A pregnant woman should only eat male fish, deer, and other species. If she ate eggs or female meats, her baby's body would be born "confused." Teasing certain animals produced twins or malformations like a hare lip.

Four examples, all transvestites named by their locations, were from Upper Skagit; Lyman on the lower Skagit River; the Snohomish River; and, across the Cascade Mountains, the Okanogan River of eastern Washington.

Upper Skagit (named šələlux̌ʷəx̌al) "wanted to be a woman and he couldn't make it [because] such a person must go out and rustle for fish, but when he gets home he acts like a woman" (Snyder 1950s: Box 109, folder 5:86 CA).

Lyman (named yalx̌ʷahad) was flacid; acted, dressed, and worked as a woman, making baskets, mats, and other household crafts; and submitted sexually to men. "She" once eloped with a Nooksak man, but was brought back by the father and brothers of "her" large family (Snyder 1950s: Box 109, folder 4:54 LW).

Snohomish had a white father, but his native mother so wanted a daughter that she dressed him as a girl and they lived together until death. He was tall and big, doing both male and female work, and had painful erections when he would "holler loud and cry and cry." He was a x̌ʷstubšəp, "really like a man" but not a saliʔap ('two ends') of both genders, though other women thought so and did not like "him" (Snyder 1950s: Box 109 folder 4:54, 81, 82 LW).

Okanogan was a transvestite with a "small member," who played around with boys until "he got a child on the stomach, his stomach got real big. . . . He died because the baby didn't have any way to come out." While a tumor seems likely, his sexuality led to his fate of being well remembered on both sides of the mountains.

The nearest female equivalent, however, only behavioral, not biological, was a woman at Darrington on the Stillaguamish River who hunted successfully just like a man (Snyder 1950s: Box 109, folder 5:86 CA).

Space ~ Place ~ "mud"

In terms of the overall Puget Basin, Marian Smith (1940a:7), relying on her fieldwork among the Puyallup and Nisqually, devised a spatial model, based on units of decreasing size, for describing how native peoples related to their watersheds. She explicitly recognized that the greatest allegiance and loyalty coincided with the entire drainage system of Puget Sound. Taking these units in reverse or increasing size, better indicates the progression (see p. 21, this volume, for native terms).

Therefore, within each watershed, group cohesion, loyalties, and affiliations grew in terms of (a) hearth mates eating together at the fires within; (b) a household; (c) residents of all neighboring houses; (d) birthright locals—those born there as distinct from in-laws; visitors, and foreigners; (e) seasonal settlements, camps, and resorts; (f) wider community networks; (g) tributary waterways; and (h) the entire drainage of a river.

Each river constituted a "tribe," designated by the endings of -bš (-bsh) (if more cohesive) or as -bix̌ʷ (-byuh) "bunch" if more dispersed. The ending -mish in English (Snohomish, Skykomish) is the same as -bsh in Lushootseed. Rivers and streams with side trails linked all of these together, while trails along and across ridges gave access to separate tribes.

Membership within each drainage derived from the subtle, discerning, and valued appreciation of customs such that insiders, in contrast to outsiders, understood the complexities of "the feud, the snub, the verbal innuendo" and accordingly "were appropriate guests for a ceremonial feast" (Roberts 1975:79).

Traditionally, the crux of the entire system and the basic reason for gathering people together was the display of bonds with particular immortal powers. No one could be successful without such help. For centuries, leading families had bonded with the most powerful spirits in their locales. Lesser family members, some commoners, and even a few slaves could also have spirit partners, but these were less powerful than those of the leaders.

Kin

In addition to considerations of space and place ("mud") within an overall drainage, Lushootseeds also traced kinship through the bloodlines of both parents. The immediate family grouping (derived from four grandparents) is technically called a *kindred*, while the huge extended family, which was and is transnational or intertribal (through eight great grandparents), is technically called an *intersept*.

Among ordinary kinspeople, a nodal kindred was formed around its senior member(s), often the grandparents as a married couple. After the death of the last surviving spouse, the kindred regrouped around the marriage of their oldest child—if fit and able—and so on, through a generation or two. Leading families, however, formed a *stem kindred*, which continued across generations because the stem consisted of the line of holders of its famous, renowned name, conferring control ("management") of locations and resources that made up the "estate" of these nobles. Influence from Wakashans of Vancouver Island may have led to occasional *ramages*, descent based on birth order, especially a line composed only of eldest sons or eldest daughters.

Traced through all of the bloodlines of great grandparents, an *intersept* had its own network that even now extends beyond space and time, as a "nondiscrete, nonlocalized, property-holding group" (Suttles 1987:210). It existed wherever its members lived, and included ancestors from the past and children yet unborn. It had neither fixed size nor place, except in family lore explaining the origin of its famous names. It was managed by the oldest able elder (male or female), who provided guidance and "advice" about the proper use of resources and the transmission of names, positions, and artifacts within the kindred. If it held a famous name, stories about past holders of that name and their fea(s)ts served to specify places where the kindred indeed had a birthright through past actions, particularly on-going partnerships between the spirits of these places and family members. These most powerful spirits (conferring wealth, power, bounty) dwell in remote locations, either high up in the mountains or deep in the water, either ocean or river. Its most prized possession has been called "advice" (xwdikw [xʷdikʷ], also teachings, know-how, wisdom), which included special formulae (*dicta*) to control activities for good or ill, genealogical details, and a body of stories from the beginning of time.

House

Major nodes in this overall system were cedar plank houses, once located along the shore near spots rich in local resources, such as a salmon stream, berry patch, and hunting territory. Even spirit beings lived in such houses, though only special people could see them. Beyond this house node were and are at least three concentric rings occupied by allies, by competitors for regional status, and, third, by strangers (Roberts 1975:82). During the late 1800s, officials broke up these communal homes. Instead, single family dwellings were built with milled lumber, though many people shared these rooms. Today, these households are conceptual and symbolic, though periodically reconstituted inside local school gyms, tribal halls, and ceremonial smokehouses when they host family namings, potlatches, and other displays of their generosity and upholding of traditions.

These community halls, sometimes inspired by styles of ancient housing, are still used for ceremonies, feasts, and gatherings, particularly in winter. These buildings and events continue such traditions. Regional networks also continue, now discussed according to modern reservations instead of former watersheds, though there is considerable overlap between these past and present locations due to treaty provisions.

The park-like old growth forests and the rugged terrain left few level spaces where people could live, so each house in every town had about fifty occupants, with placement within the house reflecting rank in local and regional society. Thus, with a door at the front or side, the owner of the house and his family had the best protected spot in a back corner, away from the drafts at the doorway. They constituted nobility, providing leaders for varied community tasks (Miller 1997a). The hallmark of nobility was being hard working, steady, and reliable.

Along the sides were families of ordinary common folks, who contributed food and upkeep to the household in return for the prestige of living with wealthy relatives. The least desirable and most exposed places in the front of the house harbored slaves, who had been captured in raids, purchased, or born to their lot. Each family had its own hearth fire along a side of the house, since eating together as a "commensal unit" was what defined close, caring, trust relations. Nobles usually had more than one wife, but each seems to have had a separate fireplace hearth to feed her own children and their playmates.

On important occasions, particularly during winter, the head of the house hosted public events on behalf of all the residents. Accordingly, most families moved out to other accommodations, either nearby homes or mat tents, to make room for guests. Two or three large, public fires were lit down the middle (along the long central axis) of the big house. Huge amounts of food—gathered by slaves and housemates and prepared by women under the direction of the senior wife of the host—were served throughout the festivities.

Changes in social status—such as naming, puberty, marriage, or death—provided the occasions for hosting, for inviting in guests. The more prominent a family, the more people would be invited from furthest away. Important families had far flung networks of friends and kin, forged by marriage, adoption, gifts, help, trade, and social obligations. They also named their infants at the youngest possible moment, when it was clear the heir would live.

Today, all of the religions and sects of the modern world can be found among the native peoples of Puget Sound, but they co-exist with much more ancient beliefs and practices based in the landscape. Even the modern churches, however, have distinctly native features because families and communities continue to worship together. In the northern sound, assigned to the Catholic Church for 150 years, cedar boughs freshly cut from the forest and flutes carved from cedar limbs are used during the Mass. Similarly, Protestant churches on reservations will feature native designs and concepts such as the "Great Spirit" in their services.

Two modern religious expressions, moreover, continue ancient beliefs and traditions associated with the spirits of the land. One is sometimes called the Smokehouse Religion because it uses public buildings in the form of ancestral, communal, cedar-plank houses. It continues the tradition of personal spirit helpers and special regard to certain places, often remote and sacred, on the land and in the water. The other is the Indian Shaker Church—founded near Olympia in 1882 by the death and revival of John Slocum—incorporated under the protection of Washington state law in 1910. It blends ancient beliefs with those of Christianity into a distinctive pattern of worship now spread from California to Canada and Montana (Miller 1999b).

Resources

Lushootseed natives had an extremely complicated social life which was comparable to the complexity of farmers elsewhere in the world. Here, however, they largely lived by harvesting (without the effort of planting) the bounty that nature provided for them. They did enhance plots and fields of plants with edible roots, such as wild carrots, onions, camas, and other bulbs; but this wise cultivation of nature was not the same as intensive farming (Miller 2005a). When natives encouraged the growth of certain wild plants, they unobtrusively left seeds and roots in moist locales. After traders from the Hudson's Bay Company introduced natives to "Irish" [Andean] potatoes, these prior talents at tending wild foods allowed them to quickly raise such tubers as a cash crop (Suttles 1987:137–151). Traditionally, people moved with the seasons to camps near available natural foods. The climate was mild, due to the offshore Japanese and California Currents, and rainy, so the region abounded with plants and animals.

Chief among these foods were five species of salmon which (more properly, who) spawned and died in the rivers each year, although some years the runs were more abundant than others. By working hard for a few weeks, a household could catch and dry enough fish to meet winter needs of the family and its guests. Yet people did not live by fish alone. After the summer fish runs, families went into the uplands and mountains to collect dozens of kinds of berries, which were also dried and stored for winter use. Men hunted a variety of mammals, both sea and land, during the fall and winter, depending on where they lived. In the spring, fresh greens and early fish runs enriched the diet of stored supplies. By prudently and generously using resources which were locally "anchored," a household could add to their "radiance" throughout a larger region (Miller 1999b).

K^w askadub

The best-known name from fieldwork, fieldnotes, and documents is that of Kwaskadub [k^waskadəb] "roasted, burnt head." Chiefly names are usually distinguished by the endings -qd [-qn] 'head' or -qs 'nose, point' indicating their duties as deciders or leaders (Bates, Hess, and Hilbert 1994:127, 178, 179).

The lone appearance of this name in print is dramatic. In his dictated autobiography, John Fornsby, a shaman, told how, as boy picking berries near Skagit City, he entered the overgrown feasting house of his great grandfather, and found him still laid out on the rear platform. Later, the body was reburied behind this house and then moved to the Swinomish Catholic Cemetery. After this potlatch house washed away in a flood, one of its carved houseposts (3x4x8 ft.) was later found and installed by Lummi workmen paid by Fornsby at a famous potlatch when graves from a nearby island were moved to the same cemetery.

That Kwaskadub was a famous trader with several homes at strategic locations. His winter and thus primary home was on Penn Cove at Coupeville on Whidbey Island.[5] The home at Skagit City where he lay in state was at the lower end of a two-mile-long logjam that forced migrating salmon to pool before they wove their way upriver. Local gardens grew huge nettle plants (some eight ft. tall), processed into fiber for nets and other fabrics. These nets were specifically adapted to microhabitats. This logjam re-routed canoe travel into other nearby rivers until it was dynamited away in 1878 (Collins 1974:39).

Kwaskadub had several adult children who forged dynastic marriages. More famous and much better documented is the son named Sneatlum (sditbb in Lushootseed), who was a fur trade middleman for Fort Nisqually, founded in the south Sound in 1833. Sneatlum was also a Catholic lay leader. At least one of his wives was Makah, from the far northwest tip of Washington state.

After Sneatlum died 16 December 1852, a carved wooden effigy dressed in his own clothes was set up on what became known as Sneatlum Point on eastern Whidbey Island (Gibbs 1877:203). Another Kwaskadub son flaunted the rules of rank by taking up with a slave girl, who thereafter was named "mistake." One of his daughters married into Chehalis.

Kwaskadub's nephews (sibling unknown) included Goliah, a community spokesman drafted by Governor Isaac Stevens into signing the 1855 Treaty of Pt Elliot (Mukilteo) as "chief" of northern Sound tribes. As an official speaker, though not of noble family, Goliah, having the advantage of some English fluency, appealed to American authorities.[6]

Goliah's brother, known only in fieldnotes, was Sadoəhebix, who maintained a fortified home at Quartermaster Harbor between Maury and Vashon Islands, an important portage in the south Sound. Both Penn Cove, the Lower Skagit homeland, and Quartermaster Harbor were sheltered bays deep into islands, providing portage shortcuts. Famous as a warrior and slaver, he also had crucial access to the fur trade at Fort Nisqually. Because he raided the nearby Duwamish for slaves, his fort was under constant threat so in old age "this village moved to Gig Harbor. The movement took place not long before the treaty" (Smith 1940a:11).[7] Throughout this region, competition took many forms, not all of them involving weapons and warfare.

Moreover, a clearer view of the international and intertribal complexity of the region is shown by the ability of important families to set themselves up in foreign territory and to take advantage of slaving upon locals and trade at the British fort. Of especial note, via intermarriage among local chiefly families, these famous hereditary names thereby become legitimately claimed by heirs of great ability.

Both Kwaskadub and Sneatlum appear in the Fort Langley journal during June, July, and August of 1830 as "the two Scadchats Chiefs—Neetlum & Weskienum" (Maclachlan 1998:150, 156). On Friday, 10 August, Sneatlum's son married the daughter of a Cowichan leader, variously known as Joshua, Josia, Old Joe, or Shashia. In 1847, Paul Kane painted portraits of him and his son Cul-chil-hum. At least one other son is mentioned, but the father died blind and heirless in 1870. Cowichans, then as now, had winter villages on Vancouver Island. After Fort Langley was founded by the HBC in 1827, its journal noted that these island villages had permanent camps on the mainland along the Fraser River to take full advantage of salmon runs.

Between 1780–1810, Ba'da'ɫ (ma'na'yɫ in Straits Salish), a granddaughter of Kwaskadub, was captured by Klallam raiders from Dungeness who quickly realized her rank and married her to a noble son. At the wedding, the groom wore an enormous rawhide mask. Kwaskadub gave the groom's family ten slaves, a seagoing canoe, and many blankets, and, in return, received twenty slaves, a canoe, and other goods (Elmendorf 1993:108–110).

Alice Campbell, married to the Upper Skagit chief descended from the famous prophet Captain Camel (Campbell), explained the upriver source for the name Kwaskadub.

> Long ago there were people who turned into rocks [in the Flood]. This Kwaskadub was the name of one [of them] way up on the Skagit. It is the name of one of Andrew Joe's relatives. They came up to ask the people there for a name (certain people used to go to certain places to obtain a name). If they had known, they could have asked the Sbalix here [natives at Concrete, WA] for a name. (Snyder 1950s: Box 108, Folder 5:58)

What is noteworthy about her report is the transport of a renowned name from an earlier era into a later one. Kwaskadub survived the Flood by being carried upriver and then turned into stone, with his powers intact. When the renewed coastal family came looking for an ancient name, they were reminded of the upriver rock and so revived that name, neatly bracketing the all-important salmon runs between the downriver resource site at the lower logjam and the farthest point upriver where (sockeye?) salmon came to spawn.

Elsewhere in the notes, the "begets" of the name itself are listed, descended from the first being sent down from Heaven to what became Sneatlum Point. As founders of the pedigree of human chiefly lines, these "renowned names" (Collins 1966) constituted the hik^w $si'ab$ (highest rank), based on words for "big, high, most, very" and "wealth, rich, treasure, abundant" (Bates, Hess, and Hilbert 1994:15, 109).

The first ancestor of the Lower Skagit, sent down by the Creator to this point, was named KeKedab [kəkədəb]. He sired three families, each living within a compartment of a huge cedar plank longhouse inside a stockade. Like the Iroquois whose symbolic longhouse paralleled the Mohawk River across central New York, the Skagit occupants of each section settled along the Skagit River, with those in the back of the house furthest upriver, as compared to those who stayed in the middle, and those in the prestigious front section who took over the river mouth, delta, and islands (Snyder 1950s: Box 108, Folder 10:33 AJ).

Each compartment took along or developed specialized artifacts and technologies appropriate to the ecology of their new homelands. Such distinctions are most clearly indicated by different types of nets. Those out in the saltwater used the reef net (sx^walo) named for the twisted willow bark that formed its tough cordage. In the lower river, the weir net ($ql'its$) also of willow bark was used, and upriver the trawl net ($shubid$) was woven from a grass that had to be traded from afar. Both river nets were suspended from a pair of canoes working together, but the weir also included a wide pocket to contain the fish. Today, native fishers, protected by federal and treaty laws, rely on commercially manufactured nets and motor boats to accomplish the same ends.

Of note, the plain straight net of the $shubid$ was deployed effectively in the water, as well as in the air and on land. Set above the ground at strategic locales, it caught flocks of waterfowl as they rose in flight, while set across game trails it took deer and other mammals. Sometimes, as on Whidbey Island, these nets were once set up before communal deer drives.

In the very beginning, other beings already lived on the earth, including an underwater Wealth spirit, who took on the appearance of an ugly, pitiful young man or of a tiny baby. Using mind control (through $dicta$), he compelled the family of KeKedab to adopt him. The daughter who nursed him eventually became pregnant, and he married her in the guise of a handsome, hard-working man. Again using $dicta$, he enabled his wife and son to live underwater with their affines until the boy was old enough to quest for spirit power on land. The son fasted for a year and received "help" at both Sneatlum Point and the bottomless lake across from Greenbanks, a portage. Arriving outside of his own home, he sent his fasting cousin to tell his parents to "clean out" their home so he could publicly dance and sing his newly acquired powers. As he did so, the beach filled with fresh foods (Snyder 1950s: Box 109, Folder 2:12–13, 39–40 AJ). Thereafter the Lower Skagits were known as a wealthy, powerful, and generous tribe. Those inheriting the name KeKedab managed all of the trade along the Skagit River through an upriver partner at Concrete who was also inheriting a single name through time.

Descendants of the first founder, with a bewildering set of names, married into nearby communities, beginning with the Swadabsh [true Swinomish] and Samish to beget seven named grandchildren. These in turn married further away into Lummi and other villages. Since these sons were wealthy, they had many wives, all of whose children stood to inherit their own renowned names. The names of daughters were equally renowned and pass to females along bilateral lines. The only bar to sharing a name within a kindred was proximity. Siblings and cousins who lived far apart can share the same ancestral name as long as confusion about identities is kept to a minimum by distance. In time, these names passed to known historic personages, such as Goliah who signed the treaty. In the begats, this name originally belonged to the son of a woman from Oak Harbor on Whidbey Island, married to a grandson of the founder KeKedab. Oak Harbor itself was founded by someone named xachded (Snyder 1950s: Box 108, Folder 2:96 AJ). Such ancestors might be preexisting beings, animals, or geological features changed into mere humans, and thereby in need of spiritual aid to be successful.

Among the many descendants of KeKedab were famous standouts, such as the boy who was renowned as an endurance warrior, who trained by spitting on a rock, running around Sneatlum Point, and returning before it had dried (Snyder 1950s: Box 108, Folder 2:97 AJ). He easily outran deer, elk, cranes, and eagles. Much later, as part of U.S. Coastal defenses, the strategic lookout used by this warrior eventually became fortified by concrete encasements as Fort Casey.

The heirs of KeKedab suffered through many crises, including the periodic destruction of the known world. Four major eras include 1) a primordial one of real or semi-spiritual beings who marry humans to create descent lines; 2) lawless times when humans and dangerous spirits were punished for damaging general wellbeing; 3) Changers who prepared the world for present conditions, and, most recently; 4) the world as now known. The high god system for transferring power through other beings goes back to the beginning of the world.

Specific communities have traditions of particular disasters. Northern Lushootseeds tell about Glacier Peak in the North Cascades—a volcano that erupted 6700 years ago. A flood of its ash and debris formed Sauk Prairie and rerouted the Sauk River itself from the Stillaguamish into the Skagit (Vance 1957:309).

For Skagits, the earliest Changers were four brothers, oldest to youngest, named Shield, Knife, Fire, and Baby. Each taught ancestors along the river important skills, such as defense, butchering, cooking, and child care. The immortals (spirits) system of power was another result.

Starchild and Diaper Boy created orderly time by becoming Moon and Sun, while their heirs formed chiefly families across the region, receiving the first *dicta*. Before they settled in the sky, they incinerated the world and used the ashes to more evenly scatter resources for use in the next era.

Lower Skagits share the story of Robe Boy, whose family survived the Flood in a canoe. The many victims of the Flood probably established the ghost system of power. As this scoured landscape slowly revived, Robe Boy and his dog hunted for the meat of tiny animals, sewing these pelts into his robe. Later, a voice from above told him to gather up scattered animal bones and, using *dicta* while waving the robe, create new people. They arose dull and very cold, so he waved the robe over charcoal to recreate fire. Herring swarmed in the slough to feed them, and a mountain goat provided wool for fine warm clothing. They lacked sense until Robe Boy took up local dirt to make brains for them (Snyder n.d.: Tale 68 AJ). Eventually these dull humans wandered away, and Robe Boy discovered that his parents were alive and had taken refuge on Sneatlum Point where they were mourning for their children presumed to be dead.

Robe Boy married a human woman and had two sons, First Light and Daylight (Lehalbid). Much later when plague from the east threatened all the people, Lehalbid envisioned a protective song and dance. As a prophet, he led the community at La Conner in constant services until the pestilence passed over them. Holders of this name maintained at least four houses around Fidalgo Island—near the present Swinomish police station, in a fort on Sullivan Slough, on Pull And Be Damned Road along Martha's Bay, and at Snee-osh Point. They shifted by season to these "resorts" to benefit from local foods as these reached peak conditions for harvesting.

The founding of the Indian Shaker Church in 1882 provided the most recent system of power, which was linked with the universal one of Christianity. As such, it renewed the primordial power from the high god, closing the loop that began at creation.

Conclusions

The very mention of King Arthur, Brünhilde, El Inka de la Vega, King Philip (Matecom), Jesus, Malinche, Wovoka, Fatima, Panini, Slocum, and so on identifies these famous names with a place and a time, as well as a gender. Each represents a moment in world history, with the understanding that namesakes partake of the qualities and personalities of all their eponymous ancestors. Eskimos (Inuit) remain empathic on this unifying concept that names partake of the personal fates and characteristics of all their holders.

Similarly, names, especially renowned ones, are at the very heart of Lushootseed culture. Regardless of the loss of language, of territory, and of community health; these names continue to be passed on to appropriate heirs. Associated with them are symbolic households, resource estates, art forms, and histories. Upholding these institutions on either side are the mainstays of "blood" and "mud." As a name serves to infuse a person with all the past, present, and future of prior namesakes, so Andrew "Span" Joe evoked the eternal fusion of mud and of blood when he said that Robe Boy made the "brains" of his revived people from the very earth of that place. Among Lushootseeds, as most other native peoples, the mind is located at the heart not the head of a person, at the very center of being, so these brains involved the core of a person.

Hereditary name + titles have long been recognized as vital features of the complex matrilineal cultures of the North Pacific Coast, and regarded as distinct from the ambilateral and bilateral cultures to the south. Yet the regional elites consistently have intermarried, and continue to do so. The pedigrees established are based on the ownership of traditions based in hereditary names. Given this context, it is not at all surprising, in hindsight, that esteemed ancestors—founding chiefly blood line upon rich mud steeped in the past—were as crucial to the Salish as to their neighboring potential affines.

NOTES

[1] The prime trove of these fieldnotes comes from the amazingly productive years in the early 1950s when Sally Snyder, a graduate student of Melville Jacobs, worked on the Swinomish reservation and among (then) landless ("unrecognized") Skagits and Sauks living upriver. Her life nor career was never easy so we are especially fortunate that copies of her notes are preserved in Special Collections at the University of Washington, though they were long closed to the public and their use required permission from a board of trustees and a family member. My admiration of her notes has been confirmed by thirty years involvement with these communities, where I am honored to be a friend of current Goliah, Lahalbid, and Kwaskadub.

[2] Lushootseed (Puget) belongs to the Coast Salish Branch and, for English speakers, seems daunting because of its complex phonemes, the same sound often pronounced with four variants, and a confusion of the sounds of B and M, D and N that confounds the ethnohistoric record.

[3] This paper builds upon my prior work with Tsimshian eras (Miller 1997b) for the matrilineal north coast, and vastly improves my prior discussion of kinship and

naming among Lushootseeds (Miller 1997a, 1999b). More recent effort has used native names from fieldnotes to reconstitute aboriginal villages burned out so that prime "vacant land" could be homesteaded (Miller 2000).

[4] The significance of high-rank names are better known closer to the northern coast. Wilson Duff (1952:85) noted their importance among the Sto:lo of the Fraser River, while commenting that each researcher (Franz Boas, Diamond Jenness, Charles Hill-Tout) was given a different list and pedigree of these important hereditary names—indicating that the actual name was merely a marker for the crucial concept of rank. Creation epics are reported in some detail for the Sto:lo, from Old Pierre, a shaman, and for the Nuxalk (Bella Coola), as summarized in Miller (1999b).

[5] Penn Cove was also the home of Pat Kanim, the pro-American Snoqualmie leader, whose distinctive house was round with wedge shaped cubicles for his wives and allies, presumably because his primary power was Mountain Goat and this round house was like its cave den described in stories.

[6] A remarkably detailed census by local agent Fay at Penn Cove in 1856 lists Goliah as being six foot, slim, and thirty-five. He died 25 February 1857, after dictating a letter of instructions to Agent Fay. Instead of residing at the Washington, D.C. National Archives, the companion Snoqualmie roll at Holmes Harbor by Nathaniel Hill remained with him at Port Townsend and is now in their historical society.

[7] *The Puyallup-Nisqually* (Smith 1940a:11), based on Marian Wesley Smith, Microfilm Roll 3 (Reel A1738), British Columbia Archives, MSS 2689:Box 6, Folder 9 (Houses 26); Royal Anthropological Archives, MSS 2794, Houses p. 26.

PART III. BIOGRAPHIES

Focusing on named individuals, as well as transgenerational collective holders of a famous name, this section deals with the Tsimshian great name, generally and specifically, with a rare glimpse into the life of an unusual slave, and, lastly, with an academic biography of Vi Anderson Hilbert, the foremost Lushootseed elder scholar.

Ligeex: A Tsimshian Dynasty / Ligeex ~ Tsimshian High Chief: A Comparison of Native and Scholar Views

Because the name title of Ligeex figures strongly in Tsimshian ethnohistory, two articles, general and specific, present my studies of the nature of Tsimshian chiefship, especially the role of the name title of Ligeex, once the highest in rank as confirmed by a series of unique claims and privileges. Worked out in these two parallel efforts, they were not published because, like my study of the chronology of the *adaawx* (sacred epics), they are highly sensitive (Harris 1997). In particular, during the 1980s, several rival claimants were negotiating to revive the Ligeex name (none did). My ethno-ethnohistory (Miller 1998) was published because great effort went into sorting out the episodes, each associated with a chiefly name, and it followed from the work of Ray Fogelson on Cherokee ethnohistory that appealed to the editor of the journal at that time.

Dr. Simon: A Snohomish Slave at Fort Nisqually and Puyallup

Slavery was a Northwest institution whose economic contributions were long an academic concern of Viola Garfield at the University of Washington. Stigmatized, slaves were most often named after the tribe, town, or community of their origin—as a depersonalizing insult. Actual names and biographies are rare. Finding this life of Simon in the notebooks recounting the native town of Minter, dictated near Tacoma by Jerry Meeker to Al Smith, set me to adding this gem to the literature once I had substantiated him in other documents. Since its publication, Simon, 60, has been found on a 30 June 1891 Puyallup census listed along with his wife Lucy, 65, and daughter Annie, 30.

Vi Ta^{w}šəblu Hilbert ~ The Language of Growing Tall

My biography of Vi Hilbert is included here because of her role in motivating other publications in other outlets, including her own Lushootseed Press. It was originally asked and done with her for a linguistics journal that wanted more nuts-and-bolts linguistics that would have taken too much time from her other more community-oriented work. Periodically, I have offered it to editors and web sites, but its length has worked against its availability.

Vi Hilbert was especially fond of Neah Bay, where her family fished over long weekends, incongruously, after a long drive with camper and boat, as relaxation from the grueling demands of her beauty parlor. Several of her clients had complained about the lack of good material on local natives for classroom use, and that nudged Vi toward her eventual career and the founding of non-profit Lushootseed Research to assure that her native language was among the best documented in the world. For her life's work, she earned awards as a state and national treasure, though more for her story telling than for her unique research, with a printing outreach to provide bilingual editions. I helped edit most of these, so my Puget Sound research appears there and in university press books, not in *NARN* or *JONA*.

Journal of Northwest Anthropology, Memoir 9:88–98   2014

LIGEEX: A TSIMSHIAN DYNASTY

ABSTRACT

The chiefly line across centuries maintaining the preeminence among Tsimshian of the Ligeex name title of the Eagle crest is placed into general context, with particular attention paid to his ~ their unique claims, events, confrontations, and privileges during the Fur Trade era of the first half of the 1800s.

Introduction

The antiquity and character of chiefs, and, in particular the high chief, of the Coast Tsimshian of northern British Columbia have been largely misunderstood by academics.[1] Each held and holds a hereditary name that is regarded as immortal by Tsimshian and their North Pacific neighbors, but it is often difficult to separate out the series of actual human holders, although the actions of each served to exalt or tarnish the fame of that name.[2] For natives, however, the *adaawx*, a sacred history precisely told by the head of a "house" (matriline) possessing its leading hereditary name, indicate that the titled name of Ligeex was held by a succession of Eagle crest (matriclan) leaders of the Gispaxlo'ots (People of Elderberry), which, through his efforts, became the foremost tribe in historic times (Marsden n.d.; Marsden and Galois 1995).

This name is first mentioned in *adaawx* referring to events about five hundred years ago, but the most famous bearer, known as Old Ligeex, was active about 1800–1840 during the peak of the land-based fur trade (Robinson 1996).[3] The impetus for this dynasty seems to have been the dispensing of membership in spiritual guilds or secret orders (known as *wiihalaayt*) inherited by the founder from his Wutsdaa (Bella Bella Heitsuk) father but wrongly attributed by Marius Barbeau to Old Ligeex of three hundred years later.

A chief bearing the name of Ligeex, apparently about 1830, was the originator of the secret societies among his band. These fraternities of mutually helpful craftsmen and raiders were his own device to break down the resistance of hostile clan chiefs opposing him and to bring about his domination among the northern tribes. They progressed the more easily among the Kwakiutls for the lack of opposition, in the absence of clans. The potlatch, an ancient system of native transactions and social entertainment, everywhere became the vehicle of new ambitions of conquest, prestige, and power. (Barbeau 1990:65)

In the normal course of North Coast diffusion, such guilds had been spreading from Bella Bella, speakers of a Northern Kwakiutlan or Wakashan language, to the south and to the north, where they had already been placed among the Southern Tsimshian. By intermarrying at Kitamaat and Wudsdaa, Ligeex was able to bring these orders into the Tsimshian heartland to add to the prestige and fame of his house.

However, the murder of Old Ligeex's designated heir in May of 1839, precipitated a bitter rivalry between his own brother and nephew (sister's son, later baptized as Paul), both with claims to matrilineal succession.

Several academics, however, mostly relying on the records of the Hudson's Bay Company (HBC) trading at Fort Simpson, though built on land donated by Old Ligeex, have denied evidence of his primacy. Behind their arguments, moreover, lurks a misunderstanding of Tsimshian leadership, wrongly assuming a consistent royal imperiousness appropriate mostly to European monarchs. While impetuous and ambitious, the Ligeex line were neither tyrants nor autocrats, but rather successful negotiators skilled in the selective use of force.

For Tsimshian, a chief has, minimally, two contrasting management styles. Inheriting an unblemished pedigree from a long line of prior chiefs in the matriline, each holder of a famous name was expected to be "skilled in all things, energetic and ambitious" (Garfield 1966:17). Overall, chiefs were "able leaders, good speakers, haughty and proud before strangers, and humble and generous toward tribesmen. The ideal leader was an able organizer and speaker, and a model of good taste and conduct" (Garfield 1966:27). From a native perspective, a chief had to prove wisdom ('wii ho'osxw), kindness (ammagoot = "good heart"), and strength (daxgyet) in order to gain respect (antlx'ooms) (Gitsegukla 1979:37).

The Tsimshianic language family is composed, in the interior, of Nishga (Nisga'a) on the middle Nass River and Gitksan of the upper Skeena River and, downriver, of Canyon, Coast, and Southern Tsimshian. Since hard and fast boundaries are a convention only in state societies, as elsewhere in the world, Tsimshian border zones were, at least, bicultural and bilingual. Southern Tsimshian leaders were as fluent in Wakashan as Tsimshianic, while Gitksan knew Athapaskan and Nishga used Tlingit. Some of the Tsimshian chiefs spoke Haida and/or married there. Such dynastic marriages united the chiefly families along the entire coast, overarching differences of town, tribe, or parent language.

Viola Garfield, the classic Boasian Tsimshianist, estimated thirty Tsimshian tribal chiefs, each heading the major house of the tribal town (Garfield 1966:26). While immortal names conferring rank were and are almost always male; in the absence of a close male heir, a woman could and did "carry" the name and was accordingly treated as a "man."

Before Christianity, each leader had four named spiritual aspects, often distinguished as sm- "real." As smgigyet ("real people") house chiefs, they coordinated summer economic activities and conducted feasts and namings; as naxnox dancers, they sponsored and/or performed in fall masked ceremonials. As smhalaayt, with a carved frontlet on the forehead, a woven blanket over the shoulders, and a raven rattle in the hand, they initiated young people into ritual roles of the crest. As 'wiihalaayt leader of one of the four secret guilds, they ritually confirmed the royal rank of children and adults" (Halpin and Seguin 1990:279).[4]

Beneath these chiefs, several hundred lineage and house heads managed the societal routines and made up the nobility. Each tribal chief was advised by a council of these nobles, together with craft and resource specialists such as shamans, carpenters, carvers, painters, musicians, composers, herbalists, midwives and astronomers (MacNeary 1976:156; Miller 1992c). With the advice of these specialists, overall efforts were coordinated by the chief of the leading house of that town.

Since each Coast Tsimshian tribe functioned in terms of its constituent ranked houses, all territories and trade routes were controlled by the house chiefs. Both water and land routes were owned and defended by a house, although marriages among royalty forged trade alliances to provide access to a variety of desired resources.

In general, coastal towns specialized in various kinds of seafoods and marine goods (dried cockles, clams, grease, dried candlefish, seaweed, dried herring eggs, shells) traded to interior chiefs in return for prestigious furs, hides, and copper. Throughout the coast, potlatches relied heavily on such inland pelts, particularly of marmot.

Along with marital ties, such alliances were strengthened by exchanging names and privileges, by feasting, and by ceremonial displays. At strategic locations along inland trails, chiefs built feast houses where friendship-making (*ne-amex*) rites (a kind of *halaayt* ritual) could be held to warn against poaching.

The crucial importance of trade for Tsimshian society is further indicated by the use of seven numbering systems to readily specify the type and quantity of goods involved.[5] As merchants, Tsimshian were seasonally mobile, arguing against the proposition that seasonal rounds were post-contact phenomena in the Northwest. Based on archaeological surveys of Vancouver Island, Inglis and Haggarty suggest that the prehistoric density of town sites there indicated local control (ownership?) of all local resources, which were harvested by residents and circulated only through trade. After European epidemics and dislocations destabilized the Nuchahnulth population, however, survivors began a pattern of seasonal movements to harvest available resources in various locations (Inglis and Haggarty 1987).

Extensive archaeology along the Skeena River and Prince Rupert Harbor indicates occupation for thousands of years leading to historic Tsimshian (MacDonald 1979; Coupland 1988; Matson and Coupland 1995). In particular, a dense concentration of town sites along Metlakatla Passage indicates a thousand years of joint winter residence by a dozen Coast Tsimshian tribes. In the spring people moved to the Nass for the candlefish run, rendering their trade mainstay of oolichan grease. In summer, towns moved to their territories along tributaries of the Skeena River until they all gathered together at Fall Place (*spaksuut* = "Fall place," Port Essington) for festivities before wintering back at Metlakatla.

Each year, summer was devoted to economic activities under the leadership of the chiefs of four crests—matrilineal clans forming semi-moieties of Orca-Wolf and Raven-Eagle (Miller 1978, 1981a, 1981b). Crest celebrations, hosted by chiefs, were potlatches, when the *adaawx* of the household was recited and displayed on carved poles (Miller 1989).[6] During the winter, chiefs assumed their priestly names and hosted dramatizations of their *halaayt* privileges, mostly elaborated visits to Heaven. The autumn gathering was devoted to presenting wonders, enactments of an encounter between an ancestor and a supernatural spirit (*naxnox*).

After 1830, Tsimshians relocated to a trading post and then an Anglican mission, adding to the three social classes of nobles, commoners, and slaves characteristic of the entire Northwest Coast Culture Area. Thus, historically, Tsimshian developed a fourth class of royalty, tribal chiefs who arose from the ranks of the former town leaders when heirs were placed in charge of either old or new locations. To reinforce their increased rank, royalty received initiation into one or more of the guilds and claimed new crests combining humans traits with fabulous creatures (Halpin 1973, 1978, 1994, n.d.).

During 1787 to 1805, the fur trade was ship-based and concerned with sea otter pelts, so coastal chiefs had the advantage, particularly the Kitkatla Orca named Ts'ibasaa, who served as Southern Tsimshian high chief. Another leader in an advantageous position was Txagaaxs ("World Raven," also named 'Wiiseeks) who became a rival of Ligeex until killed during the 1836 smallpox epidemic. With the shift to beaver pelts during 1805–1825, Old Ligeex came into his own by maximizing his links with the interior.

Seeking a land base, the HBC built Fort Nass in 1831, but the site was too exposed to freezing winds. There, in particular, Ligeex benefited from the marriage of his daughter Sudaał to

Dr. John Frederick Kennedy, physician and resident trader.[7] For two years, she talked to her father about a better locale until he offered his camp "at The Wild Roses" for Fort (Port) Simpson, built in 1834 (Grumet 1975, 1982; Meilleur 1980). By 1840, when Old Ligeex vanished from the record, the other Coast Tsimshian tribes had each founded a neighborhood there in lieu of Metlakatla. By claiming a monopoly over the entire Skeena River, as well as ready access to the Hudson's Bay Company, Ligeex rose to prominence over all the Tsimshian royalty, based not on his might but rather on his generosity by sharing these resources with his fellow chiefs.[8]

Outsiders, of course, saw mostly his imperious aspect, particularly his brilliant military strategies. As Chief Heber Clifton noted:

> Ligeex was a most ferocious warrior and he had no respect or feeling for anybody, just like his Eagle warriors, mostly all Gispaxlo'ots. He was dreaded by all. Women from other tribes used his name in their nursery songs to instill fear into their children. The Ligeex warriors were a vicious group. (Barbeau and Beynon 1987b:69)

Among the Tsimshian themselves, however, the Ligeex title was specially honored because of its succession of able managers, potlatch hosts, *halaayt* initiators, dynastic marriage brokers, and war lords (Garfield 1939:201–204; Miller 1997b:86–87).[9]

In contrast, academics have consistently misread statements from Henry Tate to Franz Boas about the history of the Ligeex line (Boas 1916b:510), which need to be reconsidered carefully. In particular, because it fit with European notions of chronology, a false link was made between the Kitamaat origin of the name and the Ligeex six generations back from 1888 who painted his claim on a Nass River cliff. Therefore, the introduction of the Ligeex name, probably about five hundred years ago, was distinct from the momentum provided by the European fur trade, about 1750, to move that name into primacy. What Boas actually wrote was this:

> Thus the highest in rank among all the Tsimshian chiefs was Ligeex, the chief of the Eagle group of Gispaxlo'ots. His family alone had the right to perform certain ceremonials corresponding to the highest secret societies of the Kwakiutl. Tradition says—and it is undoubtedly correct—that an Eagle woman of the Gispaxlo'ots tribe eloped with a Kitamaat chief (the tribe of Kwakiutl affinity inhabiting Gardner Channel), whose family assumed membership in the highest ceremonial society. After her return to the Skeena River, the woman was given the name K'amdmaxł ("ascending the mountain with a costly copper"). The name Ligeex is said to be a Kitamaat name (perhaps from *la-* = "to go", *-eg.a* = "behind"?).[10] The chief of the tribe took it after the previous hereditary chief's name, Nisbalaas, had lost its standing, because the bearer had been killed by a chief of the Raven clan and his head put up in the house of the latter. (Boas 1916b:510)

Three paragraphs later—after describing Ligeex intermarriage with the Kitkatla royal Orca house, links with the Gitando, and remarking "I have also been told that the Gispaxlo'ots had the privilege of trade with the Gitksan, which they maintained successfully against the Hudson's Bay Company until the later purchased it in 1866"—Boas added "The Ligeex who ruled about one hundred and fifty years ago (the sixth back from the year 1888) had his figure painted on a vertical precipice on Nass River, a series of coppers standing under his figure."

With greater precision, Matthew Johnson,[11] chief advisor to the Ligeexs in the early 1900s, told Homer Barnett that the grandmother of Ligeex I married the Kitamaat chief, while their daughter married Hamdziit, a leading Heiltsuk (Wutsdaa, Bella Bella) chief (Barnett 1940, notebook #1:44). Thus this matriline became doubly empowered from the south by a Kitamaat name and Wutsdaa guilds from fathers whose paternal role in this matrilineal society was to extravagantly advance the public career of his children.[12] Moreover, Heiltsuk chiefs had a tradition of memorializing their fame by having a "portrait" painted on a rock face.[13] Through his mother's Eagle crest, Ligeex was also allied with the Gwinhuut Fugitive Eagles of the Alaskan Stikine and Tlingit, along with the legendary Haida princess named Omen. His crests included both the Frog Hat, held on his head by two members of his father's clan, and a cane topped by a Frog, together with the Beaver Hat, which was held on Ligeex's head by a member from each of the four crests to show that Ligeex "was the highest in rank among all the clans" (1916b:267, 272, 512). For Tsimshian, this public act of cooperation among the four crests is regarded as proof of his primacy.

Moreover, Ligeex had many *naxnox* and *halaayt* privileges uniquely his own. One *naxnox* involved two enormous hands that reached down from the roof and lifted a man toward Heaven, while another, called Crack of Heaven, was a mask that made the house divide in two, move apart, and rejoin. His *halaayt* names included *txagaxsm laxha* (Heaven Body), *hanatana*, and *gaguliksgaax* (Boas 1916b:513, 556; Barnett 1940, notebook #2:21–22, 1942).[14] Needless to say, these feats were spectacular beyond those of other chiefs.

The men called Ligeex participated in dynastic marriages; Old Ligeex married very well (Marsden and Galois 1995:Figure 2). Before 1800, he wed Maskgaax (Meksgaax) of the House of Saxsa'axt of the royal Gitwilgyoots, who had sea otter beds and traded with the Masset Haida. One of their sons married into a Raven house of the Gits'iis, then married A'maa'tk, a sister of Nisnawaa, a leading chief of Kitselas from the House of Senaxaat, trading with Kaigani Haida and Gwinhuut Tlingits. One of their sons married a royal Gitzaxłał Raven with trading privileges into the Tongas Tlingit. After 1800, Old Ligeex allied with Nts'iitskwoodat, a niece of Sgat'iin, a Wolf chief of the upper Nass River. One of their daughters was Sudaał, who married Kennedy of the Hudson's Bay Company, and another wed Txagaax, the former rival. This third wife lived well as a trader until dying in the 1836 smallpox outbreak, when the Hudson's Bay Company provided her coffin and grave. At his apogee, Old Ligeex married NaseLiyoontk, also known as Ksmgyemk (Lady Sun), of the Kitkatla royal Orca house of Ts'ibasaa (Hale), who, in turn, wed Ligeex's eldest sister (named K'amdmaxł for their mother), and their Eagle son, Ligeex's heir, was named Hatsksnee'x (Long Fin).[15]

Through trade and ritual exchanges, the Ligeex received enormous cedar canoes from Haida Gwaii (Queen Charlotte Islands noted for huge cedar trees) to transport large loads of trade goods along the Skeena.

The keepers of the gateway to the furs of interior Gitksans and Athapaskans were the Kitselas at the Canyon of the Skeena. Their royal house was founded by a Fireweed from legendary Temlaxam (Prairie Town) with extensive kin ties. Later Githawn (Githoon, Salmon Man), a famous chief, founded an Eagle royal house there, fostering alliances with Ravens upriver among the Gitksan. Each spring, the Kitselas formally opened the annual trade with the Gitksan; only then could Old Ligeex impatiently begin his monopoly.

To circumvent this ritual requirement, Ligeex several times tried to vanquish the Kitselas and upriver towns. During one foray, he arrived in front of Kispayaks using the first umbrellas as a *naxnox* display to lure these townspeople into an ambush, which was brutal but indeterminant. Instead, over time, Ligeex used his own and other marriages, along with feasts, to regularize a successful alliance with the Kitselas.[16]

Yet, for all his preparations, Old Ligeex's well laid plans went awry just before he died about 1840. From 22 to 29 May 1839, a skirmish between Tsimshian and Skidegate Haida rocked Port Simpson. Among the many casualties was probably the designated heir to Old Ligeex, leaving the succession uncertain. When the old chief died a year later, his own brother (Hatsksnee'x, the proper name for the heir) and nephew (probably a boy) vied for the position with equal matrilineal claims.[17]

During this fierce rivalry, Ts'ibasaa tried hard to humiliate the boy, who was sagely protected by Xiyoop, his Eagle spokesman and guardian who once purchased the Cormorant Copper from the Haida with his own resources to best the Kitkatlas.

In time, the boy himself seems to have taken the name Xiyoop and continued to prove he measured up to his responsibilities. In keeping with family tradition, he married a Kitselas woman named wałk,[18] who had lived for four years in Victoria and could advise him about the ways and supplies of European fur traders.[19] He became a skilled warrior and plotted to confirm himself as Ligeex by massacring Skidegates in revenge for the lost heir. As Ligeex, he had a special house built where these Haida would be invited to a feast, trapped, and killed. Instead, however, at its completion, Niswiksunash, Gitlaan chief, threw eagle down on him in public, thereby forcing him to remain peaceful.[20] In 1865, his rival uncle was taken by the Gitando to be the Eagle chief named Sgagaweet.

Meanwhile, other major changes were taking place. Sponsored by the Church Missionary Society, Evangelical Anglicans, in 1857, William Duncan, a lay missionary, arrived from England. After devoting a year to learning Tsimshianic from Clah inside the fort, he began preaching in Ligeex's own house until they had an angry falling out when Duncan persisted in ringing his bell during the enforced silence of the *halaayt* initiation of a Ligeex daughter. In 1862, to protect his converts, he led them to found a wealthy cooperative community back at Metlakatla, where Ligeex joined them and was baptized Paul Legaic I (Usher 1971, 1974; Murray 1985). After two decades of success, however, differences with an imposed Anglican bishop drove Duncan and most of his converts to New Metlakatla in Alaska, seeking religious freedom under United States protection.

Frustrated and shamed after his Haida plot went askew, his councilors advised the soon-to-be Paul to join Duncan's community of Christian converts, where his primacy was still valued. At Metlakatla, all the houses looked the same so everyone would be equal before God, yet Paul was allowed to have a house larger than the others because of his rank. Named *Walp Hawhaw*, it bore a lion head carved at the end of its ridgepole and a sign written by Duncan, "This is the Lion House."[21]

While Paul played a prominent role in the Christian community until his death, over time, Duncan himself usurped the primary role of Ligeex, as evidenced by his oratorical fluency in the native language, his care and welfare for the community, and his constant industry—all traditional marks of chiefly status (Usher 1974:109). Indeed, he was explicitly called "Chief."

After Paul joined Metlakatla, his councilors at Fort Simpson made his nephew Awx his surrogate among the traditional chiefs until his inheriting of the Ligeex name in his own right when Paul I died in 1869. As he assumed the English name Paul Legaic II along with the elite name title of Ligeex (Brock 2011:205, 207), he hosted and, in return, was feasted by other First Nations since highest prestige comes from outside the local community. In 1869, at Fort Simpson, he was feasted by Kaigani Haida serving pilot bread and molasses, and Paul, in response, hosted whiskey feasts. At the end of 1870, he has stockpiled gifts and goods for a major potlatch, inviting Tlingits, Kitkatlas, and others. In February of 1871, Paul gave away all that he owned, including elk skins, 60 coppers, and 710 trade blankets.

As Ligeex, Awx married a Kitkatla woman and potlatched a new-style milled lumber house when their first child was born in 1872. After his wife died, he moved to Victoria, where he died, perhaps also known as Paul. When he died in 1891, his tribe gave away $800.00 in rifles, $650.00 in blankets, and $150.00 in clothes, in addition to new coats, shirts, pants, and stockings to those who attended to the body. In challenging response, the Gitando gave out $3000.00. In 1892, a marble monument to the entire Legeex line was set up at Port Simpson, where it still stands as an utterly unique marker among Tsimshian royal name titles.

The Ligeex title next passed to Marite (Martha, Wułish), a niece of sixteen, who died of measles two years later. In 1895, through his mother Diiks, sister of Paul I and wife of Taylor Dudoward, William Kelly inherited the Ligeex name until he died 29 September 1933. In lieu of a clear succession, the Gispaxlo'ots formed a committee of fourteen members to perform the powers of this chiefship[22] until in 1938, his son William Kelly assumed the name by right of his father adopting him as a nephew (sister's son).[23]

Against this historic native record and continuing Tsimshian regard for this great chief, several academics have argued against any primacy of the Ligeex line nor any claims to a Tsimshian chiefdom, despite two thousand of years of interactive winter occupation by allied tribes at Old Metlakatla. In particular, written reports mentioning other natives trading along the Skeena are taken as denials of any Ligeex monopoly, but this view is ethnocentric. Native sources are clear that anyone could trade along the Skeena, provided that they paid a tariff to Ligeex for this privilege. Thus, while these other traders may have been seen, their payments to Ligeex were not.

In one *adaawx*, a Nishga Wolf Chief named Łitux went overland and traded so successfully with the Gitksan that he had to attempt to come down the Skeena after the spring thaw. Forewarned, Ligeex sent word to his Eagle clansmen at Kitselas that this Wolf "was eating out of my food box." Intercepted, Łitux's canoes were smashed and his goods confiscated. Later, in consequence, revenge battles were fought on the Nass until peace was restored.[24] Yet, this Nishga's offense was not that he traded, but that he had the bravado to evade the tariff.

Nevertheless, Donald Mitchell (1983), relying on existing records from Fort Simpson, has argued that the Tsimshian had "a tribal level of social complexity and that to characterize it as a chiefdom is to misinterpret its significance for an understanding of cultural evolution."

> These thirty years record at least 32 different trading excursion up the Skeena River. Seven refer only to Tsimshian trading; ten identify the traders as Gispaxlo'ots... and 15 make specific reference to Ligeex as the trader.... It seems clear that Ligeex and his group, the Gispaxlo'ots, did monopolize the Skeena River trade and that they did so for at least 30 years. . . . It seems undeniable that Ligeex and his people—the Gispaxlo'ots—had some kind of exclusive right to carry the fur trade up the Skeena River and into the interior. It also seems obvious that Ligeex was or became the individual of highest rank among the Metlakatla Tsimshian lineage heads. In this sense he was the "principal chief" of the Tsimshian although he may not have attained this status until the 1840s. (1983:60)

> But the contemporary observations of Fort Simpson traders make it seem most unlikely that Ligeex headed a political unit that could in any useful sense be termed a chiefdom. He ruled over no group but his own, and even there his hold seems fragile. In short, there was no chief and I would argue that the Tsimshian case provides us with no evidence of Northwest Coast chiefdom. (Mitchell 1983:62)

Similarly, after another intensive study of the written record, Jonathan Dean (1993, 1994, n.d.) determined that at Fort Simpson three chiefs were most prominent: Neshoot of the Gitzaxłaał; Txaqaaxs (Wiiseeks) of the Ginaxangiik; and Ligeex of the Gispaxlo'ots, but only Ligeex survived the 1836 smallpox epidemic, in part because he was vaccinated by the Hudson's Bay Company. As noted above, however, Old Ligeex finally coopted these very chiefs through strategic marriages:

> While Ligeex reportedly enjoyed a 'monopoly' in this time, this cannot be understood in Western terms, as a complete shutdown of all but Gispaxlo'ots commerce, but might have consisted of nominal control. Even after the rise of Ligeex in 1840, strangers from the Interior continued to use the Skeena to bring trade down to the fort, and the Nass river valley also continued as a very important venue. Beginning in the 1850s, the managers at Fort Simpson employed Neshaki— a Nishga noblewoman—to conduct the trade and transport furs from her village at Caxatan, and she continued to freight for the Company on the Nass after Ligeex left to join William Duncan at Metlakatla in 1862. By the middle 1860s Neshaki was even operating on the Skeena River, in Ligeex's 'backyard.' (Dean 1994)

More specifically, in an unpublished study of the career of Ligeex, Dean suggested that Ligeex became more famous in memory after the name lapsed and the Gispaxlo'ots would not reciprocate with feasts, gifts, and potlatches, using past glory to justify present inactivity (Dean n.d..:20).[25]

Yet living memory among all the Coast Tsimshian, particularly as enshrined in the *adaawx*, makes it clear that the matriline of Ligeex high chiefs contributed to their overall cohesion during the trying times of the fur trade, Duncan's mission and flight from the Anglican bishop, and the imposition of Anglo-Canadian law and bureaucracy. Today, as all British Columbia First Nations prepare for their long overdue land claims and treaties, the name of Ligeex continues to be invoked as reminder of the superior leadership so characteristic of the Tsimshian from ancient times.[26]

Motivation

Lastly, the Ligeex climb to the top should be considered. While all chiefs were driven to excel, this line did more. Several hints indicate why. First, they were vastly and well connected. Hamdziit, the father of I, was a high ranking Heitsuk, a tribe so known for their supernatural powers that they are sometimes called wizards or enchanters. Second, the Gwinhuut Eagles were a royal house but small, so they probably tried harder. Third, the primary Gwinhuut Eagle chief among the Gispaxlo'ots before Ligeex was Nisbalaas, who became eclipsed. Boas wrote that a later Nisbalaas had been beheaded by Ravens (Boas 1916b:355–370).[27] Thus, to overcome this shame, the Ligeex name was advanced at a time of great stress and managed to overtake all rivals. Four, like Chief Seattle, the early Ligeexs served as an intertribal war lord for concerted Tsimshian engagements. Over time, military success led to loyalties that advanced this name among all the other chiefs.

At apex, Ligeex provided an orderly system to channel the flow of furs, power, and largesse so that these other chiefs could expect to benefit from his generosity and skill as an effective manager. Other chiefs had other prime specialties, such as Ts'ibasaa opening the winter ceremonial season or Sgagaweet leading the cannibal *halaayt*. Yet when outsiders were involved, all united behind Ligeex.

ACKNOWLEDGMENTS

Study of these disparities between academic piecemeal and Tsimshian holistic treatments of Ligeex owe much to conversations with Susan Marsden, Viola Garfield, John Dunn, Christopher Roth, Ernest and Lynne Hill, Ray Fogelson, Marjorie Halpin, Jonathan Dean, and Chiefs Tom Brown and John Clifton.

NOTES

1. Tsimshian is an ethnonym deriving from *ts'm* 'inside' and *ksyaan* 'Skeena River.' Basic sources on the Tsimshian (including Southern, Gitksan, and Nishga) include tens of thousands of manuscript pages by the Tsimshian chief William Beynon (Gwisk'aayn). Another important source on the Ligeex line is Homer Barnett (1940).

2. In keeping with its importance, the name Ligeex has no easy translation. Among Tsimshian, the more important a name, the more interpretations it has in order to consume time and energy. According to native sense, the name means "impassability, invincibility, impenetrability, what cannot be overcome." The Ligeex spelling used herein was approved by literate Tsimshian for publications used in tribal schools and by the Tsimshian Language Authority. Europeans have spelled this name as Legaic, Legeek, Ilegauch, Illgayauch, Legaeek, or, recognizing its cohesiveness, the Illegaich Gang, but all versions have been standardized in this article.

3. In this generally garbled account of this dynasty, Old Ligeex is called Legaik 2, but IV would be more like it (Robinson 1996).

4. For Marjorie Halpin and Margaret Seguin (1990), their Tsimshianic spellings have been updated.

5. These counting systems are distinguished as 1) general; 2) animal or flat (as pelts); 3) humans; 4) long objects; 5) canoes; 6) people in canoes; and 7) unit measures. See Dunn, *Sm'algyax* (1979c:38–40).

6. A traditional chief had a moral and religious obligation to transform chaotic cosmic energy into socially useful power by being a conduit for it down through his spine, ceremonial cane, or totem pole, which, above all, was the "deed" to "his" rank, name, house, and territory.

7. One source said that her mother was a Haida wife of Ligeex, but every other authority indicates that her mother was Nishga. If her mother (and very identity) had been Haida, the Hudson's Bay Company records would have been very different. Instead, Haida traders at the fort often had to be guarded and escorted during their visits. Barnett (1940, Notebook #1:8) gives her name as Ashigiumk, with a son called Taawiis, who went with his father after the wife died. Matthew Johnson (Barnett 1940, Notebook #1:49) recalled that Kennedy supplied his father-in-law with the first shingles, pants, and other trade specialties ever seen among the Tsimshian, including a gun before firearms were banned. At Fort Simpson, Ligeex was "boss" of the young men cutting firewood and gardening for the traders (Barnett 1940, Notebook #1:57).

8. In the most explicit statement about the nature of this monopoly, Matthew Johnson told [8]Homer Barnett (1940, Notebook #1:31), "Ligeex made a law that only one canoe per house, to control trade with Hagwilget." In other words, Ligeex regulated the trade for all the Tsimshian, specifying that each house, roughly a crest-based matriline, could send one

and only one canoe to trade upriver along the Skeena with the Tsimshianic Gitkxan, who in turn traded with the Athapaskan Wet'suwet'en (Bulkley River Western Carrier) whose towns included Hagwilget. Each house and canoe, of course, paid a tariff to Ligeex for this regulated access.

[9] Ligeex's vital role in the *halaayt* initiations of elite children appears in Volume 12, text 179, The Halait and all the Different Kinds of Halait, taken by William Beynon in 1937 from Julia White and Mrs. R. Tate, now at the Butler Library of Columbia University, also Reel 3 of the set by Microfilming Corporation of America, 1980.

[10] According to Chief Gordon Robinson of Kitamaat (1956:24–26) the name Ligeex means "overland traveler" and was assumed by Jasee (ts'si), a Gwinhuut Raven chief at Kitamaat whose own name had been given by his Eagle father and means "Eagle Claws."

[11] Johnson was born 5 November 1855 and was 85 when he worked with Barnett in 1940.

[12] Dr. Emmon Bach, a linguist formerly at the University of Massachusetts at Amherst and now at the University of Northern British Columbia, worked on the Kitamaat version of Northern (Kwakiutlan) Wakashan with Jeffrey Legaik, who died in 1976.

[13] A Beynon text (microfilm reel 2:111–128) places this painting on the Nass, but another or duplicate also exists on the Skeena (where I have seen it) across from Port Essington, most likely sponsored by Old Ligeex to assert the claim to his Skeena trade prerogative. The original Skeena artist's name was Dzumks, although Gaya of Gitlaan later refurbished it. The basket Dzumks stood in and the rope used to suspend it were purchased from a Skidegate Haida chief, who made the trip home and back in eight days, for five coppers and five slaves.

[14] Barnett (1940, Notebook #2:20–21) lists five wonders and eight masks.

[15] Today, Northwest natives are well aware of such parallels between the dynastic marriages of European and of Tsimshian noble houses. Royal Tsimshians specifically equate their own houses with others like the English House of Windsor, although their own, of course, are far older. It is to their benefit that Canada, unlike the U.S., honors such noble statuses.

[16] Similarly, Barbeau and Beynon (1987b) also include the origin of his crests of the Gunhuut (Gwinhuut "fugitives", including Tlingit) branch of the Eagle semi-moiety from a conflict with the Ravens at Laxsail, Alaska (Barbeau and Beynon 1987b:31–35), the origin of the Ligeex name and halait privileges from the Kitamaat and Bella Bella Heiltsuk (1987b:62–65, 69–75), his revenge against the Haida (1987b:66–68), conflict with the Kitselas (1987b:84–85), series of four ascendancy potlatches (1987b:92–94), chiefly contests (1987b:95–111, 118–126), staged cremation *halaayt* (1987b:116–117), and attempted murder of William Duncan (1987b:206–209). Other texts refer to actions by Gispaxlo'ots royal houses (1987b:213–235).

[17] Old Ligeex, his brother, and his nephew should have all been Eagles through their mothers (also a sister of the brothers in terms of the nephew), yet this Uncle has what appears to be the Orca name of the heir to the royal house of Kitkala, whose premier name was Ts'ibasaa, until he exchanged this name with a ship captain for that of Hale. Such a link to this foremost Orca house is reinforced by the intense rivalry between Ts'ibasaa and the boy Ligeex in the 1840s.

[18] Barnett (1940, Notebook #1:32, #2:27) says she was the daughter of Eks, a man who

died from miscalculating the amount of poisonous root to eat during ritual purging in preparation for halibut fishing.

[19] Barnett (1940, Notebook #1:27). While Wałk was on a visit to Port Simpson, the future Paul Ligeex decided to marry her, but she was warned that he was "mean" when drinking so she refused and escaped on the Beaver, the Hudson's Bay Company steamship to Victoria, founded in 1849, where she stayed for four years, benefiting from contact with Sir James Douglas, first governor after a long career in the Hudson's Bay Company. When she returned north, Ligeex had reformed so they married. He called together the other chiefs and reported what his wife had told him about Victoria, proposing an expedition there, which took a month in 1854, opening a whole new trade network that, unfortunately, provided the route for the rapid spread of the 1862 devastating smallpox pandemic. See also Bolt (1992).

[20] The downy white feathers of eagles or swans were and are scattered at native gatherings to enforce peaceful intent. Such eagle down was a pledge of legal and moral action free from any treachery. Antonia Mills (1994) aptly titled her book on the Wet'suwet'en Athapaskan neighbors of the Gitksan, *Eagle Down Is Our Law*.

[21] Barnett (1940, Notebook #1:53). The native word used here for lion (*hawhaw*), originally referred to a mighty spirit power until Duncan used it in a bible song about Daniel in the Lion's Den, still being sung. Since Matthew Johnson (1940, notebook #1:46) also reported that Duncan jailed natives who cut down their totem poles because they attracted tourists, he may have had a similar reason for labeling such a "curio," although respect for Paul was such that he was one of the few partners Duncan allowed into his private trading company.

[22] The Gitando also laid claim to some of these Ligeex powers because they had buried two prior Ligeexs.

[23] See Barnett (1940, notebooks #1:55–58; 2:6–10, 16); Johnson explicitly said (Barnett 1940, notebook #1:58) that George Kelly was the fourth Ligeex he knew, listing as prior Paul, Awx, and Mather (?), which accounts for a present rival claim.

[24] See *Conflict at Gits'ilaasu*, Teachings of Our Grandfathers (*Suwilaay'msga Na Ga'niiyatgm*) 6 (Prince Rupert School District 52, 1992f).

[25] Dean (ms.:20) made that charge that during the 1862 smallpox outbreak, "Had Legaic been the international specialist and the foremost chief as often portrayed, he should have taken steps to stabilize the situation (in spite of, or perhaps, because of, the smallpox) as semo'iget [*smoogyet*, real person, chief = "the real one who protects the people"] and wihalait ['*wiihalaayt'*, great priest], whose *raison d'etre* was to master temporal and natural powers." As the *adaawx* indicate, however, the Ligeex succession was then in disarray from smallpox and rival claims.

[26] During my twenty years of fieldwork, Ligeex was always mentioned with such respect that people say the title is "too heavy" for anyone alive now to carry. The man who made the most current claim for this name died in January of 1997.

[27] This disaster may have included the massacre of virtually all Gispaxlo'ots chiefs, giving Ligeex even greater incentive to advance by lavish potlatching.

Journal of Northwest Anthropology, Memoir 9:99–109   2014

LIGEEX ~ TSIMSHIAN HIGH CHIEF:
A COMPARISON OF NATIVE AND SCHOLAR VIEWS

ABSTRACT

The publication of a superb set of textbooks for use in Tsimshian schools in northern British Columbia (Prince Rupert School District:1992a-g) again raises the issue of native versus academic interpretations of history and culture. In particular, the role of Ligeex as Tsimshian "high ~ foremost" chief is reexamined in terms of his many unique ~ special privileges.

Ligeex, a hereditary chiefly name + title among the Eagle crest (hereditary art forms) of the Gispaxlo'ots tribe, passed matrilineally from maternal uncle to nephew, is, in particular, the subject of recurrent disagreements among scholars and natives. Scholars, thinking and writing in terms of European notions of politics, deny that Ligeex was anything like their notion of a high chief.

Our academic understanding of the Tsimshian has improved (Miller and Eastman 1984; Seguin 1984; Miller 1997b) so the study of Ligeex involves larger issues (Brock 2011). Generally, Tsimshian includes four divisions along the north Pacific coast and the Nass and Skeena Rivers. Near the shore were the Coast Tsimshian, ten tribes (of whom nine survive) who, for thousands of years (Coupland 1988; Matson and Coupland 1995), had summer locations along tributaries of the lower Skeena and winter neighborhoods along Metlakatla Pass. Southern Tsimshian (three tribes) lived on offshore islands and Douglas Channel (Dunn 1979a,b,c; Miller 1984b). Along the upper Nass were the Nisga'a, who moved downstream in recent centuries, and along the upper Skeena were the Gitxsan (~ Gitksan)

Summer was devoted to economic activities under the leadership of the chiefs of four crests, matrilineal clans associated with Orca Killerwhale, Raven, Eagle, and Wolf. In practice, these crests formed semi-moieties of Orca-Wolf and Raven-Eagle (Miller 1978, 1981a, 1981b). Crest celebrations, hosted by chiefs, were potlatches, when the *adaawx* (sacred history) of the household was recited and shown on carved poles (Miller 1981a, 1989). During the winter, chiefs took on their priestly names to host displays of their privileges known as *halaayt*, which were elaborate dramatizations of visits to Heaven. Fall, when people regathered from summer dispersal before returning to their winter homes, was devoted to the presentation of *naxnox* (wonders), enactments of an encounter between an ancestor and a supernatural spirit.

In the 1830s, the Hudson's Bay Company founded a fort on the Nass, then moved it to Coast Tsimshian lands controlled by Ligeex (Grumet 1975, 1982). In 1857, William Duncan, a lay missionary arrived from England and converted most of the Tsimshian, reestablishing a wealthy cooperative community at Metlakatla (Usher 1971; 1974; Murray 1985). Later, differences with his Anglican bishop forced Duncan and his converts to move across the United States border to New Metlakatla in Alaska, seeking religious freedom under United States protection.

These relocations—to fort, trading post, and mission—fostered an elaboration of the three social classes of nobles, commoners, and slaves of the Northwest Coast Culture Area. Historically,

Tsimshian also developed a class of royalty, tribal chiefs who arose from the ranks of the former town leaders. Foremost among these royalty was the holder of the name + title of Ligeex.

Scholar Views

Donald Mitchell (1983), relying on existing records of the Hudson's Bay Company at Fort Simpson from 1836-1866, argued that the Tsimshian had "a tribal level of social complexity and that to characterize it as a chiefdom is to misinterpret its significance for an understanding of cultural evolution," even though he acknowledges the special claims of Ligeek:

> It seems undeniable that Legaic and his people—the Gispaxloats—had some kind of exclusive right to carry the fur trade up the Skeena River and into the interior. It also seems obvious that Legaic was or became the individual of highest rank among the Metlakatla Tsimshian lineage heads. In this sense he was the "principal chief" of the Tsimshian although he may not have attained this status until the 1840s.

> But the contemporary observations of Fort Simpson traders make it seem most unlikely that Legaic headed a political unit that could in any useful sense be termed a chiefdom. He ruled over no group but his own, and even there his hold seems fragile. In short, there was no chief and I would argue that the Tsimshian case provides us with no evidence of a Northwest Coast chiefdom. (Mitchell 1983:64)

Similarly, after his intensive study of the written record, Jonathan Dean (1994) determined that at the site of the second fort, though the land was donated by Ligeex, three chiefs were most prominent: Neshot of the GitzaxLaaL; Tsa-qaxs of the Ginax'angiik; and Ligeex of the Gispaxlo'ots, but only Ligeex survived the 1836 smallpox epidemic.

> While Legaic reportedly enjoyed a 'monopoly' in this time, this cannot be understood in Western terms, as a complete shutdown of all but Gispaxloat commerce, but might have consisted of nominal control. Even after the rise of Legaic in 1840, strangers from the Interior continued to use the Skeena to bring trade down to the fort, and the Nass river valley also continued as a very important venue. Beginning in the 1850's, the managers at Fort Simpson employed Neshaki— a Nishga noblewoman [Neshakx ~ Mrs. Martha (William Henry) McNeill]—to conduct the trade and transport furs from her village at Caxatan, and she continued to freight for the Company on the Nass after Legaic left to join William Duncan at Metlakatla in 1862. By the middle 1860's Neshaki was even operating on the Skeena River, in Legaic's 'backyard'. (Dean n.d.:33)

More specifically, in a study of the career of Ligeex, Dean (n.d.) suggested that Ligeex became more famous in memory after the name lapsed and the Gispaxlo'ots did not reciprocate with feasts, gifts, and potlatches.

Homer Barnett (1940, 1942) collected information on the later history of the Ligeex line and the reasons behind the conversion of most famous name holder, who joined William Duncan at the Christian cooperative community of Metlakatla after being compromised by a rival for the title. He was baptized as Paul Legaic. At Metlakatla, all the houses looked the same so all would be equal before God. Only Paul Legaic was allowed to have a house larger than the others because of his rank.

After his conversion, Ligeex played a prominent role in the Christian community, but, over time, to a large extent, Duncan himself replaced the name-title of Ligeex as the paramount leader among the Tsimshian. Duncan's oratorical fluency in the native language, his care and welfare of the community, and his constant industry were all marks of chiefly status (cf. Usher 1974:109). Indeed, the Tsimshian explicitly called him "Chief."

Viola Garfield (1939:169) reported the death of the last Ligeex in 1933, although the family generally acknowledged to hold this name occasionally mentions passing it on. They continue to discuss this possibility with the other hereditary Tsimshian chiefs because their agreement or consensus will be vital to the success of the transfer.

Reviewing only written sources, scholars agree that Ligeex did have economic, social, and ritual precedence, but not paramountcy. Yet politics, as such, was never elaborately developed on the coast (Kroeber 1923).

Native Views

After several years of consultation with Tsimshian chiefs and elders, along with scholars, the first book produced by the Prince Rupert School District 52[1] (1992a:70) says "The Gispaxlo'ots were led by several chiefs of different housegroups of different clans, but, of them all, the Eagle housegroup of Ligeex was considered the most powerful. Because of this, the House of Ligeex was considered the leading House of all the Maxtakxaata Tsimshian."

Book 4 in the series, *Fort Simpson, Fur Fort at laxLgu'alaams* (1992d), explains how, after the first Fort Simpson was built on the Nass River in 1831, Sudaal, the eldest daughter of Ligeex and a Haida wife, married Dr John Frederick Kennedy, physician and trader of the Hudson's Bay Company. After two years at the exposed site, Sudaal complained to her father, who offered the site of one of his camps for the second fort, built in 1834. By 1840, the winter home of all (nine of the original ten) Coast Tsimshian tribes had relocated to Simpson from Metlakatla in Prince Rupert Harbor.

It was control of the upriver trade, "combined with Ligeex's influence over who had access to the fort, that gave this group their monopoly of the Fort Simpson fur trade from approximately 1840 to 1860" (Prince Rupert School District 1992d:55).

During this time, the Gispaxlo'ots were the main link that the people of the interior had with the new traders. Ligeex's wealth allowed him to purchase the best Haida canoes, and the largest. It was these canoes and the riches they brought from the interior that allowed the fort to thrive" (Prince Rupert School District 1992d:56).

Similarly, the second volume of *Tsimshian Narratives: Trade and Warfare*, collected by Marius Barbeau and William Beynon (1987b), has several texts about Ligeex, including the origin of his crests of the Gunhut (Tlingit) branch of the Eagle semi-moiety from a conflict with the Ravens at Laxsail, Alaska (1987:31–35), the origin of the Ligeex name and *halaayt* privileges from the Kitimat and Bella Bella Heiltsuk (1987:62–65, 69–75),[2] his revenge against the Haida (1987: 66-68), conflict with the Kitselas (1987:84–85), series of four ascendancy potlatches (1987:92–94), chiefly contests (1987:95–111, 118–126), staged cremation *halaayt* (1987:116–117), and attempted murder of William Duncan (1987:206–209). Other texts refer to actions by Gispaxlo'ots royal houses (1987:213–235).

Today, Tsimshian themselves agree that Ligeex had "first say" among chiefs, indicating that he was foremost. Yet, because he was so "high," people criticized him and his line of heirs because chiefs should not get too haughty. For the same reason, rival traders delighted in thwarting his claim to the Skeena trade, as detailed in Book 6 (Prince Rupert School District

1992f) about how Litux, a Wolf chief of the Nass, tried to bypass Ligeex but got caught and plundered at Kitselas. The next year, he took his revenge when everyone came to the Nass River to render candlefish into oil ("grease").

Chiefly Styles

At base, this disagreement about the importance of Ligeex comes down to a misunderstanding of chiefly management styles. Unlike European monarchs, Tsimshian chiefs persuaded rather than ordered. The more effectively they managed the economic and religious routines of their town and tribe, the more quickly people did their bidding. By all accounts, the holders of the Ligeex name were very skilled managers over eons. For this reason they do not fill the records of the traders or missionaries because when things go smoothly, there is little to report. Instead, what comes though the various *adaawx* and anecdotes about the Ligeex line is that, foremost among historic chiefs, they were particularly ingenious, innovative, and ingratiating. For that reason, the name of Ligeex has a special place in Tsimshian culture to this day. Judged not by ledger entries but by involvement in Tsimshian institutions like the potlatch and *halaayt*, Ligeex was indeed great.

Some changes among Tsimshian began when the ship-based trade arrived on the coast in the mid-1700s, but the major ones occurred when the land-based forts were build in the 1830s. Tsimshian left the sites of their winter villages along Metlakatla Pass and moved to the trading post at Fort (later Port) Simpson, run by the Hudson's Bay Company (Meilleur 1980). Town chiefs appointed heirs to manage either the new neighborhood or the old town, thus elevating themselves into the role of tribal chiefs. These new ranks had to be confirmed in the old way by lavish generosity at witnessed public displays called potlatches, which now took on aspects of rivalry and confrontation so as to sort out the new rankings of chiefs and their tribes.

From this melee emerged Ligeex, of the Gispaxlo'ots Eagle crest. The previous title for this tribal chief, Nisbalas, had been shamed when its holder was beheaded for insulting members of the Raven crest. An earlier disagreement with the Wolf crest had started the Gunhut migration from the Tlingit to the Tsimshian. Through potlatching, a foreign name from the Kitimat, inherited through a (captured ?) Gispaxlo'ots Eagle wife, was substituted as the tribal chiefly name (Boas 1916b:357). In the course of establishing the name of Ligeex in place of that of Nisbalas, the Gispaxlo'ots tribe moved to the forefront of the Coast Tsimshian and its chief became the high chief.

During the process whereby royalty emerged from nobility, the secret societies or *wutahalaayt* orders were borrowed from neighboring tribes and influenced by the older *smhalaayt* or "real *halaayt*" emblems of chiefly rank. In this way, the earlier triads of class and cult common to other North Pacific nations became the fourfold pattern of the Tsimshian. New crests involving humans and fabulous creatures, called combination monsters, were also being created to distinguish emerging royalty (Halpin 1984:33, n.d.).

Moreover, during these times of stress and instability, Coast Tsimshian gained confidence from their enhanced leadership. Such was the context for the angry response a Gitksan directed at John Adams:

> When I discussed my model of the conflicts created in Gitksan society by imbalances of population and the problems of succession which result, one of my informants became furious with me: Who was I to accuse the Natives of having such problems? Didn't Whites have these same problems, too? Weren't the deaths of Martin Luther King and both Kennedys due to jealousy? Why couldn't Whites

learn what the Natives had learned: that to avoid such problems it is necessary to install a king who is so high above everybody else that nobody can touch him. (Adams 1973:112)

Garfield (1966:26) estimated thirty tribal chiefs for the Coast, Nisga'a, and Gitksan. Each had an unblemished pedigree from a long line of chiefs, and was expected to be "skilled in all things, energetic and ambitious" (Garfield 1966:17). As a group they were "able leaders, good speakers, haughty and proud before strangers, and humble and generous toward tribesmen. The ideal leader was an able organizer and speaker, and a model of good taste and conduct" (Garfield 1966:27). Among the Gitksan, the Gitsegukla History (Gitsegukla 1979:37) states that a chief had to prove wisdom (*wii ho'osxw*), kindness (*amma'gawd*), and strength (*dahx'get*) to gain respect (*an thlx'ooms*).

Each leader had four named spiritual aspects, distinguished as *sm* "real." As *smgigyet* or house chiefs, they conducted feasts and namings; as *naxnox* dancers, they performed in masked winter ceremonials. As *smhalaayt*, they wore a carved frontlet and robes, and "with the raven rattle as symbol of power, they initiated young people into ritual roles. The final formal named role for a leader was the *wihalaayt* or 'great dancer,' the leader of the four secret societies, into which many of the people were initiated" (Halpin and Seguin 1990:279).

There were several hundred lineage and house heads, who managed the societal routines and made up the nobility. Together with craft and resource specialists, they made up the advisory council that served each of the town and tribal chiefs. These occupations included shamans, carpenters, carvers, painters, musicians, composers, herbalists, midwives (McNeary 1976: 156), and astronomers (Miller 1992c). Each of these specialists had responsibility for some aspect of the world, but the overall system was coordinated by the chief of the town, assisted by those of the houses.

Since Coast Tsimshian tribes and towns functioned in terms of their constituent ranked houses, all territories and trade routes were controlled by the house chiefs, who were responsible for maintaining the vitality of the traditional sacred histories. Both water and land routes were owned and defended by the house, while trade alliances were confirmed by royal marriages between households resident at the extreme ends of the rivers and tribal territories.

In addition to marital ties, alliances were also strengthened by the bestowal of names and privileges, by feasting, and by ceremonial displays. Thus, the name of Seeks, a relative of Ts'ibasaa when everyone lived at Temlaxham (mythical Prairie Town near modern Hazelton, British Columbia), was given to a Tlingit chief who became known as Shakes. Similarly at strategic locations along inland trails, chiefs built feast houses where friendship-making (*ne-amex*) *halaayts* could be held. Though based on clan and kinship solidarity rites, these particular *halaayts* were characterized by mistrust. At this ritual, a stranger was invited in, seated on a woven cedarbark mat, and entertained by a display of the host's *halaayt*, by feasting, and by gifts. Of course, in addition to forging a new alliance, the rite was also a warning about the consequences of the theft of local resources.

International Contexts

Tsimshian border zones were, at least, bicultural and bilingual. The Southern Tsimshian at Gitisu ~ Kitasoo neighbored the Kwakiutlan Xaixais, before they moved together at Klemtu (China Hat). Tlingit and Nisga'a were north of Coast Tsimshian, with Gitxsan to the east. While widely separated by Hecate Strait, particular Tsimshian towns nevertheless had close ties with Haida communities. In turn, some nations forged alliances with Athapaskan hunters further inland. Thus, the Gitksan traded with the Wet'suwet'en, who traded with the Kaska; the Nisga'a chief named Mountain monopolized trade with the Tsetsawt; and Tlingit chiefs contacted the Gunana (their term for Alaskan Athapaskans).

The Kitselas at the Canyon of the Skeena had a distinct identity which was fostered by their crucial position along the river. Their royal house was founded by a Fireweed lineage which departed Temlaxham and had extensive kin ties with royalty along the lower Skeena and at Kitkatla. Later Githawn ~ Githoon, a famous chief, founded an Eagle royal house there and established alliances with Ravens upriver among the Gitksan. Each spring, the Kitselas officially opened the annual trade with the Gitxsan.

Such trade became the "monopoly" of the Gispaxlo'ots and Ligeex, who several times tried to vanquish the Kitselas and the Kispiox. During one foray, Ligeex arrived in front of Kispiox with umbrellas, which he used as a *naxnox* display to lure the townspeople into an ambush, but, though the attack was brutal, his victory was not complete. Over time, Ligeex used feasts and marriages arranged through his daughter-in-law and other relatives to regularize an alliance with the Kitselas.

In general, coastal towns specialized in various kinds of seafoods and marine goods (dried cockles, clams, grease, dried candlefish, seaweed, dried herring eggs, shells) traded to interior chiefs in return for prestigious furs, hides, and copper.

Ligeex

For Tsimshian, Ligeex had a special position because of his transgenerational success as a manager, host of potlatches, initiator into *halaayt*, broker of dynastic marriages, and war leader.

Boas (1916b), based on fieldwork in 1888, provided important details on Ligeex, whose important crests included both the Frog Hat and a cane topped by a Frog, together with the Beaver Hat, which was held on Ligeex's head, most significantly, by a member from each of the four crests to show that Ligeex "was the highest in rank among all the clans" (1916b:512, 267, 272). Ligeex also claimed descent from the Haida princess known as Omen miraculously saved from the destruction of the town of Dji'gua. Boas (1916b:510) reported that by 1888 six men had held that title for over 150 years. The first memorialized his fame by having a portrait painted above a row of coppers on a cliff along the lower Skeena.[3]

His mother, Gandmaxł ("ascending the mountain with a costly copper") of this first name holder eloped with (or was captured by) a man from Kitamaat,[4] whose family belonged to the highest ranked of the Wakashan secret societies. This name and privilege passed to family members of her Eagle crest.

Ligeex had many *halaayt* privileges uniquely his own. One *naxnox* involved two enormous hands that reached down from the roof and lifted a man toward Heaven (Barnett 1940, Notebook 2: 2), while another, called Crack of Heaven, was a mask that made the house divide in two, move apart, and rejoin (Boas 1916b:556). His *halaayt* names included *txagaxsm laxha*, *hanatana*, and *gaguiksgax* (Boas 1916b:513).

The men called Ligeex participated in a long series of dynastic marriages. Each Ligeex's primary wife was a woman named Ksmgamk, the sister of the Blackfish chief at Kitkatla, the foremost leader of the Southern Tsimshian. In turn, this man, Ts'ibasaa ~ Hale, married the Eagle sister of Ligeex named after the mother Gandmaxł. Their son, Ligeex's heir, was named Hatsksneex. Ligeex had other prominent wives from the Haida, who provided him with enormous canoes from Haida Gwaii (Queen Charlotte Islands), which he used to transport many goods along the Skeena.

The basis for the prestige of Ligeex was his exclusive claim to trade with the Gitksan, after the Kitselas at the canyon. Among the populous coastal tribes, he dictated the trade along the Skeena River and had a boundless source of revenue.

Ligeex protected these prerogatives in various ways. He provided land for the second Hudson's Bay Company post at Fort Simpson and his daughter married the chief factor. Yet when the company built a trading post at Lake Babine, Ligeex led warriors upriver and destroyed it. The company only began to trade effectively with the inland tribes after it purchased the privilege to do so from Ligeex in 1866, providing the funds that were probably used for the elaborate potlatch described below.

Ligeex's Potlatch, 1860s

One of the Ligeex hosted a potlatch, which was notable for the formality and dignity which was required because it included so many chiefs (Garfield 1939:201-204).

A year before the event, Ligeex feasted his own Gispalo'ots tribe to announce his plans. Clan families offered to help and suggested which members should be named, elevated, or confirmed into higher ranks at the event.

Next, he held a feast for members of his father's Raven crest to ask their help and to assign some of them to certain tasks, such as announcing, organizing, contributing particular foods, or commissioning a carving.

Meanwhile Ligeex amassed foods and gifts. When the date was set, tribesmen were sent as messengers, accompanied by a lesser chief to enhance their prestige, to invite chiefs on behalf of their towns and tribes. Arriving in front of the town, this visiting chief stood in the bow of the canoe, wearing a chilkat robe, using his raven rattle, and singing a *naxnox* song to the accompaniment of hidden whistles. He called out the name of the town chief three times, inviting him (and his people) to the potlatch. The fourth time, the chief responded by sending word to invite the visitors into his own house. He fed them and sent gifts back to Ligeex.

These chiefs then gathered their families and advisors to paddle to Ligeex's town, where each canoe waited in front of the beach until Ligeex's sister and other ranking women came down to greet them by dancing and singing. The sister, wearing a mask, acted as though she were grabbing one of Ligeex's *naxnox*, called "All Calm Heavens," from the air and throwing it toward the guests. The arriving chief acted as though he caught it, wrestled with it, and threw it back to the sister.[5] Then the canoes beached and the guests were welcomed. Chiefs, in particular, were escorted or carried from the shore to their seats inside the house.

Inside the house, they witnessed displays of other names and spirits owned by Ligeex. After this dancing and singing, the guests were well fed. That night, chiefs stayed in homes of crest relatives. Other visitors camped on the beach, supplied with wood and food by the hosts.

The next day, a feast like a picnic was held on the beach. That night, a challenge feast was held with Ligeex boasting of his fame and belittling everyone else. Guests were seated by rank and some were singled out to receive huge ladlefuls of candlefish grease mixed with snow, brought from far mountain tops.

Ligeex's people came in dressed for war, with their hair bound up, but scattered eagle down everywhere to indicate their peaceful intent. After taunting songs and over-eating, gifts were distributed, accompanied by jokes about the shortcoming of the guests. Every item was counted out while a song was sung, the better to overwhelm the guests with the wealth of Ligeex. Many goods had been hidden behind a rear partition and these were now thrown into the room. Soon the pile was so high that the roof boards had to be removed. Ligeex taunted that he had thousands of items while other chiefs had only hundreds.

A Raven man, preassigned this task, then announced all of the names and histories that Ligeex claimed. All of his coppers[6] were shown and named. Children of Ligeex's crest were brought forward and named. Pregnant Eagle women were given the names of a boy and a girl to give to the newborn according to its gender.

While the guests relaxed, members of the tribe made a final tally of the remaining gifts. Bundles of sticks had previously been assembled to represent each group of guests, divided by house and crest. Quantities also varied by tribe, from most to least, according to a ranking from Kitkatla, the tribe of Ligeex's main wife, to the Gitlaan, a small group because most had converted and forsaken potlatching.[7]

The final day was spent giving out these gifts to chiefs, for the benefit of themselves and their tribes. Visiting chiefs and spokesmen gave speeches of thanks during a last feast. Then the hosts helped to pack all the canoes and the guests left.

Soon after, Ligeex gave a feast for the Eagles to thank them for their help, providing them with gifts of food.

Ligeex's Halaayt

In careful fieldnotes on a *halaayt* initiation, William Beynon (1937:Text 179),[8] Tsimshian ethnographer and Wolf chief (Halpin 1978), was told by Julia White and Mrs. R. Tate how an initiate vanished at the sound of *naxnox* secret whistles and went to Heaven to "become elevated." Later, the child returned to town riding on a representation of a family crest. While this crest was inherited through the mother, the display itself was arranged by the father. Thus, the *halaayt* made use of both crest and wonder, mother and father, to create a new identity. Throughout his writings, Beynon described *halaayt* initiation as "elevation" and initiates as "elevated," calling attention to its celestial aspects.

These events were noteworthy because they involved Ligeex, the high chief of the Tsimshian during the historic period. During the first stage of initiation, called *tsiik*, the father of the child arranged for her or him to be elevated up (*m-nya*).

At the *halaayt* house of the Gispalo'ots, five children were tended by paternal aunts until Ligeex arrived and threw his great *halaayt* power into them. Instantaneously, they disappeared, "ascending" to heaven (quickly hidden away by their aunts). Their parents then distributed much wealth to the guests, particularly to Ligeex.

On another occasion, as whistles sounded, a girl was led by her father's sister into the house of Ligeex, and formally seated. Ligeex came toward her singing and dancing, until, as he reached her, she disappeared. (Actually, her aunt took her outside and hid her in the back of her own house, where she was dressed in a small dancing garment with cedar bark rings around her neck and head.)

Previously, craftsmen (*gitsontk*)[9] had made a big swan that could open its wings and had mounted it on a small canoe. The swan was one of the foremost crests of her father. Ligeex found a young girl who looked like her enough to impersonate the initiate. The night before the girl came back from Heaven, the double was taken out in the swan canoe. Early in the morning, warned by blasts of *naxnox* whistles, people rushed to the beach to watch the girl's return from Heaven. Off shore, a huge swan appeared with the girl (her double) on its back, floated toward shore, opening its wings, and then suddenly sank out of sight. As the canoe vanished, the girl and paddlers swam underwater and hid behind boulders near shore.

Then, as whistles came from the hills, Ligeex, wearing a Chilkat robe went into the forest and came back with the naked girl. Dancing and singing, they visited all the homes in the village, before going to the *halaayt* house of Ligeex. There, her parents gave away wealth, while the girl went into seclusion. Eventually, the whistles were heard outside of her father's house. Ligeex went inside, took the cedar bark rings off the girl, and received many gifts from her father. The girl went back into seclusion, until the woven rings were removed a second and a third time, after which the girl was free to resume normal life and play.

Chiefly Allies and Rivals

The arrival of trading ships after the 1750s led to the rise of four war leaders, three of them chiefs, among the Tsimshian. Guns, clothes, and iron pots became coveted items. While Sabaen (Prince Rupert School District, 1992c), a Raven from Kitkatla, had the first reported encounter with a European ship near the southern end of Pitt Island, the most famous leader of the early era was Ts'ibasaa, a Kitkatla Blackfish chief and Ligeex's brother-in-law, who spent a year on a trading ship and learned to speak some English. Ts'ibasaa, by rank also chief of the Southern Tsimshian, eventually traded names with one of the first ship captains to visit his territory, taking the name of Hale (Hail), which still reigns in that town.

When he returned safely, he potlatched the new name of Hale and created a *halaayt* in which he wore a top hat, cutaway coat, and pants. He correctly realized that such "fancy" attire had prestige among Europeans and so adopted it as his own. He acquired a gun very early in the trade and used it to intimidate the Nisga'a at Fishery Bay on the Nass in order to retain the Tsimshian camp at Red Bluff for rendering candlefish oil (Marsden n.d.).

Early chiefs of the Ts'ibasaa line were haughty, as Mitchell (1981) showed in his reconstruction of the Kitkatla seasonal round for 1835, based on three diaries kept by employees of the Hudson's Bay Company. At least two Haida crests, Grizzly and Moon, were given to these chiefs by Ts'ibasaa, a powerful means of forging an alliance with foreigners on the islands.

Among the Gitksan, Neqt was also known for his haughty belligerence (MacDonald 1979, 1984), but he did not survive long. From his ingenious fort among the Gitksan, he raided and terrorized widely. Known as Kitwanga Fort, a natural stone knob was artificially mounded and palisaded to protect several houses. Excavations date these constructions "from about the seventeenth century until the early part of the nineteenth century" (MacDonald 1979: vi), in other words, the fort overlaps the rise of the name Ligeex and its destruction coincided with the arrival of the Hudson's Bay Company forts and the ascendancy of Ligeex. Coastal towns also had such forts where people took refuge from attackers (Miller 2011). Often they were the cones of extinct volcanos (Dunn 1978: 97, #1873), whose rich soil was later used to grow potatoes, introduced by traders, for lucrative sale to the Haida and Fort Simpson.

Neqt's mother was a Frog (Raven) from the Nass, captured and married to a Haida chief. Later, she killed and beheaded him, escaping with her son who was kept quiet by sucking on the tongue that protruded from his father's head. Reckless and cunning, Neqt controlled trade over a large region.

For the Nisga'a, Sagewan ("Mountain") arose among the lower Nass River during the 1860s. He was an Eagle and lived at Gitiks near the mouth of the Nass along the commercial routes. Eventually, he controlled the Nass River trade with the interior Athapaskans, particularly the Tsetsawt. Among Nass chiefs, rivalry focused on the height of their poles. The Wolf and Orca Killerwhale chiefs were in such fierce competition that the Killerwhale man was shot and killed. For protection, the Wolf chief allied himself with the leader of the Laxluutkst branch of the Eagles, whose chief was Saga'waan. To mark his ascendancy, Sagewan commissioned the tallest pole then on the coast, now at the Royal Ontario Museum in Toronto (McNeary 1976:52, 141).

Later, one of Saga'waan's wives deserted him to marry William McNeill, Chief Trader of the Hudson's Bay Company. She was the famous Neshakx ~ Neshaki, whose sister was married to Clah ~ T'amuks, baptized as Arthur Wellington, the man who taught Tsimshian to William Duncan. Her Christian name was Martha, but it was seldom used. Usually, she was called Mrs. McNeill in the records. After her marriage, she maintained her own trading network on the Nass, extending the reach of Fort Simpson into the interior.

To shame Neshakx, Saga'waan sent her a gift of marten skins, accompanied by a taunting song. Not to be outdone, she sent him a fine Haida canoe. To recover his prestige, Saga'waan held a potlatch to renounce his wife. She countered by erecting a memorial pole for her deceased brother, elevating herself to the status of a Wolf chief above the pettiness of her former spouse (McNeary 1976:188).

Maud (1982:55–59) mentioned that Chief Mountain converted to Christianity after his privileged ability to handle fire and red hot iron failed him. Barbeau (1951:124, Song 27), who purchased Chief Mountain's pole after his death, records the song used to shame the former wife, Neshakx, although Barbeau gives her name as Weeyae and that of her brother as Neeskinwaetk.

Regrettably, these all too human qualities of great men and women are often missing from the available literature. The highest ranking Nisga'a chiefs were left out of Sapir's list (1915), while Boas (1902) merely noted that a speaker titled Chief Mountain provided him with some Nishga texts.

Summary

In all, then, Ligeex has yet to be properly treated as "the" Tsimshian leader, nor have the leaders of the other three divisions. Ligeex may not have been as famous as Seattle, Tecumthah (Tecumsah), or Pontiac, but he too might have mobilized a chiefdom, if not a confederacy. Certainly, like them, the holders of the Ligeex name rose to preeminence as war leaders during times of threat from outsiders. His military successes offered protection to would-be allies. Moreover, the rise of the name to replace one that had been shamed certainly bespeaks a native, not an European, context for its beginnings. As Heber Clifton noted:

> Legaix was a most ferocious warrior and he had no respect or feeling for anybody, just like his Eagle warriors, mostly all Gispaxloats. He was dreaded by all. Women from other tribes used his name in their nursery songs to instill fear into their children. The Legaix warriors were a vicious group. (Barbeau and Beynon 1987b:69)

Finally, those who doubt the historical existence of a Tsimshian confederation should be reminded of the thousands of years Coast Tsimshian clustered along Metlakatla Passage, when their constant Winter interaction would have required some means of dispute resolution, particularly a leader who was the court of last resort. Such was the context in which a man grew to cosmopolitan influence among the Coast Tsimshian royalty. His Gunhut Eagle subcrest originated from the Tlingit, his name was from the Kitimat, his *halaayt* privileges were confirmed at Bella Bella, his wives and kin belonged to the Haida, Southern Tsimshian, Gitksan, and other nations, and, most particularly, he was lavish and generous to the Gispaxlo'ots and other Coast Tsimshian.

NOTES

[1] These books have now provided an "official" spelling of this name as Ligeex. Earlier records include Legaic, Legeek, Ilegauch, Illgayauch, Legaeek, and Illegaich Gang.

[2] This text says that after being married to the Kitimat man, thereby legally entitled to his crest inheritances, the Gispaxlo'ots woman was captured and married to Humchitt, a great Raven chief at Bella Bella, the center of the *wihalaayt* ~ secret society priesthoods so important among the international royal families. Humchitt became the father of the first Ligeex, an awesome pedigree.

[3] A Beynon text (Reel 2:111–128) places this painting on the Nass, but either the location is wrong or a duplicate of it still exists on the Skeena across from Port Essington (which I have personally seen). The original artist's name was Dzumks, although Gaya of Gitlaan later refurbished it. The basket Dzumks stood in and the rope used to suspend it were purchased from a Skidegate Haida chief for five coppers and five slaves. It took eight days for the chief to go home and return with the basket and rope.

[4] Dr. Emmon Bach, a linguist retired from the University of Massachusetts, received data on the Kitimat version of Northern Kwakiutlan or Wakashan from the most recent holder of the Ligeex name there. Dr. Jay Powell, current linguist to this community, adds that several prominent land forms there also bear this name.

[5] Among the Nuchahnuulth and other nations, these greeting ceremonies simulate the throwing of a flashing crystal back and forth to show that the powers of host and guest were equal, at least for the duration of the potlatch.

[6] A copper had a rectangular lower half with a raised T shape down and across the middle. The top had a curved, flared convex surface decorated with a painted or engraved figure. Considered to be alive, coppers became emblems of wealth, vitality, and permanence after catastrophic epidemics took a heavy toll.

[7] Garfield (1939:204) gives this ranking, in her spelling, as Kitkatla, Gitzaklalth, Ginakangeek, Gitsees, Gilutsau, Gitwilgyots, Ginadoiks, Gitandau, and Gitlan.

[8] Beynon (1937:Text 179, 1937). Microfilm. Interview with Julia White and Mrs. R. Tate, Reel 3, Volume 12, pp. 74–106. ("Haleyt of Legaix").

[9] Crests, wonders, and *halaayt* each had its own type of artists. Those for the crests worked in public, but those for the *naxnox* spirits, both wonders and *halaayt*, worked in secret and were called *gitsontk* = "people secluded." The punishment for seeing unfinished art or laboring artist was execution.

Journal of Northwest Anthropology, Memoir 9:110–116   2014

DR. SIMON: A SNOHOMISH SLAVE AT
FORT NISQUALLY AND PUYALLUP[a]

ABSTRACT

Field notes, fur trade ledgers, and court records provide glimpses of the career of a Snohomish, enslaved thrice, lost as a gambling bet, gifted with a shamanic spirit at Gig Harbor, freed at Fort Nisqually, and gainfully farming and doctoring as the Puyallup Reservation was destroyed to bring the railroad into Tacoma.

Introduction

Three remarkable notebooks (A, B, C), preserved in the archives of the University of Washington (Special Collections, formerly Manuscripts, Special Collections, and University Archives), provide enough details on the early life of an enslaved Snohomish man that the rest of his life can be glimpsed in the records of Fort Nisqually, outpost of the Hudson's Bay Company (HBC), and the Puyallup Agency of the Bureau of Indian Affairs (BIA). Fortunately, he quickly acquired the English name of Simon, distinctive enough to stand out in these varied records, in addition to an anglicized version of a native last name. This is remarkable because slaves usually lost any personal identity, becoming known by the name of their ancestral village or tribe, which acted as a constant insult to that community (Tweddell 1974:120). No other Simon, who clearly grows progressively older through the years, appears in these records.

The name of the notebooks' scribe—Alfred John Smith—is now known, while his close working relationship with Arthur Ballard (1950) is only now being unraveled. The elder who was the source for this information was Jerry Meeker, whose parents worked as "favorites" of pioneer Ezra Meeker (1980 [1905]). Jerry's mother was from the native town at Minter in Carr Inlet, burned out by homesteaders in 1874 (Elmendorf 1993; Asher 1999; Miller 2000a). For the rest of his long life, Jerry was a "success" at the dismantling of the Puyallup Reservation and selling Tacoma real estate. While his career was a challenge to native rights, these notebooks (C has his own selective autobiography) reveal him as well-informed on Lushootseed (Puget Sound) culture. The scribe's unfamiliarity with local history or native accented English explains spelling confusion in the notebooks over the age of Simon at his last sale (15 not 50 years old) and the name of Dr. William Fraser Tolmie (Tolmie 1963; Carpenter 1986), long manager at Fort Nisqually. Yet these notebooks are so detailed that the native community at Minter can be raised from the ashes, and, at least for the high class, repopulated by name. While the transcriptions do not conform to those in the modern linguistic dictionary (Bates, Hess, and Hilbert 1994), they are remarkably good for their time and place.

Slaves were an underclass among all of the First Nations of the Northwest Coast, the victims taken in raids to be sold far away, or those born of slave parents (Haeberlin and Gunther 1930; Blukis Onat 1984; Suttles 1987, 1990; Miller 1997). Very little is actually known about slavery, since it was not readily discussed and was legally suppressed in treaties of 150 years ago.

---

[a] This article was previously published in *Northwest Anthropological Research Notes*, 36(2):145–154 (2002).

Their lives were supposed to be filled with dull drudgery keeping their masters supplied with firewood, water, and shellfish (Ruby and Brown 1993; Donald 1997). They either slept exposed near the doorway or had to scramble each night for safe haven (Suttles 1991). Today, native elders continue to use the native term for "slave" as a dire insult against members of other families. Lushootseed, the language of Puget Sound Salishans, lacks obscenities or insults, so this word has great potency (Tweddell 1950; Bates, Hess, and Hilbert 1994).

Throughout Puget Sound, a chief was expected to have more than two slaves to meet obligations of hospitality and generosity. After death, birthplace determined fate. Souls of slaves captured in raids went to their ancestral afterworld, while those born into slavery remained in bondage after death in the afterworld of their owner (Miller 1999b:23).

By law, native slavery ended in the treaties forced by Governor Isaac I. Stevens during 1855. Puyallups (Smith 1940a) were subject to the very first Treaty with the Nisqualli, Puyallup, etc., of 26 December 1854 at She-nah-nam, or Medicine Creek, which included "Article 11–The said tribes and bands agree to free all slaves now held by them, and not to purchase or acquire others hereafter."

During the mid-1800s, the leader of Minter was a woman named Tsialtsa, working indirectly through her husband, who was politely called the chief, during that marriage. This woman, however, was unquestionably the native-born head of the community by right of family descent. Of note, though, she cooked all meals, assuring his family's continued high rank without blemish. While some of the food was provided by Simon, its final preparation and cooking was done by this high class woman. Slavery carried with it a moral taint, much like untouchables in India, where vegetarianism is a mark of high caste and cooking is carefully regulated by Brahmans to prevent contact with meat eaters.

Sally, Jerry Meeker's mother, a cousin of this head woman, was married twice, both times into other leading families. Her first husband was the son of the chief at Steilacoom and they had one surviving son, John. Her second husband was Jim Meeker from Skykomish, the northern fork of the Snohomish, but of their four children only Jerry lived.

Somewhat improved, here is what the notebooks say about Simon, with page numbers indicated by < >. Since these were working fieldnotes, more details and information were added by Meeker at subsequent sessions, which were held at Brown's Point in Tacoma.

Notebook A

Tsialtsa <A45> & chief had 2 slaves–there were only 2 slaves in the house at that time. One was from Lummi tᵘlubi (woman); one was from Snohomish dakʷilał (man) [pronounced something like da-kwee-lath].

Slaves (stoduk) The slaves left after agent made slavery impossible & both took up land on Reservation. Woman was a little older than Jerry, Simon (dakʷilał) young man became a famous doctor. He trained himself & washed himself. A real doctor (twda'b). He cured.

[Each] Lived in separate huts–8 ft square, just enough for bed. But sat at same place as others. But cook their own stuff. Gathered wood & water. Chief did virtually no hunting or fishing, the slaves did all of his work. Chief's wife always cooked the food for her family–Because "she was a woman."

Slaves were [judged to be] adopted. So gov't. deemed by living with the owner most of his life, inherited owner's property when owner died.

Got them thru raid[ing]. <A46> Mostly men [warriors], but did take woman with them. Women had the braveness power–She could call the power of braveness to the men. Most of the brave men have this power. Very few women had it (like tiger, wild cat, bear). These [two slave] people were not ransomed because they were not from prominent families.

Notebook B

Mother's <B50> first husband was a leading man at Steilacoom. Got people to back him buying back the men taken as slaves to Lummi or Tulalip. He brought them back to Steilacoom & they never had any stain as slaves. They became full men [once redeemed to host a shame-removing feast].

Simon (*dak^wilaɬ*)—Snohomish slave at Minter—came when 12 or 14. He got his power right here at Gig Harbor. Woman from Lummi was a Nisqually slave. Dr. Toldman or Tully [William Fraser Tolmie] brought the slave man from them. <B51> He was Hudson's Bay Co head. He paid so many blankets for him & had him work for him at Fort Nisqually. He kept him there until he left for Vancouver [Victoria]. Then let him free.

tsidɛ·tɛ·lq [something like tsee-day-tay-lik] brought him from k^witsa'qs [something like kwee-tsaa-ks], his original master. His power (twida'B) was doctor[ing]. He got rich over his doctor power after he was set free. Got many horses, money, clothing. I've seen older dr. [doctors] do a lot of [for] Indians. He used to use lots of herbs. Wild roots & cedar seeds. Nettle roots. Made tea from them. Also chutum wood bark – made people <B52> drink it. He used them with his power for curing. Diff[erence] between power sickness & regular physical sickness [religious vs. medical illness].

They knew he was good (when at Gig Harbor) & called him to help them even though a slave. "Seems funny doesn't it." [Jerry mused]

He worked for his master all the time, even if he was a doctor.

Sometimes slave goes out by himself to hunt. But usually went with master to help fetch things & got in canoe to[o].

k^witsa'qs was original master of the slave man and captured him. But he sold him <B53> or rather gambled [him] away & then got him back. Then sold him to Hudson's Bay man. k^witsa'qs family was very nice & treated the slave like one of their own family. He received little gifts from people he cured before he was sold to Hud[son] Bay man & freed, then became rich through his curing. He was about 50 [?] when sold to H.B. man. He broke & rode horses, farmed for Hudson's Bay Company (Had big farms where H.B. Co raised wheat, barley, oats, peas) [actually the subsidiary Puget Sound Agricultural Company].

Nisqually Records

The Indian Blotters kept at the fort do indicate that efforts were made to redeem native slaves, as seen below, a decade before the treaties:

July 1845

26
   advance Tzithlako to purchase his freedom
       8? Plain Blankets 2½ pts
       1 Com Cotton Shirt   Sheep Drs [dippers ?]
       120 ?headed half axe
  10 ch[arges] ammi[o] bins Tob[acco]s

The first appearance of a Simon, however, is May 1853, just before the treaties and a likely date based on Jerry Meeker's evidence. From then, continuing if intermittent references are made to Simon until the fort closed under American pressure and compensation was paid to the company in 1869–1870. The fort had relocated to Victoria, British Columbia, in 1849. Tolmie himself moved there to settle in 1859.

One index (Dickey 1989) to the Journal of Occurrences at Fort Nisqually (NJ) lists by year "Simon Employee, Indian boy, teamster and horse breaker NJ53, NJ54, NJ55, NJ56, NJ57, NJ58." Usually daily tasks are attributed to Indian gang, or hands, rather than to individuals. Simon is specifically mentioned by name when he is personally involved with company property such as wagons, horses, and cattle, or taking on responsibilities as a guide, but not when he is working among laborers in the fields and pastures.

1853

May

16th Monday . . . Dr. Tolmie rode out to Tlithlow, Mr. Dean commences tomorrow castrating and numbering lambs. [William] Legg and hands (Wyamock, Wilcut and the boy Simon) brought in and confined two wild cows. [added emphasis to indicate Simon's young age].

27th Friday . . . Calf cutting & marking going on well. Hands employed: Legg, Bill, Wilcut & the boys Charles & Simon. Waymoch after receiving a good thrashing has been discharged for il[l]treating horses.

1854

December 16 Saturday . . . Simon with horse cart sent out [to] Harry Dean's with rations for Shepherds.

1855

January 31 Wednesday . . . The remaining hands employed as usual. Ross and Simon each with horse wagon hauling in beef from plains. Ox carts hauling firewood and dung into swamp.

May 15th Tuesday . . . Cush, Simon and Cushcusheen started for the Cowlitz with 9 pack horses.

November 23rd Friday . . . The Indian gang was paid off this day. All the Indians living at this place went away accompanied by Mr. Simmons to proceed to an island [Squaxin ?] near Olympia. Trade dull in Sale Shop.

1856

July

9th Wednesday Fine . . . Simon killed 4 poor sheep, being accidentally hurt.

18th Friday Fine Day . . . McLeod, Squatsup & Simon killed ox—2 years—398 lbs. & 5 sheep.

22nd Tuesday . . . Very rainy night & day . . . McLeod, 2 Allards & Simon finished thrashing wheat & cleaned ? bushels.

1857

June

4th Thursday Fine . . . Simon and Rabasca ploughing the swamp.

20th Saturday Fine . . . Lieut. Rocher of H.M.S. *Satellite* arrived this morning in a large sailing boat from Victoria with a mail. He arrived here after Dr. Tolmie had left for Olympia and consequently went up there with the mail accompanied by Simon as guide. They returned later this evening.

December

10th Thursday . . . ShoweryLegg with horse wagon and Simon with ox wagon went to Steilacoom for some goods which arrived from California, brought home one winnowing machine and a quantity of sugar which is rather in a wet state.

11th Friday Gloomy . . . Legg with horse wagon and Peter Lagace and Simon with ox wagon hauled up the balance of the sugar from Steilacoom.

12th Saturday Gloomy . . . Simon left for Muck with a load of clay.

14th Monday Showery . . . Simon in from Muck with ox wagon.

1858

January

25th Monday Gloomy . . . Cush and Simon with ox wagon hauling goods from beach....

27th Wednesday Gloomy in forenoon, commenced raining in the evening . . . Huey McLeod & Simon with ox wagon hauling goods from Beach Store.

30th Saturday Gloomy . . . McLeod and Simon hauling salt from the beach.

Simon next appears in the index to the Indian Blotters for trade goods in the 1860s (Norton 1990a, 1990b, 1990c, 1990–1991, 1991a, 1991b, n.d.).

In 1862, on Monday May 5th, Simon is listed for soap, tobacco, match boxes, kettle, pewter looking glass, black silk handkerchiefs, and thread; on Saturday July 19th, for a green blanket and shirt; and on Saturday October 25th, for a blue serge shirt, regatta shirt, pair of brogans, and cloth cap.

Saturday May 9th 1863, Simon purchased 2 yds. baize, a pair of brogans, grey buttons, and boot hooks.

For 1865, on 30 September, Saturday, Simon is listed for 1 lb shot and 1 bar soap, 1 pair "gumm boots"; and on August 26th, Saturday, he bought coral handkerchiefs, sugar, regatta shirt, green baize, broad belt.

In 1866, Simon bought 1¼ lb of biscuits on Saturday, January 27th, 1 lb flour on Thursday, March 15th, 3lbs flour on Friday, April 27th, 8lbs flour on Tuesday May 8th, 2½ yds ferret[?] ribbon and a straw hat on June 30, a regatta shirt on Monday August 13th, 2 pieces worsted braiding on Saturday, October 6th, 1 ox head and 5 yrds. denim for Monday, October 8th, 3 yrds blue baize on Saturday October 13th, ½ lb tobacco on Monday October 15th, 2 ½ lb sugar on Saturday, October 20th, 2½/2 point green blanket on Saturday, November 10th, 6 cups & saucers and 3 plates (from Latham's, $1.75) on Monday, November 12th, a pair of strong pants ($6 !) and regatta shirt on Friday, December 7th, 1 "Reeding Jacket" (from Steilacoom Store, $12.01) on Friday, December 21st, and another regatta shirt on December 24th.

In 1867, he is listed for 1 gallon molasses on Thursday January 4th, 1 box gun caps (Steilacoom Store, $.75) on Tuesday, February 12th, 2½ point green blanket on Saturday, February 23rd, ½ lb tobacco on Saturday, March 9th, 1½ bushel oats, 1 pair ladies shoes, 1 lb shot, ½ lb gunpowder on Saturday, March 16th, 37 ? lb hay on Saturday, March 23rd, and a regatta shirt and bar of soap on Friday, March 29th, regatta shirt, pair of ladies shoes, ½ lb thread, 1 bar M soap, and 1¼ lb sugar on Wednesday, April 3.

Simon is scarce in 1868, but has curious transactions in 1869 for 2 pieces of soap on Friday, April 23rd, and 1 old saddle from Simon for labor to E. Huggins on Thursday, June 10th. In the totals for 1869, "Simon (Indian) Com[d] [commenced] January 4 1869" is itemized for 10 days (January), 10 lbs fresh beef, paper packs, glovers [?] needles, blue baize, sugar, tea, blankets, 4 Regatta Shirts, apples, 10 yards bleached cotton, 1 small padlock (.50), 2 beaver traps, 3 yards cotton flannel, 1 Butcher knife, gunpowder, pair of scissors; for March, strong boots ($6); for April—thread, soap, hair oil, broad leather belt, straw hat (No 2, $1.50), ladies cloth cloak ($8), regatta shirt, and 4¼ bushels oats "paid by cord [of] Wood;" for May—flour, soap, blue serge shirt, cotton handkerchief ?, and 2 skeins of thread (with the vertical notation "your order to Indian Baston").

The next page lists Lucy (Mrs. Simon) with spent wages in April and May for a white blanket, boy's shoes, spoals [spools] thread, rice, shot, woman's boots, soap, grey sheeting, and blue baize. Lucy (Lewis' Mother), at wages $8.00 a month in goods, lists blue flannel coat, regatta shirt, unbleached sheeting, black silk headband, bandana, and 12 yards print. On the next page, Mrs. Simon in July purchased a silk shawl, sugar, tin kettle, soap, and butcher knife. Inside covers listing "Women taken on to Work" include Lucy for, at least, 1865, 1866, and 1869. Because of their different listings of kinship (wife or mother), these were two distinct women named Lucy.

While the bulk commodities of tea, flour, and sugar are not exceptional, the padlock, brogans, ladies shoes, mirror, and fine clothes suggest Simon was a dandy. This is in keeping with his role as shaman (Indian doctor) because only men and women in that profession felt able to call attention to themselves. Chiefs and others were expected to be inconspicuous because their own prominence put them in danger of sorcery or malevolent magic motivated by envy, jealousy, or resentment (Elmendorf 1970; Miller and Hilbert 1993; Asher 1995). As powerful individuals, shamans attracted attention to themselves both as bravado for their abilities and to advertise for patients (Miller 1988a, 1992b, 1999b). In the native view, Simon's own knowledge of herbs also contributed to his ability to handle livestock, themselves herbivores.

Moreover, as a former slave, Simon should not have a spouse, yet he did. We know nothing of the background of Lucy, but she seems to have been equally industrious. No children are specifically mentioned, though the purchase of boy's shoes suggests the couple was raising at least one youngster. Again, fostering was an expected practice among prosperous families, where a career was passed on by a life-long apprenticeship.

During the hearings into the allotment and sale of Puyallup lands, Dr. Simon Hogalcut is identified as a Snohomish and former slave. Moreover, he was implicated as an ally of Judge James Wickersham (1892, 1896, 1898, 1899) in the testimony of Thomas Dean, who was threatened and attacked by both Jim and Jerry Meeker (Wickersham 1892:9, 16, 21, 31). Dr. Simon, strengthening his curious position, was one of three Snohomish shamans then practicing among Puyallups. Puyallup Land Commission Report (1903:13) lists his sister as Somanalish, his wife as Lucy, and her brother as John Quol-ol-i-eish. Since a slave has no "family," this sister may well have been the fellow slave at Minter taken from Lummi. Certainly, the M and N sounds in her name are distinctive of Straits Salish, which includes Lummi and Klallam but not Lushootseed (Suttles and Elmendorf 1963; Suttles 1991).

On 30 June 1887, Simon Hogalcut had 80 acres, 1 house, with 20 cultivated acres, 35 fenced acres, 50 acres in wheat, 200 acres in oats, 50 acres in potatoes, and 20 tons of hay. An 1888–1889 census lists Dr. Simon as 45 and Lucy as 40, with Jim and Sally Meeker as both 50, but these ages seem too young by a decade (Edwin Eells, WSHS, Box 3, Folder 10B, No. 11; Folder 12A No. 412, 413, 523). Except for 60 acres saved by bureaucratic error, allowing a revival in the 1930s, the Puyallup reservation was abolished in 1903. No record of Simon appears after 1890.

Summary

Taking into account that F is a difficult sound for native speakers of Lushootseed (Puget Salish), the written age of 50 for Simon when Tolmie redeemed him was probably heard wrongly and more likely 15. If he were born about 1835, captured about 1840, sold to Minter about 1845, gaining a doctoring power about 1848, and earning money for his master until 1853, he would have been last sold as a "boy" of 17. At the end of 1866, when he was 30, given his fancy purchases, he probably hosted a feast or give-away that may have marked his marriage to Lucy. Thereafter, working for the Hudson's Bay Company and receiving generous gifts from grateful patients, the couple lived comfortably until he died at about 55 years of age.

Simon was never a typical slave, as described in the available literature. His work involved little drudgery and much excitement as he earned a successful and profitable power and he worked hard to live and dress well. Having these glimpses into the life and exceptional career of an industrious slave in Puget Sound vastly expands our understanding of the complexities of native society and one virtue of the fur trade based at Fort Nisqually. Moreover, the confirmation in other documents of details in the Meeker notebooks makes all the more compelling the effort to restore the chompions (competitive eaters) of Minter to their place in Puget Sound.

VI Taqʷšəblu HILBERT ~
THE LANGUAGE OF GROWING TALL

ABSTRACT

The career of Vi Hilbert, a scholar-elder, U.S. National Treasure, Washington State Living Treasure, and Skagit resource is reviewed by using excerpts from interviews to provide background and context to her vital research and famed storytelling.

By the most extraordinary set of circumstances, Vi Hilbert, known as q̓ʷəstanya as a child and then as Taqʷšəblu, found her life and work increasingly devoted to the perpetuation of her language, Lushootseed, also known as Puget Sound Salish. Indeed, after growing up as an only child in a household where Skagit, a Northern Lushootseed dialect, was the primary language, it can be said that she was marked from birth for this awesome undertaking. In addition, her relatives, some of the foremost culture carriers of the region, provided information to a host of scholars and other interested people over the years. In time, all of these various efforts met and fused around her, utilizing her particular talents to become her own life's work.[1]

She always denied being a linguist, in part because she could not name each and every morpheme and grammatical process of the language she spoke fluently. Indeed, her forte was nuanced translation and intuitive insights rather than current trends in method and theory. The most tedious of tasks nevertheless had to be "fun" and rewarding for her to be involved. Yet, through collaborative efforts with people she called "helpers," articles, books, theses, dissertations, films, and news items have been produced because, as she often said, "Lushootseed takes care of itself." By that she meant that whenever something needs to be done for or with the language, someone with the necessary time, funds, abilities, and motivations will show up to do it.

In fact, as a result of her long-term association with the University of Washington, students, staff, and faculty have volunteered or been recruited to work on many aspects of Lushootseed research and publications. Key roles in these efforts were and are played by Drs. Thomas Hess, Pamela Amoss, Sally Snyder, and, as Devil's advocate, Melville Jacobs.

For her, Lushootseed was a palpable presence in her own life and in the lives of all other concerned human beings. It was not something to "reduce to writing" or "analyze to death," but something to be involved with, to listen to, and to live by. To explain her outreach to include formal linguistics in her life, her work history has to be considered.

Jobs as Career Preparation

"Every experience prepares us to make choices that allow us to enjoy more of what we are doing" is how Vi Hilbert described all of the efforts she made to bring in a paycheck.

Born in 1918, Vi was the only child to grow to adulthood of Charlie Anderson and Louise Bob. Her father was from the upriver mountains and her mother from the tidal downriver of the Skagit drainage. As she grew older, Vi joined them in various migrant labor tasks. Her father was primarily a logger, like most able-bodied men of his generation, and to supplement the family income, the couple spent part of each spring and fall picking strawberries, raspberries, blackberries, and potatoes. As Vi grew older, she worked beside them. Her pay was 20 cents a crate, 25 cents if she picked though the full season. After laboring, at night, she would visit with her Aunt Susie Sampson Peter, the scholarly elder of Skagit culture. Aunt Susie was blind by this time, yet she picked, and picked clean, by feeling the berries on the bushes assigned to her. In consequence, at night, her hands would bristle with thorns. Vi would carefully remove them while listening to her aunt chat. For this kindness, Aunt Susie began to call Vi her daughter. Years later, these quiet moments listening to the elegant Skagit spoken by Aunt Susie took on special relevance when Vi began to transcribe and translate tape recordings of her aunt made in the 1950s.

Like other children, she was sent off to boarding school, first on the Tulalip Reservation for a month while her parents picked hops in Yakima, and then for years at Chemawa, near Salem, Oregon. Unlike other students, she responded well to the discipline and standards imposed in these federally sponsored schools. Though denied the use of her native language, she found compensations in the classroom and outside experiences. In exchange for piano lessons and extra tutoring, she did housekeeping chores like ironing and child care.

In time, however, Vi decided that such schooling was not preparing her for life in the wider world. She left Chemawa and kept house for a childless couple in Portland so she could graduate from a city high school. In exchange for room, board, and rent of $10.00 a month, she cleaned and cooked while finishing school. On graduation day, however, this white couple ignored her success. Only a family minister and several girlfriends attended the ceremonies. Her parents could not afford to come to Portland, but they were proud of her accomplishment, even though high school was not part of their experience.

Shortly after, Vi was invited to visit Taholah by one of the girls at her high school graduation, and is where she met and married her first husband, a Quinault. They had two children, a daughter Lois and a son Denny, who died when he was 3½ years old. To keep herself busy, she worked in Indian Pete's pool hall as cook and tender. Then, she ran her own filling station and grocery. Taholah has a reputation for hostility to outsiders, but Vi managed to endure most of this exclusion.

After her son died and her marriage ended, she lived with her parents on the Nooksack River and worked briefly in a pear cannery until the unrelenting noise, ceaseless flow of pears, and long hours led her to find work in a local cafe.

With her savings, she moved to Seattle and bought a house, working as a grocery stock clerk and fancy cookie wrapper. She married a Tulalip star athlete, who worked at Boeing and they had a son Ron. After four years, they separated and she moved to Tacoma, where she was employed at a shipyard as an electric spot welder during World War II.

She met her third husband, Donald Hilbert, who was recently divorced, while his Navy ship was at Bremerton, WA, for repairs. During the war, they corresponded and, when he was discharged, they married in 1946. He proposed in a cemetery where it was a quiet place to walk in busy Seattle.

When the war ended, Vi was laid off and found work as a waitress in a Chinese restaurant, and then was a cashier for food wagons at the main Boeing plant. She then decided to learn how to work office machines and the telegraph key, just as phones replaced it. With these skills, she became secretary to the director of nursing for Children's Orthopedic Hospital, where she went out of her way to soothe and comfort the young patients. Still, Vi wanted more independence.

Vi then went to school to become a beautician, working first for two other businesses to gain experience to qualify for her own salon. A separate room was added to her new house so she could "bend hair" to earn money and to have a creative outlet. In this capacity, she took special care of her appearance and dress, while also learning to deal with opinionated customers. Some were surprised that she was native. A few who were public school teachers complained of the lack of materials to use in the classrooms to inform students about the first people of the region. She did nothing about these conversations at the time, but the seed had been planted to eventually result in a booklet on contemporary ceremonies.

During this time, her father Charlie died and Louisa became forlorn. She moved in with Vi and Don, but could not fathom why her daughter seemed to like white people better than her own mother because she spent so much time with them. In time Louisa learned to use the bus and, wandering in the Pike Place Market, met her old friend and sometimes in-law Gus Campbell and they moved in together. Gus liked to read, but only his fourth and last wife, a Pentecostal, approved of his reading habit.

Always, Vi worked long, grueling hours. Unusual for that time, her husband helped with child care and housework. On weekends, they hauled a boat for several hours to reach Neah Bay on the Makah reservation fronting the Pacific, where they rested by fishing and enjoying the serenity.

These long, relentless days of intense labor came to an abrupt halt in 1970 when she was overcome by pain, saying to her husband "fireworks are going off in my head." Rushed to the hospital, an aneurysm was diagnosed and an operation immediately performed. A long, slow recovery process began.

Vi had lost the creativity that had attracted customers to her salon. Both her Lushootseed and English were impaired to some extent, but she persisted in bringing back her languages. In 1985, a second aneurysm was treated surgically, with less devastation on her life than the first one.

This, then, was the context that led her to assume an increasingly new direction, culminating in a life's work that, over time, became recognized internationally.

A New Start

Before the aneurysm in 1967, Vi was talking with Louise George, a multilingual elder married to a Nooksack relative. Louise, a Pentecostal, was highly praising the work of a nice young man she was helping to write down the Lushootseed language. That man was Thomas (Thom) Hess, who had been collecting data since 1961 for his UW dissertation on the language. Here is how Vi described her introduction to linguistic collaboration with Thom:

> Louise George, an elder and friend of my family, spoke Nooksack, Lushootseed, and Halkomalem. Our families were close. Louise's brother, Dave Johnson, was married to my much older cousin, Minnie, the daughter of my mother's only sister, Sophie Bob Logan. Minnie's brother, Walter, was working as a loader in a logging camp when he was crushed and killed by falling logs. My mother always considered Walter like a son. Our families were that close.

> Throughout the 1960s, she [Mrs. George] had been one of Thom Hess's major sources of information because, he said, she had so much patience. For some time, Louise had been saying, "I am working with this wonderful young man who really is good with our language. He is writing it down. You have got to come and meet him. I think you could help him."

> But I said, "Oh, Louise, I couldn't help him." Finally, she insisted, "Just come and meet him. He is going to be here, this weekend." I said, "Well, I could come on Sunday" because I was busy with my beauty salon at that time. The meeting was fortuitous because Thom was just beginning to work on a tape of my mother telling a story.

Louise was living here in Seattle. I went to meet Thom Hess and he was working with Louise playing a fraction of a sentence of Lushootseed while he wrote it down. Then he would read back to Louise what he had written to get her okay that he had captured all of the sounds. Then he would ask her to translate into English what he had just written. So Louise would try to do that. Her command of the English language was not quite adequate to take care of everything that she needed to translate for him.

I could hear and understand what Thom was writing. He was indeed beginning work on a story that my mother had told to Pam Amoss. She had tape recorded a Basket Ogress story. My father had died and my mother was emotionally upset so her story had some very unsettling elements in it.

So I worked with him a little at that session. I was there mainly to get acquainted, to listen and watch him work. It felt marvelous to me that he could capture the sounds of our language in writing. That impressed me. That and the fact he had so much patience. He was delighted to find someone who could understand and translate into English what he was trying to write in Lushootseed. After our first meeting, he moved to the University of Victoria. But he wrote to me as he was working on this story, asking me questions about this and that. So we wrote to each other for several years. I began to recognize his way of writing out the language from these letters.

A lot of time elapsed and an aneurysm was part of what happened in that interval. I felt that the aneurysm had impaired me so I would be less help than I had been in the first place.

In a real sense, Vi's growing dedication to her own traditions was crucial to her healing process. In 1972, as an early offering of the American Indian Studies Program, Thom Hess was asked to teach a class in Lushootseed. He insisted that Vi join him in this endeavor, as she explained:

My responses to everything right after the aneurysm were so very slow, the slowest speed, but Thom said he would only teach this class at the university if I would help him. I did not know that I could really help him. But he insisted that my voice, as a native speaker of Lushootseed, was important for the students to hear. So I agreed to do that.

He stayed here in my home for that 10 weeks. We worked together every day on the lessons as he prepared the subject for the next day in the classroom. He drove us to and from class, where he would talk about the structure of the sentences that they were studying. He would have me speak to them in Lushootseed so they would hear the real sounds. We collaborated well.

You know what else he did? He split his salary in half for those ten weeks. He had the university give me half of what his salary would have been. I was being tutored and being paid in the process. Each time he gave the class a test, he gave me the test, also. I took the test with the students. Thom graded it with the others and handed it back. I did very well and that helped my confidence and determination. That helped to encourage me to continue learning to write. The first quarter I taught I did not feel that I knew how to write, but I did it anyway. Sometimes it takes a while for things to sink in with me.

For the next seventeen years, Vi taught Lushootseed Salish language and culture every quarter, taking the bus back and forth to campus when no driver was available. Her dedication to Lushootseed became total. Those who worked with her soon learned that her momentum alone was sufficient to inspire and execute a range of activities. She was not just the source and motivator, she was also the sustainer. Over the years, every interested questioner has received food, shelter, therapy, money, and advice in the process of undertaking a project with her. Researchers automatically are included in family meals, outings, and activities, provided that they pass the initial approval by Vi to allow them to begin research. Such judgments are based on an assessment of character, interest, sympathy, resolve, and, importantly, sense of humor and flexibility.

In this way, beginning as a sensitive translator, Vi struck out on her own to fulfill her own family's expectations about the leadership role they had assumed for generations. She always deferred to her elders and ancestors, modestly claiming only to do the work they intended. When asked a question, she, as often as not, would not respond with what she herself knew, at least not initially, but rather with a citation to a text she had transcribed or translated. Before undertaking her own work, she decided to assemble what had been done by prior scholars working with her own parents and other relatives. Doing so, however, was not easy because she had to overcome academic suspicion, particularly by Melville Jacobs, the maven of local Salish and native linguistic research.

Bearding the Lion in His Den: Melville Jacobs

As Vi describes it, convincing Mel Jacobs to provide copies (not the originals by any means) of research done by his graduate students had all the aspects of an heroic epic:

My parents told me that they have been asked to talk about cultural things and they had been told that everything that these academics were collecting from them, all this information, would be given to their daughter, me. So years after this had been collected, I tried to pursue this information that had never been given to me.

I knew the names of some of the people who had been working with my parents. So I pursued copies of their work by calling up the man who had sent his students up to work with my parents and other relatives of mine, Melville Jacobs of the University of Washington. He was a linguistic anthropologist.

But when I talked to him, he said, "No, no, I don't know where that information is." I said, "Well, I would like to come to talk to you in person. I would like to come and talk to you." He agreed, "Well, you can come to my office at such and such a time." I set a date with him. I dressed up to look my best.

This was 1968. I was wearing high heels at that time. I put on my best bib and tucker. I looked presentable to go visit this big man who had been sending students out to work with my parents. When I got to his office on campus, Pam Amoss met me. She agreed to come along since she was one of Mel's students and had worked with my parents.

I knocked on his door and he said, "Come in." I had my camera with me, too. As I came in, he looked me over from head to toe and was surprised at what he saw. He said, "I did not expect to see this." I responded, "Oh, you thought I was going to be some old hag. I expected a long bearded old professor." He was quite presentable himself.

I said, "You know, you people always take pictures of my people. I'd like to take a picture of you." And so I did. He allowed it. I took a picture of him and I took a picture of him and Pam. I gave her a copy.

I said, "My parents told me that Sally Snyder promised to give copies of everything that she did with them to me. I have never received the copies. And I am here to ask where they are."

He had two students [Sally Snyder, Virginia Mohling] that he had sent out. Virginia to tape record my dad singing songs and Sally, to tape record the literature. I never received copies of any of these things. I said, "When people make promises, I expect them to keep them."

"Well," he said, "I don't know where those materials are. You will have to ask Sally about that." I said, "Where is Sally?" He told me that Sally was out teaching someplace, but she will be here for the conference held downtown soon. It was the American Anthropological Association Meeting in 1968. One of the big hotels downtown was full of all these academics.

I decided then that I would meet with Sally Snyder. So how do I find Sally Snyder when she is here? I called the hotel where this conference was taking place and asked to talk to her. She was delighted to receive my call. She said, "I have a date with Margaret Mead but if you are going to come in, I'll break it." And she did.

She had known my parents and they had sort of taken her under their wing as the naughty child that she was. My mother mothered Sally and others who were out in the field working with my parents and others.

I said, "I came, Sally, because my parents told me that you promised them that copies of all the material that you did with them would be given to me. I am here to ask if indeed you meant what you said about those copies." She replied, "Oh, yes, Vi, of course. Those copies are in Mel's office." I said, "Mel told me he did not know where they were." So we went and found Mel and she said, "Mel, you know where that material is." "No, I don't, Sal," was his response. "Yes, you do, they are in such and such a drawer in your office files." So then he said, "Well, I guess we could go to my office to see if they are there."

I said, "When?" He said, "I do not have a car." I said, "I do. I have a car. I will take you. Now. I will take you both." So I loaded them in the car. We went to his office, where Sally said, "Here is the material, right in here." So he was in a corner. He said, "I can't give you these copies. I'll have to wait and have copies made." I said, "Maybe Pam Amoss can help." He did not trust me to take those copies and make others. So Pam Amoss was the one who got the copies made for me. Mostly what I got were tapes of the songs sung by my dad. Mel was very, very nice about it after I got him in a corner. I did not take no for an answer. These were promised.

Later on, before she died, Sally Xeroxed some information that she said was mine. Interviews with my parents, both my mother and dad. So she arranged for those copies and gave them to me. She said, "You know, Vi, you have my permission to use any of my material," but she did not put it in writing and her brother has denied me further access to her papers, but I have other ways of getting at a lot of that material [he relented years later].

The pages that she copied are very valuable because they carry information that I never heard my parents talk about. There were a lot of things about illustrious ancestors and important positions [first salmon priest] held by my family. My parents never told me about these because that seemed too much like boasting and that is not proper behavior for our people. I also used some of the information in the classroom. Other knowledge I shared with my elders. There were also some family names that I could show to their living relatives so those names could be passed on to the younger generation.

Indeed, throughout her work, Vi was acutely concerned with reintegrating her materials into the local native community. Any family member of anyone she had on tape or paper is, she felt, entitled to a copy of the information from that ancestor. She called this "archiving" and, from a native perspective, it is just that because it achieves a communal sharing of this knowledge. Some academics have also been privileged to receive such materials for archiving. In all cases, however, the decision to provide such material is based on a character assessment of that individual. People with the good sense and balanced perspective to know when and where to share such data have been the ones to receive it. By taking custody, they agree to talk or not talk about the information based on their assessment of the time, place, people, and attitudes involved. Fully aware that "a little knowledge is a dangerous thing," such decisions to archive with a person rely on judgments about her or his discretion, particularly the absence of any character flaws encouraging defensive regard for arrogance, possessiveness, proprietary sense, or other false claims.

It is just this sense of archiving *copies*, but never the originals of such data, that brought her to confront Mel Jacobs. In consequence, there are always several copies of materials, particularly from her parents, at many locations, further insuring that the information will be preserved.

It was, in fact, the opening up of another collection, archived in the European sense, that earned Vi status in her own right. She came into her own as an international figure when she undertook the transcription and translation of tapes collected from her own elders by Leon Metcalf in the 1950s and then built upon this familiarity to return these and other stories to the oral tradition, speaking to both native and mixed audiences.

Leon Metcalf was a Seattle teacher who took an early tape recorder into the homes of various native elders. With the help of Martin Sampson, Aunt Susie's eldest son, he identified those speakers who were most knowledgeable. He recorded not only stories and histories from these elders, many of them related to Vi, but, remarkably, he put the recorder at their disposal. In this way, elders who had not visited each other for years were able to send each other taped "messages" about themselves, their families, and local situations. These messages, unique among such early recordings, provide a sense of the natural use of Lushootseed, along with glimpses of speech etiquette and registers not otherwise available from these now-dead fluent speakers.

Because of her childhood spent with these elders, Vi was the ideal person to undertake the translation of the Metcalf tapes after they were deposited in the Washington State (Burke) Museum. In the process, she renewed her contacts with the elegant Lushootseed of Aunt Susie, the family history of her Tulalip son, and the difficulties of translating without understanding the full context of an utterance. Overcoming tapes of uneven quality and distortions, wearing out two tape players in the process, Vi typed up separate English and Lushootseeed versions. More recently, others have rendered these efforts into a computer format with parallel bilingual columns. By so-called "format migration" some tapes have become digitized, making them available for a wide range of sound, volume, and speed enhancements.

At all times, Vi deferred to these recorded elders as the best teachers. When she finished a first draft of her efforts on a story or account, she visited living relatives of the speaker she had long known, probably as a playmate. She went over her work and asked for their help with difficult passages. When all were satisfied, she did a final draft and gave them a copy.

In the case of the voluminous tapes by Aunt Susie, she went over each and every one with Martin Sampson, her son, who provided context and commentary for each translation, particularly valuable because it too is in the native language. Currently, Martin's own grandson, John, is basing his dissertation at Seattle University on her tapes.

In all, only a native speaker could have achieved this kind of nuanced translation and commentary. That Vi was also working with material from close relatives was a dividend resulting from the native repute of the ancestors of her family. In particular, these relatives included the most famous of modern shamans, who lent his support to her efforts and helped to lessen any criticism from some segments of the native community.

What Vi herself has contributed, above all, is the return of these stories to the spoken language. With poise and dignity, she has brought the family tradition of story telling onto the modern stage, a living oral tradition beyond publications and videotapes. Because of her, Lushootseed lives in a much wider world and, with each accolade, reminds the local native community that their vanishing speakers nevertheless have continuous importance.

Working Style

Building upon the firm foundation taught by her parents and elders, Vi forced herself to go to a city public school, work with the general public, learn about fashion and style as a hair dresser, and deal with haughty academics and their concerns. After the near fatal aneurysm, she redirected her life. Her salon became the "brain room" filled with computers and printers to carry out her plans for Lushootseed Research. Scholars replaced customers in these new endeavors.

Certain aspects stand out of her working style. Except when she was on the computer, a mastery she developed slowly despite two aneurysms, she generally worked at the dining room table in the midst of family activity. She did not seem to require the isolation favored by most academics. Even during interviews and collaborations, she would pause to make sure others had food or coffee. The setting, therefore, was a visit rather than an imposition. Since she always worked long hours with little sleep, her quiet times came in predawn hours while she prepared for the day in a bath.

While she has long lived in Seattle, several hours drive from some reservations, she maintained close ties with her relatives by phone and visits. With the help of drivers, she remains active in the winter ceremonial system, often serving as a witness speaking to verify transfers of positions and knowledge. In lieu of living in a native community, the steady accumulation of mileage testifies to her involvement. Because she had been steadily employed, constant cash contributions and "love offerings" to various ceremonial leaders and organizations assured continuity in many instances, particularly during slow downs in the logging or fishing industries where many natives were employed.

She responded to any and all invitations to attend native gatherings, where she spoke in Lushootseed. Always adverse to anything she regarded as "boring," she used these speeches for thoughtful commentaries of interest to the elders and challenges to the young. Sometimes her actions bordered on the outrageous, seeking to enliven an event or spark greater interest. She once coerced a room full of baulking linguists at a conference to tell stories, insisting that if they studied oral literature, they should be able to recite examples.

Unlike most scholars, however, thoroughness or exhaustiveness was not a prime criterion of her finished research. Since knowledge is on-going, there can be no final summary statement. Instead, she intended to epitomize the best and most compelling of her information. While her data and archives were unusually complete, she was well aware that a full presentation of such information would overload most readers. Instead, she presented the "bullets," the main topics, to inform those interested in a subject.

Often, a telling image served to make the point. Since she was often asked to speak to professional gatherings, such pithy analogies cross disciplines and interests. Two examples, long recalled by their hearers, illustrate this practice.

In 1986, The Conference on Salish and Neighboring Languages was held at the University of Washington. As always, after days of linguistic presentations, Saturday was an open session for talks about native language programs and other research. Vi played a prominent role making other Native Americans feel welcome at these sessions. Attending that year from the Tsimshian language classes at New Metlakatla, Alaska, were Arnold Booth, an accredited Alaska high school teacher, and Mary Guthrie. Sensing their unfamiliarity with its conference format, Vi spoke soothingly to them and other native speakers present with a powerful image still used throughout the region, despite today's digital cameras.

> One man said, "We have heard a lot about Vi Hilbert, and I would love to hear her talk." I think that is what affected me, knowing that they felt inadequate, feeling out of place with these very knowledgeable linguists talking. They felt that they did not have any place being there. And I felt the same. I too did not have any business there, even though I had known and worked with them for ten years at this point. I still did not feel I had any business there. So when that Booth man sat down, I stood up and I thanked him for his important words.

> I said, "Now you will hear Vi Hilbert speak. I will tell you how important it is for you to be here because the information that these people are looking for could not ever be put down for the future without you. See, you are the camera that is providing the negative for them to develop."

> That is what I said. Then they understood how important native speakers and teachers are to the future prospects of linguistics.

> Another time, The Native American Art Studies Conference was meeting at the University of Washington and I was asked to speak by the local organizers. I carefully listened to these papers because I did not know what art historians were all about. I listened for two or three hours. I remember thinking, What in the world could I say to these people? What could I say to them? As I listened to them, it came to me what I could say to them.

> Some of them were lifting off layers and layers of stuff to get to the bottom layer that was underneath there. The tedium that had to be part of the discipline of that work really made me respect them. They had to practice patience to find information that was buried under layers and layers of stuff. Knowing that, I said to them, "In my culture, the most important things are whispered to people who should have the answers. So what I have perceived here as I listened to you is that you are looking for

ways to hear the things that have been whispered to maintain valuable information." I remember how happy I was that I could make that analogy.

Taking Stock

In addition to the many story-telling sessions she provided to native and mixed audiences, Vi spearheaded many efforts to assure that Lushootseed is one of the best documented of Native American languages.

Her earliest efforts were explicitly designed for use in the classroom. Beginning with the two-volume textbook and professional articles in collaboration with Thom Hess, she assembled three volumes of oral literature, called *Yehaw*, *Huboo*, and, published by the University of Washington Press, *Haboo*. A booklet, published by the educational branch of United Indians of All Tribes, describes contemporary public ceremonies and is intended for use in regional schools. Her final class sessions on the language were videotaped for posterity. During her teaching career, she always invited elders into the classroom and was sure to videotape their presentations.

Her dignified story-telling style snowballed over the years to take up more of her time, beginning with annual presentations from 1983–1987 at the National Association for the Preservation and Perpetuation of Storytelling at Jonesborough, Tennessee. Other invitations followed, taking her to Canada, England, Europe, and all over the United States. In 1983, with the help of a Yakama lawyer (Jack Fiander) who had been her student in respect for his own Puyallup ancestors, Vi incorporated a not-for-profit corporation called Lushootseed Research to collect money, sponsor grants, and publish the results of her life's work. A laser disk of her archives was to be one of its major undertakings. While academic helpers have received grants administered through Lushootseed Research, Vi preferred the independence gained from raising her own funds. To this end, she held concerts, elders gatherings, and silent auctions. For the 1992 Quincentennial, she gathered elders and artists at the Seattle Art Museum and St. Mark's Episcopal Cathedral to share Lushootseed traditions with a large and appreciative audience.

Attempting a regular media outlet, four issues of a newsletter were produced by helpers using camera-ready computer output. The time, money, and effort was judged too consuming, however, and articles in the Seattle *Ethnic News* were substituted instead. She hosted annual family salmon bakes, which included speech making and had them filmed. She gathered elders together to tell stories and had the session videotaped.

As a result of her inspired teaching, several of her students, ranging from undergraduates to faculty members, have undertaken the completion of various projects she initiated. Her contacts have also been extended by serving as an advisor to several local museums. Among the most noteworthy of her efforts in this context was a back translation from florid English into laconic Lushootseed of the famous speech attributed to Chief Seattle.

In her last years living in Seattle, she mobilized two new programs. Lushootseed Press will publish about eight books, including the traditions of Aunt Susie Sampson Peter, Ruth Shelton, and other elders. Five volumes of a Lushootseed canon have been projected, although only the first saw publication through the University of Nebraska Press. A revised, expanded dictionary appeared in 1994.

She was motivated to start this press, in part, because of what she came to call "academic barnacles," by which she meant things long delayed or not finished by academics that irritate native people. In particular, she found fault with the academic tendencies to take "forever" to publish, to rewriting Indian or Red English, and to lay possessive claim to material that was never theirs to "own" in the first place. While all information should be shared with discretion, people who are not members of that family can have no special claims on it.

Once published, these Lushootseed Press books became available to both native and other buyers. As she said, "Pasteds (Boston's, Whites) are encouraged to buy the books so they can have something to respect."

Her last project, Lushootseed Theater, responded to the presence of more VCRs than books in native households, intending to produce video tapes, now DVDs, of each story, along with commentary. To stimulate this work, Vi asked members of the native community and interested others to "adopt" their favorite story and memorize it. Since stories, along with other family treasures are "owned and copyrighted" by members of those kindred, only they can claim the rights of possession. By having people "adopt" a story, however, native copyright is respected, particularly because the adopter must name the original narrator as part of the presentation. In July of 1995, the adopters gathered at the Upper Skagit tribal center to tell their stories in front of cameras. Under the care of Katie Jennings (1995), as producer and director, these and other sessions became a DVD on Vi's life and work that was partially financed and shown first on Wales TV.

Her intention, always, was to make her traditions readily available to the native community in whatever format they can most easily use. Since the printed word has proved limited, video tapes became increasingly available. For example, Vi made commercial audio tapes and a children's book based on stories from her family.

Her dynamic efforts resulted in numerous awards, both locally and nationally. She was named a Washington State Living Treasure in 1989, and won the 1993 Nancy Blankenship Pryor Award for contributing "vision and time to the literary culture of Washington and the Northwest." In 1994, she was awarded an honorary Ph.D. from Seattle University for her "accomplishments as a language teacher, a storyteller, a translator, a researcher, and a traditional elder." Also in 1994, Hilary Rodham Clinton personally presented her with a National Heritage Award (which includes a $10,000 fellowship), along with induction into the National Folk Arts Hall of Fame.

While linguists and others gain satisfaction from working out the grammar and theoretical points of native languages, there is also that pleasure of providing a native community with something that it will long treasure. Above and beyond this contribution, however, is the joy of knowing that a member of such a community has taken these materials and breathed even more life into them. In this regard, Violet Anderson Hilbert epitomized all that is valuable in a native speaker, scholarly elder, and linguist's native linguist.[2]

Vi's papers are in Special Collections at the University of Washington in Seattle, her aural and video tapes are now at the University of Washington ethnomusicology archives, with a website at: <http://www.music.washington.edu/ethno/hilbert/collection.html>.

Vi died 19 December 2008 but her funeral was delayed for a week by iced-in conditions throughout the region, in keeping with her family tradition of weather workers. Remarkably, her name has not been tabooed because it is simultaneously held by her granddaughter, now a student in Santa Fe at the Institute of American Indian Arts.

NOTES

[1] The interviews quoted throughout this article were conducted in November 1994 in Vi's home in south Seattle. One of the key examples of Vi's linguistic proficiency was her skillful use of the "reflexive" (-cut^3 referring to the "self") as well as her inability to ever remember this term for it.

2 In addition to the abundant goodwill generated by her storytelling and hospitality, Vi made academic contributions of her own (Hilbert 1974, 1979, 1980a–b, 1983, 1985a–b, 1991a–b, 1992a–c, 1993); in collaboration (Hess and Hilbert 1976a–b, 1977; Hilbert and Miller 1996, 2004, 2008a–b, 2009); to Amoss (1978), Miller (1985a–c, 1988, 1992a-b, 1999a-c, 2005), and Yoder (1992); and correctives to Collins (1974), Sampson (1972), Snyder (1964), and Seaburg (1982), as well as great effort in two dictionaries (Hess 1976; Bates, Hess, and Hilbert 1994).

128

PART IV. FOOD FACTORS

The practicalities and symbolism of two very useful artifacts lead off this section, followed by a thorough summary of what is known and thought of a very ancient "fish," whose primary defenders as its numbers dwindle are native peoples. In the face of negative aesthetic judgments, tribes are using casino money to restock their rivers and creeks with a food that in England remains a royal delicacy.

Dibble Cultivating Prairies to Beaches: The Real All Terrain Vehicle

For its sheer practicality, the multipurpose applications of the seemingly-simple dibble amazed me, and led me to pull together a variety of data to make their remarkable efficiency better known. Simple tools they are not; elegantly precise they are. Key figures in Northwest research and legal documentation had also mentioned its importance, but dibbles were not generally known. T.T. Waterman had made a collection of dibbles for the Heye Foundation, then located in New York, now moved to Washington, D.C. Bob and Barbara Lane also called attention to dibbles in their legal reports for native fisheries, including their use in digging for shellfish.

Weirs and Gear as Widowers: Fishing Symbolism across Native North America

The recurrent discovery of weirs and stone-tooled stakes along miles of the Washington coast, led me to look into the literature. Like other finished human products, I realized they were in some sense alive and aware, but I had not expected a particular life cycle status. Finding three widely-spaced cases over a span of three hundred years attest to the identification of fishing gear as a "person" who is a "widower," either a spirit or transformed primordial human, in greater need of food than someone with a wife to cook and sustain the family. Since time is a strong factor during migratory runs, this symbolism balances out the engendered labor and duties for preserving fish. It is also an exercise in recovering exploded pieces scattered across the Americas.

Lamprey "Eels" in the Greater Northwest: A Survey of Tribal Sources, Experiences, and Sciences

During current research projects, repeated and enthusiastic references to lamprey as food and medicine by Chehalis elders, together with exciting all-night eeling at Rainbow Falls, urged me to drop everything and concentrate on lamprey traditional ecological knowledge (TEK) while it remained actively in use. Aided by the sympathies of the *JONA* editor, we were able to get the article into press in a timely fashion because, after half a billion years on earth and surviving four major mass extinctions, lampreys are more than threatened today.

Though called eels for ease, they are millions of years older. "True" eels are boney fish that are streamlined, and they are catadramous, the opposite of anadramous lamprey and salmon, who breed in freshwater and mature in saltwater. Eels breed in the ocean (Sargasso sea) and mature in freshwater.

Moreover, e-mail responses to this paper, especially from coastal Oregon by Patricia Wheat Phillips, add more native names to the roster:

Pacific lamprey	"Night" eel	"Day" eel
Hanis	*sínkwit, səə´n'gwəət*	*shmǽy*

Miluk	*sinikwtæ*	
Siuslaw	*mə´tkwisi*	*shmáyya*
Lower Umpqua	*łqasí*	*shmáyya*

She added, "Night eels were preferred; it was not healthy to eat many day eels as it was believed they would cause skin sores. Night eels were only supposed to be cut with a knife made from freshwater mussel shell, otherwise the eels would feel insulted and fishermen might not catch any more of them."

The use of rock pens for lamprey by Spokan, and perhaps Nimíipuu ~ Nez Perce, reported in John Ross's massive ethnography (2011), adds another detail to the ethnographic record. The strongly symbolic use of lamprey as medicine for young children has led to my growing awareness that some of the great antiquity of this species was being transmitted to children—a sincere hope that they will benefit from such longevity.

Throughout the Northwest, I continue to ask native fishers if they see any lampreys in their streams and rivers, and have learned that a few are still in the Stillaguamish and the Baker, which is a tributary of the Skagit. Stillies, in particular, have a cultural understanding that involves interspecies morphing. Accordingly, steelhead spawn and change into lamprey which then spawn and turn into black snakes "who" move up the hillsides to live out the summer. Only the sequential bodies die. At least some of this complex understanding is well-informed according to biology and climate, since steelhead do spawn in the upper tributaries, with lamprey spawning even farther up at the start of hot weather. These sunny days, of course, also draw out cold-blooded snakes from hibernation to warm up. Since lamprey die and decompose quite quickly, the continued presence of black snakes seems all the more to be the result of these aquatic disappearances.

Lastly, as testament to the former abundance of lampreys, the name of Asotin County, in the southwest corner of Washington State, perpetuates the Sahaptian (Nimíipuu, Nez Perce) place name meaning "Place of Lamprey Eels."

Journal of Northwest Anthropology, Memoir 9:131–134 2014

DIBBLE CULTIVATING PRAIRIES TO BEACHES: THE REAL ALL-TERRAIN VEHICLE[a]

ABSTRACT

Repeatedly, ethnography and court records insist that technology was the limiting factor in the skillful use of resources throughout the Northwest. By implication, this was due to habitat and locale, but that is too facile. A telling example is the dibble, or digging stick, used by women throughout the region for both gardening and shellfishing (clamming). More than a mere tool, dibbling is an indicator of the scale to which they were cultivating the native landscape.

Introduction

Throughout Puget Sound, prairies were "owned" (by use), managed, and maintained by native women, who were cultivating a variety of foods there (Collins 1952b; Turner 1975; Norton 1979a, 1979b, 1985, 1990a; Krieger 1989; Theodoratus 1989). Though not well reported in print, this cultivating was intense—much more than a light or selective tending of "wild" species (Blukis Onat 2002). Not quite farming, it was definitely gardening. Nels Bruseth, a Skagit settler long-employed by the U.S. Forest Service, called it reverse farming since people took out (weeded) from nature rather than put in (planted) to enhance the crop. While many of these species were endemic to these same prairies, others were moved to this locale to make it more easily available. In particular, willows (which had many practical usages as twine, medicine, braces, etc) were replanted in wet areas. In prime conditions, nettles were grown eight-feet tall (Willoughby 1889:271) and the processed fibers were sold or traded to make all-important nets.

Such cultivating combined technology with ideology. A successful gardener relied on her own training, labor, and skills, but in combination with the guarded *dicta* (the special words or formulae that enhanced plant wellbeing), and rituals of thanksgiving. Specific spells could be purchased at the cost of canoes, slaves, and hundreds of dollars worth of goods.

Dicta belonged to families but were known to only one or two members in each generation. *Dicta* (enchantments, incantations, formulae, spells, charms) influence the world and its inhabitants (Miller 1999b:76). These special terms controlled (or compelled) the minds and hearts of all living things. Often the terms were paired into male and female versions to influence affections. In this manner, wayward spouses returned or lovers were attracted.

A warrior in the midst of a fierce fight would pause to slap his thighs, arms, chest, and head while naming each one with so-called "charm words" to renew the strength and stamina of each section of anatomy. When a storm began to swamp a canoe, a paddler would slap the sides and call them by special terms to keep the vessel strong and steady. Similarly, a woman working in her garden, used *dicta* to enhance her crop. While such "garden magic" is well known from the Trobriands and other Pacific Islands, this Salishan usage indicates that it was circum-Pacific.

---

[a] This article was previously published in *Journal of Northwest Anthropology*, 39(1):33–39 (2005).

Lushootseed Dialects

Language played a vital role in all aspects of the culture. The native language of Puget Sound belongs to the Coast Salish Family. Once called Puget Salish, it is now better known as Lushootseed, based on is own native name derived from łəš meaning Puget Sound and –utsid for anything dealing with the mouth or openings. An extensive bilateral kinship system related people throughout a large region. Economic factors provided a delimiting anchoring at a specific locale, from which other social institutions radiated outward, with religious expressions being the most dispersed (Snyder 1950s, 1964, 1980, 1981; Collins 1979, 1980; Miller 1999b).

The language was localized in dialects, generally distinctive of a river or waterway. The spirits and lands in that locale responded best to prayers and dicta in that dialect. Each community had preferential vocabulary (Snyder 1981:277), a few words that set them apart. Two word examples relate to the coiled basket and to the tumpline.

> (This [coiled] basket was called yiqʷus in the Skagit river villages as far up river as skəwixʷ; at this village and above it was called spučuʔ) (Collins 1974:68).

> The pack rope [tumpline] was called čabatəd by duhwaha, saxʷstəbš by Upper Skagit, and sƛidaučəd by the really far Upper Skagit. (Charlie Anderson to Sally Snyder, Box 109-5-79)

Because this region was densely inhabited for centuries and special words had to be invented during certain conditions, such as mourning, not every community had the same words for the same thing. By treaty times (1850s), moreover, the north shores of the Sound had been resettled by speakers of Straits Salish languages from out of the San Juan Islands. These are the Lummi, S'Klallams, and Samish. The Lushootseeds and others who had lived in large villages along the shore were destroyed by epidemics. The Samish moved onto the shoreline of the territory of the Lushootseed Duwaha (Nuwaha, dxʷa'ha).

The Lummi moved onto the lands of the Stockades, who were probably downriver Nooksack (speakers of another Coast Salish language, not Lushootseed). Lummi had specialized in the use of reef nets, suspended from canoes at fixed location. Therefore, they did not know how to build river weirs, knowledge that most properly involved prayers and rituals than mere technology. After various threats and negotiations, Lummi colonists hired Stockader survivors to build weirs. This exchange continued until a few Lummi married, adopted, or befriended Stockaders to learn for themselves how to make weirs. Subsequently, this knowledge and the all-important *dicta* were passed down through families with Lummi descendants (Miller 1999b:17–18).

Gardening

> Edible bulbs and roots were the sole source of food starch. They were semi-cultivated through transplanting, plant cuttings, and cultivating the soil around the plants. Bulbs grew in large prairies in the vicinity of Coupeville on Whidbey Island, at German (Jarman's) Prairie on the Samish River, Sauk Prairie, and in several smaller mountain meadows." (Snyder 1981:225)

Women farmed native root crops, particularly wild carrot (*cagʷic*), tiger lily (*cagʷičəd*), and camas (*c'abid*). An important staple was bracken fern roots (*sʔaqʷ*), the source for the tribal name for the community on the namesake Sauk River, as well as the Lushootseed name for the Nooksack.

These plants were maintained in several prairie areas, two adjacent ones, German Prairie and Warner's Prairie, north of Sedro Woolley near the Samish village of duwaha and one at the village of bakᵂalb on the Sauk River. In these meadows, Upper Skagit [a gross misidentification] women planted the stems of the tiger lily and the wild carrot. As soon as the blossoms dried up in August, they dug the roots and buried the stems. They weeded the plots after taking the roots. . . . Digging in one of these plots all day, a strong women, according to Alice Campbell, could get ten roots; a weak one, six. (Collins 1974:55)

Use rights were based on descent; during the late summer, women with such rights came from widely scattered villages to the plot of their mother. At bakᵂalb [bakᵂab] on the Sauk prairie, each plot was from three to four acres in size. The roots grew "thick like onions," according to Jackson Harvey, who lived near the prairie. (Collins 1974:55)

As described with admiration by Alice Younkin,

The Sauk Prairie, a few miles east of Darrington, has always been a strange land formation. It is a plateau of over three hundred acres with no trees on it, except for a few cottonwoods along a creek bisecting it. Few trees had ever grown there, but the soil was deep and rich. This was the "Indian's Garden," and had been theirs for generations. Many Indians lived there where they would raise much food for the tribe, with a minimum amount of work. To the south rose Prairie Mountain covered by dense forest. On the north was also forest on the side hill that dropped to the lowland along the river. This was an Indian paradise, with plenty of fish, clean water, open rich ground for planting, and plenty of wild animals and birds for food. A short distance away was the river abounding in several kinds of fish in their season. (Younkin 1980:33–34)

Once settlers saw the growing potential of this prairie, they drove the native Sauk off. Suffering great hardship, they took refuge in the region (Fish and Bedal 2000). Sauk Prairie is said, by locals, to have been cursed by this tragedy. On 30 March 1911, it was the setting for a vicious massacre among the settlers themselves (Younkin 1980:34–36).

Churning Soils

Lushootseed makes both broad and fine distinction with regard to aboriginal cultivating. A "prairie" is $xʷbaqʷus$ from the root $baqʷ$ (Bates, Hess, and Hilbert 1994:34, 340). Because of a deliberate sound change, B replaced an M sound in Lushootseed. As a result, this native word for 'prairie' now appears on modern maps in place names such as Mukilteo and Muckleshoot. An exposed "beach" is $sxʷadač$ in Southern Lushootseed (Bates, Hess, and Hilbert 1994:249, 288), while a "sandy place" is $sgʷistalbdup$ from the word for 'sand' and the -dup distributive suffix, quite logically meaning sand spread around (Bates, Hess, and Hilbert 1994:85, 103).

Kinds of digging are distinguished from each other. For example, $ʔaxʷuʔb$ is from $ʔaxʷuʔ$ 'clam,' with the clear meaning of "dig clams, clamming" (Bates, Hess, and Hilbert 1994:8, 304). Plant root digging has two forms. One is $ciqʷ$ "dig roots" in the sense of pry up, related to the root ciq "poke, jab" (Bates, Hess, and Hilbert 1994:46, 47, 304). The introduced use of a plow is referred to by using the root $\underline{x}^w i\check{c}$ "plow, scratch, mark up" because of the scars it left on the landscape.

The most interesting words for digging, because they have the full sense of cultivating, are $p\partial d^l$, 'earth, sod, to plant, bury' and $\check{c}a\partial b$ from the root $\check{c}a\partial$ which includes digging to loosen and soften soil around a plant, a key factor in the gardening success of these women. Significant extensions are the words, $\check{c}a\partial alik^w$ where the suffix indicates something done with finesse, and the name for the month of May ($p\partial d\check{c}a\partial b$) using the prefix $p\partial d$- meaning "time of." Its homonym $p\partial d^l$ has extensions $p\partial daaliik^w$ 'farming' and $p\partial dalik^wac$ 'seed,' literally farming rooted (Bates, Hess, and Hilbert 1994:68, 161, 304).

Timing was a concern of both prairies and beaches. The regular burning off of meadows and prairies seems to have scheduled for late winter when the ash nourished the new spring growth. Beaches were regularly clammed to manage the species populations, while oyster shells were returned to the shores because of a belief that they generated the next generation. (For marine biologists, they anchor the spat and thus allow the growth of more oysters.) Shellfishing took place in accord with the movements of the tides and the moon. Lushootseed women were particularly aware of the moon because of their menstrual cycles. During a girl's puberty seclusion, she was made aware of the dark and light phases of the moon. Her face was painted red on dark days (Collins 1974:236).

Dibbling

Yet all of these distinctions fuse or collapse on the basis of an extremely important observation by a Skagit woman, Jesse Moses. In reporting how gardens were cultivated, she noted that the dibble, a sharpened and fire-hardened digging tool,

> was just like a skilu [*sqal\partial x*], a digging stick for clams and things. (Jesse Moses to Sally Snyder, Box 109, Folder 4, 184 8/25)

Thus, in a single fortuitous remark, the underlying unity of women's work among the Lushootseed was made explicit. The same dibble, and presumably the same openwork baskets used to drain clams, served for the harvesting of their gardens. A thorough review of the literature indicates only one type of dibble, not a range of varieties customized by size and shape to various purposes. The length, however, was proportional to the age and size of the user. Jesse Moses, a few sentences after the one just quoted, said that men sometimes used the dibble "as a shovel." It was indeed multipurpose. Only one source, and that an expectably thorough one, made this significant connection in a passing sentence in the section on fishing equipment. "Such a stick was used to dig clams on the salt water beaches as well as to dig roots and bulbs" (Lane and Lane 1977:93).

T.T. Waterman (1973:51–53), as usual, astutely noted for Puget Sound that a digging stick "was of vast service" for vital roots, bulbs, cedar roots, and clams. On beaches, for shellfish, older women flexed their hips when digging; while in prairies, for roots, an elk antler handle, set as a crosspiece (Waterman 1973:Plate XXXIII), was used to provide a two-handed grip that was braced against the chest. The "few specimens" he obtained are now in the Suitland, Maryland, facility of the Museum of the American Indian. Two are from Sammamish prairie near Seattle (10/215 now 100215.000, 100215.001), one is from Tacoma Narrows (098539.000), and an elkhorn handle (10/199, now 100199.000) is from West Seattle.

In sum, therefore, for Lushootseeds, women's work was never done, but it was eased by a basic tool that used the same motor skills on both beaches and prairies.

Journal of Northwest Anthropology, Memoir 9:135–142   2014

WEIRS AND GEAR AS WIDOWERS:
FISHING SYMBOLISM ACROSS NATIVE NORTH AMERICA

ABSTRACT

Weirs, as stationary fishing gear set across suitable waterways, are more than bits of wood and latticework. They were "persons" alive with intent to help or harm humans in need of food. Three widely-spaced cases over a span of three hundred years attest to the identification of fishing gear as a "person" who is a "widower," either a spirit or transformed primordial human, in greater need of food than someone with a wife to cook and sustain the family. This symbolism underscores the balanced and engendered roles associated with fishing during time-constrained migratory runs.

Introduction

Aligned fish weir stakes were revealed at deep levels on Grays Harbor during recent testing for a new Washington State Department of Transportation (WSDOT) graving basin, to make and float the multi-chambered cement pontoons needed to repair floating bridges in western Washington (Friederich 2010). This discovery led to a literature review which has bolstered claims by local elders that a weir has a spirit and is a living "person" (in some sense). Three cases from the American Northeast, California, and Northwest, moreover, suggest that such catchment gear is further personified as a 'widower.'

Weirs were constructed of stakes pounded into a shoreline and braced with latticework panels or brush to guide upriver-bound fish into impounds, net pens, basket traps, or other containments (Stewart 1982:98–123). Once completed, rituals blessed and consecrated the new weir as a fully-formed person. Trapped fish were extracted with gaff hooks or nets and distributed communally for drying or smoking for winter use. Archaeologists have a general sense that these contraptions have "consciousness, social sense, and agency" consistent with belief in animism (Losey 2010); linguistic sources describe construction details as well as the mortal dangers of attack from upriver communities, especially their shamans, to downriver builders who block off entire fish runs (Andrade 1931:7–8, 152–155).

When not actively engaged in fish harvesting, panels from weirs were removed to deactivate its personhood and consciousness, as well as to allow fish easy passage upriver rather than suffer the moral harm of dying unused in a neglected weir. During the early 1800s, at the mouth of the Nooksack River, locals were paid by in-migrating Lummi to rebuild and spiritually prepare weirs until subsequent intermarriage enabled descendants to inherit the rights and rituals to consecrate these weirs for their own successful use (Miller 1999b:17–18).

Weirs have a world-wide distribution (Connaway 2007), but this paper focuses on three cases from Native North America.

Huron

The earliest report comes from the Jesuit Relations of the late 1630s, written by Fr. Paul Le Juene in Huronia (modern Quebec), and concerns an empty seine or fishing net. Le Juene gained fame when he overwintered with a Huron family, learning the language and survival skills at first hand. Readily available references in standard ethnographic summaries are presented before the actual, more detailed texts. These summaries specify an explanation in a dream, while the texts emphasize shared interspecies intelligence as the basis for such communications.

CEREMONY OF THE MARRIAGE OF
TWO VIRGINS TO THE SEINE

Only one calendric ceremony, to insure successful fishing, is mentioned by the Jesuits. In the spring, two young, virgin girls (in at least one case these were about six or seven years old in order to insure they were virgins) were married to the Seine. At this feast, the Seine was placed between the two girls and told to catch many fish. In consideration for their marriage with the Seine, the families of the girls were given part of the catch. This [p. 80] ceremony was introduced into Huronia by some neighboring Algonquin, the latter having gone to fish some years before and having caught nothing. Surprised and astonished at this unusual event, they did not know what to think. Then the *oki* (i.e., spirit) of the Seine appeared to them as a tall, well-formed man, who said, "I have lost my wife, and I cannot find one who has not known other men before me; that is the reason why you do not succeed, and you never will succeed until I have been given satisfaction in this respect." The Algonquin then held a council and decided that to appease the Seine they should present him with girls so young he would have no reason to complain and that they should give him two for one. This done, the fishing succeeded. The Huron, their neighbors, having heard about this, took up the custom and repeated it every year. (Tooker 1964:79–80)

A ceremony in which two girls who had not yet reached the age of puberty were married to the spirit of a fishing net. This ceremony, which was said to insure good fishing, was reported to have begun among the Algonkians when the spirit of the net appeared to a man in a dream asking for a bride to replace the wife he had lost. The ceremony then spread to the Huron. In return for consenting to the marriage, the girls' families were given a special share of the season's catch. The marriage apparently lasted only for a year. (Trigger 1969:33)

While these texts specify a net, the intent seems to include any impounding fishing gear, from net to trap to weir. As the most complex apparatus, moreover, a weir includes other types of gear such as baskets, nets, and impounds. Huron seines were deployed both in open water and at gaps in weirs.

The actual translation of Fr. Paul Le Juene's French includes more details, including the month when fish runs arrived, particularly of herring. Later in the year, whitefish were taken. The motivation for Jesuit inquiry is made clear because a girl convert was to be involved, her family was to benefit ("profit") from the catch, but, in the end, no rite was held that year. The spirit personification appeared in human guise, though probably of a more shimmering appearance. In 1636, he wrote:

Let us come to other mysteries. [p. 197]

In the middle of the month of March, the season having arrived for fishing with the Seine, they talked of marrying it, according to the custom of the country, to two young girls, or rather to two children, who had never had intercourse with men,— and then [p. 199] of celebrating the nuptials or feast, at which, according to the formality, the Seine would be in the middle, and the two young girls beside it. On this occasion, then, the Seine is vigorously exhorted to be of good courage, and so to act that the fishing be successful, as has been more amply told in preceding Relations.

They had in mind, among others, one of our little Christian girls, four or five years old, to be one of the two brides. We are informed of this, and immediately begin to investigate the matter, in order to understand what we ought to say about it. We have ascertained, then, that some years ago the Algonquians,—who are neighboring people, very intelligent, and excelling in all kinds of fishery,—having gone at this season to fish with the Seine, at first took nothing. Surprised and astonished at a result which was for them so unusual, they knew not what to think. Thereupon, the Soul, the Genie, or the Oki of the Seine, for our Savages [sic] call it by all these names, appeared to them in the form of a tall, well-formed man, greatly dissatisfied and in a passion, who said to them, "I have lost my wife, and I cannot find one who has not known other men before me; that is the reason why you do not succeed, and you never will succeed until I have been given satisfaction in this respect."

The Algonquians, thereupon, hold a council and decide, that to appease and give satisfaction to the Seine, they must present him Girls so young that he would no longer have reason to complain,—and that, for his greater satisfaction, they must present him two for one. They do this, then, in the manner that I have related above, at a feast; and immediately their fishing succeeds wonderfully. [p. 201]

The Hurons, their neighbors, no sooner got wind of this, than lo, there was a feast, and a solemnity was instituted, that has ever since continued, and is celebrated every year at this same season. This being so, I leave it to be imagined what we said and counseled to the parents of this Girl, and lo, there ensued a grievance. For, as the whole family profit considerably from such a marriage,—part of the fish caught reverting to them in the year when it takes place, and being then due and appropriated to them, in consideration of such an alliance,—to refuse their consent to such a marriage is to deprive and defraud an entire family of the greatest pleasure and the best opportunity that can be found in the country.

I do not know whether God were pleased to intervene especially in this affair, and break it up altogether or not; at all events, the ceremony did not take place, in any form. (Thwaites 1897a)

In 1639, the Jesuit added observations about the incompatibility of the dead with vitalities concerned with the feeding and care of mortals. Such taboos also kept women away from actual fishing sites. Instead, they butchered and processed fish away from the water, doing heavy, sustained work that lasted the fish run, as explained below:

They hold that fish are possessed of reason, as also the Deer and Moose; and that is why they do not throw to the Dogs either the bones of the latter when they are hunting, or the refuse of the former when fishing; if they did, and the others should get wind of it, they would hide themselves, and not let themselves be taken. Every year they marry their nets or Seines to two little girls, who must be only from six to seven years of age, for fear they may have lost their virginity, which is a very rare quality among them. The ceremony of these espousals takes place at a fine feast, where the Seine is placed between the two virgins; this is to render them fortunate in catching fish. Still, I am very glad that virginity receives among them this kind of honor; it will help us some day to make them understand the value of it. Fish, they say, do not like the dead; and hence they abstain from going fishing when one of their friends is dead. But lately, when they took up from the cemetery the bodies of their relatives and carried them into their Cabins, on the [168] occasion of the feast of the dead [Kettle], some brought into our Cabin their nets alleging as a pretext the fear they had of fire,—for it is usually in this season that fire often ruins entire Villages; that in our Cabin we were almost always moving about, and slept very little; that we were at some distance from the Village, and consequently were in less danger in that respect. But all this was talk; the true reason was, as we learned afterwards, that they were afraid their nets would be profaned by the proximity of these dead bodies. That is something, to be sure; but here is the foundation of a greater part of their superstition. (Thwaites 1897b)

Saanich

In the Northwest, the nearest parallel appears in unedited, unpublished fieldnotes from the Saanich of Vancouver Island, speakers of Straits Salish and users of specialized reef nets made from willow bark (*sgwala*, updated as *sx̱ʷalu'*).

for the sockeye and humpbacked species they [Saanich] used a larger purse-net called *sgwala*. The top and bottom ropes of this net were generally made from twisted cedar boughs, and the meshes from willow, gathered in May or June, peeled, and split into thin strands that were then twisted together to form a long rope; but the Westholme natives fashioned their purse-net from a flax-like plant that grows on the mainland. Stone made convenient sinkers, and blocks of light cedar served as floats. (Jenness 1935:14)

In the origin story by 90-year-old David Latess accounting for this gear, a young man provides the model to his in-laws. Of note, his bride has singed hair, a sign of mourning that is being observed by the women in that settlement, strongly suggesting that they were mourning another woman. The youth may also be more serious than his mates because he is still mourning for his first wife. While the link to her widower is not specified, this mourning context is clear. A diagram of a deployed reef net appears in Stewart (1982:93–94).

Origin of the willow fishnet (Jenness 1935:14):

A Saanitch [sic] couple and their marriageable daughter joined some relatives on a fishing excursion to Blaine, in the state of Washington. There the girl used to wander outside the rush wigwam and sit by herself at night while her parents were sleeping. One night someone approached her, and, before leaving, arranged to meet her again the next night. Thereafter they met night after night.

Shortly afterwards some strange youths began to join the girl's brothers and cousins as they played around the camp, and she wondered whether one of them might not be her nightly visitor. Towards evening, therefore, she smeared red ochre on her hands, and when her suitor joined her, playfully rubbed them on the back of his clothing. The next day she noticed in the crowd of players a youth who seemed more serious than the others, and when he turned his back to her it was red.

When night came her suitor urged her to go away with him, but she refused unless he first spoke to her parents. He was afraid that if he spoke to them they might be angry and send him away, and suggested that it would safer if she herself told them. She did so, and her father consented to their marriage if they remained for a time with her family. So she married the youth, who thereafter ceased to play with the other young men and occupied himself with serious matters about the camp.

Soon afterwards fish became very scarce, and the community was threatened with famine. The youth then said to his young wife, "Tell your father and his people to bring me a lot of sgwale." No one knew what he meant by sgwale; all the names, indeed, that he gave to the various plants and land animals were strange. They brought him bundles of one plant after another, but he rejected them all until they brought him bunches of willow. From its bark he made a net sgwale, showed them how to use it, and taught them the expressions that should accompany its handling. Then they were able to catch plenty of fish again."

Now that they were prosperous once more, he proposed to his wife that they go to his home. With the consent of her parents, the two of them embarked in a canoe, taking with them a large number of mats. However, instead of heading for some point or island in the distance where one might expect a village, he steered the canoe toward a very deep place in the sea not far from shore, where it vanished from view. Not many days later the girl reappeared above the surface of the water, showed herself to her people, and vanished again. They knew who it was from her singed hair, for along with other women of the camp, she had been mourning the death of a relative. But she never returned to them, because she married the fish-spirit *sgwala*. (Jenness 1935:14)

The implications are that this young man was a spirit fish living deep in saltwater but with an affinity to willows, which thrive in freshwater.

Klamath River Yurok

The association of fishing gear, especially a weir, with a widower is most detailed for the famous Kepel Fish Dam on the Klamath River of northern California. Within a broader ritualized context, Salish tribes of the Upper Columbia River provide details about the recognition of weir construction stages. "Prior rites of thanksgiving were held for the trees cut to make the weir, for the dried poles carried to the stream banks, and for the completed weir. The salmon tyee [priest] spent five nights at the [p. 266] trap praying and singing to consecrate its use" (Miller 1998a:265–266).

On the Klamath, at Kepel, a priest called *Lo'* directs the activities, with one or more assistants. Men live separately from women during this time. The fish weir is built over a ten day period, used for ten days of the salmon run, and then allowed to come apart, so salmon can go upstream to spawn and be caught locally by tribes farther up.

On the first day, everyone stays indoors while *Lo'* travels around the area to prepare the land. *Lo'* cuts three ten-foot stakes that will mark the ends and the middle of the trap. Then he enters the sweatlodge for four days. He cannot look at women or the fire for the duration of the rite. His wife cooks one meal a day that he eats after dark.

Meanwhile, everyone is gathering materials, which they bring to the location on the fifth day. *Lo'* builds a sandpile topped by a flat rock in a secluded location. This pile becomes his seat where he can see the work but not be seen by the workers. A boy who has never before helped build the weir crouches low as he carries the center stake to *Lo'*, who splits it. Everyone yells and begins to split all the stakes they have brought to the site. Visitors cannot look at the weir while it is under construction, presumably because they are not assuredly "of one mind" with the builders.

Every morning the materials to be added to the weir are prepared, and then installed in the afternoon. They bring to the site only what they will use that day, as apportioned by *Lo'*. They build from the ends towards the middle. Ten gaps or "gates" are left, each one opening into a trap built by a team of men who jointly divide and share its catch.

On the ninth day, men go to gather redwood boughs to plug the bottom of the weir. They encounter a <u>widower</u> [underline emphasis added], who receives a new "wife" and tokens in return for allowing the cutting of the boughs. On their return, men have a canoe race, with the winner taking any rejected stakes across the river to be burned. The boughs are passed through the smoke, and the fire's charcoal residue is turned into face paint worn on the final day.

On the last day, the boughs are packed along the bottom of the weir, the women dance before rejoining the men in daily interaction, and the *Lo'* is capsized in a canoe. Though T.T. Waterman wrote he did not understand this event, it clearly evokes the familiar story of salmon leaving their homes beyond the horizon in the form of humans paddling canoes, which tip over to transform them into salmon.

Songs, dances, and joking occur at all stages of these preparations, adding to its sanctity and communal empowerment. Once the builders have amassed winter stores of dried salmon, the weir is abandoned for another year and salmon freely reach the upper waters of the Klamath River.

In all, the symbolism connected with this weir is extremely complex. On the ninth day, when the redwood boughs are gathered, compensation is offered to a man acting the part of a widower. He seems to be a stand-in for the redwoods themselves, who are transformed humans: "they are redwood trees, they were persons" (Waterman and Kroeber 1938:69).

Construction materials are gathered by upriver or downriver teams. Three variant accounts describe these efforts and their association with widowerhood. Everyone from downriver of the trap gathered up flat stones, representing valuable obsidian blades, and took them into a certain stand of redwoods. Of note, such compensation is doubled at successive offers (2 for 1). A rock represents the hoped for permanence of the new wife.

> At the redwoods the party builds a fire. Next a man is chosen "to lose his wife." He sits down and begins to cry, accompanied in chorus by the whole group. In the fashion of a regular mourning party, they plaster his hair with mucus. Then they get ready to take the redwood boughs for which they came, but the mourner objects on the grounds that it interferes with his "sad" feelings. They proceed to offer compensation for the injury, tendering a payment of two "obsidians." He refuses, and they offer four. The mourner says he will agree if they will give him a woman plus two additional flints, plus a fishing place called *oterä'u*, together with a spring, *tere'qsūr*, which is to be found near it. The fishing place is a very good [60] one. . . The bereaved man is finally offered all that he demands. The woman named in the bargain is invariably some well-known character; for example, some lazy woman, or a famous woman at Blue Creek who has no nose. When the bargain is struck,

someone suggests that they have a Deerskin Dance (Waterman and Kroeber 1938:59–60).

When they [downrivers] are at Kepel-ito flat, they designate one who [is to pretend he] has lost a wife. He sits apart from the rest, who are congregating, and begins to cry. They say, "Let us pay him, so that we can dance." They send a man to him. The messenger takes mucus from his nose, rubs it on the mourner's hair, and says, "It is too bad you lost your wife." "Yes." Then he comes back. Another goes to him. Many go to talk to him. Sometimes one takes four [imitation] obsidians [of ordinary stone] to him. But the mourner says, "I won't accept them, I want a woman." The messenger agrees. There is an old woman at *oyoL* who has no nose; they say they will give her to him. He answers that he will accept her if they also give him the spring on Kepel bar [where all the women bathe when the dance is over], because when the women wash there he wants to peep at them from behind. When they agree, he himself begins to dance because now he has a new wife and the spring too—then they go a distance up Kepel creek, make camp, and sleep there (Waterman and Kroeber 1938:66).

Then some of the dam workers start to go uphill while some stay at the redwoods for which they have paid. Those on the hill cut sticks, small firs and pines, for the dam. As they come down again, they hear crying and stop.

The old men say, "Well, I think someone has died here; I hear crying." Then they send a man to where the crying is. He comes back and says, "The man lost his wife; he is a redwood, and he wants pay, before we dance again." They agree and send him obsidians. The messenger comes back to say, "He wants one more obsidian and a woman." The old men are prepared with obsidians, knowing how many will be needed. They also pick up a fair-sized rock, which they call a woman. This is taken to the tree, which says, "Good, I'll take her." Then everything is settled; they have been paid twice, just like head men owning the dam at Turep. Then they dance again on the flat on the hillside opposite Kepel. (Waterman and Kroeber 1938:69)

The tree that lost his wife cries and says, "My wife is dead." The old men have picked out several who stayed at the trees when the rest went uphill after sticks, and have told them how to cry. One cries for his wife, another acts as his brother, and others as his relatives. As they cry, they take the mucus from their noses and rub it on the head of the one who acts the widower until it is covered, so that it looks as if he were really in mourning. When they all start back to the dam, they bring the brush cut on top of the hill. (Waterman and Kroeber 1938:69)

For other areas of the Americas, clear body fluids such as tears and mucus are associated with fragile qualities of life and vitality and so are emphasized in mourning rituals (Miller 1988a, 141, the progression is breath, clear fluids, blood, flesh, hair, nails, bones). The generative power of mucus is attested by the story cycle involving Mucus/Snot Boy of the Klallams, who is named for his source substance ejected by a grieving mother (Gunther 1925:125–31). Mourners do not dance in ceremonies nor participate in fun activities for a year after a death, as a sign of their grief. Others intent on enjoying themselves will gift mourners for that loss while acknowledging their own freedom to enjoy fun.

Summary

Fishing is a cross-gender activity, especially during the brief time of an intense fish run, as when salmon or herring are available in abundance. The hard work of weir construction and use is the responsibility of men, while the sustained effort of preserving fish is the work of women. Children help as age and size allow. Fish themselves are often equated with children, as English does with "schools" of fish. While the "blanket" of fish flesh is removed to feed humans, with proper treatment and handling, the spirit or soul of a fish returns to its home, reborn from its skeleton for another season.

Bodies and outer forms can change, while the soul remains the same. For Hurons, a seine spirit assumed its ultrahuman form to appear in a dream. For Saanich, a fish willow spirit took human form to court and re-marry. For Yurok, humanoid spirits assumed the shape of redwoods, and a rock was identified as a woman intended as a wife. The emotional ties are such, moreover, that the widower grieves and observes the rules and taboos associated with mourning for mortals, such as no dancing, fun, or frolics for a year. To assure continued reincarnations, a series of rituals are held as equipment is readied at various stages, as well as to welcome the fish leader at the first catch.

Spirits are engendered, but paired on the basis of mutual attraction and aid, not for sexual union. Sexuality is an attribute of mortals, not of immortals. By marrying a seine to underage girls, who will still be underage when their year of marriage is over, mutual obligations are met without the threat of sexuality. Gender is the basis of labor such that men generally provide valued food and women prepare it. Children need food from a mother, so a widower represents a particular plea for pity. He can harvest fish, but he can not prepare it for storage, and he may not be able to prepare it for meals, either, given certain taboos that apply during a run as well as the mourning period.

Fishing gear, especially weirs, therefore substitute for human fishers, and add to their efficiency during times of need and scarcity by appealing to humans in need of female mates who are industrious, loyal, and dedicated.[1]

NOTE

[1] An interesting aspect of the role of weirs in cosmology appears in Native California where a Hill Patwin woman reported that Lame Bill, their prophet during the spread of the 1870 Ghost Dance, preached that a flood would destroy the world but the Indians would be saved by a big fish trap as everyone else was washed away (Du Bois 2007:151).

Journal of Northwest Anthropology, Memoir 9:143–159 2014

LAMPREY "EELS" IN THE
GREATER NORTHWEST: A SURVEY OF
TRIBAL SOURCES, EXPERIENCES, AND SCIENCES[a]

ABSTRACT

Pacific Lamprey, an ancient and underappreciated "eel-like fish" that is endangered globally, is an important source of medicine, food, and heritage for Northwest tribes. Usually described by non-natives as "ugly," with sucker-like "mouths" and muscular snake-like bodies, their significance along the Columbia River and its tributaries, such as the Umatilla, is becoming better documented. Their diminishing catch at Rainbow Falls on the Chehalis River is documented here for the first time, followed by summaries of comparative traditional ecological knowledge studies for the Cowlitz, Yakama, Umatilla, and Klamath tribes. A review of biological data in the interests of "scientific" cooperation, relying heavily on urgent studies of invasive Atlantic Sea lamprey devastating the Great Lakes fishery, is followed by a brief consideration of the pros and cons of impacts from current federal laws, regulations, and memoranda of agreements. After millions of years as the major biomass of many Northwest rivers, hydropower dams and urban development, as well as impaired water quality, threaten to extinguish lamprey populations at the same time as local tribes underscore their need to preserve and protect them after centuries of cherished reliance on them.

Introduction

Pacific lamprey have been a mainstay of the diet of Northwest (and other native) peoples for centuries, but, like so much else, their lives are now endangered. Officially designated in fisheries literature as "noncharismatic," these otherwise "ugly" snake-like, slightly slimy, faceless, primitive fishes, are understudied. While scientists increase research into these species, the bio-cultural traditional ecological knowledge (TEK) of resident tribes reminds us of their continuing and past importance to native economies and raises additional concern for their decline. After summarizing data from the Chehalis, Umatilla, and Klamath Rivers, main points of scientific research are reviewed, followed by federal management plan concerns and imminent threats from more dams and other construction projects.

Pacific Lamprey (*Lampetra tridentata*), locally called "eels" by natives and others, are vitally important to Northwest tribes such as the Chehalis, Cowlitz, Quinault, Yakama, Umatilla, Yurok, and Karuk (Fig. 1). They have been largely ignored in print and research (Smith and Butler 2008). Increasing concern is reflected in a change of its scientific names. This species is *tridentatus* "three toothed," while the genus was *Petromyzon* and now *Lampetra*, both derived from Greek and Latin roots meaning "rock sucker," with *Entosphenus* "inner wedge" shifting from synonym to valid genus (Clemens et. al 2010).

---

[a] This article was previously published in *Journal of Northwest Anthropology*, 46(1):65–84 (2012).

The Pacific lamprey live at sea and in coastal rivers on both sides of the north Pacific, from Siberia to northern Japan and from the Aleutian Islands to Baja California in Mexico. Lampreys also occur in the southern hemisphere. For example, New Zealand Maori have funnel traps and zigzag weirs for catching lampreys and eels (Best 1952:275–281). Native throughout their range, they coevolved with their host species, such as salmon, assuring that they drop off before killing their nutrient source and transport. By contrast, the recent invasion into the Great Lakes by Sea lamprey (*Petromyzon marinus*), the much-better-researched Atlantic species, illustrates the damage done by entering new habitats (Clemens et. al 2010).

Lamprey are jawless fishes (*Agnatha*) representing an ancient lineage with a fossil record dating back several hundred million years (Hardesty and Potter 1971; McAllister and Kott 1988; Brown et. al 2009). Many lamprey species, but not all, are parasites for a portion of their life cycle. Without stomachs or bones, they use suction-cup-like oral disks (bucal funnels, "mouths") to attach onto a fish or sea mammal to feed after the tongue has filed a hole through the skin (Fig. 2). Once full, the eel drops off and the wound heals, though the whole fish is seen as damaged by the scar and cannot be sold commercially for maximum profit. Typically, only a small portion of the catch is affected. But motivated by supposed lost revenue, lampreys have been poisoned and otherwise eradicated by state and private agencies serving commercial interests.

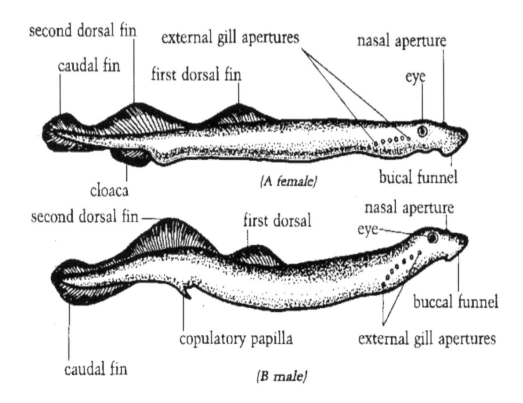

Fig. 1. Lamprey side view identifying each gender (pastiche by Jay Miller).

Fig. 2. Lamprey suctioning aquarium wall (photograph by Jay Miller).

(F)EEL

To the touch, lamprey skin is most like that of a true eel or catfish, slick and slightly slimy. While most illustrations emphasize their three teeth set inside their closed mouth (bucal funnel), their oral cavity is usually open, looking like a suction cup with fleshy lips. At Rainbow Falls, on the Chehalis River in Washington, when grabbed behind the head, their long body whips around and they struggle and feel like a resisting muscular hose (Figs. 3 and 4). If the head touches human skin, it will latch on by suction until pulled off, leaving behind an inch-round, reddish bruise not unlike a "hickey." Once inside a burlap sack, it will struggle for a minute or so, then remain still until suffocation in the air.

Cleaning involves impaling the upside-down head between the eyes upon a nail driven through a long board, then cutting up from a vent to open the belly, flattening out the body with skillful parallel knife cuts, especially through the short cartilaginous ribcage, removing the few internal organs (most noticeably the liver and notochord), and lastly cutting off the head behind the nail (Fig. 5). Females have egg sacks held together by fine membranes that need to be carefully removed intact. Enigmatically, lamprey are said by elders to have thirteen hearts, though only a tiny one can be seen clearly. A hooked nail is used to extract the notochord unless the eel is to be eaten or smoked immediately because, while adding flavor, it goes "rancid" very quickly. Eating "day eels" (see below for "day"/"night" distinction) without removing the notochord causes temporary white spots to break out on the eater's face (Fig. 6). Once cleaned, the body flesh can be boiled, baked, or smoked, before eating, canning, or dry storage. Generally, a dozen or more filleted lampreys have to be ready before they are smoked together to justify the time and expense in firewood and effort, though small store-bought smokers can prepare as few as four (Fig. 7).

Fig. 3. Rainbow Falls, major eel fishery on the Upper Chehalis River, showing rocky outcrops providing traction for lamprey (photograph by Kurt Reidinger).

Fig. 4. Rainbow Falls, showing holes left by Changer to hold lampreys (photograph by Jay Miller).

Fig. 5. Lamprey impaled on a nail, with initial incision along the underbody prior to flattening out (photograph by Jolynn Amrine Goertz).

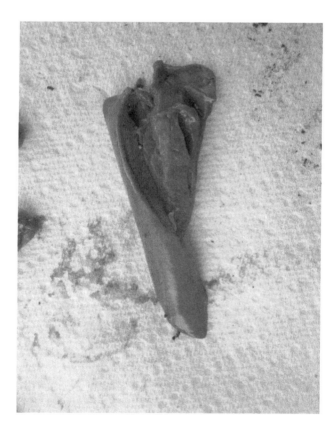

Fig. 6. Lamprey liver, largest internal organ, followed by a tiny heart and long, thin notochord (photograph by Jolynn Amrine Goertz).

Fig. 7. Lamprey filets, cleaned, and washed; note flattened cartilage ribcage at bottom left (photograph by Jolynn Amrine Goertz).

To produce a supply of medicinal oil, cleaned lampreys are baked in a pan without any seasoning or salting at all. As they bake, the oil is poured off from a corner of the pan into a storage jar. Used as a skin ointment, ear ache remedy, and tonic, the oil has long been valued for home use and trade. It is also still used as waterproofing, but dried bodies are no longer used as candles or illumination.

While visiting Chehalis villages in 1841, the Wilkes expedition noted "Hanging around their lodges were hundreds of lamprey eels, from a foot to eighteen inches long, and about an inch in diameter. We were told that these fish are caught in great quantities, dried for food; they are also used for candles or torches; for, being very full of oil, they burn brightly" (Wilkes 1845).

In the Pacific Northwest, Pacific Lamprey pass from the ocean into the Klamath, Columbia, Umatilla, and Cowlitz Rivers, and through Grays Harbor on their way up the Chehalis River, where they are taken at certain narrow riffles associated with particular families and at Rainbow Falls, a public park where they usually swarm on the first hot day in May. Chehalis know to look for them when big carpenter ants appear, or wooly caterpillars if they are later.

Umatillas mention ripened chokecherries and the "eel" ant as indicators of when lampreys should run in that river (Aaron Jackson, personal communication 2011).

Chehalis TEK

While most Northwest native languages have only a single word for lampreys, Chehalis (Tsamosan Coast Salish) has three, as well as a fourth for an eeling platform. Two kinds of adult are distinguished: night eels and day eels. Those swimming at night, called *ʔaqʷ*, are silvery bluish, bigger, and taken at Rainbow Falls on the Chehalis River, especially while resting in two deep holes in those rocks that were left there in mythic time by Coyote (*Speelyai*) (Kinkade 1991:215, K653—hereafter K# for numbered word in this dictionary, for example, K46.1 is *ʔaqʷsaliwan* eel oil). Day eels are called *kʷupa*, meaning "old man", and are brownish, and taken at riffles (K653). Today, some Chehalis "eelers" only use a gloved hand or a gaff hook to give eels a fair chance to escape (like giving a fish a chance "to spit out the hook"); others use dip nets on long handles to take dozens at a time. Chehalis has a third term for "baby eel" (*mé•ʔawt* K1111.4 "water worms" (looks like eel)), technically called an ammocoete (Fig. 8).

Fig. 8. Chehalis lampreying in the mid-1900s by torchlight and bonfire, using detachable gaff hooks on a line, while, on the right a child points to one, and others are packed together in an openwork basket. Today, gloved or socked hands do the grabbing, and pillow cases provide containers (Chalk on velvet by Hazel Pete, Moe Family collection, photo by Jolynn Amrine Goertz).

Lampreys go through several life stages (mentioned briefly here before expanded treatment below): hatching as an ammocoete (blind larvae) that filter feeds in freshwater silt and gravel for four to seven years until it becomes a macropthalmia (smolt with eyes and toothed mouth disk) that migrates to saltwater for a few years until it becomes a lamprey that returns to its home stream to build a redd (nest), spawn, and die. They are eyeless at the start and blind at the end of their lives.

In 1927, both Franz Boas, and his student Thelma Adamson were among the Chehalis collecting materials on linguistics, ethnography, and oral literature. As Peter Heck {ph} told Thelma Adamson (1927, cited as ThA after page number and the initials of the elder's name, such as {ph}), eels (lampreys) go upriver at night. Any lampreys that traveled by day were no good [cf. below, they are no longer photophobic]. They were caught below Dryad on the Chehalis at the dark of the moon using a pitch torch, mostly in April when the new leaves appeared {ph 102 ThA}. They were caught by hand, with five fern roots spread across each palm for traction, and bitten below the eyes to snap the backbone [notochord]. The use of knives was forbidden [at the riverbank]. Eels were sometime caught from a platform built across the river.

Franz Boas (1927; notebook 10:606) recorded the word for such an eel platform as kwa•x̣untEn [regularized as $k^w ax^w ntn$ K618]. Boas (1927; notebook 1, page 1′; notebook 4:199) learned "$ag^u s$ = eel (he is younger brother of spring salmon)," while *kupa* are black or daytime eels, which were caught and wrapped up for good luck and medicine after being dried. (The siblingship of day eel and spring salmon relates to a story of their taking flesh and oil from Steelhead, cf. Adamson 2009:72–74).

In 1942, Emma Lucier told J.P. Harrington "where the bridge just this side (s.) of piyell [Pe Ell] it was full of Indians [unreadable word] in shovelnose canoes. They have to catch those eels at night time & put moss in hand to grasp, & the next day they have to smoke them." (Harrington 1942, reel 17, frame 0720)

Mary Iley {mi} added that eels wanted to be cooked with their head off. The cut-off heads were roasted on sticks. If you throw a head far off, it will live for a long time. If you throw it close, it dies quickly {mi 5 ThA}.

On the Chehalis River from Oakville upstream, the stick was put through the eel's mouth [bucal funnel]; maybe from around Oakville downriver, the stick was put through the neck {ph 38 ThA}. Eels were dried on sticks, up to 10 eels on each. Mary Iley's father never ate eels because they were like his [own] power. Eelers observed ritual celibacy out of respect for their prey giving up their lives (more specifically their bodies but not their souls), as was expected during other life-taking activities requiring personal sacrifice.

The verbatim wording from the notebooks of Thelma Adamson for this summary is as follows:

> Eel said, "When I am cooked, leave my head off. Throw the head on the stick. If you throw it far off, it will live for a long time. If throw it close by, it will live only a short time. If they eat me well, not mash me before eating, they will live" {mi 5 ThA}.

> If Taitnapam throw me up, can't [go] through head or mouth. Go [naturally through as] any excrement? No eels on the Cowlitz. Eels up in Taitnapam country in the Fall. Father said, "Do not eat eels." My aunty said, "Never mind, it is food. That is his spirit power [K93]. Just he did not eat it. It wasn't really eel, but so nearly like it that he couldn't eat it because this power was a person when he found it. One person could not eat another, so my aunty explained. It was sik'vlxaiyo = snake [cf K156] {mi 5 ThA}.

Eels. From Oakville up the Chehalis River. The saqan [stick] was put from the mouth straight through the body, back to the tail. Perhaps, although this is not certain, from below Oakville, the saqan was put from his neck back through the whole body. There were at least 2 rules on the Chehalis river. Heck does not know from where the 2d one begins {ph 38-39 ThA}.

Eels. Same way with hunting salmon or for anything. Some doctors are celebate [celibate]. Must not have intercourse.

Women had their own designs for slicing and hanging eels to make them look pretty. In August, eels were big and spotted. Eel oil was used to soften and water-proof moccasins. Today, as noted, both day and night eels are caught by gaff or net (Miller 1999a).

Cowlitz TEK

Lamprey eels once spawned in the Kalama and Lewis Rivers, and the Cowlitz River tributaries of Toutle River and Mill Creek. Boys would jump into flooded holes so the eels would boil out, experiencing the sensation of getting butted and bumped into by eels rushing to escape. From visiting Yakamas, some Cowlitz families learned to put a cotton sock over the hand to better grab eels. At the mouth of Mill Creek, near the Mayfield Dam and the Cowlitz Salmon Hatchery, the silty sands held lots of baby eels or ammocoetes.

Yakama TEK

Sahaptin speakers use regional terms for lamprey: *asúm* (*asm*) on the Yakima River and below Rock Creek on the lower Columbia River, *ksúyas* above Rock Creek along the mid-Columbia River. Their "strength is uncanny . . . using their sucker mouths as feet." Considered a delicacy and medicine, they are often roasted fresh over a fire on mock-orange-wood stakes, while others are smoked or air dried. "For best results the eels were cut in an aesthetic geometric pattern, then spread with cedar splints." Yakamas also know of the advantages at Rainbow Falls, where, as trash rather than game fish, eels lack legal regulations (Hunn 1990:160–3, 315). Denied former access at Bonneville Dam, Willamette Falls became a more important eelery for the Sahaptians. Portland General Electric's diversion of the falls flow into turbines in July benefits eeling access at this location (Barnard 2011).

Umatilla TEK

Lampreys are culturally important to the native people of the mid-Columbia River Plateau (Close, Fitzpatrick, and Li 2002). Umatillas of eastern Oregon report for their own waterways that lampreys travel at night (Close et. al 2004). Like the Chehalis, they recognize two kinds, one that is long, bluish-grey, and nocturnal; the other is short and brownish. They prepare lampreys roasted on a stick by a fire, air dried, canned in jars, or boiled to remove oil before being baked. Preserved, they are a snack food and trade item, while the oil serves as a general tonic, medicine, rub, and drip for earache. Umatillas are alarmed by the collapse of the lamprey runs, and are particularly critical of the misuse by federal and state agencies of Rotenone, a commercial piscicide or poison used to kill off "trash fish." It is derived from jicama and other bean-family roots, and was long used to stun, kill, and harvest fish by natives in South America. Rotenone was used liberally because state agencies were worried that lampreys and other "trash fish" would out-compete those steelhead/salmon re-introduced by the state. Furthermore, lampreys were considered a nuisance for irrigation operations, clogging up diversion screens.

Klamath River: Yurok and Karuk TEK

Lampreys, of six species, are believed to have once been the largest biomass in the Klamath River of northern California (Lewis 2009). Yuroks (meaning *downrivers*; current population 4,029) call Pacific lampreys *key'ween*, while the Karuk (*uprivers*, population 2,702) name them *akrash*. Lewis (2009), working closely with a staff member of the fisheries departments of the Yurok and of the Karuk, reached fourteen conclusions about Klamath River lampreys and TEK. In addition, he highlighted a few distinctive features of the Klamath, such as dying lampreys moving gravel to mound over their redd after spawning there. Attention is also called to the "popping noise" produced when suction is released by a lamprey's mouth disk as it moves up along a hard surface. As thousands of dead lamprey rotted to return nutrients to the environment, at least one old couple would gather up bodies and boil them for oil that they used to saturate their dugout canoe to make it more waterproof (Lewis 2009:3, 29, 31–33, 34).

Lewis's fourteen TEK items are paraphrased as follows:

1. Two morphologically distinct lampreys were noted for the mainstem, larger bluish or smaller darker, while only the bluer one is reported for the Klamath River mouth or only the darker one upriver. This suggests the blues are entering the watershed, while the darks are ready to spawn after freshwater residence.

2. Adults respond to changing water conditions (temperature, flow rates, particulates), using a breathing hole at the top of their body in muddy conditions. They follow the leader, climbing over it to form a wedge to "leapfrog" over rocks and dams.

3. Groups follow a specific "trail" that depends on changes in the water and habitat.

4. During lightning, solar flares, lunar eclipses, and other electromagnetic activity, lampreys move deeper into the water or swarm up on to exposed rocks.

5. A normal run on the Klamath begins in late November at the mouth, at Somes Bar at the end of March, and upriver at Scott River by late July.

6. Lamprey mostly spawned in tributaries, higher up than steelhead. This is shown by the dead bodies floating down rather than actual observation of the redds or spawning.

7. Lamprey are lazy swimmers, so eeling is flow dependent and relies on specialized gear such as gaff, dip net, trigger net, platform, gloved hand, or woven basketry trap. The hand was once wrapped in fern fronds that grew to full size at this time.

8. The demise of eulachon runs that preceded the lamprey collapse is attributed to toxins from human activities, and should have given forewarning.

9. Seals and sea lions prey on lamprey unchecked, protected by the 1972 Marine Mammal Protection Act, while in prior times they too were hunted.

10. The population collapse began 40–50 years ago, impacting ammocoetes, adult, and dead lampreys. It is attributed to intensified upslope management practices, such as logging, herbicide spraying, dams, fire suppression chemicals, and wetland destruction. Acting like sponges, wetlands regulated water levels by slowly releasing or retaining

water. Extreme fluctuations in water released over dams stranded ammocoetes in shallow pools, killing them.

11. Impacts from intensive logging, hydraulic mining, wetland destruction, water diversions, loss of spring freshets to clean debris and willows out of channels, and road building were further aggravated by episodic floods (in 1955, 1964), scouring away spawning and rearing habitat.

12. Fire suppression has increased forest density, retaining water in root systems that once was modulated by routine annual burning by natives.

13. Lampreys were once a huge biomass playing a significant role in the overall integrity of this ecosystem. In their early stages, they fed salmon fry, while living and dead adults fed sturgeon before these bottom fish spawned. Their dead bodies contributed marine-derived nutrients and organic matter to the nearby soils.

14. Lamprey arrival was once signaled by environmental signs, varying with location, such as dogwoods blooming, crickets singing, frogs croaking, fern frond full growth, or swallows return. Today, many of these indicators are either out of sync or gone.

In all, these TEK findings are especially helpful for understanding the distinct native names for two different kinds of Pacific lampreys. The larger bluish one has recently entered freshwater from the ocean, while the darker shorter one has been resident in the river and is preparing to spawn.

Lamprey Evolutionary Record, Biology, and Current Research

The Columbia Basin and rivers in western Washington host at least three species: Pacific lamprey, western brook (*Lampetra richardsoni*), and river lamprey (*Lampetra ayresii*). Each full adult has two large eyes, one nostril atop the head, seven gills, and two dorsal fins. A lamprey goes through several life stages, as noted. It hatches from the egg as an ammocoete (blind larvae) living in freshwater silt and gravel for four to seven years by filter feeding. After a period of years, Pacific and river lamprey metamorphose into the macropthalmia stage when they develop smolt-like (osmoregulation) capability, with eyes and a toothed mouth disk. Emerging from the river bed, they migrate into saltwater, and become a parasitic lamprey over a course of two to three years (Beamish 1980). The western brook lamprey, however, is non-parasitic and remains in freshwater its entire life. Once mature, ocean lampreys return to freshwater streams (May to September) to spawn, moving upriver by swimming and resting by sucking onto rocks. They are important ecological components of river systems, with larval forms becoming food for juvenile salmon, while adult lampreys are prey for marine mammals (Close, Fitzpatrick, and Li 2002; Scott and Crossman 1998). *Freshwater Fishes of Canada* (Scott and Crossman 1998) provides additional life history information in detail.

Like salmon, they do not feed during this up-migration, and die after spawning. A mated female lays 10,000 to 200,000 eggs in a shallow redd (nest) made by the pair whisking their tails and moving small rocks with their mouths. Pacific lampreys are dark bluish-grey when they arrive in freshwater, then turn reddish brown when spawning. These color changes are the basis for their Chehalis (Tsamosan Salish) names (Fig. 9).

The family of northern hemisphere lampreys (*Petromyzontidae*) includes *Petromyzon* and *Entosphenus* genera, with the former the most ancestral with a degree of mitochondrial DNA that suggests divergence at least 9–13 million years ago. Details of their biochemistry from Clemens et. al (2010, internal references removed) follow:

> Pacific lampreys develop as endogenous-feeding embryos before spending 3–8 years as filter-feeding larvae (ammocoetes) in soft stream sediments. During the late summer and early fall, a number of exogenous and endogenous signals cue transformation of the ammocoetes into macrophthalmia with functional eyes, sharp teeth, and silver body coloration. Macrophthalmia become entrained in the water column during freshets and appear to emigrate in a passive fashion to the lake or ocean where they parasitize hosts. After 1–4 years, they cease feeding and migrate back into freshwater streams to spawn and then die. (p.585)

> [They] can reside in fresh water for as long as 2 years [probably as] a function of the larger river systems on the west coast. (p. 585)

> Lampreys are photophobic during their upstream migration and they migrate almost exclusively at night . . . [climbing] vertical surfaces by attaching with their oral disc, contracting the body, and then releasing [with a "pop"] and reattaching a few centimeters higher; they are thus able to ascend continuous, perfectly-vertical, wetted surfaces . . . In fact, Pacific lampreys are capable of ascending the 12 m. high Willamette Falls in . . . Oregon. (pp. 585–586)

> [They] orient to a larval (migratory) pheromone, which leads them to streams with quality spawning and rearing habitat. The pheromone appears to work in concert with other factors, such as rheotaxis and temperature [and] a longer period of sensitivity to the major lamprey bile acids. (p. 584)

> Photoperiod appears to play a role in stimulating the hypothalamic-pituitary-gonadal axis during maturation and spawning. (p. 586)

> In males, spermatogonia proliferate and develop into primary and secondary spermatocytes, and in females, vitellogenesis [yolk forming] occurs. The final maturation processes, resulting in mature eggs and sperm, occur during the non-feeding, upstream migration. (p. 588)

> The hypothalamus controls reproduction through the release of gonadotropin-releasing hormone (GnRH) . . . secreted from the pituitary. Changes in levels of GnRH in the brain are correlated with season (photoperiod and temperature). There appear to be three isoforms of GnRH (GnRH-I, -II, and -III) that control sexual maturation and reproduction in lampreys. . . . Estradiol, but not testosterone, appears to be a major steroid regulating reproductive maturation and functions in both sexes of the sea lamprey and Pacific lamprey. (p. 588)

> . . . growing evidence [is] that all lampreys produce gonadal steroids that are different from those of other vertebrates, by possessing an additional hydroxyl group at the C15 position. Furthermore, there is evidence that 15α-hydroxyprogesterone is a hormone in lampreys, and that androstenedione, a precursor to vertebrate androgens, is the main androgen. (p. 589)

> Spermiating male sea and Pacific lampreys attract ovulating females to nest sites with a mating pheromone that is released through the gills. The primary component of this pheromone is 3-keto-petromyzonol sulfate . . . and 3kPZS, albeit at much higher concentrations. (p. 589)

During the spawning period, the lampreys are nearly blind, and the lampreys will spawn during daylight hours. Female sea and Pacific lampreys orient across the nest while the male initiates a "gliding-feeling" motion prior to attaching to the female's head, wrapping around her, and squeezing the eggs out while fertilizing them. (p. 387)

Lampreys and other primitive fishes have made important contributions in the study of endocrine system development and reproductive biology, particularly how hormones coupled with environmental cues like photoperiod and temperature serve to trigger events in the development of gonads of individual fish, leading to final maturation and spawning. The essentials of these endocrine systems are conserved in higher vertebrates, so their study in lampreys opens a doorway to understanding how they work in other animals (Clemens et. al 2010; Sower 2010).

Additional research has indicated how lampreys communicate and signal their presence using larval pheromones during their spawning migration. These inquiries are aimed at understanding the use of attractants to control lampreys invasive into the Great Lakes where they are exotic pests (Bjerselius et. al 2000).

Fig. 9. Photograph of Lamprey spawning; male begins to wrap around the feeble female to force out the eggs to be fertilized.

Pacific lamprey homing mechanisms appear to promote a high degree of population mixing (Goodman et. al 2008). Pacific salmon appear to seek the characteristics of their actual natal environment, resulting in high fidelity to their home streams. But lamprey are pamicitic, attracted to larval pheromones, not the stream itself, and so may seek any suitable stream with resident ammocoetes. This attribute works against the evolution of reproductive isolated, unique populations.

Like salmon and smelt, however, lamprey populations have declined due to urban development, habitat destruction, water pollution, forestry practices, and dam blockage. Studies have recently been carried out to understand Pacific lamprey climbing behavior in order to design better fishways at dams that will aid their upstream migration (Moser, Ogden, and Peery 2006; Reinhardt et. al 2008; Kemp, Tsuzaki, and Moser 2009; Moser et. al 2010, 2011).

Lampreys had commercial uses in the Pacific Northwest such as raw-ground hatchery food, vitamin oil for livestock and poultry, and scientific research into medical anticoagulants. This commercial fishery first harvested in 1941 at Willamette Falls, which has become the first Traditional Cultural Place (TCP) in Oregon because of its ongoing cultural associations with native lamprey harvest.

Recent Federal Involvement

Federal laws and relicensing regulations are now involved in plans to safeguard lampreys. Tacoma Power was granted a new 35-year license by the Federal Energy Regulating Commission (FERC) in 2003 for their Cowlitz River projects when the emphasis was on transport of salmonids to upper watersheds without concern, however, for lamprey protection. FERC subsequently responded to recent heightened tribal concerns for lampreys. Grant County's 2008 license for the Priest Rapids project on the Columbia River requires a lamprey management plan, at the insistence of the nearby Sahaptin Wanapum community.

The Columbia Basin Fish Accords, partly consisting of three memorandums of agreement (MOA), were signed 2 May 2008. They are intended to last for ten years, promising nearly a billion dollars of federal funds to deliver specific, scientifically-valid biological benefits for the region's fish. Based on Endangered Species Act BiOps (biological opinions) by NOAA Fisheries, they respond to a rewrite order by Judge James A. Redden, U.S. District Court of Oregon, of May 2005. Federal 'action agencies' signing an MOA are the Bonneville Power Administration (BPA), U.S. Army Corps of Engineers (USACE), and Bureau of Reclamation (BR). The last two operate and maintain the Federal Columbia River Power System (FCRPS). One MOA was signed jointly by the Confederated Tribes of the Umatilla Indian Reservation, the Confederated Tribes of the Warm Springs Reservation of Oregon, and the Confederated Tribes and Bands of the Yakama Nation. The Columbia River Inter-Tribal Fish Commission also signed this MOA. An identical MOA was signed separately by the Confederated Tribes of the Colville Indian Reservation. The tribal MOA, Section IV B 2, second bullet point, reads: "the Action Agencies' commitments under this Agreement for lamprey actions are adequate for the duration of this Agreement such that the Tribal parties will not petition to list lamprey or support third party efforts to list lamprey as threatened or endangered pursuant to the ESA."

Consistent with intent of the MOA, the three Sahaptin nations, joined by the Nez Perce in Idaho, have proposed a lamprey restoration plan where needed modifications (possible, practical, and immediate) "include the use of 24 hour video counting, installation of lamprey passage systems, altering existing fishway structures to prevent trapping, reducing velocity barriers, reducing/eliminating juvenile impingement on screens and reducing fishway flows at night" (Nez Perce, Umatilla, Yakama, and Warm Springs Tribes 2008:2) (Fig. 10).

Summary

Pacific lampreys, like salmon, spawn once and die; their body constituents enriching nearby soils. From eggs in redds, they transform into ammocoetes resident in freshwater, macropthalmia moving from stream to sea, and lamprey returning from salt to fresh water to spawn. As sometime parasites, they improve the health and rigor of other fish stocks, with which they coevolved, stopping short of fatal predation. As primitive fishes without bones or stomachs, lamprey evolved hundreds of millions of years ago, the Pacific species appearing about twelve million years ago.

Fig. 10. Confederated Tribes of the Umatilla Indian Reservation harvesters at Willamette Falls (Associated Press story of 3 August 2011, by Jeff Barnard, widely reprinted).

Migrating lampreys are photophobic, moving upstream at night. Before spawning, their bodies produce sperm or eggs after the hypothalamus releases GnRH (gonadotropin hormones), and an estradiol steroid to achieve full maturity. Their gonadal steroids, with an added hydroxyl group, precede those of more recently evolved vertebrates. Varied pheromones help lampreys to locate suitable spawning areas and to attract a mate.

Once a huge biomass in some Pacific coast rivers, they nourished many other species, including salmon, sturgeon, and humans. Traditionally their availability was signaled by specific natural cues, ranging across plants, insects, birds, and amphibians, as listed above. Their flesh and oil provide medicine, food, lubricant, waterproofing, and trade items.

To catch them, humans devised an array of techniques and equipment, dependent on water flow, terrain, and options about giving them a fair chance. Their smooth, slimy bodies are best grasped by hands once wrapped in plant fibers or now wearing cloth gloves. Otherwise, baskets, nets, hooks, and gaffs are used. Taken by men, lampreys are processed by women for drying, cooking, smoking, and storage. Lacking stomachs, bones, or vertebrae, their bodies are sliced open to remove the few internal organs and notochord before other preparations are made.

Chehalis name two kinds, which are either returning in fresh water (silvery bluish, bigger) as spawners or departing (darker, smaller) as parasites appropriately named "old man." Lamprey begin eyeless and end their lives often blinded, with furunculosis clouding the eyes of spawners as the male squeezes the eggs out of the female into their redd, which they then mound with gravel before dying. In life, the "popping" sound of released suction as they spring upward, and the mass of their long wiggling bodies leave lasting impressions. In death, the stench of their rotting bodies once filled the air for weeks, though their remains did provide food for other fish and lubricating oils for humans.

Decades ago, their abundance once encouraged commercial sales for raw hatchery food, livestock and poultry vitamins, and medical study of anticoagulants. The unsightly wounds they left on fish, especially salmon, that prevented best prices for the catch, led to unwise use of rotenone to eradicate them.

Now described as noncharismatic (in lieu of "ugly"), they are not listed as endangered or threatened, in large part because continued dispersal of federal funds depends on the status quo. Today, native harvesting is often done by young men with tribally-issued permits on behalf of their elders and families, who then prepare the lamprey eels for ceremonial feasts, for snack foods, and for medicines as rubs, drops, and lubricants. Instead of the thousands once prepared until the 1970s, eelers today are lucky to harvest a hundred during a run and most get a few dozen.

Efforts worldwide are underway to study lampreys, intent on raising the Pacific species in hatcheries or killing off invasive sea lamprey in the Great Lakes, even as native people lament their loss in numbers and contributions to the environment. Their own TEK of lamprey must, of course, be an integral part of this recovery effort.

Lastly, in the interest of having the lamprey have its say, of sorts, the following poem summarizes its parasitic life cycle from an Anglophone socialist perspective.

The Socialist Lamprey

If I'm not much to look at and you dislike my way of life
    Remember that my childhood was full of woe and strife;
'Cos I was squeezed out of my Mum by an ultavigorous dad
    and dumped right on the gravel—its' all so very sad.

And if that wasn't bad enough my parents went and died
    And left me orphaned in this stream, an insult to my pride;
But, when I'm a little older—some say four or five—
    I'm going to change my colours and really come alive.

You may think I'm only kidding but inside my notochord
    I feel these changes coming and teeth growing like a horde;
I'll live on social welfare and I'll suck you good and dry
    A daily blood transfusion should keep me feeling spry.

Never mind your blood group—just let me hitch a ride
    Roll over if you wish to—I'll latch on to either side;
I'm not worried by your morals or your very numerous scales
    Board and lodgings quite enough—I've no interest in your tails!

Your pelagic upper class has had it good too long
    Don't forget we're not just suckers for you to string along
And now I've made my mark and it looks as if you're dying
    I'm off to spawn upriver, to keep the red flag flying.

Roger Lethbridge (1971)
Murdoch University, Western Australia

ACKNOWLEDGMENTS

The sad saga of Pacific Lamprey survival first came to my attention in Grays Harbor, the estuary of the Chehalis River, and soon focused on the continuing importance of Rainbow Falls for present-day eelers. For help, guidance, and dry clothes along the way, I'd like to thank Tom Steinburn, Mel Youckton, Ron LeGarde, Nathan Reynolds, Ed Arthur, dAVe Burlingame, Curtis Dupuis, Wayne Barr, Katherine Barr, Richard Bellon, David Burnett, Don Secena, Mark White, Harvey, Janice, Quentin, and Barron Hamilton, Jolynn Amrine Goertz, Theodore, and Ben Goertz, Marilyn Richen, Tammy Jackson, Michelle Saville, and, especially, Kurt Reidinger. Aaron Jackson (CTUIR), lead on the Umatilla Lamprey Project, provided a thoughtful review and comments.

Earnest, sometimes off track, searching for collective understanding dominates this last section. It begins with a summary of the Americanist tradition especially slanted toward the Northwest, and is followed by the sharply contrasting native versus academic views about the sharing and presentation of such information. The role of teachers as unique individuals in this learning process features four elderly women and, next, the first work of a famous native son archaeologist. In terms of institutions, missteps at the University of Washington over the past century, as well as today during a hastily hired consultation at an important sacred site, provide object lessons that should apply both locally in the state ("the other Washington") as well as nationally from Washington, D.C., more specifically, the very complexity of that local area comes into its own in the next article. Lastly, the dynamic interaction between a responsible federal worker, a local leader (lacking a "valid" ~ "official" tribe), and concerned natives of western Washington is outlined in terms of legal and archival concerns that remain vitally important.

The Americanists Tradition

Since my avowed intent, after settling there, has been to reintegrate the Northwest into the rest of Native America, it was important to survey the span of research into its native peoples and cultures, organized chronologically in terms of Frontiersfolk, Genteel Scholars, Museum Scholars, and Academic Scholars. Emphasizing long-term input from Northwest people and places helps with this refocusing.

Americanists Cross Purposes ~ Ways of Knowing

Wide differences between native and academic epistemology, sociology of knowledge, and notions of "archiving" led me to reflect on how these contrasts were brought out at a conference at University of British Columbia's residential Green College (5–8 March 1998). Modeled after English universities like Oxford and Cambridge, Green honors its place base by having a Musqueam weaving hanging above its high table where faculty eat (as at Hogwarts in the Harry Potter series) instead of a heraldic shield conferred by the monarch.

Passing the Torch: Learning from Women Elders

Rick Sprague, co-editor of the *Journal of Northwest Anthropology* (1969–2012), always encouraged my interest in the history of regional Northwest anthropology, especially since I was based in Seattle, with the University of Washington nearby. Pondering and lamenting the state of Northwest research, my early friendships with academic women pathbreakers resulted in this conference paper, "Passing the Torch." From my arrival in the Northwest, I cultivated friendships with the Americanist "old guard" of Erna Gunther, Viola Garfield, Bess Jacobs, and other Boas students living in Seattle, such as Amelia Susman Schultz, his last Ph.D. Erna lived down the hill, until a break-in led her to move to a small house on her son's property on Bainbridge Island, where she eventually ended up in a care facility, with a strong body but impaired mind because she had been an athlete and remained a strong proponent of daily exercise.

I became very fond of Viola and Amelia because of their connection with Tshimshian research. Mel Jacobs had died, but Bess continued to live in their house near campus. Verne Ray rebuffed my attempt to make contact, even after my intensive work with Colville and Plateau peoples. Years later, I realized we had common friends who could have eased my way to him and his wife Dorothy. His papers eventually went to Gonzaga University in Spokane, rather than UW where he spent his, somewhat embittered, career.

Viola in particular told the story of a new faculty member, at the annual department "meet and greet," assuring her that her life-long interest in Native Americans was "no longer fashionable." Africa and New Guinea ruled that day, not Native America, a "squeezed out orange if there ever was one." Yet her papers at the University of Washington archives, especially her volumes of photographs of totem poles, have been well-used by scholars from all over the world. And it was Viola, alone among the first faculty, who was honored by a Festschrift.

Or so I wrote, but Roy Carlson dedicated the session and the volume, *Indian Art Traditions of the Northwest Coast* (1983), to Erna as a collective tribute. In casual conversations, and a few pointed questions, I heard the names of local characters, foremost among them was the sometime couple of Helmi Juvonen, the Finnish eccentric artist, and Julius Towhy, a Paiute artist and activist from Utah. What I did not pursue, sadly, was the exciting time right after WWII when the GI Bill brought many men and women to college. The role of the University of Washington in the River Basin Surveys, dam construction, and other public works was pivotal, as shown in the appendix *Arky Epitaph*, a working outline. All of these efforts moved with Doc Daugherty east of the Cascades to Washington State University in Pullman, WA, in the aftermath of the wholesale rejection of Northwest scholarship at UW.

Startup: Richard "Doc" Daugherty's 1947 Archaeological Survey of the Washington Coast

Thirty years ago I had promised Richard Daugherty that I would write up his ethnographic notes from the Hoh to make them available. Other things intruded for some time, before I could make good on my promise. In conversation, Doc also mentioned his original hand-written notes of an archaeological survey of the Washington coast he had done first, meeting several of the tribal elders who eventually worked with him at Hoh. A thorough search of his office did not find them until the last bundle was lifted up from a far corner. Before these drafts were turned over to Washington State University, I typed them up to provide a complete set of Doc's early work on the coast, both archaeological and ethnographic. They have since been digitized at Washington State University in Pullman, WA.

Anthropology at the University of Washington: Deaths and Betrayals

This University of Washington purge of the mid-1950s was not discussed in public nor in private; wished away since the "new turks" were now mainstays of the department. The Northwest and Native America were something of an embarrassment, a vital aspect of the region but a "spent one." Only a token class or two was allowed. Yet, for Indian Country, all of this was to change radically, and soon, with the Boldt decision to safeguard the treaty right to salmon, followed in later decades by similar federal decisions about shellfish and other local resources. It very much changed with the arrival of Indian gaming and Native casinos, for nearby reservations now had money—and lots of it—to pay their way and get their wishes fulfilled. Native students on tribal and federal funds are earning needed degrees in forestry, fisheries, oceanography, and museum studies. The new push for a Native academic longhouse at the University of Washington, the only campus in the Northwest not to have one, will draw on casino funds dedicated to charity.

Synopsis, Synthesis, Skimping, and Scholarship: A Case Example from
Chehalis in the "Other" Washington

Fair, open, and thorough use of references and resources is critical to good scholarship. My awareness of the cultural and religious importance of Grand Mound, believed to be a bit of Star left behind, together with a willful shortcutting and ignoring of original sources led to this article. The flash point was the construction of a new home atop the mound without tribal review and the slighting of the subsequent protest to local permitting agencies. More than a "teachable moment," this situation serves as a textbook example of local resistance if not hostility to tribal concerns and their legal protections.

Skookumchuck Shuffle ~ Shifting Athapaskan Swaals into Oregon Klatskanis before Taitnapam Sahaptins Cross the Cascades

The language and historical complexity of southwest Washington remains largely unknown to the wider public. The Skookumchuck ("strong water") Shuffle is intended to expand that understanding, especially the role of the region as a switching point in the Athapaskan migration from central Alaska south into northern California. Since this migration out of the North was set off by volcanic eruptions, it is interesting that Skookumchuck sites indicate a continuing preference for obsidian, often traded from central Oregon. Named in Chinuk WaWa instead of a distinct tribal language, and occupied by Swaal, this river was distinctive enough to serve as a readily available boundary. The U.S. government recognized it during the 1854–1959 tenure of the Columbia River (South District) Agency which extended as far north as this river, whose Chehalis Tsamosan native name specifies it was a "fording" place.

Briefly mentioned in this article is a little known roster of Klatskani names taken down at Milton (now St. Helens, Oregon) and sent on 8 January 1856, listing these heads of families with separate columns for men, women, boys, and girls totaling 27 at a time when only a handful of survivors were usually mentioned. These names are given here, followed by the number of family members in parentheses:

Che-whâ-mauo 1st chief (2), Clo-whas-kie 2nd chief (4), Wa-nâ-kilt (3), Koo-te-ow-wâl (3), Sae-on-max-iâ (2), Wateh-mâl-kie (4), Bill (1), Mim-a-lused (2), Poos-si-yân (1), Yoo-wâ-wâ-ney (1), Mâ-ki-yoak (1), Yis-see (1), Aie-e-yas (1), and Bull (1).

Moreover, the indigenous language complexities of the Chehalis River area also implicate its role as the northernmost ice-free entry into coastal North America. Two centuries ago, this complexity increased because Yakamas, needing winter pasture for their recently-adopted horses, crossed the mountains. While the local Chehalis treaty council aborted, these Yakamas, enrolled as Taitnapams, do have treaty protections. To emphasize their treaty status, the Yakama Indian Nation took back this spelling of their name as it appears on their treaty of 1855, further distinguishing themselves from the white town of Yakima.

Charles Roblin, Thomas Bishop, and the Background of Western Washington Land Claims Cases

Most recently, the crucial significance of reviewing original documents was brought home by a hard-fought effort at the U.S. National Archives to see the original pages of the Schedule of Unenrolled Tribes by Charles Roblin, issued 31 January 1919, where a vivid array of colors made all too obvious, almost a century later, the ineligibility of certain families for tribal membership. The discovery was important enough to make the front page of the *Seattle Times*, written by Lynda Mapes, a reporter well-versed in these enrollment shenanigans.

Journal of Northwest Anthropology, Memoir 9:164–180   2014

THE AMERICANISTS TRADITION

ABSTRACT

Key figures, themes, and publications in the history of research into the native peoples and cultures of the Americas are reviewed, divided into Frontiersfolk, Genteel Scholars, Museum Scholars, and Academic Scholars, with especial concern for the early and vital role of the Northwest within these global efforts.

Introduction

Closest to the Asian continent, the American North Pacific Coast—its sea otters, salmon, and gold—fueled empires across Europe and their colonies. Nearest the Bering Strait and the most likely coast entry into North America, evidence from the Northwest should reveal earliest origins, migrations, and dispersals. Yet its anthropological understanding was slow to develop and, today, it is often treated by scholars as a region apart. While later Inuit and Dine arrivals clearly tie to Asia, the rest of the regions of Native North America were variously influenced by Mexico, especially the maize farming, ceremonialism, and vast trade of its huge population.

The North Pacific is harder to characterize: its Asian origins can be seen in its ranked societies with split-body artistic images and its continental American influences can be traced through the trade in dentalia shells, eulachon oil, and carved cedar. The earliest Americanist ethnography focused, in Russian, on Aleuts and Tlingits, with subsequent data provided by other world explorers of various nations, which may have included Chinese and Japanese. The best known sources, nonetheless, are European, then nationals from North America, continuing a writing tradition that is both indigenous and ancient.

Indeed, we should look first to native sources, especially given ancient traditions of literacy. The few writing systems of Native America, relying on Mayan glyphs and other Meso-American alphabets, have colored our understanding of Native America. While students who are about to undertake research in Asia are cautioned to scrupulously avoid anything that might be interpreted as showing disrespect to the written or printed word (such as sitting on a newspaper), students about to work in Native America must learn to emphasize the spoken word so vital to the Native oral tradition. In any literate tradition, the scholar occupies a special place which permits him or her to undertake research and publication as a matter of routine. In an oral tradition, however, it is the intellectual, especially as a narrator, who undertakes to comment upon and to encourage on-going activities, but without the aloof, mystical aura of the written word.

In a written historical tradition, it is also much easier to present the insider (*emic*) aspects of that same tradition; while in the confrontation of a literate and an oral tradition, the emic aspects of the oral one usually suffer. This has been the case with Native America. Since European contact, the richness of the Native perspective has been consistently ignored, disparaged, denied, or suppressed. There have been some notable exceptions, especially in regard to folklore and mytho-logic (what French call *mythologique*), which will be noted sporadically through this article.

It was also the earlier French who first used the term "Americanist" for those who are devoted to the study of the Americas, with the founding of the International Congress of Americanists in 1875. Other major organizations, with date of founding, involved with research in the Americas are American Philosophical Society (1743), American Antiquarian Society (1812, AAS), American Ethnological Society (1842, AES), Smithsonian Institution (1846), American Folklore Society (1888, AFS), American Anthropological Society (1902, AAA, publisher of the *American Anthropologist*, old series, 1888–1898, and new series 1899–present), Society for American Archaeology (1935, SAA, publisher of *American Antiquity*), and Society for Applied Anthropology (1941, SfAA).

As should become apparent, the knowledge, the understanding, and even the kind and quality of our "raw data" have depended upon the socially constructed premises that have been developed, and are developing via critical reanalysis, among our intellectual elders as they have interacted with each other and with external factors such as cultural systems, intellectual fashions, funding sources, and various conceptual models abstracted from these interactions. The best of these interactions have been between superior Native and academic intellectuals whose personalities predisposed them to the comparative, holistic, and transpersonal perspective that is uniquely anthropological.

A Native intellectual usually has self-assurance, curiosity, and the ability to synthesize a model of his or her culture. With proper family or personal credentials, such a person would be a candidate for the rigorous childhood training associated with tribal officials in oral traditions. Special conditions, such as blindness or a crippling injury, also predispose someone to adopt more of a life of thought than of action.

Such officials might be called tribal archivists, provided allowance is made for their more verbal and extroverted activities as compared to literate archivists in the American emic view. Tribal archivists have responsibility for such concrete and communal expressions of the tribal identity as calendrical records, winter counts, wampum belts, power packs (mystic bundles), myths, rituals, and the care of sacred shrine areas. Of course, the real function of these archivists is to maintain, perpetuate, and reconstitute, for each new generation, the tribal culture especially through the framework of its mytho-logic.

There is, however, also another locus for Native anthropologists in tribal societies. At one extreme are the valued intellectuals who function as officials and archivists. At the other are those who are marginals, inepts, deviants, or misfits. Native anthropologists have an acute sense of some of the range of human similarity and difference. Their perspective is comparative, holistic, and removed. Such a perspective also contributes much toward effective leadership. Each leader should work from an operational model that accounts for the greatest range of variation in his society if he is to avoid alienating any part of the constituency. A strong component of this variation is the marginals who are either tolerated or tacitly ignored by most members of the society. As marginals who have not yet been banished or killed (as witches) by the group, these individuals would have to know the rules and system sufficiently to dampen any latent hostility toward them and to avoid any offenses grievous enough to cause them harm or death. Marginals then quite expectedly have their own models of their society, albeit probably more tainted and troubled; less holistic than archivists.

Some of these deviants might also be Native anthropologists since their position would foster several attributes of this role, especially if they were involved in mixed marriages and multi-lingual circumstances. Parents with different backgrounds would expose their own and other children to comparative differences during the course of daily life. Children who grow up speaking several languages, in some situations, might have a marginal status that would encourage an anthropological solution to life as a survival or "coping" strategy.

But not all societies regard multi-cultural deviants as pariahs. Elite families in the Pacific Northwest were expected to intermarry across tribal, language, and ethnic boundaries in the same manner as the royal houses of Europe. The Chinook peoples of the Columbia River had such a strong mercantile orientation that they encouraged their children to gain fluency in as many other languages and cultures as possible during their lifetimes. Therefore, the Chinook valued varied outward ties in contrast to most other societies which emphasized inwardly directed relationships.

A widely reported feature of the historic (post-literate) period in Native America was the succession of a child from a White-Red marriage (or liaison) to a position of tribal leadership, the idea being that his (rarely her) mixed parentage gave understanding and access to both social systems. His followers hoped to benefit from this in terms of peaceful relations, trade goods, or successful battles and campaigns. Examples included William MacIntosh of the Lower Creeks, who was sentenced to death and executed by Creeks in 1825 for selling land to Americans, and Quanah Parker of the Kwahadi band of Comanches, who helped found the Little Moon Peyote Church. The most famous for all the Americas was El Inka Garcilaso de la Vega, who wrote classics of Spanish literature.

Leaders with an anthropological perspective are able to disseminate their cultural model among their followers so that it can be implemented in terms of objectified ideas in the events and behaviors of the society. Leaders can be considered societal magnets or foci who serve to integrate the disparate members and perspectives since their followers defer to their knowledge and ability.

Tribal leaders are often said to have a cosmic "secret" which legitimates their position. Whether or not they actually do, people think that they do and that is usually sufficient to provide a basis for politico-religious power. Among the meager data that survives from the extinct Calusa of southwestern Florida is the interesting report that when a Spanish Jesuit tried to convert the Calusa chieftain, this leader replied that a belief in the unity of the world and a single God was the exclusive "secret" of the Calusa royal line. He would not convert because his authority would crumble as a result: "Saying that in order to consolidate his position he must demonstrate that he possessed the traditional religious knowledge of a legitimate chief (Goggin and Sturtevant 1964:191)." Pueblo priests (*chaiyanyi* in Keresan) and Tlingit household leaders (*hitsati*) are said to have retained their "secrets" into the present.

Generally, deviants who are Native anthropologists generally have a less secure and influential position. But because they are known to be wise in a particular type of (often mystical) knowledge, people will patronize them for advice or occult aids to benefit often selfish motives. During periods of crisis and rapid change, both in Native America and elsewhere, some deviants have achieved exalted status as "prophets." Successful prophets seem to represent a peculiar blend of fortuitous timing, intuitive intelligence, crucial anthropological insights into the renewed functioning and manipulation of the social order, and some familiarity with the chain of command or access to authority.

Only a few of the plethora of Native American prophets can be considered, each with a strong regional impact. Examples include the Seneca holder of the Iroquois name-title of Handsome Lake; the Carrier man, who was the original Bini ("mind") among the Tsimshian; John Wilson (Moon-Head, Nishkantu), the Caddo-Delaware who founded the Big Moon Peyote Religion; the Wanapum Sahaptin sometimes called Smohalla, who founded the Washani religion; Wovoka (Jack Wilson) who initiated the 1890 Ghost Dance revival; and the Slocums, John and his wife Mary, who began the Indian Shaker Church in 1882, legally incorporated in 1910.

While academics can check statements against documents, archives, and other written records, an oral tradition can be susceptible to revisions and manipulations that can be imperceptible. All human traditions, however, have some kind of record keeping, often using artifacts as tokens and mnemonics. These range from massive panels of rock art to marked sticks. Via these tokens, possibly, continual refinements in archaeological analysis of these specialized artifacts might eventually provide clues about earlier prophetic movements, cultural shifts, or the impact of indigenous intellectual giants. Allowing for the vicissitudes of Native scholarship in the past, we can be certain that it remains represented in the esoteric lore and "secrets" of tribal archivists.

We can also achieve some sense of it by now turning to the literate tradition of Americanist research begun by Europeans. Similar accounts by Asians are harder to find, but equally likely. Brief treatments of some reputable scholars, men and women, Native and newcomer, will allow interested readers to follow such leads into areas of their own interest.

Within the Americanist tradition, there have always been different types of people, doing different types of activities. For this reason, the discussion is divided into four overlapping phases based on an interpretation of the motivations of the protagonists. In chronological order, these are Frontiersfolk, Genteel Scholars, Museum Scholars, and Academic Scholars. In the conclusion, we will take stock of the current status of the consensual basis of "reality" as it has been defined by Americanist research.

Frontiersfolk

The term 'frontiersfolk' refers to the conglomeration of explorers, missionaries, soldiers, trappers, slavers, and traders who expanded the frontier of European society at tribal expense in quest of fortune, fame, and family property. It is wrong to lump all Europeans under one heading since there certainly were cultural differences in style, values, and rapport between Natives and Europeans of varying backgrounds.

The history of the American frontier represents the emergence of European-style nation-states on the American continent. The factors involved were the quest for souls, slaves, gold, and furs in addition to the exploitation of land, water, and timber.[1] Native Americans accommodation to European models, their fall from grace, began with increasing adoption of metal, cloth, and other trade goods, especially the gun, so that after a generation or two, the Natives were locked into a dependency relationship with trading posts and gunsmiths. The relationship required the exchange of money rather than goods or services. Eventually, Natives, like other workers, were laboring less to feed and clothe themselves and more to trap animal pelts, to mine minerals, or to grow crops for the money needed to participate in the European-cum-American world.

As the colonial world shifted, allegiances had to shift also. It is simplistic to say that Europeans abused Natives or the reverse. Rather, there were complex interchanges among tribes, colonies, countries, and individuals which reflected their vested interests and diverse cultural strategies. Among the eddies in history were people and groups who refused to recognize change, who sought to return to their pristine state under the guidance of a prophet, and who fought back. The changes were more intense and radical for the Natives since the settlers controlled new or desirable values. Such changes were harder on men than on women, since females had the ongoing stability of housekeeping roles, although their children died more often and their houses changed styles and construction materials.

The initial stages of change centered on the trade in Native resources for European goods, in some cases, abetted by soldiers. Traders were the initial agents of change; control of a trading network guaranteed prominence. The strength of the Iroquois Confederacy rested on its role as middlemen in the beaver fur trade between the interior Natives and coastal settlers; their astute "playing-off" of English, Dutch, and French interests for their own benefit; and their collusion with colonial authorities against the interests of other East Coast tribes.

Only after traders had forged channels of communication through intermarriages, trade languages (pidgins), and Native dependence on the gun were there sufficient cultural and conceptual changes for missionaries to begin making converts. Colonial authority became the American, Mexican, and Canadian nation-states, with tribal autonomy subverted in the process. As a general rule, tribal institutions have shifted toward European ones in an accumulative sequence that ranges from the economic, through the social and political, to the more impervious religious and linguistic institutions. Indigenous languages have frequently been the last cultural feature to change or die.

The Spanish left an imprint on the genetics and culture of Mexico that is reflected in the Mestizo population and the *encomienda* system. The French left behind the Metis population in Canada, as well as the Cajuns in Louisiana. The Russian influence on Alaskan Tlingit and California Pomo tribes was slight, though the Aleutians include a mixed population known as Creoles. The English were generally more remote and legalistic, leaving in their wake numerous laws, treaties, American reservations, and Canadian reserves.

While Canadian reserves usually coincide with aboriginal homelands, Canadian Natives had to deal with a legal definition that formerly only granted Indien status to children of a Native father but denied Indien status to a Native woman and her children if she married a non-Native. Revisions to the Indian Act, governing Canadian First Nations, and Law C31 (1985) have since made a band's membership their own decision.

Against this general backdrop were projected the various personnel of the different European nation-states. The major thrust of European colonization was the fur trade: beaver skins bound across the Atlantic to Europe for hats and sea otter taken across the Pacific to China for robes. Later, bison hides and bones were shipped to the Northeast to become machine drive belts and flower fertilizer. The assault was therefore both economic and conceptual, since the symbolic value of the economy and the fungibility (interchange-ability) of money are crucial to European societies. In the East, the original use of wampum beads as an objectified pledge of sincerity became converted into a form of currency under European modes.

We cannot rule out early Asian influences through Trans-Pacific contacts and colonies, but the evidence for Trans-Atlantic contacts is stronger in terms of Norse exploration between 700–1100 A.D. and at the archaeological site at L'Anse au Meadow, Newfoundland, which has been equated with the semi-legendary Vineland. Suspicious gaps in the records of the City of Bristol in the 1300s suggest its men were cod fishing off the Grand Banks of Newfoundland.

Spanish

The socially constructed history of America begins with the arrival of Christopher Colon (Columbus) and Spanish claims to priority. Leaving from Spanish colonies in Cuba, Hernando Cortez and his small band of conquistadors took the Aztec capital in 1519 considerably aided by Native allies disaffected with the Aztecs and by traumatic epidemics. Intellectually, however, we are much more indebted to Bernal Diaz de Castillo for his *True History of the Conquest of New Spain*, a description of the campaign and Aztec society written in idiomatic Spanish.

From new settlements in Mexico, expeditions were sent north in quest of reported riches and souls, as well as slaves. About 1540, the Coronado Expedition traveled through present New Mexico and the Kansas plains, giving us early descriptions of Pueblo, Plains Village, and other tribes, in addition to novel animals such as the bison. Hernando de Soto (1539–1546) provided early descriptions of Southeastern peoples, establishing a baseline for understanding the devastating collapse of chiefdoms into mangled tribes of the historic period. The lower coast of California was explored by Juan Rodriguez Cabrillo in 1539. Many Spanish records do not survive in the originals, but instead were copied (plagiarized in modern terms) heavily in official reports, such as the *General and Natural History of the Indies ~ Historia General y Natural de las Indias* (partially published 1526, Toledo, 1535, Seville, fully 1855, Madrid) by Fernandez de Oviedo y Valdes (1478–1557).

Aside from such bravado, the best contribution to our understanding came from scribes such as Castillo or the accounts of clergy such as Father Bertalome de las Casas (1474–1566), who authored *In Defense of the Indians* (Casas 1552) and other tracts which helped to convince Catholic authorities that *indios* were human and had souls. De las Casas, in *Apologetica Historia ~ In Defense of the Indians*, also mentioned Ramon Pane, a priest from the 1493 second Columbus voyage who made the first record of a native religion, in this case the Arawak of Haiti, whose concept of *zemis* simultaneously referred to a building, idol, and power effusion (Bourne 1906). With the exploration and settlement of La Florida, other coastal chiefdoms such as the Calusa and Timucua enter the written record.

In the Papal Bull of 1537, Pope Paul III said *indios* had souls and should not be treated as work animals in Spanish mines and haciendas. In consequence, malaria-immune African slaves were imported from West Africa to replace *indios* as the labor pool. All human societies are ethnocentric enough to deny full human status to foreigners, as Americans recently did to the Viet Cong and Vietnamese in their own country. Therefore, de las Casas was not changing the Spanish definition of humanity, but only manipulating it to include Natives. He only expanded the definition and used it to legitimate the work he and others were doing to convert the Natives to Catholicism or other forms of Christianity. Since *indios* had souls, they could become Christians. In modern Spanish, the term *cristiano/a* is synonymous with 'person,' to be Christian is to be a person.

The most impressive ethnography from colonial Mexico is the *General History of the Things of New Spain ~ Florentine Codex*, in both Spanish and Nahuatl (Aztec), by native scribes and block print illustrations done by Native artists in the workshop of Father Bernardino de Sahagun (1579).

Early observations of Nootkan and Californian Natives are scattered in the accounts of Spanish settlers who occupied Nootka Sound on Vancouver Island in 1789 and others who established the string of California presidios and 21 missions built between 1769–1823 from San Diego to Sonoma to support and protect the Manilla Galleon (1565–1815). In Spain, a theoretical coup was struck by Father Jose de Acosta in 1588 when he correctly deduced that Natives probably entered the New World via a northern passage from Tartar (Siberia). True to his Bible, however, he decided that the animals and plants they encountered in their new home had been left there by the Ark.

French

The 1524 voyage of Giovanni da Verrazano (1485–1527) instigated French claims in the Northeast. Inland exploration was then undertaken by Samuel Champlain along the St. Lawrence River in 1603 before he founded Quebec in 1608. Large native populations for New England (called Nurumbaga by the French) were soon to be devastated by epidemics in 1618. Also in Champlain's wake came lower class recruits working in the fur trade, who lived with natives to save expenses. Traders formed "a complex hierarchy of *voyageurs, coureurs de bois, hivernants,* and *manageurs de land,* under the direction of the *commis* or *bourgeois*" (Holder 1970:7, 8).

Of special ethnographic relevance were the French Jesuit missions to the Huron, Iroquois, and other Northeastern tribes. Each priest submitted an annual report on his labors in New France, to be distributed in France to raise money and goodwill for the missions. These reports over the period 1610–1791 have been collected into seventy-odd volumes known as the *Jesuit Relations* which abound in useful ethnographic information, especially on the Hurons who survive into the present only as widely-scattered Wyandot communities. Huron life before their 1649 devastation has been reconstructed from these reports (see Tooker 1964; Trigger 1969).

Father Joseph Lafitau (1685–1740) correctly described the form of Iroquois matrilineality and, in 1724, compared American Natives to primitive Europeans (Honigmann 1976:86). Iroquois matrilineality has been a recurrent "discovery" throughout the Americanist tradition. French soldiers and traders have left us accounts from the Louisiana colonies that include data on Southeastern chiefdoms such as the Natchez.

Russians

Russian claims to the Pacific coast of America stem from the 1741 voyage of Vitus Bering. The German naturalist along was Georg Stellar, who named and described Arctic species in Latin. Russians colonized Alaska and built a trading post (Fort Ross) in 1812 on the Russian River in California. Fort Ross was sold to John Sutter in 1848, who owned a huge empire based on native labor. Discovery of gold on his Sacramento lands precipitated the California Gold Rush (1849–1851), which became lethal to many natives. The Russian fur trade was originally handled by the ruthless roustabouts called *promishleniki* until the Russian-American Company was established by imperial Charter of the Czar in 1749. Our earliest full Native American ethnography is the 1840 description of the Aleut, with some notes on Tlingit, by Ivan Veniaminov, a Russian Orthodox priest who later became the Metropolitan of Moscow (a pope-like status) and has been canonized by his church as St. Innocent (on 6 October 1977).

British

John Cabot (born Giovanni Caboto in Italy)[2] explored the northern Atlantic coast for Britain in 1497. After Henry Hudson claimed the Hudson (then called North) River for the Netherlands on his 1609 voyage, he sailed under the British flag in 1610–1611 when he discovered Hudson Bay, where his crew mutinied and set him, his son, and loyal crew adrift in these icy waters. Sir Francis Drake explored the California coast in 1528 while plundering Spanish galleons. James Cook (in 1778) and George Vancouver (in 1792) mounted famous British scientific expeditions which circumnavigated the globe in quest of knowledge and advantages. The Cook voyage brought the sea otter pelts from Nootka Sound to Canton, China, which initiated the lucrative global trade in sea otter skins that reduced them to an endangered species.

British interests in North America prospered and expanded as a result of military victories in Europe and America. The Dutch surrendered New York City in 1664 when British Indian policy was put into the hands of such capable men as Sir William Johnson (1715–1774), who wrote an account of the Iroquois for the American Philosophical Society in 1772. He also encouraged the careers of Mohawk siblings, Joseph and Molly Brant. Molly was a clan matron and his "wife," while Joseph translated Church of England liturgy into Mohawk. British policy favored the Iroquois and Cherokee, but only in terms of European legalistic and exclusion attitudes.

Unlike the French and Spanish who readily mixed with Natives, the British had to offer financial rewards in 1719 to encourage British-Native marriages. Patrick Henry ("Give me liberty or give me death") introduced a bill into the 1784 Virginia House of Delegates to provide free education, tax relief, and money for the children of anyone who would marry an Indien (Sheehan 1973: 175). However, when two educated Cherokee men married white women in Cornwall, Connecticut, the town rose up and the local Indian school was closed. One of these men adopted the name of his patron, Elias Boudinot (1802–1839), and became a famous Cherokee newspaperman. One grievance behind the American Revolution may have been settler indignation over the Treaty of Easton (1756) in which the British tried to safeguard their Native allies by halting any European settlement west of the Allegheny Mountains. The Royal Proclamation of 7 October 1763 defined Native rights as original land owners, and remains a mainstay of Canadian Law. The political context for this move was French defeat and withdrawal, and the unsuccessful Pontiac Rebellion (1763) attacking British forts.

Samson Occum, an ordained Mohican, served Native converts around Connecticut and Long Island. He was educated at Reverend Eleazar Wheelock's Charity School at Lebanon and Hebron, Connecticut, and sent on a fund-raising tour of England (1765–1767), where he raised 11,000 pounds for Native education. Wheelock used the money, however, to found Dartmouth College (1769). Occum opposed this diversion of funds, but he was overruled. Despite a bout with alcoholism, Occum was able to gather together many of the Native converts from the New York metropolitan area and to join them with the New Jersey Brothertons, then living with the Oneida Iroquois near Lake Oneida, New York. Eventually, they all relocated near Green Bay, Wisconsin. Occum felt these moves were necessary to protect the converts from the bad influence of local settlers. Illegalities of this move have allowed Oneidas to reclaim some of their ancient homeland in central New York.

Autobiographies of famous Midwest chiefs, such as Black Hawk, were dictated to writers, often school teachers. Later, Warren Whipple wrote a history of his Ojibway (Chippewa) people, as did John Joseph Mathews for the Osages, one of the finest blendings of written and oral sources available. Natives who early earned degrees in anthropology include the Rev Henry Roe Cloud (HoChunk), tragic William Jones, a Fox (Mesquakie) (see below), and Edward Dozier (Tewa).

Artists

In addition to the information that can be gleaned from these and other frontier writers, a wealth of more detailed information lies in the pictorial record left by frontier artists. Many are major figures in the Americanist tradition. Our record for the southeast begins with the paintings of Jacques Le Moyne (folio done in 1564–1665) and John White (folio in 1585–1593). Paul Kane (1810–1871) traveled through the Northwest in 1846–1847. The Plains peoples were documented by George Catlin (1796–1892) especially for the Mandan, by Alfred Jacob Miller (1810–1874), and by Karl Bodmer (1809–1893), who traveled through the upper Missouri with Maximillian Alexander Philip, Prinz Von Wied-Neuwied in 1833.

For the Northwest, depictions begin with the Spanish, such as Atanasio Echeverria and Jose Mariano Moziño at Nootka Sound. George Vancouver explored with Henry Humprys (1774–1799), Thomas Heddington (1774–1852), John Sykes (1773–1858), and Zachary Mudge (1770–1852). Sponsored by the Hudson's Bay Company, Paul Kane (1810–1871) sketched and painted the Northwest (1845–1918). George Gibbs (1816–1873), linguist and ethnographer in the Northwest, 1849–1860, was also a sketch artist, while James Swan (1818–1900) worked in watercolors, with many now at Yale.

Important photographic collections were made by William Henry Jackson (1843–1942) for the Plains, by John Hillars (1843–1925) for the Great Basin, and by Edward Curtis (1868–1952) for most of Native America, though he sometimes added props or airbrushed out modern details.

Genteel Scholars

The genteel scholars, therefore, were primarily theoreticians studying Americanist data for insights into the overall human condition, especially as it related to their own philosophical positions. Their contribution to our intellectual endeavor was to generalize from the specific to the global.

Americanist genteel scholarship has its roots in European intellectualism: wealthy European scholars who were analyzing eye-witness ethnographic accounts to achieve our early theoretical and comparative insights. In his *Second Treatise on Government* (1689), John Locke expressed the perennial European fascination with America: "in the beginning all the world was

America." There one could study the original, unencumbered human condition before literacy and divine-right kingship overwhelmed it. Jean-Jacques Rousseau (1712–1778) based his model upon reports by frontier folk of humans living in a state of nature (Noble Savages), before the Social Contract bound them to a ruler.

The key Americanist genteel scholar was Thomas Jefferson (1743–1826). He personally initiated the earliest rigorous archaeological, linguistic, and ethnographic research—or else arranged to have it done by his African slaves. His close associates made equally significant contributions. Jefferson tried to develop and foster a philanthropic program for the benefit of Natives, but it was doomed to failure since it concentrated on individuals rather than on the communal or tribal context. For a time, the only successful exemplars of his program were the Cherokees.

Jefferson intended a program of gradual Native accommodation to "civilization" and "improvement" that moved from the acquisition of domestic animals and farming, through training in household arts, private property, money, arithmetic, and writing. They were encouraged to read, initially, popular books and, later, religious and moral texts (Sheehan 1973:125).

Jefferson was a protagonist in two controversies important for the growth and development of the Americanist Tradition, as well as sustaining his own researches. As Minister to France (1785–1789), Jefferson participated in the European intellectual scene. Shortly after, he was drawn into a Trans-Atlantic debate with Georges Louis Leclerc (Compte de Buffon, 1707–1788), who wrote in his monumental *Natural History* (1791) that American Natives were never a developed "civilization" because the American soil had inherently defective "vapors," supporting only small animals and child-like people with small genitals. Because he was a patriot, Jefferson marshaled contrary evidence, mentioning gigantic animals and sexual ardor in his *Notes on the State of Virginia* (Jefferson 1785). If Buffon had been correct, then the inherent deficiency would have also affected the settlers, as it was supposed to have affected the Natives. This would have been a blow to Jefferson's and other patriots' pride in American vitality, ingenuity, expansion, and success.

Jefferson became embroiled in a second controversy centering on the so-called Mound Builders, who were said to be a "superior race" destroyed by American Natives. As settlers began to plow up the Northeast, especially the Ohio River Valley, they leveled thousands of huge earthen mounds containing human remains and exquisite artifacts made of stone, mica, copper, and clay. The settlers began to argue that such artifacts indicated a technology that must have belonged to a group, superior to the Natives, who came to be called the Mound Builders. Several intellectuals, in contrast, felt that the Mound Builders were the ancestors of historic Natives. Jefferson "undersaw" the systematic excavation of one such mound (by his slaves) on his own Virginia plantation and established to his satisfaction an unbroken continuity between the earliest burials and the most recent ones. Further, survivors of Virginia tribes continued to visit this mound, bringing its recognition into the present.

It required, however, the extensive later work of men like Ephraim George Squier and Edwin Davis, before they fell out, and federally funded excavations under Cyrus Thomas to discredit the popular image of a distinct "race" of Mound Builders. Even so, one can still find rural Eastern farmers who are not yet convinced. What is even more to the point is that historic Southeastern confederacies, survivors of chiefdoms menaced by de Soto, continued using platform earth mounds for temples and the houses of chieftains at the very same time that early settlers were speculating about the Mound Builders. The French knew of the use of mounds by the Natchez, as did the British for the Cherokees and Creeks. Yet somehow this continual use of mounds, though smaller in scale, went unnoticed or ignored by most people in the Northeast.

Jefferson is further noteworthy for his detailed set of instructions to the Lewis and Clark (1804–1806) Expedition, during his presidency (1801–1809). Lewis and Clark were told to collect all possible linguistic and ethnographic data, including choice artifacts. Jefferson also assisted Ben

Franklin in the founding of the American Philosophical Society (1743) at Philadelphia, which remains a major vault for Americanist data. Jefferson had intended to analyze, after his retirement, the linguistic material collected by Lewis and Clark and other sources, but the stout trunk holding these materials was stolen from the banks of the Potomac while awaiting transport to Monticello, Jefferson's Virginia plantation. A very few pages washed up on the river bank, preserving almost all of the data we have for the Molala language of Oregon.

Linguistic studies were embraced by Jefferson's friend, Albert Gallatin (1761–1849), who was Secretary of the Treasury (1801–1813). He sent out questionnaires to frontiersfolk in order to collect 600-word vocabularies in many Native languages. His analysis of these resulted in the first major classification of Native language stocks: *A Synopsis of the Indian Tribes within the United States East of the Rocky Mountains, and in the British and Russian Possessions in North America* (Gallatin 1836). This work was later augmented by the studies of Horatio Hale and Albert Gatschet before linguistics became a distinct academic profession.

Protestant missionaries tended to use a standardized series of characters devised by John Pickering to transcribe Native languages so as to publish Christian scriptures. While a valiant attempt, the Pickering system was entirely too rigid to accurately record the diverse languages of Native America. Catholic missionaries, on the other hand, often spoke several European languages, giving them more linguistic sensitivity. Usually, they preferred to devise a special writing system for each language. Among early scholars, genuine insights into the grammar and philology of Native languages were provided by the work of Peter Duponceau at the American Philosophical Society.[3]

Many conclusions have not withstood the test of time as more information became available, but some attempts did have a wide popularity. In *History of the American Indians* (1775), John Adair wrote about his observations as a trader among the Chickasaw and other Southeastern tribes, drafting his book while living in a native village now under Tupelo, Mississippi.[4] While his data are generally considered to be reliable, he presented them as aspects of a detailed comparison between Natives and Biblical Hebrews to prove that Natives were descended from the Lost Tribes of Israel. While such a theory has some appeal for some Christians, it is preposterous. Nonetheless, this notion still haunts the American consciousness, as evidenced by some folk beliefs and the 1970s movie "Cat Ballou." Other theories derived Natives from a lost Alexandrian Greek fleet or a twelfth century Welsh band led by a prince called Madoc.

But not all influence went from settlers to Natives in colonial America. During the Albany Convention of 1754, one Iroquois Chief explained the functioning of the League of the Iroquois to Ben Franklin. Some say Franklin was inspired to base the American bicameral Congress on the Iroquois Leagues division into Federal Chiefs (royaner) of the 50 name-titles (cf. the Senate) and into Merit (Pine Tree) Chiefs of variable numbers (cf. the House). Despite all this cooperation, it was also Franklin who advocated the use of hunting dogs to track down "wild or bad" Natives who opposed the Americans.

Important successors to Jefferson were Henry Schoolcraft (1793–1864) and Lewis Henry Morgan (1818–1881). Schoolcraft became Superintendent of the Sault Ste Marie Chippewa Agency (1832–1841) where he was befriended by the local trader, John Johnson. Intent on making discoveries, he traced the Mississippi to its headwaters, which he named Itasca (from the Latin verITAS CAput). In time, Schoolcraft married Jane, a Johnson daughter who had both been raised in the Chippewa (Ojibwa) traditions and language of her mother and educated in England. Schoolcraft also learned the Ojibwa language, publishing a grammar and a folklore collection. In explaining the Ojibwa concept of the *dodem*, he introduced the seminal topic of the totem and totemism to the literate world. His second wife, a biased Southern lady, thwarted these earlier cross-cultural efforts.

In addition to a successful political career, Schoolcraft extended his studies to other Algic (Algonquian) tribes related to the Chippewa-Ojibwa and published his work as *Algic Researches* (1839). Henry Wadsworth Longfellow read it and wrote a poem, inspired by the Finnish national epic, the *Kalavala*, blending it with features from the Chippewa Charter Myth. He chose instead to name his hero after one of the founders of the Iroquois Confederacy: Hiyawantha (Hiawatha). Schoolcraft also rediscovered Iroquois matrilineality.

A paralysis that left him an invalid occurred in the same year that his major work was published in six quarto volumes: *Historical and Statistical Information Respecting the History, Condition and Prospects of the Indian Tribes of the United States, Collected and Prepared Under the Direction of the Bureau of Indian Affairs* (Schoolcraft 1851). For all of his valid information, it was also Schoolcraft who did much to popularize the saccharine, romanticized image of the Native through his collection of legends called *Oneonta: the Indian in His Wigwam* (Schoolcraft 1844).

Another view of Great Lakes traditions was provided by William Whipple Warren (1825–1853), an Ojibwa Metis ("mixed-blood"), who wrote *History of the Ojibways, Based upon Tradition and Oral Statements* (Warren 1855) which is based on interviews conducted in his own language. This work is all the more remarkable because Warren died at the age of 28, after marriage, 4 children, and election to the Minnesota legislature.

Lewis Henry Morgan has been called the father of American anthropology for his monumental contributions to the emerging field. He began his career as a lawyer in Syracuse, New York where he belonged to a men's club called the Gordian Knot. Another member was Ely Parker, a Seneca Iroquois who was a soldier and civil engineer, before he later became the first Native Commissioner of Indian Affairs and holder of the Seneca Iroquois Federal Chief name-title "Holds The Door Open." Parker and Morgan revamped the club to imitate the Iroquois Confederacy. Morgan's curiosity was piqued such that he visited the Seneca reserve near Buffalo, staying with the Parker family and collecting data for a comprehensive ethnography: *The League of the Iroquois* (Morgan 1851). While this study is often called the first Americanist ethnography, it came out a decade after that by Rev. Ivan Veniaminov (St. Innocent) in Russian. Morgan did, however, provide the first one in English.

Fascinated by the intricacies of kinship, especially matrilineality, Morgan used the personal wealth he amassed from investments in Western railroads to tour the West in 1859, collecting data on kinship and social organization from representatives of numerous tribes. While he was enroute, he received word that his daughters were gravely ill. Knowing that he could not return before they died, he continued his journey. Such was his dedication to scholarship that he turned a personal tragedy into an ethnographic triumph from which we have all benefited.

Later his kinship questionnaire was sent around the world by the U.S., producing the data for his comprehensive *Systems of Consanguinity and Affinity of the Human Family* (Morgan 1871). He later expanded on the links he perceived between kinship terminologies and social organizations by publishing *Ancient Society* (Morgan 1877), which was supposed to trace the salient characteristics that distinguished "savagery," "barbarism, and "civilization." Lower Savagery became Middle Savagery with the addition of fire, Upper Savagery with the addition of the bow, Lower Barbarism with pottery and farming, Middle Barbarism with domesticated animals, Upper Barbarism with iron tools, and Civilization with writing. While the data he assembled remains valid, his schema is not because it was both racist and too constrictive. While anthropologists now distinguish six types of cousin terminologies—of which five occur in North America (Hawaiian, Eskimo, Iroquois, Crow, and Omaha) and one (Sudanese) does not—the initial contributions of Morgan to kinship, the framing skeleton of all human societies, are justly famous.

Museum Scholars

These men were largely self-trained anthropologists motivated to preserve and understand the tangible evidences of North Amrican tribes they perceived to be dying out. Museums were the first institutions to hire people to be Americanist anthropologists and archaeologists. Hence many early ethnographers began their careers as museum geologists, marine biologists, ornithologists, and other natural scientists who were assigned new ethnographic duties.

Aside from being independently wealthy like Morgan or having another income like Schoolcraft, museum employment was the earliest way to support an anthropological career. The collection of "things" (long before artifacts became recognized as objectified ideas) by outsiders in a "cabinets of curiosities" led to the development of museums, which encouraged the training of professionals to assemble, study, preserve, and describe these relics of a "vanishing" people.

Two key museum Americanists were Frederick Ward Putnam (1839–1915) and Major John Wesley Powell (1834–1902).

Putnam organized the anthropological collections of the Peabody Museum at Harvard, the 1893 Chicago Columbian Exposition (which became the Field Museum); the American Museum of Natural History in New York; and the Museum of Anthropology, Parnassus Heights, San Francisco (now at University of California, Berkeley). Much of the actual labor involved was apparently done by his "boys"—amateurs and professionals loyal to him. Among these were such well-known anthropologists as Franz Boas, Frank Speck, Mark Harrington, and Arthur Parker. Parker (1881–1955) was a grand nephew of Ely Parker (see above) and a professional noted for his work in museology and in Iroquoian archaeology and ethnology.

Putnam helped finance the excavation of some important American archaeological sites, especially mid-western mounds, which produced spectacular copper, shell, and stone artifacts to enhance both his own fame and museum collections. He also led the drive to purchase and preserve Serpent Mound in Ohio by Boston ladies.

Likewise, his 12-year-support of George Volk's excavations around Trenton, New Jersey, helped to settle the so-called Abbott Farm controversy. In 1873, Charles Abbott, a Trenton physician inspired by ancient finds in France, claimed he had found Paleolithic stone tools in the gravel deposits on his farm. Such finds were creating much attention in Europe, so Americanists were hoping to find similar evidence in the New World to show that the Americas had an equally great antiquity of human occupation. The work of Volk and others such as Leslie Spier denied the antiquity of the Trenton artifacts, determining instead that they were roughed-outs blanks intended for more carefully finished knapping. Putnam also trained William Jones, a Fox (Mesquakie), who received a Ph.D from Harvard.

Jones did fieldwork among various Algic tribes and then, from Chicago, began research in the Philippines where he was killed; toward the end of his stay, he threatened members of the tribal community he was studying to have them finish some museum specimens and he was beheaded in the ensuing argument. In time, Jones's notes were taken up by Edward Dozier, a Tewa with a Ph.D in anthropology who worked in both the Philipines and the Southwest. Initially he was told that objective science prevented him from researching in his own community, but the value of his connections and intuitions eventually won out.

John Wesley Powell is the more important figure because of his leadership of the Bureau of American Ethnology (BAE, 1879–1964), which encouraged the research and publication of detailed ethnographies in numerous massive reports and bulletins of the bureau. Powell lost his right forearm at the Battle of Shiloh but went on to become nationally famous for his exploratory rafting down the Colorado River, the last "blank spot" on the map of the U.S. His fieldwork concentrated on the Numic tribes in the Great Basin, although his notes long went unpublished

(Fowler and Fowler 1971). Most recently, the Crum family has done much to expand our appreciation by providing a collection of lyrical *Hewe Hupia* ~ Shoshoni poetry songs (Crum, Crum and Dayley 2001) and a general history (Crum 1994).

Powell spent much of his time as director juggling various monies to maintain funding for the bureau. One such juggling left Franz Boas jobless for over a year. Powell's commitment to "science" included a bet with WJ McGee (always without punctuation, an affectation), his friend and thwarted successor, as to which of their brains were larger. Rumor has it that McGee won by a fraction of an ounce. An analysis of Powell's brain has been published (Spitzka 1903).

After Powell, directors of the bureau were William H. Holmes (1902–1910), Frederick Hodge (1910–1918), Jesse Walter Fewkes (1918–1928), and Matthew Sterling (1928–1964).

The bureau employed several women and Natives, who often worked together. J.N.B. Hewitt, a Tuscarora, continued the Iroquoianist work of his colleague, Erminnie Smith, after her death. Hewitt, a meticulous scholar who rarely published, remained critical of the hasty work of Arthur Parker, a Seneca. While he was known to refer to "anthropologists and other suspicious characters" (Judd 1967:51), Hewitt was an energetic fieldworker, especially among the Iroquois. After a lifetime, Hewitt (1920:543–544) summarized his findings, providing strong support for the importance of gender symbolism among the Iroquois. Their tribal unity was based on this complementarily since the Iroquois Confederacy was "endowed with definite biotic properties and functions, as the male and female sexes, fatherhood and motherhood, mind, eyesight, dream power, human blood, and the possession of guardian spirits for its two highest organic members: man and woman." Hewitt further clarified that the Great Beings were "man-beings" (males) and "woman-man beings" (females), nicely catching their exclusive and inclusive relationships.

Other bureau employees were Alice Fletcher (1838–1923) and her adopted Omaha son, Francis La Flesche (1857–1932), who published together on Plains rituals and society, especially for the Omaha, Osage, and Pawnee. La Flesche also wrote a classic account of his boyhood at an Indian boarding school: *The Middle Five* (La Flesche 1963). Other women at the bureau were Matilda Coxe Stevenson (1850–1915), who aggressively studied the Pueblos, particularly Zuni and Sia, and Francis Densmore (1867–1957), who recorded and analyzed Native songs and music for over 50 years; and Densmore published on about 2,400 songs (Lurie 1966; Hofman 1968) in a dozen BAE bulletins, calling attention to the profound belief in the importance of song as a measure for the pulse of the universe.

Hers was a tremendous insight. The native world was and is possessed and permeated by song; there were "songs with games, dances, legends, and folk stories, but those phases of their music were apart from its chief function—their communication with the supernatural, through which they believed that they could secure aid in every undertaking" (Densmore 1953:223). Songs are expressions of knowledge, power, and life. After one old man recorded his vision song for Densmore (Densmore 1953:220), "he bowed his head and said tremulously that he thought he would not live long as he had parted with his most precious possession." Another man offered to put his song on tape, saying it would bring the rain whenever it was played back and so, for a price, was willing to share his song for the benefit of others (Densmore 1953:220).

The invention of recording equipment encouraged research on native music. In addition to the voluminous work of Densmore, Alice Fletcher recorded Omaha songs before 1884, Franz Boas collected Inuit music in 1883-1884, Jesse Walter Fewkes preserved Passamaquoddy songs in 1890, and James and Charles Mooney taped many southern Plains songs in 1894. More recent work, by scholars who have come to be called ethnomusicologists, includes the efforts of Willard Rhodes, David McAllister, and Gertrude Kurath.

Men who worked for the BAE included James Mooney and John Peabody Harrington. Mooney published extensively on the Cherokee and the Plains Ghost Dance. He correctly understood this prophetic movement as the reaction of defeated and invaded people. This insight owed much to his own Irish ancestry, career as a newspaper reporter, and strong Irish nationalism. Harrington was a brilliant and prolific linguist, but, as his former wife (Laird 1975) makes clear, he was often insensitive, rude, and oblivious to those around him, including Natives. He is a classic example of how the all-consuming quest for data (before it disappears) can further warp some individuals and become an obsession for others. He published only when forced by his bosses to finish a manuscript, yet his thousands of fieldnote pages recover lost languages and traditions across the Americas.

The most important publications of the BAE are the *Handbook of North American Indians* (BAE-Bulletin 30, in two volumes: A–M (Hodge 1906) and N–Z (Hodge 1910), *Classification of Native Languages* by Powell; *Games of the North American Indians* by Culin; *The Ghost Dance Religion* by James Mooney; the linguistic bibliographies of source documents by James Pilling on Eskimo, Siouian, Iroquoian, Muskhogean, Algonquian, Athapaskan, Chinookan, Salishan, and Wakashan; and the full ethnographies of many Great Lakes, Plains, and Southwestern tribes.

While the bureau staff was mostly concerned with descriptions and classification, two other museum-based scholars were more speculative: Otis Tufton Mason (1838–1908) and Daniel Garrison Brinton (1837–1899).

At the United States National Museum, Mason was noted for his research into the process of invention, especially of types of fire-making equipment around the world. His classification of Native America into twelve ethnic environments was one of the first to recognize the limiting and permissive role of ecology, countering erroneous but then popular ideas about environmental determinism. These dozen were the Arctic, Yukon-Mackenzie, St. Lawrence and Lake, Atlantic slope, Gulf coast, Mississippi valley, Plains, North Pacific Coast, Interior Basin, California-Oregon, and Pueblo (in Hodge 1906, 427–430). Mason's book, *Women's Share in Primitive Culture* (1894), is an enduring statement on the global significance of female roles and tasks.

Brinton trained as a physician, but became increasingly interested in a broad definition of anthropology and in Native, particularly Delaware and Mayan, literature. To his detriment, Brinton tried to assert "the" characteristic feature of all Native languages, an intention that was at best superficial and at worst impossible. He argued that this was "incorporation," the subordination of other grammatical features to the verb stem by means of abbreviation, contraction, or addition. Congruent with his era, he made evolutionary pronouncements based on his interpretation of language forms, such as considering "incorporation" inferior to the "inflection" characteristic of European languages. A Swiss-born contemporary, Albert Gatschet, also suggested that languages that had terminology for parts of speech were evolutionarily more advanced than languages that did not have such terminology. Nonsense such as this became prime targets for Franz Boas and his new generations of academic scholars in their initial attack on the ethnocentric theories that retarded the development of better evolutionary theory.[5]

Academic Scholars

Franz Boas (1859–1942) was indeed the indisputable university-based founding father. As a liberal German Jew, Boas was well prepared for the marginality and contradictions inherent in an anthropological career. Trained in physics and geography, his dissertation was on the coloration of sea water. He was converted to anthropology by a year-long fellowship to the Baffinland Eskimos of Cumberland Sound (1883–1884). While an assistant in the Berlin Museum of Ethnology (1885), he began linguistic work with some visiting Nuxalk (Bella Coola) and learned firsthand about the many vowelless words in this Salishan language.

Boas was ever after drawn to the Pacific Northwest, later concentrating on the Kwakiutl (Kwagyuł, kwakwakwa'wakw). His colleague was George Hunt of Kwakiutl and Tlingit ancestry. Among the Tsimshian, Boas, at first, relied on Henry Tate, whose work was marred by his commoner status, and of William Beynon, a Wolf semi-moiety chief who blossomed as a skilled Native anthropologist through his collaboration with Boas, Marius Barbeau, Viola Garfield, and others.[6]

Boas held an editorship at *Science* Magazine (1887), an academic appointment at Clark University (1888–1892), and museum positions at the Chicago Columbian Exposition (1893) and the American Museum of Natural History (1896–1899) before settling at Columbia University (1896–1936). He became curator at Chicago's Clark Field Museum (1894), which was the renamed 1893 exhibition building and permanent repository for the collected artifacts, but he lost this job to W.H. Holmes when the BAE budget was cut and Powell had to find a position for Holmes. Holmes later succeeded Powell at the BAE over the public objections of Boas and McGee. Despite some bitterness over his lost job, Boas used the bureau as a later outlet for some of his publications. He edited and published through the BAE the significant *Handbook of American Indian Languages*. Bulletin 40 consisted of part 1 (1911—grammars of Hupa, Tlingit, Haida, Tsimshian, Kwakiutl, Chinook, Maidu, Fox, Datoka, Eskimo) and part 2 (1922—Takelma, Coos, Lower Umpqua, Chuckchee). Published separately were part 3 (1933—Tonkawa, Quileute, Yuchi, Zuni, Coeur d'Alene) and part 4 (1941—Tunica).

Worthy successors and students of Boas particularly include Alfred Kroeber (1876–1960), known for *Handbook of the Indian of California* (BAE-Bulletin 78) and the awesome *Cultural and Natural Areas of Native North America* (1939); Ruth Benedict (1887–1948), associated with development of the Americanist focus on culture and personality and on configurationalism through her book *Patterns of Culture* (1934); and Edward Sapir (1884–1939), usually remembered as a multi-faceted, wide-ranging linguist. A strong Boasian ally was Elsie Clews Parsons (1875–1943)—heir to a fortune amassed by her father's association with J. Pierpont Morgan—prolific ethnographer of the Pueblos, and patron of folklore. Her *Pueblo Indian Religion* is a massive, two-volume compendium on the Southwest (Parsons 1939).

Many academic scholars are associated with a single tribe, language stock, or culture area. The following brief selection of the most famous of these, for convenience, is arranged by nine culture areas: **California**—Edward Gifford, Thomas Waterman, Alfred Kroeber; **Southwest**—Ruth Bunzel, Leslie White, Jesse Walter Fewkes, Elsie Parsons, Fred Eggan, Juan Delores (Papago), Edward Dozier (Santa Clara Pueblo), Alfonso Ortiz (San Juan Pueblo); **Great Basin**—Julian Steward (1902–1972), Omer Stewart (1908–1991), Tony Tillahash (Numa); **Plateau**—Verne Ray, H.H. Turney-High, Archie Phinney (Numipu); **Subarctic**—Cornelius Osgood; **Pacific Northwest**—Franz Boas, Homer George Hunt (Kwakiutl-Tlingit), William Beynon (Tsimshian), Homer Barnett, Philip Drucker, Erna Gunther; Viola Garfield, Wayne Suttles; **Plains**—Clark Wissler, James Murie (Skidi Pawnee), Robert Lowie, Leslie Spier, Ella Deloria (Nakota); **Northeast**—Frank Speck, Gladys Trantaquidgeon (Mohegan); and **Southeast**—John Swanton (at BAE), William Sturtevant, Raymond Fogelson.

More topically oriented academics include Harold Driver on the statistical treatment of Native American comparisons; Carl Voegelin on language classification; Stith Thompson on the typology and motifs index of Americanist folklore; Fred Eggan on kinship and social organization; and the Spindlers, George and Louise, on psychology and personality.

In a summary of personality types, an endlessly controversial topic, the Spindlers provided a listing of features that are fairly common among Natives:

> non-demonstrative emotionality and reserve accompanied by a high degree of control
> over interpersonal aggression within the in-group; a pattern of generosity that varies

greatly in the extent to which it is a formalized social service without emotional depth; autonomy of the individual, a trait linked with socio-political structure low in dominance-submission hierarchies; ability to endure pain, hardship, hunger, and frustration without emotional evidence of discomfort; a positive valuation of bravery and courage that varies sharply with respect to emphasis on highly aggressive daring in military exploit; a generalized fear [respect] of the world as dangerous, and particularly a fear of witchcraft; a "practical joker" strain that is nearly highly channelized institutionally, as in the common brother-in-law joking prerogative, and that appears to be a safety valve for in-group aggressions held sharply in check, attention to the concrete realities of the present . . . practicality, in contrast to abstract integration in terms of long-range goals; a dependence upon the supernatural power outside one's self—power that determines one's fate, which is expressed to and can be acquired by the individual through dreams, and for which the individual is not held personally accountable, at least not in the sense that one's "will" is accountable for one's acts in Western culture. (Spindler 1957:156)

In addition to these general features, there is also a specific injunction not to take gender attributes too literally, at least for the Myth Age. In a perceptive statement, Archie Phinney, a Nimíípuu (Nez Perce) educated in Russia, who collected and published folklore told to him by his own mother, remarked "The Indian does not visualize the characters of a tale as being animal or human. No clear picture is offered or needed. If such tangible features were introduced, a tale would lose its overtones of fantasy, its charm. To these personalities are attributed only a certain few necessary qualities and facilities or animal or human being" (Phinney 1934; ix).

With such native commentary to guide us, and with the background of this review, we can proceed further. Generally, the Americanist Tradition might be said to have been characterized by a continuous reanalysis of its comparative, holistic, and explicit aspects. It is comparative in the sense that we have gained a substantive understanding of tribal and areal patterns over time and in place. It is holistic in that researchers have more and more tried to comprehend and describe the full ramifications of a cultural system, even if they were focusing on only a particular aspect of it. Explicit with regard to the detached, balanced, detailed, coherent, and often insider (emic) presentation of information (although real insights are few and far between). Admittedly, these are only trends in the tradition, and individuals vary with regard to how closely their work represents these tendencies. In all, considerations of motivation, personality and process have influenced the social construction of Americanist reality.[7]

Theories

In terms of changing intellectual fashions or academic theories, Americanists began with a concern to record and preserve a record of languages, peoples, and customs that were rapidly becoming extinct. Salvage was therefore the first concern. Social Evolution was a second, from a racist, Eurocentric perspective that put colonialists on top. Culture History, local and regional developments from the archaeological to ethnographic (called the direct historical approach), was long a concern and seems to be coming back with more sophistication thanks to DNA tracings. Mainstream academic theories about functionalism, configurationalism, and culture and personality all had their vogue. Today native communities are supporting their own research for land claims, treaty rights, cultural resource management, and sovereignty. Academic concerns focus on personhood, world capitalist systems, ethnohistory, and ethnopoetics (analysis of linguistic aspects of aesthetics patterning). Ethnogenesis or the amalgamating of cultural survivors over time seems to be the present version of culture history. Complex excavations contributing to our understanding of Americanist prehistory have taken place at Windover in Florida, Ozette at the coastal tip of Washington State, Chaco Canyon in New Mexico, and Cahokia on the middle Mississippi near St. Louis. Using state archaeological databases to track the Hernando de Soto entrada has also been enormously informative.

As academics continue to specialize, relying on other disciplines for support, native communities have shown their own vitality by amassing their own interviews and archives with casino funds, and applying these data to reviving rituals and traditions from their past.

In all, because Franz Boas favored the Northwest Coast of the American Pacific, its people have come to occupy a central role in Americanist tradition. Early and important have been the active participation of those born in the Northwest, including enrolled Indiens, in continuing that tradition into the present. Since Seattle remains the last bastion of unadulterated Boasian research, though its survival is in doubt, this article serves as a reminder of what was, has been, and can be when the Northwest is reintegrated into the other culture areas of the Americas.

NOTES

[1] Naval stores of turpentine and wooden spars.

[2] Nations maintain specialized monopolies, such as Italian captains for exploring the newly-revealed new world. Today, global fiberoptic cable laying is dominated by British engineers.

[3] He distinguished these languages as agglutinative (blending together) vs. incorporative (adding on).

[4] Now famous as the birthplace of Elvis.

[5] A generally ignored aspect of the history of the Americanist tradition is the Culture Element Distribution survey which Kroeber started at Berkeley to concentrate on Native Californian data but which expanded to embrace most of Western Native America. The voluminous, if pigeon-holed, data which were collected appeared in the *Anthropological Records* series. Because such data are so disembodied, they remain of dubious value, although the occasional gem does stand out after laborious review.

[6] A key process involved in growing understanding is transculturation; adopting the culture of another society. Because many tribes have formal adoption procedures, captives were often successfully integrated into a community to the point where many white captives refused to return to Colonial society. Extreme examples of transculturation include Kateri Tekawitha, a Mohawk woman who followed an Iroquois penchant for mortification of the flesh after her conversion to Catholicism and who has been included in the roster of Roman Catholic saints, and Frank Hamilton Cushing, a bright but sickly BAE scholar who became a Zuni Bow Priest. Other transculturites are discussed by Hallowell (1963).

[7] In Canada the academic tradition included scholars of such high caliber as Diamond Jenness (1886–1969) and Marius Barbeau (1883–1969) at the Museum of Man in Ottawa.

AMERICANISTS CROSS PURPOSES ~ WAYS OF KNOWING

ABSTRACT

A conference of Canadians and Americans to discuss First Nations literature, oral and written, held at the only Northwest residential college, itself inspired by the ancient British model of Oxford and Cambridge, set into sharp focus the profoundly different if not opposed strategies for gaining and handling knowledge by academics vs. Native scholars. These principles of epistemology are assessed here in stark general terms because, there and then, two venerable and situated ways of knowing clearly stood out.

Attending the Green College (University of British Columbia) conference on native literature, both oral and rewritten, raised acute awareness of the profoundly opposing knowledge strategies of Natives vs. academics.

Distinguished scholars discussed their life's work in terms of gratuitously over-emphasized Western preoccupations with individuality and maximization, concentrating information in some amassed fashion, bagged and tagged in their own way to make it accessible mostly to themselves. Through such talks, along with publications and grants, they established their "unique claims" to this material, traditionally based in native communities.

I do not mean "appropriation," which I think of as largely apart from anthropological and linguistic scholarship because, these fields, at least by intention, keep things within a context of original form and expression. Appropriation, to me, means what is done by people in self-proclaimed Humanities (English, History, and the Arts), who remove from context and enveloping native language to exploit for their own gain, often by deflecting concern from more serious issues of economic excess and native integrity.

Native presenters, both schooled and self-expressive, on the other hand, dealt with only a facet or two of their subject, deferring to others, often elders, in the audience and implying a much larger community sharing in that theme. They attacked or criticized outsiders, but rarely made judgments about each other, assuming a native birth right to such material.

At one time, I recognized these different strategies as singular amassing or plural diffusing, but further reflection recalled research teams or lone writers who did not fit that mold, though it was generally true.

Western positivist approaches do assume that the whole is greater than the sum of its parts even as they disconnect and reduce these pieces into analytical units. The result is a butchery of a topic, a death wish driven by obsessions. Only rarely does a scholar serve instead as surgeon, keeping the patient alive after such dissections rather than leaving behind some kind of a bloody inert mess.

The native attitude is much more subtle. Because a proper person constantly evidences careful concern for the entire universe of beings, knowledge is not merely diffused, broadcast, or scattered. Instead, it is carefully arranged where it will, or will be assumed to, do the most good. In the *Popul Vuh*, it is called sowing, sprouting, and dawning (Tedlock 1985), but it really means "bestowed". Every family should have someone with the linchpin, key, or core bit of wisdom to make it all fit together.

Among Navajos where sheer population size has preserved aspects once vital to all native societies, such a crux is withheld until ready for death.

> In the Navajo way, much lore about the land is esoteric, passed from a medicine man or woman to the few apprentices that he or she may have in a lifetime. Even old people who aren't specialists wouldn't pass on their most powerful stories, prayers, or songs until they felt ready to die. The reason in both cases is that indiscriminate spread of knowledge lessens its power. The person to whom you tell your secrets should already know enough about Navajo beliefs to use your secrets in the right way. (Kelley and Francis 1994:3)

Similarly, the power = force = energy vitalizing the universe is regarded as arranged in rings and rays around one or more tysic (**t**ime = **s**pace = **c**enter), either place, person, or sacred thing. From the source and summary at this nexus, power is apportioned in varying degrees, greater at nodes and rays, yet lesser at outer rings. Only the most powerful, of course, are aware of the overall array in this careful placement of spaces and connections, but others can assume it from their own much more limited perspectives.

Spatial regard was its clearest expression, much as Rock Creek hunters insist on keeping their camps sacred by arranging the bones and bits of their prey in trees where immortals can clearly witness their sincere intent (Brightman 1993:1).

Temporal regard can be even more difficult to grasp, but as agreed by both Gary Witherspoon (1977:33) in *Language and Art in the Navajo Universe* and James Faris (1990:22) in *Nightway*, Navajo recognize unaltering constancy despite continual change because "ceremonial knowledge is non-expanding and fixed—All there is to know about this world is already known because the world was organized according to this knowledge." Thus, zen-like, if something is knowable but not to you, then automatically someone else must know it because everything knowable is already known.

In other words, immortal knowledge structures and informs this world through all time, and only seems a paradox until you realize that every note of music has always both existed and been used in songs. If notes are finite in patterning yet infinite in arrangements, so too is knowledge, with the strong implication that wisdom is stored in organized units, ready to be sorted, retrieved, and recombined according to various customized needs of certain members, moments, and motions.

The great consolation of this for natives, of course, is that no one ever dies. Your own family gives you a starter set of births, whose members then transmute and metathesize as every name assumes another form over the course of your lifetime and all those who choose to follow in it.

Of course scholars do share their knowledge with colleagues and classes, but they do so in very specialized, privileged ways that are anything but open because of jargon and rapidly shifting fads of "the next hot thing."

In America, you get more if you already have more, might making more right. In Native America, however, pervasive balance and harmony mean that you get more if you have less, at least temporarily. As Yup'ik Eskimo say, you are responsible for making up what is lacking in the universe. Human duty in their moral, fully aware universe required supplying other "persons" what they lacked, such as fresh water to seals, light and heat to belukha whales, sea-smelling seal oil to land animals, and dry land to fish (Fienup-Riordan 1990:186). Ghosts also wanted fresh water because the tears of mourners had made their own so salty.

Understanding this need to compensate, respectfully and generously, helps to explain the need to fast, mortify, and suffer during vision quests and other purifications. Here, immortals themselves make up for these deficiencies and lacking conditions.

I well remember my first startled shock to Skagit elder Vi Hilbert's definition of archiving, which consisted of giving Xerox copies of a document to a variety of people who may or may not be interested in it at the time and place. She called it spreading the wealth, but others are less sure. As often as not, this Xerox also included text in Lushootseed, her mother tongue, so that only those with knowledge of the language can fully benefit from their new possession.

Thus, full information is withheld if a receiver does not already have any preparation, despite the appearance of being most generous, democratic, and helpful. Thus it has always been in native worlds: everything is known somewhere, sometime, by someone, if it is not you. Unfortunately, such assumptions have meant that much local knowledge has been lost to any sustainable record because of the devastating epidemics from Europe and Africa that killed many informed elders before their time, preventing the orderly transmission of last minute crucial keys. Survivors were displaced and disrupted in ways that directed vital attention elsewhere, most often to issues of sheer survival.

The irony is that this amassing data has violated its previous terms of existence but also preserved it for the record of all those who want access. These communities survive with a pool of relevant information, some ancient and some new, still apportioned among members. With the loss of native languages, removal from homelands, and estrangement from a landscape, direct links with place-based aboriginal local knowledge becomes more tenuous. Yet the strategy for knowledge storage and usage continues unabated among natives. Culture survives in terms of its linkages and spacings, not in terms of what fills them.

Such insight is the singular contribution that such cross-purposing can make: structure amasses while wisdom disperses, but both must work together if either is to survive for the benefit of all.

Journal of Northwest Anthropology, Memoir 9:184–189 2014

PASSING THE TORCH:
LEARNING FROM THE WOMEN ELDERS

ABSTRACT

Mentoring and modeling by four remarkable scholarly women is discussed in terms of life lessons and insights. These were Ruth Underhill (1883–1984), Esther Schiff Goldfrank Wittfogel (1896–1997), Viola Edmundson Garfield (1899–1983), and Amelia Susman Schultz (1915–).

Introduction

Thirty-eight years after this paper was presented at an annual meeting of the American Anthropological Association (Miller 1975), three of these women have passed on. Yet the warmth and details of their lives deserves to be perpetuated and this article does that, especially because "anthropology courses have tended to gloss over the participation and contributions of many of the female practitioners of our discipline" (Gacs, Khan, McIntyre, and Weinber 1988:xiii). While fuller biographies of these women have since been published, this paper remains a more personal and intimate glimpse of their humanity and generosity as teachers of a younger generation.

Students in the field are regarded as anthropologists in process. Their advisors have already passed this and other tests in order to become full fledged professionals, ready to guide their own and younger careers. These same people, however, have also presumably entered into another series of more subtle tests involving publication, tenure, and advancement, yet the ultimate outcome of both fieldwork and academics is the same: leaving. Fieldworkers return home and academics retire. But neither should mean an end of involvement in productive education. Robert Lowie remarked that he was perpetually in the field: always watching, recording, and analyzing.

This seems to be a general characteristic of his entire generation of anthropologist since I have constantly noted this feature among four women who were also students of Boas, Benedict, and Sapir. These four have informally taught me much about the history and craft of anthropology. We are friends united by our strong commitment to cultural relativity and Native American ethnography. While all have lived the history of modern anthropology, their perspectives and careers have been very different. Two were successful academics who have passed all the tests of academic advancement. One was a scholar without academic appointment. And the other (alive at 98) left anthropology over 25 years ago for a life of social involvement.

Without the constraint of formal or departmental contexts, we have openly and calmly discussed our problems and hopes for field data and anthropology generally. We have shared a great deal, but I am convinced that the real benefit has been mine. I have come to know these women not only as anthropologists but also as human beings. I want to discuss what I have learned in terms of its commonalities and differences and to suggest important parallels between this informal training and actual fieldwork.

One of the detriments to my relationship with these founders is their extreme idealism. I realize that I am biasing my experiences, but it is important to know that these women entered anthropology with the highest and purest ideals for human understanding. As Ruth Underhill has said to me, they all live by the motto: "If you learn anything, publish and give it to the world." Even more vividly, Ruth pictured herself at Columbia as a robin pulling a worm from the ground. The worm was knowledge about people. She was given special permission to stay in the Columbia library until midnight so that she and the worm could continue to grapple long after others had given up and gone home.

This was not a naïve quest for understanding. Anthropology is a new field and our founders and elders did not begin *de novo* as members of the American Anthropological Association (AAA). Each woman came from a background of ethnic diversity, intellectual families, and liberalism. Each had experiences in another profession or career before they entered Columbia. Each tasted the real world before they entered the field. Yet their quest for knowledge was such that the breadth and relativism of early anthropology attracted their interest and dedication. This can be clearly seen in the following sketches of their lives.

Ruth Underhill

Ruth Underhill (1883–1984), whom I had known the longest, was born into an old New England family.[1] As a child she traveled in Europe and thus acquired a sense of human complexity. Following a degree in comparative literature from Vassar, she took a job as a social worker with Italian immigrants in New York. During World War I she worked in Italy. After her return to the states and a brief marriage ("Men are too much work!"), she decided to return to school in order to find out more about people. This was after considerable experience with cultural differences, but Ruth realized that she lacked the theoretical sophistication to generalize and categorize her knowledge. She entered Columbia and in the process of asking around for information, was able to talk to someone named Ruth Benedict, who suggested the new field of anthropology to her. However, her entry into the profession was not without difficulties. Some of her peers were uneasy with her patrician manner. She also had to agonize over a course in the Lakota language until she and others hired Ella Deloria, the aunt of Vine Deloria, to tutor them. Always she asked, "What are people like and what can you do to understand them." Subsequently she did research with the Papago (Tohono O'odham), Mohave, and Navajo. She was the first "public" anthropologist hired by the Bureau of Indian Affairs (BIA). At 90, she was honored by the Southwestern Anthropological Association. In spite of considerable trials, tribulations, and a very rational view of the past, she continued to regard anthropology as a noble calling. She remained very much a gentlewoman, concerned as much with anthropology as the fate of the world. Her idealism was balanced with realistic memory and her gentility with the most potent recipe for martinis that I have ever had.

Esther Schiff Goldfrank Wittfogel

Esther Schiff Goldfrank Wittfogel (1896–1997) entered anthropology by the back door as it were. After graduation from Barnard with a small trust fund, she took a job as secretary to Franz Boas. She went with him to the Southwest and incidentally began collecting data on her own. The result was a monograph on the Pueblo of Cochiti, early work at Isleta Pueblo, and several articles on the Pueblos and Navajos. Later she worked with Ruth Benedict among the Blackfeet. Esther always had an immense appreciation for the quality of data. Much of her work centered over the proper interpretation of data, the need for primary sources, and the thoroughness of data collection. She remained near Columbia most of her life, especially when married to Karl Wittfogel, and as such has a clear image of anthropology in its formative and developmental stages. She remains among the most theoretical of her peers. However, her infectious enthusiasm, her appreciation of psychology, and her own theoretical perspectives mean that any contemporary or novel interpretations must be argued pro and con logically and coherently. This is not to imply any criticism, but rather to make an observation on the strength and integrity of the Boasians.

Viola Edmundson Garfield

Since coming to Seattle, I have been privileged to learn from two other women, the first being Viola Edmundson Garfield (1899–1983), Professor Emerita in the University of Washington Anthropology Department. Her career had its beginning in the course of financial difficulties as an undergraduate. She left college and took a job as a teacher in the government school at New Metlakatla, Alaska, among the Christian Tsimshian Indians. Aspects of life in the town and her class piqued her curiosity. Among the most compelling, as it had earlier been for Lewis Henry Morgan, was a general awareness of matrilineal descent. When she returned to school with her savings, she moved into anthropology. Later at the suggestion of Boas, she entered Columbia and completed a dissertation on Tsimshian social organization, which remains a classic. Viola long remained a knowledgeable ethnographer of the Northwest Coast, especially for social organization and art. Though she never published on Tlingit, she did visit most of these villages with her husband Charles, a certified old sourdough. Her bias is toward the practical and empirical, but her sensitivities are those of a humanitarian.

Amelia Susman Schultz

Of considerable impact on my perceptions has been my friendship with Amelia Susman Schultz (1915–), the second woman I've been privileged to learn from in Seattle. Her name is less well known than it ought to be. After an undergraduate degree in psychology (from the Philosophy Department at Brooklyn College), she was encouraged by a mentor to enter anthropology because it was one of the very few fields endorsing graduate work by women or Jews. She made good on this referral by entering Columbia. In spite of very substantial setbacks and a career outside of anthropology, she continued to personally and professionally practice the ideals of Boasian anthropology with a depth of sympathy and understanding that few of my peers could equal. This is made all the more amazing because of the anguish that characterized her anthropological career. Her first dissertation was a study of "acculturation" on the Round Valley Reservation in northeastern California. It was intended as the eighth case study in the collection later edited by Ralph Linton and Benedict and called "Acculturation in Seven American Indian Tribes." Unfortunately, Amelia's contribution was dropped because of fear of litigation or slander charges stemming from her treatment of ethnocide, genocide, and land theft by white settlers (mostly in a single paragraph that could have easily been deleted). At this time, the doctoral degree was awarded on the basis of its publication. Amelia postponed her own advanced degree so that seven others could receive theirs. In return, Boas and Benedict arranged with Paul Radin for her to do a dissertation on accent in Winnebago. Her source was none other than Big Winnebago, alias Crashing Thunder. Her field work began on the boardwalk at Atlantic City where the Blowsnakes were selling beadwork and dancing for tourists. Amelia soon moved them to Brooklyn and supported them on informant fees.

Her degree (1943) was conferred shortly after Boas died in 1941. Boas also sent her to the Tsimshian in British Columbia to recheck the grammar and mythology that he had already published. In the process, she worked closely with William Beynon, the indigenous and intuitive Tsimshian ethnographer and linguist. Shortly after this, she left linguistics for a career in social work and genetics. However, she did not forget her training. While living in Switzerland she studied local dialects and peasant economy for her own interest on the GI Bill. In many ways, Amelia is a time capsule from the past, isolated from the anthropological mainstream. She nevertheless conveys a sense of the dedication, resourcefulness, and idealism that was so vital to the founding of anthropology.

The Assets of Learning from Elders

Each of these women has told me that she can recall people who entered her classes only to later drop out. All of them are careful to point out that not everyone can be an anthropologist, but they also insist that the world would be improved by a better appreciation of what it was that they have devoted their lives to: the understanding of the human condition, its similarities, its complexities, and its variations. For this reason they are willing to consider contemporary theory, data, and ideas provided that it is presented in a rational, scholarly, and unhysterical—non-confrontational fashion. They are also comfortable with provocative, political, and ingenious solutions to problems. While they are likely to chime out the Boas maxim "Where are your facts?," they are adaptable, tolerant, and intellectually stimulating. It is these attributes which bring me to a consideration of the assets of learning from such elders.

These are roughly of four types of assets: models, perspectives, advice, and insights.

Models

With regard to these elders as models, I personally find it both powerful and compelling to share in the experience of colleagues who have spent most of their lives in my profession. In composite form, they have shown me that to be an anthropologist requires a unique combination of idealism and realism, enthusiasm and curiosity, dedication and detachment, theory and empiricism, empathy and personal commitment, and an important sense of nuance and adaptability. Each of these women exemplifies these traits. I believe that each of them would also sympathize with me that the general task of anthropology is to match what people do and what people say with their unconscious—unintuitive motivations. Certainly each has attempted to fulfill such a task in her own career.

Perspectives

The perspective supplied by these women revolves around realism. They lived through the founding of modern American anthropology. If the matching of the real, ideal, and unconscious is important for our data, it is also important for ourselves as anthropologists. We are human beings, a little weirder than most, but still subject to the same emotions and motivations. The professional antagonism of Leslie White to Boas is significant for the history of the profession, but our full appreciation of it should include knowledge of the personal interaction of these two men. The same can be said for more supportive relationships, such as that of Kroeber and Lowie. I can still recall the emotional impact when I was told that Kroeber and Lowie would appear in mourning attire for graduate oral examinations and would fail a candidate on the grounds that he or she had "insufficient humanity." The story may be apocryphal but it clearly underscores the dominant perspective so dear to our predecessors. However, this humanism is balanced by a sweeping, considered realism. These are professionals who have lived through several world wars and awkward bureaucracies. Their opinion, advice, and knowledge have been tapped by state, federal, and foreign powers. Yet most of it has not been followed or even seriously considered. Each time they have rallied, learned lessons, and returned to the task at hand, perhaps with renewed optimism. Other anthropologists have left the task undone or retired in defeat. What is important to me in these confrontations with reality is the continuous integrity of the field as exemplified by the elders rather than its demographic history.

Advice

While these elders in the profession can provide models and perspectives at a distance, their advice is best given through direct personal involvement. This is necessary because the advice takes the form of autobiographical data, anecdotes about colleagues, career-oriented lectures, or just plain gossip.

Among the most useful advice I have been given relates to establishing and maintaining rapport. Examples include Ruth Underhill's introduction to the Papago through a groundskeeper at the University of Arizona and the negotiations of Boas to settle Amelia Susman among the Tsimshians (some of the details of which appear in the September 1975 Anthropological Newsletter). While my professional training prepared me to understand the natives, it was the advice of these elders which helped me to begin to comprehend the local Whites during my fieldwork. Their advice has also helped me cope with some of the comments my more obtuse colleagues will sometimes make. Ruth Underhill supplied my favorite example. When she got off the train to begin fieldwork among the Mohave, George Devereux (the psychoanalytical researcher) was there and she asked him for some sage words about conducting her research. Devereux left her with the most important piece of information he felt that she needed to know: "The Mohave strongly object to copulation under water!"

It is also from retired academics that I have been given the most useful information about intellectual growth, career development, and professional responsibilities. Competition with peers and subordination to senior faculty are just not as conducive to such transfer of advice.

An equally important contribution from the elders is unpublished data, their own and others. What may once have been noted but then regarded as insignificant, might still be recovered and rendered theoretically important. Examples include the bit of bear ceremonialism Viola Garfield once saw among the Tsimshian and the fact that Ruth Underhill's Mohave informant was a man who became a shaman late in life and was called "Raw But Burnt," ripe with incumbent raw/cooked Levi-Strausian Structuralist meanings.

Insights

The insights these women elders have given me also relate generally to anthropological theory. As an anthropologist I have the benefit of both professional and tribal elders. I am comfortable using the same term for both because they are formally and functionally the same. As elders they represent individuals who are old and wise, with a keen insight and understanding of the human condition. In a tribal context, the elders are recognized by their seniority, experience, and reflective minds. They are able to present an integrated synthesis of the society and more generally human existence. Senior anthropologists can also do the same, but their models are particularly well formulated because of their training and intuitions. But there are also areas of blending. Among the really important contributions of anthropology to the world, in my own view, has been the reinforcement given to indigenous intellectuals in the process of questioning and watching another society during fieldwork. Examples are numerous. William Beynon, Wolf Phratry chief, blossomed as a Tsimshian researcher through his interaction with Boas, Garfield, Susman, and Marius Barbeau. Crashing Thunder is another example. In such cases, however, the relations between elder and students become even more complex than usual. Among the components of such relationships are reinforcement, caretaking, and amusement. I have already discussed reinforcement in terms of a sharpened focus on traditional patterns and the creative adaptability of cultural concepts. Caretaking functions are less true now than in the past as more and more young people find satisfaction in devoting time and attention to their elders. Such was not always the case. Erna Gunther had to cut firewood for the widow of an important shaman during her early fieldwork in the area north of Seattle.

Conclusion

Amusement is a vital part of any educational situation. Generally, the source of amusement is the researcher as a sort of resident idiot who is awkward, clumsy, uncouth, interesting, and occasionally intelligent. We are all of these things without even trying and thus are all the more funny. On numerous occasions when this has happened to me, it was largely because I have not fully lived the experiences of these elders. In Oklahoma, I will always evoke laughter because I am ignorant of wide-ranging classical literature in its original languages, tackle for horse drawn teams, oil fields lingo, and local places that were significant influences in the lives of older people.

But through it all, my elders and myself have a bond that seems to go to the heart of the craft of being culturally relative: it is the bond forged by an intense personal curiosity based on diverse human experience together with considerable innate intelligence and flexibility.

Of particular note, four decades later, was the willing encouragement of these and other women, rarely if ever mentioning the slights and hardships they endured or suffered as women in a man's field; a field, as Boas well knew and practiced, that had to include women if anthropology was ever to fairly, honestly, and accurately portray those humans who "hold up half the sky."

NOTE

[1] Indeed, though it was rarely mentioned while she lived, except that Ruth would say "My ancestors were involved with Indiens," the Underhills go back to Richard, known as "Butcher of the Pequots" for his savage attack on the swamp fort of this tribe, brokers in the wampum trade which the Puritans soon took over. Survivors were forced to change their tribal name and, using a term for their own Bear clan, became the first of the Mohegans. Such is the pedigree of many other successful Colonial families, except that Ruth tried to make academic amends, as have family members of the current generation.

Lastly, her bearing as a gentlewoman encouraged Benedict and Boas to urge her to represent anthropology's cultural relativism by testifying in the murder trial of the Apache man who killed graduate student Henrietta Schmerler during a misunderstanding.

Journal of Northwest Anthropology, Memoir 9:190–197   2014

STARTUP: RICHARD "DOC" DAUGHERTY'S 1947 ARCHAEOLOGICAL SURVEY OF THE WASHINGTON COAST[a]

ABSTRACT

During the fall term of 1947 at the University of Washington, Richard "Doc" Daugherty conducted on foot the first full archaeology survey of the Pacific coast of Washington. Copies of his nine-page introduction have circulated for years, however, the original site forms, maps, and notes laid dormant among his personal records until relocated in 2010. The documents provide important additional information concerning the archaeology of the Northwest Coast and supplement the professional contributions of a major figure in American archaeology.

Introduction

During the fall term of 1947 (October to December) at the University of Washington (UW), Richard "Doc" Daugherty conducted on foot the first full archaeology survey of the Pacific coast of Washington State. Fifty archaeological sites were recorded during the survey. While his original introduction is well known, the hand-written drafts of the site forms have remained amongst his personal records. In 2010, the site forms were found together in an envelope as Doc and I were editing his Hoh ethnographic notebooks (Miller 2010). The site forms are summarized here to add to his public record of fundamental contributions in Washington and Northwest Coast archaeology. Slightly different typed site forms were added to the Washington State site record files administered by the Washington Department of Archaeology and Historic Preservation.

The training ground for Daugherty's research was the 1946 UW summer field school at Cattle Point on San Juan Island, followed by experience conducting the Smithsonian River Basin surveys that preceded Snake River and Columbia River dam construction. Doc, born and raised in Aberdeen, Washington, wondered about sites out on the coast and in 1947, funded by the Burke Museum, he undertook a coastal survey. With his wife Phyllis and baby daughter in a nearby "auto court" cabin, Doc would park his car as close as possible to the beach to be surveyed, then, in his words while reminiscing (18 August 2010), he would "walk the beach all the way up, turn around, and then go inland a ways and come back to the car." He checked "the beaches, the swamps and the bogs" of Grays Harbor and Willapa Bay, and continued north in the same fashion, paying particular attention to river mouths, moving wife and baby as he went, and ultimately reaching Cape Flattery.

"Rained like hell," Daugherty commented, looking back. "But I found a lot of sites and learned a lot." Sites including Ozette and Minard and other coastal sites that were later excavated under Doc's supervision were initially listed during this effort. Additionally, the on-foot approach

---

[a] This article was previously published in *Journal of Northwest Anthropology*, 44(2):257–265 (2010). See Gary C. Wessen's 2011 article for additional information on the 1947 survey (*JONA*, 45(1):123–127).

provided introductions to tribal elders who contributed to Daugherty's 1949 ethnographic fieldwork.

The article begins with Doc's verbatim introduction to the survey, with his original page numbers provided in square brackets. Each of the site forms is summarized below to supplement the historical and anthropological record. A list of individuals who assisted in identifying the sites is also provided (Table 1). The designations do not match the Smithsonian trinomial numbers, county abbreviations, or typed-up versions used today for these same locations. Most 1947 sites are on older forms, but a few also have a newer one (GH-1, -14, PA-1, -2; while PA-12 has only newer). A comparison of these two forms comprises Table 2 and 3. All but seven forms include a sketch of that locale (on the back of a second sheet for older forms, or on the back of newer single sheet). On these forms, directions are specified by their first letter (NE for Northeast), the number PA-9 is used twice for nearby sites, and all are in hard pencil except for a few in ink [as so indicated].

Survey of Washington Coast—Cape Flattery to Columbia River. R. Daugherty, 1947

Statement of Problem

In October 1947, archaeological research was conducted along the coastal area of the state of Washington. The object of this research was to locate and evaluate the archaeological sites, as well as to secure all ethnographic and historical data pertaining to each site.

The area included in this investigation was the entire coastal strip from Cape Disappointment at the mouth of the Columbia River to Cape Flattery at the entrance to the Strait of Juan de Fuca. Grays Harbor, Willapa Harbor, and the tidal portions of the Copalis, Quinault, Raft, Queets, Hoh, Quileute, Ozette, Sooes, and Wa'atch rivers, plus the many creeks and smaller streams entering the ocean were included.

Archaeologically the coastal area of Washington was almost entirely unknown. A number of the larger sites have been recorded in ethnographic and historical sources, but none have been archaeologically evaluated. A great number of smaller sites have escaped previous mention [p. 2].

Method of Approach

The survey was begun at the southernmost extension of the area, Cape Disappointment, and was systematically pursued northward. The survey was made on foot and the area back from the beach was covered as well as the area bordering the water.

Before the survey was undertaken, a decision had to be made as to which of two possible procedures would be followed. One possibility was to choose a more limited area and investigate each site in detail, sinking test pits to determine depth, stratigraphy, and extent of site. The other possibility was to survey the entire coastal area, stressing the locating of sites and making a somewhat less detailed evaluation. In either case the survey would include all of the ethnographic and historical information available. The latter possibility was chosen since it seemed that there was an immediate need for a complete archaeological picture of the coastal area.

I believe that some very profitable research could be undertaken by some individual who would extensively test a number of these sites in a limited area for a more definitive evaluation and also for some comparative material. Several such projects as this in different parts of the coastal area would provide information from which to draw some rather definite preliminary conclusions. It would also aid in developing a systematic plan for future major excavations.

TABLE 1. INFORMANTS PROVIDING INFORMATION TO RICHARD DAUGHERTY DURING THE 1947 ARCHAEOLOGICAL SURVEY OF THE WASHINGTON COAST

Name	Indicates Native or Indian	Location
Buck Bailey	√	Moclips
Penny Bush	√	Bay Center
Roland Charley	√	Georgetown Reservation, Tokeland
Jonas Cole	√	Amanda Park
F. Espey		Oysterville
Mr. Fisher	√	Hoh
Stanley Grey	√	La Push
Mr. Hudson	√	Hoh
Mr. Jackson	√	Hoh
Al Johnson		Naselle
Emma Luscier	√	Moclips, Bay Center
Ralph Minard		Oyhut
A. Nelson		Oysterville
Chas Nelson		Nahcotta
Ed Nelson		Tokeland
Randolph Parker	√	Neah Bay
Esop [Esau?] Penn	√	Queets
Morton Penn	√	La Push
Mrs. Petit	√	Bay Center
George Prior		N. Nemah
Mrs. Prior		Bay Center
Charles Rhodes		Bay Center
Harry Shale	√	Taholah
Bernie Taylor	√	Ilwaco
Mr. T'sailto	√	La Push
Mr. Watson		Markham

As the sites were found they were recorded on the University of Washington site survey forms. An attempt was made, in all cases, to ascertain the areal extent, depth and richness of concentration. Frequently it was found impossible or impracticable to accurately [p. 3] determine the depth due to the extensive excavation that would be necessary or to heavy vegetation covering the site. In some instances the dense vegetation covering the site prevented an accurate measurement of the length and width. One or several photographs were taken of each site, depending on the circumstances, and the photographic data were recorded on the survey forms. A simple schematic line drawing was made of each site and the immediate surrounding area, including prominent reference points, on the reverse side of each site sheet.

Unfortunately no really good maps of the area in a desirable scale were or are available. It was decided that the best maps of all those available, upon which to record the site locations, were the State of Washington Department of Highways maps.

While proceeding with the physical survey, a determined effort was made to contact all available informants for all areas. These informants were contacted for site locations. Ethnographic data were not secured at this time as time did not permit. The plan was to secure the ethnographic data at a later time so as to be able to complete most of the physical survey in the initial period.

Whenever possible, data as to the Indian name of the site, number of houses, their location and orientation, number of occupants of site, date of last occupation, and other pertinent information was obtained.

A list of informants [consultants] is appended to this report (Table 1).

At present most of the physical survey has been completed. Only those areas remain that have to be reached by boat, or were inaccessible due to the high winter tides and stormy weather.

Most of the existing and available historical material has been [p. 4] carefully investigated for any and all mention of the sites. A small amount in the form of diaries still remains to be investigated. All of the existing ethnographic material has been investigated and information bearing on the various sites extracted. [p. 5]

Areal Description

Topographically, the coast of Washington changes radically from south to north. The southern area is characterized by broad sandy beaches bordering the ocean, with the rivers flowing sluggishly through broad valleys. The adjacent land has little elevation.

As one proceeds northward the beaches become narrower and are bordered by abrupt cliffs, rising in some localities to several hundred feet. The character of the beach changes from sand to rocks. A number of swiftly moving streams flow through rather narrow, well-defined valleys. It has become apparent that these topographically and geological differences markedly influence the locality and character of the sites.

In the southern area, the low land bordering the rivers, bays, and ocean is generally characterized by open meadow lands, marshy flats and areas of dense brush with but few large trees. The hills in back of this low land are, however, densely wooded.

To the north in direct contrast, the forest growth comes within but a short distance of the ocean and grows to the very banks of the rivers. This is also a limiting factor.

In an analysis of village and campsite locations certain factors are immediately apparent. Rarely do the sites occur in places where there is no creek or river. Never are they inland away from all water. The largest sites occur at the mouths of the major streams or at some other economically strategic point along the bay shore, ocean, or banks of the upper river.

A great number of the sites situated on the bay shore or bordering the ocean beaches have been almost entirely destroyed by being [p. 6] washed away due to the subsidence of the coastal areas. Frequently only a slight deposit remains of a site which may once have been quite extensive. This is true along with whole coastal strip, but due to general topography of the southern sector, the damage has been greatest there. [p. 7]

Preliminary Hypotheses and Conclusions

The views presented here are based entirely on surface indications and deal mainly at this point of the investigation with the physical nature of the sites. With further investigation it is possible that these preliminary hypotheses may be considerably altered or proved untenable.

One of the most significant factors that has become evident is the apparent lack of depth exhibited in most of these sites. Some of the major sites indicated by ethnographic and historical sources are at present but a few feet above sea level. Is it to be assumed from this that it indicates only a very recent occupation of the area, or a very sparse population, or both? Or perhaps only a relatively recent adaptation to a diet consisting of sea food?

I offer here an alternative view. If one is to reflect on the location of the major village sites, it becomes apparent that the locations are for the most part at the mouths of the major streams. These streams are constantly altering their courses near their mouth. I believe this constant shifting of the river's course never allows a great concentration of material to occur in one particular spot, and that the village has slowly and unapparently moved about, always maintaining its position near the river's bank. Evidence of this shift is found near the mouths of the Chehalis and Queets Rivers. A site was found one and one-half miles north of the mouth of the Chehalis River which at one time was directly on the river's bank near its mouth.

The identical situation has occurred at Queets, probably in more recent times. A shell deposit was found on the shore of a small slough which at one time was part of the main channel of the Queets River. [p. 8]

The general subsidence of the coastal area, I believe, gives an apparent lack of depth to some sites located on Willapa Bay. I believe it entirely possible that some of the sites that are now practically awash at high tide, extend in depth below the present water level. It is of course apparent that these postulations need further supporting evidence and examination in the light of future excavations.

A rather marked difference is noted in the character of the deposits in the northern and southern sites. However the change is a gradual one. The concentration of shell in the deposit is greatest in the sites around Willapa Bay and Grays Harbor. From Taholah northward a lesser amount of shell is found in the sites. At La Push there is evidence of a great amounts of sea mammal bones in the deposit. Whale bone is most apparent. Mussel shells are much more prominent in the more northern sites. This undoubtedly is correlated with the distribution of shellfish and the amounts of each type in a particular area, as well as cultural emphasis of an economic nature. [p. 9]

Site Inventory

Grays Harbor County

GH-1 Pestle found at shell mound site West of Westport Airport, 29 October 1947, sketch

GH-2 House pits in pasture, no date, sketch

GH-3 Shafter Roberts place shell mound, no date, blank

GH-4 West end of Bay City bridge owned by hunting club, 27 October 1947, sketch

GH-5 West end of Bay City bridge, north of cannery, 27 October 1947, sketch

GH-6 Bay City shell mound, no date, blank

GH-7 Bay between Bay City and Ocosta, shell mound, 27 October 1947, sketch

GH-8 Low rise on old road to Ocosta, shell mound, 27 October 1947, sketch

GH-9 Roberts Cattle ranch, NE of Ocosta, shell mound, 28 October 1947, sketch

GH-10 Markham, mouth of John's River, NE bank, shell mound, 28 October 1947, sketch

GH-11 O'Leary Creek mouth, shell mound, 29 October 1947, sketch

GH-12 100 yards of Breckenridge Bluff, shell mound, no date, sketch

GH-13 Chenois Creek, E bank, shell mound, 3 November 1947, sketch

GH-14 Burial ground, 1 mi. W of Chenois, last used 1932, overgrown, from Walter Allen [2/15/48 on newer form] blank [Walter, who settled at Quinault, was the African-American driver for wealthy native Sampson John family]

GH-15 Minard Ranch, shell mound, 3 November 1947, surface artifacts and remains, sketch

GH-15x Ridge ½ mi. NE of Oyhut, no date, sketch

GH-16 Pt Damon, shell mound, 4 November 1947, sketch

GH-17 Connor Creek hill, graveyard, 5 November 1947, last used 1931, sketch
GH-18 Copalis village shell mound, 24 November 1947, sketch
GH-19 Curve in highway 3/10th mi. N of Copalis, burial, shell mound, 5 November 1947, sketch
GH-20 Yakima ranch, hammerstone, shell mound, 4 November 1947, sketch
GH-21 Shell mound near first Copalis rocks, 4 November 1947, sketch
GH-22 Copalis Rocks, shell mound on bank, 5 November 1947, blank
GH-23 Sunset Beach, shell mound, 20 November 1947, sketch
GH-24 Moclips shell mound, 21 November 1947, Jonah Cole says where houses were now washed away, sketch
GH-25 Taholah village, 21 November 1947, sketch
GH-26 Taholah burial N bank, 21 October 1947, sketch

Clallam County [Now Abbreviated CA, CL Is Clark]

CL-1 La Push shell mound village, 19 December 1947, sketch
CL-2 Sooes rise, shell mound house site, 21 December 1947, blank
CL-3 Portage Head, mussels, 21 December 1947, blank
CL-4 Waatch River mouth, N bank, 1st bench, shell mound, 21 December 1945 [sic], blank [Ozette should be here, but has no form in Doc's packet]

Jefferson County

JE-1 Queets village, 17 December 1947, sketch
JE-2 Queets, former island, shell mound, 17 December 1947, sketch
JE-3 Queets, "playa" island, house site, 17 December 1947, sketch

Pacific County

PA-1 Fort Canby Cove, W side, shell mound [older form not dated, 4 October 1947 on newer form], blank
PA-2 Oysterville village, from Verne Ray's Lower Chinook Notes [older form dated 5 October 1947, newer form blank] both have sketches, older bigger in pencil, newer smaller in ink
PA-3 S Oysterville, W shore [older form not dated, lists BB Salinders farm, has sketch; newer form has 6 October]
PA-4 Between Nahcotta and Oysterville, shell mound village, 7 October 1947 information from Mr. C Nelson, site old and rich [older form dated 7 October 1947, has sketch; newer form, blank]
PA-5 Round "Baby" Island, burial, cairns, Oct 13, 1947, local reports that Indians removed [tree and other canoe] burials about 25 years ago, sketch
PA-6 Long Island, S end, shell mound, 13 October 1947, sketch
PA-7 Long Island, low rise, shell mound, no date, sketch
PA-8 Diamond Point shell mound, 10 October 1947, sketch indicating both PA-7, PA-8
PA-9 BB Saunders Home, W 300 yards, peeled cedar [CMT], 11 October 1947, sketch
PA-9 Mill Ranch, N end Naselle bridge shell mound, no date [in ink] sketch
PA-10 Lynn Point, shell mound, 9 October 1947, sketch
PA-11 Bay Center, shell mound, no date [in ink], sketch
PA-12 Bay Center, shell mound village, 14 July 1948 [sic], only newer form, sketch
PA-13 Bruceport shell mound, no date [in ink], sketch
PA-14 Georgetown [Shoalwater], shell mound, 25 October 1947, allotted land, chief is Roland Charlie sketch [in ink, with 3 possible spellings of allot]
PA-15 Georgetown, field at base of hill, shell mound, 25 October [in ink], sketch
PA-16 Kindred Island, N Willapa Bay, 25 October, sketch

TABLE 2. ARCHAEOLOGICAL SURVEY OF WASHINGTON FORM USED IN 1947

Archaeological Survey of Washington

Reconnaissance Data Form   Site No.
            centered township, range, and section recorded in ink   Photo No.
                                                                             Artifacts

LOCATION
        U.S.G.S. or Hydrographic [map]
        Place Names
        Directional indicators
DESCRIPTION
        Geographical
        Habitation Potential
        Geological
SITE
        Type of site – shell mound, rock shelter, burial ground, house site, cairns, petroglyph or
        pictograph
        Description
                Direction site trends
                Natural coves
                Depressions
                Mounds
                Type of soil
                Other features
        Measurements
                Length (specify)
                Width – maximum   minimum   average
                Depth – maximum   minimum   average
                        estimated   unknown   [page 2]
        Testing
                Test pits
                Artifacts – location
                Excavations made
        Condition – eroded, wave cut, disturbed, white occupation
        Accessibility –
                Roads
                Paths
                Nearness to habitation
                Availability of work [workers]
                Edgement of site
        Owner
                Observer   Date
REMARKS
        Accompanying sheets
        Brief description of artifacts
        Additional information
Site sketch on back of second sheet, third page of form.

TABLE 3. UNIVERSITY OF WASHINGTON FORMS USED AFTER 1947

ARCHAEOLOGICAL FIELD FORMS

County   Site No.

1. Map reference
2. Type of site
3. Cultural affiliation
4. Location
5. Owner and address
6. Previous Owners
7. Tenant
8. Informants
9. Previous designations for site
10. Site description
11. Position of site and surroundings
12. Area of occupation
13. Depth and character of fill
14. Present condition
15. Previous excavation
16. Material collected
17. Material observed
18. Material reported and owner
19. Recommendations for further work
20. Photography Nos.
21. Maps of site

Recorded by   Date

[Along right margin] County   Site No.

ACKNOWLEDGMENTS

Thanks to Richard Daugherty, Ruth Kirk, Gary Wessen, Richard Bellon, Laura Phillips, and Mary Barbara Collins for starting to sort out the history and anthropology of this foundational survey.

Journal of Northwest Anthropology, Memoir 9:198–209   2014

ANTHROPOLOGY AT THE UNIVERSITY OF WASHINGTON: DEATHS AND BETRAYALS[a]

ABSTRACT

Anthropology at the University of Washington was initially charged with preserving a full record of the Native Northwest. How it lost its way in favor of globalization around the Pacific Rim involves tensions among its founding Boasians as well as deaths that left unfilled gaps for important sources of knowledge, later broached by other Seattle cultural institutions. Reviewing anthropology's first century in Seattle makes this particularly clear. Ironically, the other major universities in this region, Berkeley and University of British Columbia, acknowledge their respect for their "native hosts" at all public events and by native art in key locations.

Introduction

Anthropology was brought to Washington from without, though there was also and still is a homegrown gaggle of local collectors of Indien lore, baskets, and surviving artifacts that looked prehistoric, transacting sales in simplified Chinuk WaWa pidgin instead of learning the richly complex local languages. Organized as pioneer societies, town history buffs, pot hunters, and unlabeled museums, they lacked comparative perspectives and cultural relativity, and were deeply suspicious of professionals from "back East" who periodically swept through region buying for big city museums. In Washington state, a few of these amateurs were transplants from Ohio, well aware of rich archaeological "treasures;" others were New England Yankees intent on curios. One even "collected" artifacts from native hands under the gun barrels of his revenue cutter. Yet, from the start, organized anthropology also suffered from these same second-hand, derivative impulses.

The University of Washington (UW) was founded in 1861 by the subterfuge ("kidnapping") of Arthur Denny and Daniel Bagley to locate it in struggling Seattle. Its first president, Asa Mercer, started by grubbing out stumps and toting lumber for its first building, before he went East to recruit marriageable women after the Civil War killed off many suitors. Its first head of the regents, James Tilton, was a Southerner whose own slave Charlie had escaped successfully to Victoria, British Columbia, in 1860, becoming free once he stepped onto British soil. In 1895, the UW campus moved from Denny's Knoll (now the valuable downtown Olympic tract) to its present home on Portage Bay between Lakes Union and Washington. At that time, John Cheshiahud (also Indien John, Lake Union John) and his second wife Madeline lived across the way. Edmond Meany, self-styled historian and "Indian expert," reported a meeting with John while botanizing along Montlake. Dwelling on tragic "Poor Lo" aspects of "doomed" native life, home-grown Meany lacked the training, understanding, or insight needed to draw vital data from John, who died in 1910.

---

[a] An earlier version of this article appeared in *Northwest Anthropological Research Notes*, 36(1):103–12 (2002). Because this topic remains so problematic for the whole Northwest, we revisited and revised it again for this memoir.

John Peabody Harrington Kicks It Off

The same year Indien John died (1910), the first academically trained anthropologist arrived at UW to teach two summer classes on campus, devoted either to migration to the New World theories or to native languages. His start-off migration class has proved prophetic for Washington with the growing realization of the Chehalis River as the most likely coastal entry into North America. His most famous claim to fame, however, is as a brilliant linguist. Trained (1902–1906) at Stanford, Berkeley, Leipzig, and Berlin, he was also a John: John Peabody Harrington (1884–1961), a legend in his own time, famous for both his nuanced transcription of native languages as well as a weird and secretive lifestyle. He is portrayed in just such conflicting light by his ex-wife (1916–1922), Carobeth Laird, who was in her mid-70s when she began writing of their life together (Laird 1975). She divorced him during fieldwork to marry their informant, George Laird, a Cherokee long resident among Chemehuevi, and, though dirt poor, raised a highly successful family of native leaders.

Harrington remained devoted to California and Southwest fieldwork, with forays near and far. In 1940, he visited Melville Jacobs in Seattle and undoubtedly there was talk of their founding studies. Edmond Meany (1862–1935) must have provided bemused subject matter since his own papers at UW include a nasty and baffled plea for a set of simplified letters for writing native languages, ignoring their great phonemic complexity. He also took great exception to Harrington's use of beef tongues in his linguistics class to illustrate the actual articulation of sounds in the vocal tract (which must have gotten student's attention).

In Harrington's sprawling notes are Lushootseed place names for the area around the university, along with the native names of Lake Union John and both his wives. I had assumed that Harrington had worked with John himself until I was able to use a photograph in what was then called UW Manuscripts, Special Collections, and University Archives (MSCUA) to locate the graves of Indien John and his first wife Lucy Annie, with inscribed birth and death dates, in a Seattle cemetery famous (once notorious) for allowing the adjoining burials of different "races," long before this was legally mandated in the 1960s. Most likely Harrington worked with Jenny, John's daughter living in Suquamish, who must have returned to her home grounds on occasion, as her family continues to do today. Of special note, the death of Indien John only months before Harrington arrived was the first of many death-missed opportunities for local anthropology.

When his second wife, Madeline, died in 1906, John moved to Suquamish, near a daughter, were he died in February 1910. He was carried across Elliott Bay to be buried beside his first wife Lucy Anne in Seattle at Washelli Cemetery, near the hillside graves of early pioneer David Denny, who did learn indigenous Lushootseed, and his family. In addition to being a leader, guide, jokester, and culture broker, John was also a canoe carver. The extent of the gap he left behind was revealed in 2008, when the Seattle Art Museum featured both one of his canoes and his great granddaughter speaking about him on a video in the welcoming section (Brotherton 2008). Ironically, that woman has an anthropology BA from UW, continuing a very long family tradition immersed in the place-based ethnography of the UW campus site. Most recently, a dozen photos of John making a canoe were found during an inventory of early photographs at UW Special Collections, where they await study by someone from afar with the necessary knowledge.

Basic Boasians

Franz Boas, a German physicist turned anthropologist, instituted graduate academic training in anthropology at Columbia University after 1899. Students schooled elsewhere by his own graduates, if promising, came to Columbia for their PhDs. His primary heir, Alfred Kroeber set up the program at Berkeley in 1901, building that major department over time but diverging from Boas's main precepts.

In 1916, Boas sent Herman Haeberlin, the man who was mostly likely to be his handpicked successor, to the Tulalip Reservation north of Seattle. While engulfed in fieldwork, his health deteriorated. Concerned, Boas had Leo Frachtenberg detour from his own fieldwork with coastal Quileute (a special language isolate) to join Haeberlin, guiding him in field techniques as well as taking him by ferry into Seattle to consult an MD, who diagnosed him with diabetes. Insulin was just about to be discovered, but, becoming ill too soon, Haeberlin barely managed to publish interesting aspects of his notes before he died in Boston in 1917. In his letters, he seems determined to stay on the East Coast, near the intellectual centers of the U.S. and Europe. I feel certain, however, that Boas wanted to place him at UW to pursue local fieldwork and look for interested natives and students to take up such research, as he did elsewhere with key native scribes such as George Hunt, William Beynon, and Ella Deloria. In all, the death of Haeberkin was a serious setback for Americanists, and a second gaping hole for the Northwest, though others, including myself have mined his notebooks once I found all of them (Miller 2005b).

Devoted to the Northwest Coast, along its entire length, Boas was keen to have at least one student work among the complex Salish communities of British Columbia and Washington so they would not continue to be lumped with the matrilineal north Pacific tribes, who early overwhelmed our knowledge of the Northwest Coast because of their fine arts and elaborate social institutions of rank, clan, and initiation degrees.

Waterman Watershed

After earning a BA in Hebrew from Berkeley, Thomas Talbot Waterman was sent to Columbia University to work with Boas in 1910. He was assigned a comparative study of the "explanatory element" in Native North American folklore for his PhD. Back in California, Waterman worked with tribes of that state. In 1918, he moved north to UW, undertaking local research in Washington and southeast Alaska, particularly continuing his interest in place names begun in publications on the Yurok worldview of northern California.

By that time, Ishi, the Yahi who surrendered to civilization on 29 August 1911, had died of tuberculosis on 25 March 1916. The Waterman family had often hosted Ishi in their home, and still keenly felt his loss (Heizer and Kroeber 1979). Once in Seattle to teach general anthropology (Waterman and Kroeber 1919) and Salish linguistics, Waterman did indeed connect with local natives. He visited and fished with them, seeing their hardships. Later, at least one couple starved to death over the winter of 1920 on a float home inside the city of Seattle because the dredging of the Duwamish waterway killed off smelt and other vital fish runs. Waterman worked with Jenny Davis and again collected place names around UW, remarking on the long residence of Lake Union John there. It is noteworthy that both of the first professionals to be hired were expected to teach the linguistics of local languages, a challenging task only realized with the founding of a separate UW linguistics department fifty years ago.

UW undergraduate students had long been recruited for local research, and anthropology followed suit. When he was denied research funds, Waterman organized his UW students into study groups to plot the distribution of native canoes, houses, tools, and other traits. Geraldine (Gerry) Coffin Guy, who retained the manuscript of Christine Quintasket's autobiography until she gave it to me for publication as Mourning Dove (Miller 1990), was a student of both Waterman and then of Erna Gunther, remaining a life-long friend of each. But she kept encounters with Erna's partner Leslie Spier to a minimum because he was, she assured me, a "womanizer."

Leslie and Erna had, instead of a marriage license, a legal contract of set duration so he was not "technically" a married man.

Gerry described Waterman as red faced with a small white mustache, blustery manner, and a runny nose that he was constantly blowing. His greatest criticism of fellow academics was that their work "read like a hardware catalogue." He then had a wife and two children, but the marriage was not going well and he was often off fishing and doing fieldwork or avoiding handing in grades in a timely fashion, increasing the irritation of Prof. Woolston, chair of the Sociology Department that included anthropology until they separated in 1923. When Waterman had a chance to return to Berkeley in 1920, he took it. Negotiations with Paul Radin and Diamond Jenness, an Oxford-trained New Zealander, failed, forcing the dean to phone Berkeley for a quick replacement.

Spier to the Heart

At Berkeley, Kroeber talked Leslie Spier into taking the UW job (1920–1927) in lieu of the one-year replacement position he was about to assume at Berkeley. Erna Gunther, his "wife," went north with him. Leslie soon disliked all the rain, so he moved to the University of Oklahoma in 1927, but Erna in turn hated Oklahoma and so worked from New York City on an index to Southwest folklore for Else Clews Parsons. UW and the University of Oklahoma often exchanged faculty during those years. Vernon Parrington, now revered for his time at UW, had been fired from Oklahoma by its regents in 1908. Today the central oval on the Norman campus, nevertheless, honors his name with a plaque giving a wry account of his coaching baseball and falling out with the University of Oklahoma regents.

His long-term plans frustrated again, Boas met with UW President Matthew Lyle Spencer (1927–1933) and Graduate School Dean Frederick Morgan Padelford (1920–1942) in 1927 while doing fieldwork among the Chehalis at Oakville. In response, two of his students were asked to stop by campus for interviews. These were Melville Jacobs (1902–1972) and Thelma Adamson (1901–1983). Jacobs probably had a romantic interest in Thelma, but she was already secretly married to a physicist, Edward O. Salant.

A gentleman of his times, Boas assumed a married woman would be supported by her husband, so he only sought jobs for his male and unmarried female graduates. At UW, Boas arranged that part of their faculty duties would involve fall and winter terms off for time devoted to local fieldwork for "preserving a record of the lost civilizations of Washington State." UW provided $3,300 for salaries and $600 for department funds, while Boas, through the Carnegie Foundation, supplied $1,900 for fieldwork and $100 for supplies.

Melville Jacobs Commits

After work among Yakama speakers (then spelled Yakima), Jacobs launched his life-long coastal Oregon research, while Thelma Adamson worked among Chehalis and Nooksak, teaching at UW from April to September of 1928. She returned East and wrote a dissertation on Salish Tricksters and Transformers, but soon she suffered from tuberculosis and then depression. Ruth Benedict and others edited her collection of stories for publication in 1934 but she was too incapacitated to assist them. Finally, she was institutionalized in 1941 for the rest of her long life (Seaburg 1999). Serious though brief consideration was given to Ruth Benedict as Thelma's replacement at UW. Manuel Andrade, a linguist of Quileute and later a famous Mayanist, was being recruited to UW when Kroeber somehow interfered, probably because Waterman had told him about working conditions there.

Jacobs, who had never been out of New York City, apparently thought of this job as an exile, until his fellow student Frederica de Laguna (personal communication), reminded him, "It will be OK, Mel, there are lots of Indians out there." Once he was in Seattle, moreover, provincial students gawked at their first look at a Jewish New Yorker. His campus office was in the state museum, a legislative finesse by Meany in 1899 (Frykman 1998:88), where Jacobs became increasing upset with the neglect of the collections, particularly baskets, by the director. He successfully maneuvered to have an anthropologist appointed as head, which is still required to this day, though now any academic must also have administration experience. Budgets indicate the director earned $4,000, associate instructor (Jacobs) $2,300, museum attendant $720, stenographer $960, teaching assistant $600, readers $120, with additional funds for supplies $300, publications $1,000–1,500, and $2,000–2,500 for buying additional artifacts.

Gunther Returns

After approaching Irving Hallowell, who turned them down and remained at the University of Pennsylvania, the headship of the joint museum and department at UW was offered to Spier to return. He accepted (at $4,200), effective July 1929, but asked for a year's leave for fieldwork on the Gilbert and Ellis islands in the Pacific, with Erna as interim replacement (at $2,300). On Leslie's return, they "divorced" because their contract had expired, dividing their two sons between them. Erna's earlier published comparative work on the first salmon ceremony and her detailed ethnography of the Klallam and Makah soon took a poor second place to her increasing administrative work (Ziontz 1986a, 1986b; Amoss 1988). Assisting the work of others superseded her own research. Over time, Gunther, at both the museum and department, maintained three cars and two boats to assist graduate research.

Spier later married Ann Gayton, a famous Berkeley ethnographer from a wealthy California family. In the 1950s, her nephew Peter Kilbourne became a graduate student in UW anthropology, specializing in the Arabic Middle East. Trained as a librarian, he was tragically murdered in 1986 during an assault on the U.S. embassy in Beirut. His fellow graduate students uniformly remarked on the evenhanded treatment that Erna gave him, even though he was a relative of her ex-spouse's current wife. While the son who stayed with Leslie in turn became an anthropologist, the one with Erna specialized in media at Boeing.

Erna served as host to many visiting anthropologists, as well as putting up those bound to or from Alaska through the Seattle gateway. On one memorable occasion, as she once told me, she met Yale's Cornelius Osgood returning from interior Alaska fieldwork. As the ship docked, he shouted from the upper deck, "Erna, those damned Athabaskans have clans." His major insight has since generated considerable scholarly attention, though he later specialized in Korea.

In 1929, UW instituted student evaluations. Having just recruited Gunther to the faculty, Jacobs probably expected some sympathy from her concerning his low ratings, but she assured the administration that Jacobs had failed to heed her own firm advice on gaining popularity in the classroom. Concerned with building support for the museum and her projects, Erna was always publicity minded and Mel's science first, last, and always attitude did not appeal to the masses. Though he later became an engaging, elder-statesman-type of lecturer, Jacobs saw Erna's lack of support as a betrayal that ever after strained any hopes for their cooperation (Seaburg and Amoss 2000:12).

Verne Ray and Viola Garfield: Junior Faculty of a Certain Age

The first of UW's own students to be hired by the UW anthropology department were Verne Ray (1905–2003) and Viola Garfield (1899–1983). Ray was born in Spokane but graduated from a Seattle high school. He began his Sanpoil research in 1928 as an undergraduate, and continued at UW for an MA, before completing a famous PhD at Yale in 1937 on Plateau interrelations. He was UW instructor in 1933; full professor in 1947; associate dean of the Graduate School (1948–1954), with a year off to direct the Human Relations Area File at Yale; acting executive officer of anthropology (1960–1966); and retired after 33 years at UW. Frail, he long lived in Port Townsend, married to Dorothy Jean Ray, an anthropologist of native Alaska. His "retirement" years were devoted to tribal land claims, and the federal recognition of the Cowlitz, who formally honored him with adoption when they were successful in 2000.

Viola Garfield, a freshman in 1919, ran out of funds and went to teach in Alaska in 1920 at New Metlakatla among ex-Canadian Tsimshians, who were given religious asylum in the U.S. She married in 1924 to a much older man, who, after she tired of being house-bound and childless, encouraged her to look for a career. She returned to UW in 1925 to earn a BA in 1926 and MA in 1928. She continued on at Columbia, earning a PhD focused on Tsimshian in 1935, though not awarded until its publication in 1939. Until World War II, a Ph.D was not official until the dissertation was published, in keeping with what was regarded as the unique status of graduate scholarship as contributing to global knowledge (see p. 186, this volume).

Her specialties became kinship and art, particularly aesthetics, since that drew considerable enrollment. This interest continued in the very popular Northwest Coast Art class taught by Bill Holm, who took a degree in art augmented by classes with Gunther and Garfield. Today, Robin Wright, a Holm student, continues this last shred of the founding tradition. The 1932 move from UW to Sarah Lawrence College by Dorothy Demetracopoulou Lee (of the Whorf-Sapir-Lee hypothesis), left a permanent faculty position, which was then occupied by Viola.

Of particular note are the hardships endured by Viola Garfield for the sake of her career. As a married woman, with a husband tied to Seattle's fur exchange, she was "trapped" at UW and paid less salary from 1935, when she finished writing, to 1939 when *Tsimshian Clan and Society* was published at UW. She was essentially a teaching assistant at $95/month from 1917 to 1939, the "lowest rung" serving as undergraduate advisor; teaching 5 different 3 hour classes a week for a 15-hour load, many of these new preparations; and fulfilling numerous outside lecture and club responsibilities. Today, Viola would have a range of community and private colleges in and around Seattle, which are now providing more local hire options, though UW counts on its regional prestige to hire at lesser salaries and benefits.

Viola taught the first archaeology and physical anthropology courses on campus, staying just ahead of her students by cramming each summer. Her training excavations took place in the trash dumps at the north end of the Arboretum, now under the Montlake highway links and empty ramps leading onto the 520 bridge across Lake Washington.

Ballard Bulwark

Another recruit was strictly local, a homegrown talent willing to learn professional standards, an amateur in the best sense. Members of the Ballard family had founded both the town of Ballard, now a Seattle neighborhood, and Slaughter, now called Auburn, where grandson Arthur Ballard attended other local colleges before he graduated from UW with a degree in Latin in 1899. As a child, Arthur had learned the local native language, Lushootseed, from his nanny. Though his own family and friends thought it suspect, Arthur maintained an interest in local native culture for his entire life. In 1910, John Harrington met and encouraged him. Later he and Waterman co-authored a collection of tales, now archived at Berkeley, that eventually developed into texts published by Ballard (1927, 1929, 1950, 1951, 1957, 1999) through the *University of Washington Publications in Anthropology*. At his death, his children suppressed his major work, *Listen My Nephew* which was then in press. It was a betrayal of his whole life's work, though Erna tried to save it, but arrived at the press half-an-hour too late.

Full Service to the Whole Region

With remarkable gender balance, these four UW faculty divided up the region, with Jacobs responsible for coastal Oregon; Ray for the interior Plateau; Garfield for Alaska and British Columbia; and Gunther for the local tribes, abetted by Ballard. Jacobs also did linguistics, Ray did theory; Gunther did technology, ethnobiology (Gunther 1945), and museology; and Garfield taught everything else from art to religion to archaeology to physical anthropology. Alexander Goldenweiser at Reed College and anthropologists (mainly Homer G. Barnett and Ted Stern) at the University of Oregon undertook ethnographic work in Oregon. Later, UW added William W. Elmendorf for local native languages and cultures, Arden King (later at Tulane College) for archaeology, and Fred Hulse (later at University of Arizona) for physical anthropology.

Boas continued to send students to Washington for dissertation work. In 1935, both Marian Smith (slightly handicapped from polio) and Ethel Aginsky were in the field at Puyallup and Skokomish. From UW, Jay Ellis Ransom was working on Flathead language and Roger Ernesti was researching local technology and plant lore. The Swedish publication of a Flathead Selish grammar, preempting that field, forced Jacobs to relocate Ransom to Muckleshoot, where he worked with Julia Siddle. She was born on or near the UW campus as the child of Lake Union ~ Indien John and Lucy Ann, his first wife. Brief notes indicate that Claude Schaeffer conducted an archaeological survey of the Puyallup Valley.

In 1936, the Bryn Mawr philosopher Grace de Laguna, who was raised in Tacoma, and her daughter Frederica (Freddy), a Boas PhD, spent a year in Seattle. Freddy (personal commication) was particularly impressed that Viola Garfield was older and "knew things."

Ruth Underhill lived in Seattle for a year "picking everyone's brains" to write her booklet on the Northwest for the Bureau of Indian Affairs (BIA) schools (Underhill 1945). For a time, she was a guest of Erna Gunther at her home on Mercer Island, linked by ferry to Seattle. A colleague had "stolen" and misused field data from Underhill and she chose to work out her frustration by writing a murder mystery. A spiral staircase led upstairs. One morning, on her way down, Erna almost tripped when she heard Ruth shout out "Now I know how to kill her." After a shocked silence, Ruth had to explain her fictional motivation.

During the war years, a few graduate students, such as Francy Fox Calhoun, a Bryn Mawr BA, continued with classes and fieldwork, but most students were in the armed services. With the end of WW II and the GI bill, several students from families that could never have sent them to college were able to enter graduate school and earn advanced degrees.

In 1948, Cal Burroughs was hired from the Southwest to direct a regional archaeology program, which was connected with the Smithsonian. Using UW boats and facilities at Friday Harbor on San Juan Island, he began active surveys and excavations. He recruited John and Marcia Winterhouse from the University of Utah to undertake a survey of southern Puget Sound as their honeymoon in 1948. Only the present location of their final report provides any evidence of this as a UW project (see Appendix B, Arky Epitaph).

The first anthropology department PhDs were Richard D. Daugherty, a champion swimmer from Aberdeen, and Wayne Suttles, from a dairy farm on Bear Creek near Redmond who was initially intent on China Studies. Daugherty conducted ethnographic fieldwork among the Hoh, a coastal language isolate related to Quileute, in 1949 (Miller 2010). Daugherty soon, however, concentrated on archaeology. Funded by excavations prior to federal dam constructions, he built a major anthropology department at Washington State College in Pullman. Suttles pioneered ethno-ecology, building on Gunther's work, seeking the ethnographic background for the Friday Harbor archaeology. At Suttles's defense, Ray stormed out because he felt that the detailed maps of resources and thick description of Straits Salish economic strategies were not sufficiently theoretical. Of note, Viola Garfield was his chair, as she was again burdened with the most labor-intensive jobs in the department.

Looking for her own successor, Erna Gunther selected Daniel Sutherland "Suds" Davidson (1900–1952), a graduate of the University of Pennsylvania interested in the comparative study of Australian aboriginal culture traits, especially technology diffusions. She was keenly aware that UW needed faculty who had worked around the globe, but who would also continue the departmental tradition of data-rich researches. At a meeting at the University of Oregon in Eugene, she went to a pool party, dived in and surfaced just in front of Davidson, "inviting" him to UW by asking "How about moving to Seattle?" He agreed, and became an engaging teacher until fate intervened, and his death truly changed history. The American Anthropological Association formerly met during the week between Christmas and New Year. That year, 1952, the meeting was in Philadelphia, where, staying with his mother, Suds dropped dead. His Australia specialty was eventually assumed by the ever-colorful LaMont West, whose unconventional UW career goaded two Seattle ministers into a shootout.

Gunther remained as museum director until 1962 and department chair until 1966. She then moved to the University of Alaska at Fairbanks where she engaged in translations of classic works on the region written in German and French, which she spoke as a native because her family came for a contested region of Europe that often switched sides. Her only setback was the loss of her car in the massive 1968 earthquake.

Aftermath and Intervention

In the aftermath of Davidson's death in 1952, the administration stepped in to "rework" the department and make it "global." James B. Watson, then fresh from New Guinea after fieldwork at Hopi and in Brazil, was a leading proponent of acculturation theory. He was hired as "executive officer" of the department. Initially, Jacobs was ecstatic to have such a "progressive, scientific" colleague. Soon, however, Jacobs soured on this hope and was himself up on charges of pro-Communist sympathies by a state committee, gutting his career for some time. Eventually, he shut himself off from politics and devoted his later years to editing and publishing his extensive language texts. He also refined his theory of folklore as a drama, anticipating the ethnopoetic work of Dell Hymes, who carried on coastal Oregon research.

Correspondence indicates that Gunther, Garfield, and the "old guard" retreated to the Washington State Museum, diehards in upholding local research, while Watson began hiring Africanists and others to banish any academic attempts to pursue the original mandate. Those few students who continued along that local line of research found jobs in local community and "lesser" institutions, further demeaning and weakening any local appeal. Another UW hire for his New Guinea work, Mick Reed, whose own fieldwork appears in two novelized accounts, devoted his keynote address at one Seattle yearly conference to a parody of local research called "The Squeamish and the Squamish." A particularly bitter exchange between Watson and Gunther concerned the repair of a mimeograph machine that had been shared by the department and museum, but no longer worked for either.

The Purge of 1955

The showdown came when four junior faculty with Americanist specialties (Elmendorf, McClellan, Massey, and Osbourne) were up for tenure or rehiring. All four were dismissed in the "Purge of 1955," and tenured faculty, such as Frederick Hulse chose to go elsewhere. Later, William Elmendorf had a long career at the University of Wisconsin at Madison, where Kitty McClellan also joined him, writing extensively on the Yukon. For a few years between Seattle and Madison, he taught at Washington State University, which published his Twana monograph in 1960 (Elmendorf 1960, reissued 1992). William Massey went on to collaborate with Harold Driver on comparative studies of Native North America. Douglas Osborne, adored by local amateur archaeologists, worked in the Southwest, especially Mesa Verde, and later taught in the California system. Jacobs was particularly nasty at the time, accusing Elmendorf of so neglecting the Twana language that he allowed it to die. Fortunately, three solid tomes on Twana have vindicated Elmendorf's early efforts. Gone were the days of release time from teaching to pursue research as a defined part of the job. Ironically, Jacobs himself espoused a life-long academic strategy of devoting one's youth to amassing data and old age to analyzing and publishing it.

No anthropology was taught when UW was downtown on Denny Knoll, and after 1895 everything was in Denny Hall until the Alaska Yukon Pacific Exposition of 1909 provided space to expand into its more permanent buildings. The museum moved into the Forestry Building, constructed of logs still covered with bark. Smoking was strictly forbidden in what has aptly been described as a tinderbox, an unlikely and ironic location for precious artifacts and specimens. Later, predictably, voracious termites forced it to be condemned.

The department and the entire college library then shared the State Building, two stories fronted with impressive white columns that turned out to be very hollow when a delivery truck backed into one of them, as Viola Garfield recalled. Once Suzzallo Library was built, the books moved there. After the State Building was condemned, the museum holdings were scattered into spaces all over campus until the Burke Museum was built. The department moved to the top floor of Thomson Hall, now the Jackson School, where it expanded through the 1950s. Viola and graduate students shared an office, with a row of bookcases dividing their space in half. Next, the department moved to the top of Savery Hall, where there was a suicide, then in the late 1970s back to Denny Hall, where everything had started.

Death Reigns

A well-liked graduate student named Roy Webb died of throat cancer about 1950 and his family donated his books to Suds Davidson to become the core of a departmental library, added to by friends and later donors. Typically, Viola Garfield was made Roy Webb librarian, as part of her responsibilities for undergraduate advising and note taking at faculty meetings.

Another student, Paul Fetzer, was amassing ethnographic and linguistic materials from Nooksak when he also died of cancer. Barbara Efrat, Pam Amoss, Donna Gertds, and Brent Galloway have progressively relied on his notes, though nothing substantial has appeared in print, except for a recent study of Nootsack place names (Richardson and Galloway 2011).

In the 1960s, the department hired a series of psychological anthropologists, including Ray Fogelson, who quickly moved on to a long career at the University of Chicago. David Pavy was hired from Tulane in 1968, but, within months, a "demoniacal suicide" left him hanging in his office. In the late 1970s, after she had briefly taught China classes at UW, Judith Strouch also committed suicide while at Tufts. Wilson Duff (UW MA 1952), founder of sustained anthropology in British Columbia, shot himself in his University of British Columbia office in 1976. He had strongly encouraged field work among British Columbia communities, and remained loyal to the UW Boasian who guided his MA, so this pivotal source for local research left behind a huge gap. Carol Eastman, progressively faculty, chair, graduate dean at UW, then provost at University of Hawaii, succumbed to swift cancer in 1998. At faculty insistence before her tenure vote, she undertook research with the Haida language spoken by Alaskans living in Seattle, augmenting her Swahili expertise, but her efforts were at best half-hearted, having been forced upon her.

During the 1970s, ethnic studies programs were started at UW, as elsewhere. With a sense of relief, anthropology delegated Americanist teaching to classes shared with American Indian Studies (AIS) at UW, which briefly offered classes in state Salishan languages. The AIS encouraged Skagit elder Vi Hilbert to teach her literature in English, though she was also hosting local elders and shamans in her classroom. Vi was recruited by linguist Thom Hess (UW PhD 1967), who wrote the textbooks used. She continued teaching alone, but was treated rather shabbily and only welcomed back by UW AIS at high ceremonies. Still, the UW high tech center in the humanities center, with sponsorship by William Seaburg, produced CDs and archival copies of a bit of her Lushootseed materials. Today, Navajo is taught in the AIS Center; local native traditions are all but ignored, unless purchased by tribal casino money. Further diffusing and dissipating local import has been Women's Studies, seeking to globalize without any respectful grounding on home turf.

Native Support

Native involvement in the original Anthropology Department is quite intriguing. Erna Gunther was famous for putting aside anything else to welcome and address visiting school groups and delegations from local reservations. In 1929, attempts to hire Louis Shotridge, a Tlingit then collecting for the University of Pennsylvania Museum, were rebuffed by a curator there, though he was not spared a lonely, tragic end. Manuscripts by Martin Sampson of Swinomish, Joyce Cheeka of Squaxin Island, and Marian Vincent (pen name Mary Ann Lambert) of Klallam were reviewed by Jacobs and Gunther. Howard Rock, an Alaskan Eskimo, gained pointers in Art about 1937–1938, and later edited *Tundra Times*. During the 1940s and 1950s, Henry Allen, a Twana elder who worked closely with William Elmendorf, would visit his UW classes, where his flattened head, a mark of high class, endlessly fascinated. Both Viola and Amelia Susman Schultz, the last Boas PhD, had close ties with William Beynon, a Tsimshian chief who wrote volumes of native texts and ethnography, but mishandled money.

Along with the Washington State Museum, now renamed the Thomas Burke Memorial Museum, the last strong bastion of local interest and resources is the library itself, especially the UW Special Collections (UWSC), Archives, and Northwest Collection (formerly MSCUA), which houses the papers of several of these early faculty and students, protected even as they are neglected by local students and would-be scholars. Today, instead, it is academics from around the world who regularly journey to Seattle, particularly in the summer, to consult the notes of Jacobs, Garfield, Gunther, Ransom, and Helmi Juvonen.

Consequences

By mid-century, UW switched from an academic strategy of allowing a department to grow and graft under the watchful eye of Boas at Columbia to one of aggressive efforts by deans to lop off and lever in. Given its founding mandate to concentrate on "Washington native civilizations," whether lost or not, the department was remarkably Salish-phobic, though Salish is much the predominant group in the state. While Jacobs himself encouraged early work, he sent student drafts off to Boas for evaluation. Later, he sent Dale Kinkade to Carl Voegelin at Indiana University

Bloomington for Chehalis dissertation work. He never felt assured or comfortable with their very difficult sound systems. An even greater oversight was Chimakuan (Chimakum–Quileute), the languages unique to Washington State. While Harrington and Boas did rescue some Chimakum, only the timely work of Jay V. Powell, long at British Columbia, provides Quileute for posterity.

Factionalism and specialization betrayed the UW mandate, seeing in globalization a beacon for professional fame, when, in truth, the future will continue to curse such foundations built on sand because most of what UW continues to do is second hand. Betrayed by fate, by climate, by circumstance, and, most especially, by ill-timed deaths, UW anthropology lacked anyone competent to teach regional anthropology at the turn of this millennium and, whether by denial, curse, or betrayal, shows only too well that decades of mistakes become compounded into an anthropology of hollow promise. Today, after the death of Vi Hilbert, the "authority" on local peoples, cited and quoted is a Seattle parochial school teacher. The department itself has the dubious honor of serving as the inspiration for a murder mystery entitled *Fieldwork,* in which several of the more nasty members of the faculty are killed off; it was published in 1961 by two sociologists writing as Maria Danielle.

Of all lasting consequences, the greatest legacy, appropriately enough, is that of Viola Garfield, put-upon and unsung in her own time, yet now the revered ancestor of a large, diverse, global, and productive cohort of Tsimshianists. She was also the only early member of the department to receive a Festschrift (Miller and Eastman 1984), though a volume of essays on native art was dedicated to Erna Gunther (Carlson 1983).

Jacobs invested in real estate and, though his wife sold it at a loss after he died, set up a research fund based at the Whatcom County Museum in Bellingham, which also received his basket collection. With additional funds at the deaths of his mother and wife, the Jacobs Fund continues to finance modest Americanist research projects. A parallel account in Canada was established at the death of Dale Kinkade. The Jacobses "had originally determined to leave their estate to the Anthropology Department at the University of Washington, but Jacobs's growing disenchantment with the direction of scholarship in the department led him to look for an alternative venue" (Seaburg and Amoss 2000:10).

Ronald Olson (1895–1979), a logger turned anthropologist (UW BA 1926, MA 1927) whose introductory classes swelled enrollments at Berkeley, left money for a graduate scholarship at UW, but its intended purpose for local scholarship has been seriously misdirected to Asia.

The greatest irony, of course, is that the nearest "major" universities at the University of British Columbia (Duff) and University of California, Berkeley (Kroeber) innately respect the anthropology of their own locales. At the new Green residential college at the University of British Columbia, a Sto:lo Salish weaving hangs above the high table where, in Europe, there would instead be a venerable coat of arms. At Berkeley, whole rooms in central locations hold data on California languages and cultures, sharing space with scholars working around the world and training students for leading academic positions. Except for quick grants and hit and run field studies based on expedience, UW long ago sold its soul outside the region and turned its back on any sense of place so that it no longer "belongs" in Seattle.

Rehashes

Why bother to rehash the past, yet again? For a decade, writing up and publishing a vast collection of fieldnotes has been my primary motivation. Having largely finished those from Native Americans and First Nations, this article begins work on the "other guys." Increasing despair over the future of continuing Salishan and Northwest ethnography, where no interested students can be found, has encouraged me to spend time putting Washington ethnography to bed in a pretty thorough fashion. The hope is that later generations will be drawn to improved collections at UW Special Collections and a range of recent publications finally presenting UW research from the past century (Chehalis, Suquamish, Puyallup, art). These subjects have been sufficiently trivialized that they are now better represented in classes at community and tribal colleges than at any university. Local reservations looking for interviewers to record their elders and for expert witnesses for court cases have repeatedly told me there are no interested graduate students nor any prospects of them. That "well" is very dry, one official assured me, and this article begins to explain why.

Hope has returned, however, in Canada among the spiritual heirs of Wilson Duff, where the University of British Columbia under Bruce Miller, the University of Saskatchewan under Keith Carlson, and the University of Victoria with John Lutz have inspired a new crop of regionalists, though more in history and ethnohistory than anthropology.

As bleak and gloomy as the situation was when I began writing, there have been a few rays of light. The Burke was briefly led by a new director, George MacDonald, a Northwesternist well qualified to return to Northwest anthropology to Seattle before he left hastily for Canada. For the times just after 1950, an amazingly large number of the students trained in those decades remain alive and only too willing to set the record straight in conversation, but not yet in print.

Yet, with peaks there are troughs, and UW managed to stay true to form. When MacDonald moved to Canada, he took with him the remnants of the Roy Webb Library, founded as a memorial by his family and added to by friends and faculty ever since. In need of space for computers, Julie Stein, now director of the Burke Museum, ordered the destruction of the library, with theses and dissertations sent to the UW Library, books on the shelf offered for sale (full discloser, I bought several classics), and a vast collection of reprints by everyone and anyone ever associated with UW purchased by the MacDonalds, along with the remaining books, to be saved for posterity across the border. As the first "Guardian of the Roy Webb Library" I took special umbrage that the collection, donated by his widow, of Clyde Kluckhohn books, all signed, scattered in this mess.

Most recently, the Environmental Studies component of the department has imploded as core faculty took better jobs and another potential local interest vanished. The mainstay of Northwest Studies at UW, of course, has been its Press, though more as a distributor than an originator of titles, particularly those of the Canadian National Museum. But here too there have been serious gaffs, such as the absurd contrast between the two scholarly Lushootseed Dictionaries and *Native Seattle*, with its atlas of place names (1/3rd of the book) in a writing system that looks like jibberish mixing upper and lower case letters with numbers. It is, expectedly, portions of this atlas that have been recopied by local sports and governmental organizations, illiterate of accuracy and respect. Everywhere else in the country, when such simplified writing is presented, it appears beside the technically correct system. In all, the consensus among academics is that UW has always been derivative, following, not always wisely, trends at major universities. In this light, then, it is understandable why it consistently ignores as "provincial" what is indeed original and indigenous in its midst, except, that is, for some tokenism. It will be the last campus in the Northwest, for example, to have a native-style longhouse.

While the UW Anthropology website once included a brief history by Simon Ottenberg, an Africanist who spent his long career there and served as Acting Chair, today the website (http://depts.washington.edu/anthweb/welcome) includes only a brief paragraph that starts a decade too late and ignores any of the dynamics among the founders:

> The Department of Anthropology at the University of Washington was launched in the 1920s by Leslie Spier and Melville Jacobs. Both were students of Franz Boas, as was Erna Gunther who took the reins in 1929 and under whose lively leadership the department grew for a quarter of a century.

Journal of Northwest Anthropology, Memoir 9:210–215   2014

SYNOPSIS, SYNTHESIS, SKIMPING, AND SCHOLARSHIP: A CASE FROM THE CHEHALIS IN THE "OTHER" WASHINGTON[a]

ABSTRACT

Special places need extraordinary treatment. Grand Mound—between I-5 and the Chehalis River in southwest Washington—is, for native peoples, "proof" on the landscape that a Star spirit left behind a bit of itself. Interrelated with its presence is the regional epic about the Moon and Sun, fathered by an old Star and themselves the ancestors of local chiefly families. These connections and clarifications are explicit in original materials from Thelma Adamson, but slighted in my 1999 condensation of them (Miller 1999a).

Introduction

Source evaluation is critical to the pursuit of knowledge, both within and without academia. A key example, recently raised, has to do with the protection of Grand Mound (literally named 'star' [*łačis* Kinkade 1991:#63, #818]) in the Chehalis area of Washington State, a landmark vital to the people of the Confederated Chehalis Reservation and beyond. *Northwest Anthropological Research Notes* (*NARN*) published my boiled-down synopsis—reduced to 1/5th of its original length—of 1927 ethnographic fieldnotes of Thelma Adamson (Miller 1999a), a graduate student of Franz Boas from Columbia University (Seaburg 1999). The *NARN* article has been subsequently used by those involved in Traditional Cultural Properties ~ Places (TCP) and Cultural Resource Management (CRM) studies. A golden opportunity, however, has been missed because Grand Mound, this holy landmark, has not received its proper scholarly due, nor have our foremothers such as Thelma Adamson in the profession.[1]

Instead of going back to Adamson's original notes, recent TCP and CRM reports have relied on my précis of these materials. Admittedly, the Adamson materials once required special access by written permission (now lifted) within the Melville Jacobs Collection at the University of Washington libraries, but competent scholarship requires rigor. Rigor and respect, as with the non-academic example of a collection of Cowlitz stories lifted in whole from Adamson and Melville Jacobs without a shred of thanks, attribution (except to story teller), or bibliography (Wilson 1998). Unusual places need special attention, rather than receiving routine pro-forma treatment.

As a telling example of such minimal scholarship, this article explores the integrated understanding of Grand Mound as what native peoples themselves call a "proof" of their own cultural tenets. It also explores the ramifications, so underappreciated, of the Star Child epic for establishing the pedigree of chiefly families and their dynasties throughout this region. A separate

---

[a] This article was previously published in *Journal of Northwest Anthropology*, 43(2):171–178 (2009).

article (see p. 12, this volume) explores the overlooked significance of the downriver Tsamosan culture hero Misp[h], who has escaped any recognition in Northwest literature (Miller 1989, 1992a).

Tsamosan (once called Olympic Salish) is the subgroup within Central Coast Salish consisting of Quinault-Queets, Lower Chehalis, Upper Chehalis, and Cowlitz. The late Dale Kinkade, the authority on this subgroup, named it for the words for the numbers 2 and 4 shared by its daughter languages. Upper Chehalis had three dialects: Satsop, and dividing at Grand Mound, Upriver and Downriver.

Background

To explain the motivational background of the 1999 Adamson synthesis, several paragraphs from the original introduction (Miller 1999a:1–3) have been selected and reprinted below:

As preparation for my book-length overview of Puget Sound ethnography (1999b), following up a prior study of its major ritual—the shamanic odyssey to the land of the dead—the 1927 notes on Chehalis, Cowlitz, and neighbors by Thelma Adamson were typed into a computer and boiled down into the present work. Similar efforts also produced Suquamish notes based on those of Warren Snyder. Strongly motivating these contributions has been increasing despair that anthropologists, especially in the Northwest, have been actively denying their own founders, even as local native peoples constantly remind each other not to forget their elders. This growing contrast only adds to the larger sense of loss.[1]

. . . The bulk of this description was collected by Thelma Adamson as a graduate student at Columbia University under the famed Franz Boas. After collecting folklore texts in 1926, she turned more to ethnography in 1927. Almost sixty years later, all that remains of her Chehalis ethnography is a carbon copy of roughly typed notes divided up according to materials given by named individuals. The original notes are lost, but the carbon was saved, like so much else, by Melville Jacobs of the University of Washington.

In an attempt to make these notes more useful and available, Jay Miller typed them into a computer during December 1994 and January 1995. The original order of source (elder, informant), sometimes date, and unarranged subjects under a centered heading was revised by creating new computer files according to topic, combining materials from several sources on the same topic unless they were substantially different. As a result, any slight repetition that may appear involves variations of basic data.

Segments of information are identified by page number and initials of source inside curved brackets, such as {000 jm}. When topics were only coded by some form of a Chehalis word, such as that for first menstruation, a substitute such as M1 replaced it. The time frame was clarified whenever possible, and references to "now" were changed to "1927." Native phrasings "directly" copied are indicated by quotation marks. . . . After twenty five years of research in Washington State, Miller was also able to qualify and better present whatever comparative information was supplied to Adamson when she was very new to this region . . .

. . . Since the surviving carbon is irreplaceable and indispensable for scholarship, these topics are arranged by page number of the carbon followed by the initials of the elder. Their initials were taken from the *Upper Chehalis Dictionary* by M. Dale Kinkade (1991), which reproduces all of the linguistic forms attempted by Adamson in these notes and in her 1934 published collection of texts, *Folk-Tales of the Coast Salish*, a Memoir of the American Folk-lore Society (Adamson 1934). Indeed, through the kindness of Kinkade, these notes were typed from the very same photocopy of the carbon which he used to extract the words that appear in the dictionary. The continuous page numbers, penciled in by Dr. Kinkade, provide the citations used here for the entries

. . . In October of 1995, Miller boiled down the rearranged topics into understandable English summaries which are presented here in a fifth of the original space. The intent was a close paraphrase of the information, with "exact phrasings" always marked by quotation marks to indicate they are in a native voice.

All of the Chehalis words (but not the Cowlitz, Taitnapam, or Lushootseed [Puget Salish]) in these notes appear in the Kinkade 1991 dictionary as correct forms, but the most significant ones are included here, along with its corresponding number in the dictionary. Where the technical spelling of a word is reliable, it appears in **bold**, while those that remain uncertain are in *italics*.

. . . Adamson's material represents an impressive early ethnography and is particularly useful for religious and theological topics. The work was done as an aspect of the research for her doctoral dissertation on Tricksters and Transformers under the direction of Franz Boas, who also arranged for Thelma Adamson, along with Melville Jacobs, to become founding members of the Anthropology Department at the University of Washington in Seattle. In 1927, both Boas and Adamson were conducting fieldwork with the Chehalis. (Miller 1999a:1–30)

Understanding Grand Mound, Sky and Sun

At issue are six paragraphs published in the 1999 *NARN* article (Miller 1999a), extracted from the fuller sections under Sky and Moon composed from the original Adamson notes.

The following three paragraphs were included in The People section under the Upper Chehalis subheading:

Grand Mound, where part of a Star came to earth, had a spring half way up the side. The Star was too big to live on the earth so it only left a small bit behind. Just to the east are many small mounds that once were porpoises [1612] before the Flood.

Brush Creek divided Grand Mound Prairie and was known for its winter abundance of red salmon. It was dry in the summer.

At Lequito [Claquato], Moon was born, according to the epic. Before the Flood separated everyone into animals and humans, birds were the boss of all the people. Moon changed all that. (Miller 1999a:7)

The following paragraph was included in the Environment section under the Sky subheading:

Morning [Moon] was a baby stolen by two women at Lequito and taken west before being rescued by Bluejay to become the Moon {58 md}. His brother became the Sun. Everything bad was burned {386 js}. This is the story of the founding of the chiefly lines {345 js}. (Miller 1999a:16)

The following paragraph was included in the Society and Rankings section under the Royal Chiefs subheading:

Chiefs were royal in the old days. Their line was founded by Moon while he was on earth. Sometimes they were called *taiyiman* from the Chinook jargon word for chief or leader, tyee. No matter how much money a person had, they could not be a chief, "not in their hearts." A chief was born not made. A chief, first and foremost, kept things going smoothly within the tribe and dealt with outsiders whenever they came. He had to be smart, know about all the families in the region, and speak many languages {372 ds}. (Miller 1999a:22)

The following paragraph was included in the Tales section under the Background subheading:

Story tellers would visit widely to expand their repertoire, making a business of it. Of course, stories got borrowed and changed this way. Star Husband belonged to the Upper Chehalis, but the Snoqualmie put it together with their own version. Spider told the girls they were married to Stars and helped them escape back to earth when one of them gave birth to the Moon at Lequito {345 js}. (Miller 199a:53)

Vital to understanding these abstracts is the Star Child (Star Husbands) epic, most completely treated in Miller (1999b:54–57, 152 note 8, 153 note 10), with a crucial prelude found only in Adamson's book of Chehalis tales (1934:379–384; fieldnotes 58 md [Marion Davis]) and identified as such by Dale Kinkade. Important sources for contextualizing this epic include Hilbert and Miller (1994, 1996), Miller (1989, 1992a), and Palmer (1925).

Star Child tells the story of two girls who "wish upon stars," one red and one white, to marry them and wake up beside these husbands in the sky. The Red Star is young and vital but the White one is old and has rheumy eyes, though having the potency to become the father of Star Child. Birds and females dominate the earth, so the birth of this boy at Claquato sets off a series of events that lead to his kidnapping by two women who become his wives. In grief, his mother goes to a stream to wash out his last soiled diaper and finds a twisted child, Diaper Boy, in her hands. Raven then claims both as his slaves, until Star Child is rescued by Bluejay, returns, straightens out his brother, and avenges the family by turning the braggart into the present shiny black bird. Together the twins decide the world needs a "soul" and become the Sun and the Moon after incinerating the earth and making it ready for humans to become the pivotal species in this "new world."

Today, among members of the Confederated Chehalis Reservation, the Bluejay episode is closely associated with the Sanders family (Andrew, George), who had links with Taidnapam, Nisqually, and Chehalis. Indeed, Bluejay as trickster has a Plateau "feel" since the Klikitat (Taidnapam kin) name themselves after the Stellar jay. Rather than being altruistic in rescuing Star Child/Moon, however, Bluejay was seeking access to power for his own use. Instead, as usual, his actions have the unintended consequence of helping to reform the world. George Sanders was also the source for the remarkable narrative that integrates many episodes into the coherent Transformer epic published by Palmer (1925).

Simultaneously "finishing off" pre- and post- aspects of the world is a Changer or Transformer, known variously as Xwane among Chehalis, Xels among Sto:lo, and Dukwibulth among Lushootseeds. He created from Salmon milt the two girls who stole and married Star Child. Later he provided tools, foods, and resources along each of the major riverways.

Missing from any of this discussion is the concurrent native belief in a "proof" left on the landscape to confirm the authenticity of each epic, much like the Rainbow testifies to Noah's Flood in Biblical tradition. Known proofs include the sky rope tumbled to earth that became Big Rock for the Skagit (Highway 9 at mile post 538), or a quarried rock near Mount Si for the Snoqualmie. Of note, only Grand Mound is a Star, itself coming to earth and deciding to leave a bit of it(him)self behind.

As the original notes make clear, the mound itself is called by the same word as a "star" [łačis] in the Kinkade Chehalis dictionary (Kinkade 1991:#63, #818) because the star, too big to occupy that space, left a token of itself embedded there:

> Grand Mound on Grand Prairie, with a spring half way up, was a star that came down to earth, but it was too big, left just a little because it was too big to live on the earth. Star [63, 818]. The mound there is also called the same word. Just east of Star are many little mounds, each from a small whale, they travel 4–5 in one stream (English equivalent unknown) [1612, porpoise]. When the flood was here, they were dried there and are called [1612], are dried (into little mounds) there in the woods. MD, dolphin?, porpoise? {37 ph end}

Also in the original notes under the heading Moon are the following entries:

> {50 md} Belief in the Moon. People used everything that he said to do.

> {345 js} Moon. Is the story of the chiefs. All the chiefs always know it because Moon is the chief. Fire is also a great chief, but it is a story of the girls.

> {386 js} Warrior. The Moon burned everything he killed, turn it into ashes. This is a rule of this tribe, to burn anything that is bad. Mostly every tribe has it. [For other tribes, evil beings were turned to stone by a Changer.]

> {80 ph?} Moon [909]. Moon changes everything to how it is today for the Indians. People did not know anything. Birds and animals were ahead of them. When Moon changes, the people know what to do. Indians, animals, and people could talk to each other before that.

> {81 ph?} After Moon changed animals and birds, they can not talk the language of the people. Some tribes have it a little different, how the Moon was. Moon and Sun were brothers, all they knew, Chehalis never worshiped both. Can't seem to get any functional idea of Sun and Moon.

Conclusions

It is always best to go back to original sources, fortified by improved understandings and accumulated data, especially when places of great cultural and religious significance are the focus. As Tribal elders are respected, so too must be our academic ancestors. While a handy and useful overview of traditional Chehalis traditions, my 1/5th "boil down" neglected to specify that Grand Mound is itself called "Star" and is a willful embodiment of an ancestor of the Chehalis Royal line. Its seat was upriver at Claquato (Łequato), where Moon was born as Star Child and Diaper

Boy was conceived from a soiled garment washed in the river. Untwisted and made handsome by his spiritual twin, he became the Sun. Moon left behind chiefly children from his first marriages, and took his third wife Frog into the sky with him. She can still be seen on the face of the Moon. Subsequently, these chiefly lines spread far and wide to become important dynasties around Puget Sound and neighboring areas of Canada. Both international and extraterrestrial, these leaders are regarded as very distinct from ordinary humans. As proof of their claim, Big Rock and Grand Mound remain to mark the tribal landscape.

The routine and the ordinary serve as defaults for most conditions, but special instances require unique efforts.

NOTE

[1] In the latest egregious example of the University of Washington's disregard of its own Anthropology founders, then Dean Julie Stein, an archaeologist, destroyed in May 2004 the Roy Webb Memorial Library (named for a much mourned graduate student), replaced it with a computer lab, and gutted the entire collective memory—represented by complete reprint files, all dissertations, and classic books donated by everyone ever associated with it.

ACKNOWLEDGMENTS

The late Vi Hilbert was instrumental in my understanding of Star Child and his widespread chiefly progeny. Katherine Barr opened my eyes to Thelma's sessions with her dying father, eager to have his stories recorded at that critical juncture. Richard Bellon of the Confederated Tribes of the Chehalis Reservation has been a helpful and insightful reader, as well as advisor. Gene Woodwick revealed aspects of the natural landscape. Bill Seaburg, Laurel Sercombe, and Bob Walls share my enthusiasm for increasing our recognition and respect for Thelma Adamson's life and work.

SKOOKUMCHUCK SHUFFLE:
SHIFTING ATHAPASKAN SWAALS
INTO OREGON KLATSKANIS BEFORE
TAITNAPAM SAHAPTINS CROSS THE CASCADES[a]

ABSTRACT

Southwestern Washington—drained by the Chehalis, Cowlitz, and Columbia Rivers, including the estuaries of Grays Harbor and Willapa Bay—is the interface of five language stocks and a crossroads in a vast trade network relying on a trade jargon now known as Chinuk Wawa. This Tsamosan homeland saw the in-migration of Taitnapam Sahaptins across the crest of the Cascade Mountains into the foothills region as traders and horsemen, which is well known. A prior out-migration of Swaal Athapaskans is not well known. By vacating the basin of the Skookumchuck River before C.E. 1800 to become the Klatskanie in Oregon, they left an occupational gap that may have helped draw Sahaptins from the Yakama area across the Cascades. Sequencing these population and language shifts in Southwest Washington restores the understanding of this region achieved by Franz Boas, James Teit, and colleagues a hundred years ago. Today, drivers along I-5 cross this river at Centralia, looking down on the Borst blockhouse from the Treaty War, set incongruously beside current outlet malls.

Regional Tribes and Languages

Southwestern Washington, at the southern edge of the Olympic Mountains and Peninsula, is the intersection of five language stocks (Hajda 1990; Wray 2002). These are Tsamosan Coast Salishan, Chinookan and Sahaptin Plateau Penutian, Makah-Nootkan Wakashan, Quileute-Hoh Chimakuan, and Pacific Coast Athapaskan. As a crossroads in a vast trade network, the region relied on the trade jargon now known as Chinuk Wawa, originally based on words from Penutian Chinook and Wakashan Nootkan, but later adaptively including Hawaiian and European languages, especially English, French, and Spanish. Long the Tsamosan Salish homeland, Makah and Quileute once came as visitors, raiders, and slavers, and more recently as spouses and honored guests. Of particular note, the well-known migration of Taitnapam Yakamas across the crest of the Cascade Mountains into the foothills region as traders and horsemen was preceded by an out-migration of Swaal Athapaskans vacating the Skookumchuck in the late 1700s to become the Klatskanie in Oregon.

Southwestern Washington accordingly has a complex prehistory, due to its large rivers. Over ten thousand years ago, continental immigrants coming south down the Pacific coast could

---

[a] This article was previously published in *Journal of Northwest Anthropology*, 46(2):167–176 (2012).

have first entered the continent through the mouth of the Chehalis River. Later, passage was facilitated by the Cowlitz corridor between Puget Sound and the Columbia River, and, in reverse, the Salish Funnel downstream along the lower Chehalis River (a landscape considerably broadened by the outflow of the massive Puget Sound glacier). Coast Salishan Tillamook ancestors first moved onto the coast along this route prior to Tsamosan settlement (Thompson and Egesdal 2008), named for its basic words for the numbers 2 and 4.

As a subgroup of the Central Coast Salish branch within the larger Coast Salishan language family, Tsamosan (formerly called Olympic Salish) consists of four languages within coastal and inland branches. Coastal includes Quinault-Queets and Lower Chehalis; inland includes Upper Chehalis and Lower Cowlitz. Upper Chehalis includes five bands speaking three dialects—Satsop, as well as Downriver Oakville (ch series, Bays and Oakvilles) and Upriver Tenino (k series, Teninos, Boisforts, Ilawiqs~Claquatos) splitting at Grand Mound. Satsop, while speaking Upper Chehalis, interacted more with the Lower Chehalis because of the Satsop trail into Hood Canal. Upriver used back of the mouth sounds (k k̓ x), whereas downriver used front of the mouth sounds (č č̓ š) in the same words. For example, the word root for "slender" is čema–downriver and k̓ema– upriver, producing variants for a 'narrow trail' such as čemašuɫ and k̓emašuɫ (Kinkade 1991:40, #502).

Cowlitz are multilingual and multicultural, comprised of three distinct communities and language stocks, though identified together as a single tribe among themselves and by others (Ray 1966). At the mouth of the Cowlitz River were originally Chinooks (Ray 1937, 1938); only a short distance upriver lived Tsamosan Lower Cowlitz. After disastrous epidemics decimated the Chinooks by 1830, Cowlitz moved downriver, in accord with Morey's Law (Dobyns 1983:306–10). The Willapa-Swaal lived in the Willapa Hills, drained by the river of the same name. The Swaal spoke Athapaskan and were known locally as Willapa, Kwaliokwa, Mountain Cowlitz and Klatskanie (Clatskanie, Tlatskanai), but the situation was much more complex, as elaborated below.

Cowlitz River headwaters were on the slopes of Mount Rainier, near others flowing into eastern Washington, with four mountain passes within twenty miles. Through trade, marriage, and opportunities for horse and livestock pasture, Yakama Sahaptins moved across the Cascades in the early 1800s to become known as Taitnapams or Upper Cowlitz on the Lewis (Kathlapootl) and Upper Cowlitz Rivers (Boyd 2011). A century ago, many Taitnapams "returned" under threat of force to the Yakama Reservation to settle, others continue to form a constituency within the Cowlitz Indian Tribe, recognized by the federal government in 2000. George Gibbs explained:

> After the depopulation of the Columbia tribes by congestive fever [malaria], which took place between 1820 and 1830, many of that tribe [Yakama Klickitat] made their way down the Kathlapūtl (Lewis River), and a part of them settled along the course of that river, while others crossed the Columbia and overran the Willamette Valley, more lately establishing themselves on the Umkwa [Umpqua]. Within the last year (1855), they have been ordered by the superintendent of Oregon [Joseph Lane] to return to their former home, and are now chiefly in this part of the Territory. The present generation, for the most part, look upon the Kathlapūtl as their proper country, more especially as they are intermarried with the remnant of the original [Chinook] proprietors. No correct census has at any time been made of the Klikatat, but they are estimated at from 300 to 400, exclusive of the Taitinapam. (Gibbs 1877:170–171)

In all, relocations to the Yakama reservation took place in 1856, during the Treaty War, and again between 1910–1912 when Natives were recruited to claim and settle lands about to be lost as a result of the Dawes Allotment Act.

Smallpox repeatedly swept through the region, perhaps starting in 1520, but certainly in 1781, 1801, 1824, 1836, 1852, and 1862 (Boyd 1999:22). Those in populous areas, such as the Columbia Chinooks, were hardest hit, with high mortality and settlement shifts to concentrate survivors. Sparser inland communities survived better, and some moved downriver to benefit from abandoned land and resources, in accord with Morey's Law that healthy upriver people repopulate decimated lowland communities. An initial suspicion that some Washington Athapaskans moved to Oregon to take advantage of such emptied lands is not borne out, particularly since the lure of the Clatskanie area, with historic fluctuations, is an abundance of game, especially deer and elk, as local tree farmers still complain. The Chinookan depopulation made the move easier, but it does not seem to have directly propelled it. Good hunting did.

Pacific Coast Athapaskans: Willapas, Swaals, Kwalhioqwa, Klatskani

The Athapaskan diaspora was precipitated by the C.E. 803 White River eruption on the current Alaska-Yukon border, and featured small narrowing-stem points, rectangular houses, and possibly microblades. Earlier eruptions there in C.E. 50 and 450 may have also set off migrations (Matson and Magne 2007).

Pacific Coast Athapaskans split from the Canadian branch, after it split from the Alaskan homeland. A scattered population, these Diné speakers occupied uplands from the Columbia River to northern California, including the Upper Umpqua, Tututni, Galice, and Tolowa. Like others of the diaspora, they retained their own language while also speaking those languages around them and borrowing features of economy and technology. They continued a concern with death taboos, and with girl's puberty, but shifted the focus to the menstruant herself rather than her potentially dangerous impact on the larger community. Unlike the matri-emphasis of other Athapaskans, Pacific Coast communities were more patrilineal and patrilocal, with settled towns and territories. Land hunting remained important, though some coastal tribes regarded sea lions as "ocean deer" (Perry 1991:40–49). Over four hundred years after the dispersal, Pacific Coast Athapaskans had come to rely on a stored salmon-acorn economy (Matson and Magne 2007:151).

The Lower Columbia Athapaskans, called "upstreamers" or "inlanders" by Chehalis, spoke Salish with Chehalis and Athapaskan with the Pe Ells, a headwaters group given that name post-contact because they lived at a site where a French-Canadian named Pierre settled but shifted the R sound to L in their pronunciation of his name (Adamson 1927; Miller 1999). More generally they are called Willapas and Mountain Cowlitz, with the eastern branch sometimes written as Su'wal, though Swaal is a better spelling. Dale Kinkade (1991:155, #2189) rescued this proper linguistic spelling of the Swaal tribal name from the fieldnotes of John Peabody Harrington, a master linguist. A link with the word Thelma Adamson and Franz Boas wrote for the Satsop term for "arrowhead" (.swāāls, Kinkade 1991:155, #2174) seems likely because of the strong associations of this group with hunting. They called themselves Xanane (Boas and Goddard 1924:41, #29).

The Oregon branch originated from the Skookumchuck Valley, and moved south, potentially along the Cowlitz River corridor: "According to a tradition recorded by [George] Gibbs, [Edward] Curtis, and [James] Teit, the Clatskanie once lived on the Skookumchuck River but migrated across the Columbia where the hunting was better" (Kraus 1990:530).

The Swaals were probably best known by their Chinookan names of Kwalhioqwa in Washington and Klatskanie in Oregon, though that place is spelled Clatskanie (Welch 1983). The names Kwalhioqua and Klatskanie (Tlatskanai) are Penutian Chinook words, the first a village name meaning 'lonely place in the woods' and the second meaning 'those of the place of little oaks' or 'little-oak-ers.' Horatio Hale with the 1841 Wilkes Expedition "estimated them at about 100, said that they built no permanent habitations, but wandered in the woods, subsisting on game, berries, and roots, and were bolder, hardier, and more savage than the river and coast tribes" (Hodge 1906:I, 746). Hodge later described the group as follows:

> Tlatksanai. An Athapascan tribe that formerly owned the prairies bordering Chehalis r., Wash., at the mouth of Skookumchuck r., but, on the failure of game, left the country, crossed the Columbia, and occupied the mountains on Clatskanie r., Columbia co., Oreg. [Anson Dart, Oregon territorial Indian agent, in 1852 said] "This tribe was, at the first settlement of the Hudson's Bay Company in Oregon, so warlike and formidable that the company's men dared not pass their possessions along the river in less numbers than 60 armed men, and then often at considerable loss of life and always at great hazard. The Indians were in the habit of extracting tribute from all the neighboring tribes who passed in the river, and disputed the right of any persons to pass them except upon these conditions." (Hodge 1910:II, 763)

In their defense, as new comers to this region abounding in game, itself probably depleted by epidemics, their aggressiveness reflects their necessary assertion of possession of new territory.

George Gibbs, as federal treaty secretary and avid linguist, collected material on the Willapas in the 1850s, which was published after his death:

> Of the Willopah (Kwalhiokwa) or, as they call themselves, Owhillpash, there are yet, it appears, three or four families living on the heads of the Tsihalish [Chehalis] River above the forks. According to the account of an old man, from whom the vocabulary was obtained, the Klatskanai, a kindred band, till lately inhabiting the mountains on the southern side of the Columbia, and now also nearly extinct, formerly owned the prairies on the Tsihalis at the mouth of the Skūkumchuk, but, on the failure of game, left the country and crossed the river. Both these bands subsisted chiefly by hunting. As before mentioned, they are of the Tahkali stock, though divided by nearly six degrees of latitude from the parent tribe. The fact of these migrations of the Klikatat and Klatskanai within a recent period is important, as indicating the direction in which population has flowed, and the causes inducing this separation of tribes. (Gibbs 1877:171)

It is noteworthy that Gibbs was aware of these recent population shifts, though he did not appreciate the importance of their sequencing. James Teit (1910), while on a reconnaissance of Washington Tribes for Franz Boas, wrote him a long letter, describing his own findings:

> Whilst working with some old Cowlitz people I learned a family of the Willapa people lived only half a mile away consisting of an old woman, her daughter, and her grand children. . . . She remembered an old woman of the Willapa having heard her people telling of the splitting of her tribe as follows.

> A long time ago a man of her [p. 4] tribe was tracking an elk in the mountains and got lost. As he did not return and his people could not find where he had gone they

concluded he was dead. He had traveled south to the Columbia River. Somewhere in that country he fell in with another tribe and married a woman there. He had a number of children by this woman. After a number of years he returned to see his people, and after staying with them some time he went back again to this country of his adopted tribe taking a good many members of his own tribe with him. He had told them the country was better where he lived, and the surrounding people more friendly. Afterwards descendants of these people were met from time to time by members of the parent tribe. These people were called Tlakatskanei-a.

The Cowlitz tribe tells nearly the same story about this incident. They say "formerly some of the Su'wal got lost. They wandered off to the south. Afterwards a man and a woman (or a man and his daughter) of these people were met on the Columbia River and recognized. This man's people of the country they lived in was called Tlats kats kaneia." The Cowlitz called the Willapa Athapaskcans Su'wal or Su'wall and say they formerly inhabited [p. 5] the upper Chehalis and upper Willapa with headquarters near a high mountain called łikaiEks [Mud Mountain?, Sam Henry?] some also lived in other spots near the mountains. These people also call themselves Su'wal but say this was the name of those only who occupied the upper Chehalis (southern and western headwaters of the Chehalis River). The tribe on the Willapa river was called wElapakoteli by the Su'wal. They spoke the same language as themselves but with slight variations. They used at one time to go right to the mouth of the Willapa at certain seasons but made their headquarters up the river in the mountains. They say both tribes as far as remembered were never very numerous. . . . She said the Su'wal and the wElapakoteli were originally one people living together, and also the Tlatkatskanei-a, who were a branch of the Su'wal. According to all the information I have gathered so far Gibbs extends the Willapa (viz. Su'wal) too far east and north.

The eastern [Swaal] division [8b] of the tribe occupied all the western head waters of the Chehalis River down to nearly as far as Newaukam. It appears a number of them made their headquarters around Pe Ell and perhaps the majority wintered near Mud Mt. According to their own traditions they were never a powerful people nor very numerous, and formerly long ago were attacked by many enemies. For fear of these they used to live in holes in the ground [pithouses or dugouts, see below]. According to the Satsop, a band of people called <u>tcutsaia</u> lived on Chehalis River someway not far above themselves. They were a mixture of Upper Chehalis and upper Willapa (viz. eastern division of the Willapa). This is the only trace I found of the tribe occupying country outside of the territory above defined. It seems this band was absorbed by the Upper Chehalis. According to the upper Willapa, the Klatskanai of Oregon are an offshoot from them that migrated south, and the Cowlitz and Chehalis have traditions to the same effect. According to the Cowlitz the head quarters of the upper or eastern Willapa was around Klabur [Klaber] & Bafo [Boisfort, with Gallicized pronunciation "bwafo"]. I obtained no flood tradition from the tribe, and no tradition of their having lived further east or north in the Interior. According to the flood tradition of the Chehalis, they either anchored themselves at LekaiEks mountain or drifted against it, and when the flood subsided they came down and lived in the adjoining country. This mountain is said to be south east of Klaber [Sam Henry?, Boisfort Mt ?] and appears to be the Indian name for Mud mountain. A comparison of their language with that of the Nicola, and other northern Athapascans, appears to show they were closely related at one time. (Teit 1910)

In his collection of Kathlamet Chinook texts from Charles Cultee, Boas (1901:187–195) includes an 1894 account of a vicious leader of the Willapa, the tribe of Cultee's father's father. In part it helps explain why Swaal were said to roam and not have any houses. Instead, for gatherings, they used impromptu semi-subterranean halls. Here is a paraphrase:

The TkulXiyogoā′ike [upper Willapa Diné]

PōXpuX, chief at Nq!ulā′was, drowned all his sons at birth, allowing only his daughters to live. One boy was disguised wearing a coat, to be raised by his grandmother, who trained him rigorously to dive into lakes until he succeeded in catching much dentalia. Grandmother asked house to house for sinew to sew up his tattered woodchuck blanket, but it really was to string these shells. She asked many households, and all gave her sinew, which she strung dentalia on for days and nights. Strings of short dentalia were buried in one hole under the bed, and long dentalia were buried in another. After days of asking for sinew, people became rude so the grandmother and the grandson invited them to their home and gave away all the dentalia strings. Thunderbird was his patron, and he left the boy a whale in the middle of a prairie to feed everyone. A husband from the coast had to tell the people what the whale was. "Then the chief made a potlatch. He made a long ditch. He put planks on top of the ditch and covered them with dirt. He made a door at the entrance to the ditch. It was a long hole. There the people went in to dance. They disappeared in the hole underground. They came out again at the door of the ditch." He hosted everyone to become a high chief named Waq!awiyas, ancestor of those at Nq!olā′was at the headwaters of the Willapah River. PōXpuX was humiliated into insignificance.

Cowlitz leaders were multilingual, though migration, hostilities, and epidemics so reduced the number of speakers of Kwalioqua~Swaal~Willapa that Cowlitz Salish speech predominated among the survivors. Washington Athapascan word lists were collected by Gibbs in the 1850s and by Franz Boas and his students a century ago (Boas 1910). In 1898, Maria Harris, living at Boisfort, was one of the last speakers of this language. Today, no local families have come forward to claim Willapa ancestry, though a few decades ago, an elder at Shoalwater is said to have done so.

The never-ratified treaties by Anson Dart includes that of 9 August 1851 with the Klatsksnia band of Chinook [sic], pledging an annuity of $30.00 for 10 years, with $50.00 in cash and the rest in merchandise.[1] The identification of Klatskania as a band of the Chinook was a political expedience of the U.S. but had no cultural or geographical validity. The names of the two native men who signed this Klatskania treaty were Tuckamaack and Winnawah. Boyd (2011:163, note 6), however, has called attention to the names of 27 Clatskanie in a 1855 census of the Milton refugee camp by Thomas H. Smith for Joel Palmer (Records of the Superintendent of Indian Affairs for Oregon, reel 14, frame14).

Today, *skookumchuck* is the most prominent Chinuk Wawa place name in the southwestern Washington region, meaning "strong water or current," aptly describing this steep waterway. While named *the-a-woot-en* in Tsamosan according to Gibbs (its residents = *the-a-woot*) and, more accurately, by Kinkade (té•wtń "ford place"), the current use of its jargon name probably stems from its former mixed occupation by Swaal Athapaskans who vacated it in favor of Oregon to become the C~K~Tlatskanie.

Conclusion

American colonization and Indian policy have forced the consolidation of different groups into one place, with a corresponding loss of small-group cultural identity. While the complexity of the synchronic occupation of southwestern Washington has been well known, its diachronic aspects, especially the split from Swaal by Klatskani, has not been fully appreciated. Realizing this population shift occurred between smallpox epidemics and before the Taitnapam immigration enhances understanding of the complex and dynamic cultural history of the region, and ensures persistence of unique Swaal group identity in the historic record. This case study provides much-needed light on the outcome of the Athapaskan diaspora for the Swaal people, which is relevant to all aspects of the diaspora that placed Apache and Navajo in the Southwest and other Diné groups in the Plains, Plateau, and Pacific Northwest.

NOTE

[1] Nathan Reynolds, Ecologist for the Cowlitz Tribe noted: "The Dart treaty with the Wheelapa names Kwalioqua directly. Plus, in exchange for the cession of Wheelapa lands, Dart tried to set up a general reservation for all Chinook and Chehalis who are willing to give up their reserved rights as established in other treaties. The Kwalioqua are twice mentioned directly in the 1855 failed Isaac Stevens treaty at Cosmopolis" (Nathan Reynolds, personal communication, 18 May 2012)

ACKNOWLEDGMENTS

Thanks for help with unraveling this complexity to Richard Bellon, Ron Kent, Tony Johnson, Jolynn Amrine Goertz, Elaine McCloud, Ann Schuh, Nathan Reynolds, Gene Woodwick, Justine James, and Drs. Dale Kinkade, Marilyn Richen, Jay Powell, Amelia Susman Schultz, and Roy Carlson.

Journal of Northwest Anthropology, Memoir 9:223–230 2014

CHARLES ROBLIN, THOMAS BISHOP, AND THE BACKGROUND TO WESTERN WASHINGTON LAND CLAIM CASES

ABSTRACT

The national and local backgrounds, quoting archival resources, of the 1930s native Puget Sound Land Claims are reviewed, with attention to its two key players and its more bizarre legal aspects. Growing out of a (still) messy attempt to allot lands at Quinault to "fish eating Indians" and thwarted land claims, Washington natives evolved a firm identity based in their legally superior treaty rights, especially to fish, hunt, and harvest plants.

A century ago, educated Indiens began mobilizing on national and local levels of the United States. On Columbus Day 1911 in Columbus, Ohio, at Ohio State University, the Society of American Indians (SAI) was formed, with at least three of its founders holding degrees and jobs in anthropology. Among its recruits was Thomas Bishop, who organized at Tacoma in 1913 the Northwestern Federation of American Indians (NFAI), modeling its 1914 constitution on that of SAI with the notably addition that membership was organized by tribes, the source of treaty rights. Scheduling depositions with many elders to chronicle property destruction and theft, prior to pursuing land claims in federal court, Thomas had the willing support of Charles Roblin, an unusually conscientious Bureau of Indian Affairs (BIA) Special Agent. Indeed, the resulting 31 January 1919 Roblin Roll of landless tribes has become the basis of several base rolls for Washington tribes later federally recognized.

Since the roles of Bishop and Roblin in these exciting times after World War I is not well known, a wider context is herein provided for understanding these early political activities, often taking on the local BIA. In summarizing their efforts, this article relies heavily on direct extracts, always set off as "indented within quotation marks."

As background, at Tulalip, during U.S. Grant's Peace Policy (1872–1887), BIA Indian agents had to be recommended by the Catholic Bishop of the Diocese (Seattle), as this reservation was one of the few that was assigned to Catholic missions. U.S. policy was overwhelmingly Protestant. Then, between 1886–1893, political appointees served as agents. Thereafter they were drawn from the newly-formed Civil Service and their title was changed to "school superintendent."

The first school superintendent at Tulalip was the former agency MD, Charles Buchanan, who served from 1 July 1901 until his death 18 January 1920. During his tenure, Buchanan collected Puget Sound ethnographic and linguistic materials, and wrote for scholarly journals. He generally supported Native rights, as well as, in time, the formation by Thomas Bishop and others of the NFAI, which lobbied for the work eventually done by BIA Special Agent Charles Roblin, who annotated his notes in red ink.[1] Bishop was also a notary public who preferred green ink, and many of the applications include a power of attorney form with blanks filled in with that telltale green.

Bishops

The Bishop family (McDaniel 2004) descended from Bonaparte, a Snohomish leader and treaty signer who moved into the Chimacum Valley near Port Townsend, across Puget Sound from Seattle, after its native Chimakuan speakers had been devastated by epidemic diseases and raids. The Bishops became wealthy farmers and ranchers, always politically astute. Of the brothers, William Jr. became a state senator, while Thomas worked for native rights on the national stage. For a time, he had a strong ally in Charles Roblin, who was a transplanted Canadian. Thomas and SAI triumphed with the native right to vote, passed in 1924 in response to native contributions during World War I.

While Thomas first spoke of forming native "unions," the NFAI organized communities, both off and on reservations, as "tribes" since that it how treaty signatories were legally based. With the help of key Natives, such as Martin Sampson, a Swinomish working at the Puyallup federal school in Tacoma, Ed Davis in Fall City, Jerry Kanim at Tolt, Lawrence Webster at Suquamish, and others, he mobilized landless natives by tribe to pursue their treaty claims, once the BIA had completed a tally of those claiming to be landless and unenrolled.

The serious lack of land, schooling, and health left many native feeling "wronged," and NFAI sought remedies: "perhaps allotments, perhaps cash, perhaps respect" (Harmon 1999:181). Members would collect bits of money to pay his expenses back to Washington, D.C. to lobby the BIA and U.S. officials. He was always resourceful, for himself and others, as need be. Once, when he ran out of money, he worked as a butcher to earn his return fare from D.C.

In 1915, Thomas published the landmark "An Appeal to the Government to Fulfill Sacred Promises Made 61 Years Ago" to call attention to ignored or mangled treaty provisions from the 1850s (Harmon 1995, 1999). Similarly, reservations began Treaty Day celebrations during January, calling attention to their continuing respect for these federal documents. In 1919, Washington State Representative Lindley Hadley saw the Court of Claims bill through Congress, allowing Indiens to sue, though its judicial implementation did not occur until 1925. Depositions were taken in 1927, and published in 1933. Organizing this suit was Seattle attorney, Arthur E Griffin, who had to be voted on by each of the tribes. Afterwards, he drafted constitutions for landless communities, such as Duwamish and Snoqualmie, that remain in force in some form.

With his family living in Salem and his recent work at Suiattle and Quinault, Roblin readily stepped in to begin the enrolling of would-be claimants for unknown redress. In his cover letter to the finished Roll of 31 January 1919, Charles Roblin summarized his efforts for this enumeration, remarkably unbiased and undertaken in the interests of general welfare and kind intent.

Quinault

Under threat of losing "excess" lands after 1911 allotments, Quinault, as it is now spelled, hurriedly added members to save as much reserved land as possible. The tribal council, as Roblin wrote, meeting 4–6 April 1912, got "carried away with the spirit of generosity and 'adopted' whole families, in some cases containing scores of members, without properly considering the merits of the claims advanced" for over 500 applicants. After Roblin finished his study, the council again reviewed all these files on 18–20 December 1918, acting to limit membership (M1344):

> The passage of the Act of Congress of March 4, 1911, authorizing the allotment of
> land on the Quinaielt [Quinault] Indian Reservation, Washington, to the members

of the Hoh, Quileyute, Ozette, and other tribes of Indians who are affiliated with the Quinaielt and Quileyute Indians in the treaty of 1855 and 1856, crystallized this movement into one for the allotment of all persons of Indian blood, hitherto unalloted, on the Quinaielt Reservation. . . . This movement ripened in the organization of the Northwestern Federation of American Indians. The leading spirit of this organization is Mr. Thomas Bishop, its president. . . . Mr. Bishop and his colleagues immediately took the position that all unallotted Indians living west of the Cascade Mountains in western Washington could be allotted on the Quinaielt Reservation; and they spread this word broadcast. This, too, was the position taken by Mr. H.H. Johnson, Superintendent then in charge of the Quinaielt Indian Reservation; and it thus obtained official backing, which lent it impetus.

Mr. Bishop organized the Northwestern Federation of American Indians and sought membership applications, and dollars, from all Indians of western Washington who had not had their "rights." Meetings were held in many places in the State, extravagant promises were made, unwarranted hopes were raised, and the organization prospered. Hundreds of mixed-blood Indians, who had not thought, theretofore, of making any claim against the United States Government for land or money, now put in claims; family trees were studied and great expectations were raised.

Some one seems to have estimated the value of an allotment on the Quinaielt Indian Reservation at six thousand dollars [$6000]; and, as many claimants did not want land on that reservation, because they had been raised and lived in the more pleasant climate of the Puget Sound country or southwestern Washington, it was stated that demand would be made for an allotment of land or its equivalent in cash. So, today, many of these people are looking for a cash payment from the Government of six thousand dollars to each person of Indian blood who is not allotted. It is surprising how general this understanding is. I found it prevalent in every part of western Washington. . . .

The full-blood Indians, and those mixed-bloods who are living under true Indians conditions, seem to have been very well taken care of, with very few exceptions. [Nooksack, Skagit, Snoqualmie, Cowlitz, Clallam, Chinooks ~ Shoalwater Bay ~ and associated bands, Mitchell Bay.]

There are many members of other tribes, in the Puget Sound country especially, who are not allotted; and some few who are not enrolled. I have prepared schedules of those I found who are not enrolled, but have excluded from the schedules those who are now enrolled, even though not allotted. (Roblin 1919)

In a letter to Tulalip Agency of 10 May 1926, Roblin provided background:

I was to investigate and report on unenrolled Indians of Western Washington. This matter arose as follows: For many years Thomas G. Bishop, and the "Northwestern Federation of American Indians" had made claim that there were many thousand Indians in western Washington who had never shared in any of the benefits derived from any of the treaties of early days and who were entitled to *some* recognition by the Government and some remuneration for lands taken from them, either in the shape of an allotment on the Quinaielt Reservation, or by the payment of the cash equivalent of such an allotment. These were supposed to be "Indians" who were not enrolled at any agency on the coast. Mr. Bishop made several trips to Washington on behalf of these homeless Indians, and was advised by the Office that there were no records in the Office showing who these Indians were and that there was no foundation for a request to Congress for relief for them. In 1916, Mr. Bishop urged the Office to have an enrollment made of these Indians, so as to get such information in the record. The Office agreed to have such an enrollment made, with the distinct understanding that such an enrollment would not be a recognition of any claims made by the Indians; but an endeavor to have the record show what their claims were. Dr. McChesney was first detailed to this work, but he died in Portland soon after taking it up; and I was detailed to it [by telegram of 16 August 1916 to Elbowoods, ND, arriving in Seattle 2 September].

The Office, in instructions to me, dated 17 November 1916, combined the two tasks; and the first five pages of their letter deals with the matter of Quinaielt adoptions. Then the Office continues:

As the recent decision of the Department restricts the enrollment and allotment with the Quinaielts to the *fish-eating tribes* of the immediate coast, and the other bands and tribes mentioned in the said Treaty of 1855–1856, the Executive Order of 4 Nov. 1873, and the Act of 4 March 1911, many of the applicants whose cases are submitted by Mr. Bishop for enrollment and allotment at Quinaielt will, of course, have to be excluded. However, the Office desires that a separate enrollment be made of all applicants who, under the decision mentioned, cannot be enrolled and allotted at Quinaielt, to the end that should Congress so request, a full report might be made as to such unattached and homeless Indians who have not heretofore received benefits from the Government. (emphasis added) (Roblin 1926)

Land Claims

To further seek their goal in the Court of Claims, Duwamish et. al. (F-275) was instituted by jurisdictional act of 12 February 1925 (43 Stat 886) to allow suit by Washington State Indians and Tribes living west of the Cascade Mountains, an estimated population of 4597 in 1940. The nature of the claims was one of general accounting for funds ($71,496.45) allegedly still due under treaty stipulations, compensations for lands taken, and hunting and fishing rights. The report of 933 pages was forwarded to the Department of Justice on 17 November 1931; the court on 4 June 1934 (79 C Cls 530) dismissed this claim, arguing that it was eliminated by financial and service offsets provided to the plaintiffs. Appeal was denied 27 May 1935 (81 C Cls 976, 295 US 755).

This was a suit by 19 Indian tribes or bands, or remnants of tribes or bands, residing in the state of Washington, to recover a vast sum of money upon 103 separate causes of action. The total amount sought to be recovered as set forth in the petition was $73,365,416. In the plaintiffs' request for findings this amount was reduced to $69,703,466.69.

Stated briefly, the claims of each of the 11 tribes parties to the Point Elliott Treaty (Duwamish, Lummi, Whidby Island Skagit, Upper Skagit, Swinomish, Kikiallus, Snohomish, Snoqualmie, Stillaquamish, Suquamish, Samish) dated 22 January

1855, 12 Stat. 927, were that no considerable portion of the amount of $150,000 as provided by Article VI of said treaty had ever been paid to or expended for its benefit; and that merchandize furnished was charged at grossly excessive prices; that the United States failed to reserve for the Indians, all of the lands specified by Article II and III thereof; that the United States failed to expend any portion of the sum of $15,000 for the purpose of clearing, fencing, and breaking up lands on the reservation created by the treaty; that the United States failed to establish and maintain a school with instructors, to establish a central agency, to provide a blacksmith and carpenter shops and furnish them with tools, and to employ a blacksmith, carpenter, farmers, and physicians; that the United States failed to appraise and pay for improvements as provided by Article VII of said treaty; that the United States failed to set aside a general reservation for the Indians, parties to the treaty; and that the United States encouraged white settlers to take up and live on plaintiff's lands; that said settlers depleted plaintiff's forests of game and their streams of fish.

The claims of the two tribes of Indians, parties to the treaty of Medicine Creek (Puyallup and Squaxin) dated 16 December 1854, 10 Stat 1132, were substantially the same as the claims advanced by the Indian tribes who were parties to the Point Elliott Treaty.

The claims of the Skokomish tribe of Indians, party to the treaty of Point-No-Point, dated 16 January 1855, 12 Stat. 933, were substantially the same as the claims advanced by the Indian tribes who were parties to the Point Elliott and Medicine Creek treaties.

The claims of the five tribes listed as nontreaty claimants (Upper Chehalis, Muckleshoot, Nooksack, Chinook, San Juan Islands Indians) are that white people, encouraged so to do by grants of valuable lands from the United States, destroyed the wild game and fur-bearing animals, depleted the rivers and streams of fish, destroyed their buildings and excluded them from their homes and cultivated lands; and that no payment had ever been made for said lands.

The court held that the plaintiffs were entitled to a judgment under Findings XI, XVI, and XXI, in the amount of $71,496.45 as follows:

Finding XI. The following tribes and bands abandoned the number of houses herein set forth of the value of $259.00 each, when they removed to their respective reservations set apart under the treaties, and have received from the United States no payment therefor[e], viz:

1	Skokomish, 15 houses	$ 3,750.00
2	Squaxin, 6 houses	$ 1,500.00
3	Puyallup, 45 houses	$11,250.00
4	Suquamish, 28 houses	$ 7,000.00
5	Duwamish, 56 houses	$14,000.00
6	Snohomish, 12 houses	$ 3,000.00
7	Snoqualmie, 11 houses	$ 2,750.00
8	Stillaquamish, 12 houses	$ 3,000.00
9	Kikiallus, 8 houses	$ 2,000.00

10	Whidby Island Skagit & Upper Skagit, 26 houses	$ 6,500.00
11	Swinomish, 6 houses	$ 1,500.00
12	Samish, 14 houses	$ 3,500.00
13	Lummi, 19 houses	<u>$ 4,750.00</u>
		sum $64,500.00

Finding XVI: There is due the Indians under the treaty $1,535.04 (Treaty of Point Elliott).

Finding XXI: When the Puyallup School was discontinued certain equipment formerly used therein was sold to the Salem and Tulalip Indian schools. To the Salem school the authorities sold equipment of the value of $27,250.13, and to Tulalip school equipment of the value of $6,096.50, making a total sum of $33,346.63. The plaintiffs are entitled to 10.16% of said total sum, i.e., $6,389.21, less $927.80 heretofore paid them, and a judgment will be awarded for the difference, $5,461.41.

The court further held that, although the plaintiffs were entitled to a judgment of $71,496.45, the defendant on its counterclaim, was entitled to an amount in excess of this sum, and therefore, that the petition should be dismissed." (Smith 1947)

Outraged by such duplicitous findings, the newly-formed National Congress of American Indians urged Congress to set up a separate Indian Claims Commission, which heard cases from 1946 to 1978, when those lingering cases were transferred back to the US Court of Claims. Northwest tribes received cash settlements for these cases in the 1970s, though some are still pending.

Under the US Constitution no state or federal court had jurisdiction over Indian land claims. Each individual case had to be authorized by a specific act of Congress and then brought to the U.S. Court of Claims. The average case took 15 years to wend its way through the system. . . . During the existence of the commission from 1946 to 1978, over 852 claims were filed. (The commission's life was extended four times.) . . . Over 800 million dollars was awarded. . . . Although . . . the express purpose [was] of providing Indians with the opportunity to obtain redress for the loss of tribal land, the tribes could only receive money, not actual land, based on the value of the land at the time it was taken. (Nies 1996:346–348)

Records of the Indian Claims Commission
(Record Group 279) 1946–1983 [109970 ICC]

Docket 25	Box Snoqualmie
Docket 92	Boxes 187-191 Skagit
Docket 93	Box Snoqualmie
Docket 97	Box 193 Sauk Suiattle
Docket 98	Boxes 194-196 Muckleshoot
Docket 109	Boxes 206-7 Duwamish
Docket 110	Box Lummi

Docket 125	Box 229 Snohomish
Docket 132	Box Suquamish
Docket 155	Boxes 1531-38, 303 Quileute
Docket 161, 159	Box Samish
Docket 203	Box 346 Puyallup
Docket 207	Box Stillguamish
Docket 117	Box Duwamish
Docket 218	Box Cowlitz
Docket 234	Box 383 Chinook
Docket 237	Boxes 2193-97 Upper Chehalis
Docket 242	Box 2208 Quinault Queets
Docket 262	Box Tulalip
Docket 263	Box Kikiallus
Docket 292	Box Skagit
Docket 293	Box 2632 Swinomish
Docket 294	Box 464 Lower Skagit
Docket 456	Box Kikiallus
Docket 475	Box Upper Skagit
Docket 658	Box Muckleshoot

Charles Roblin

Lastly, because his personnel file is missing from federal employee records at Saint Louis, something must be said about Charles Roblin himself, based on U.S. census records. That he was a Northwest transplant, based in Salem, adds to our understanding of the conscientious job that he did on the Roll.

Charles Edward Roblin (1870–1953) was a naturalized U.S. citizen who immigrated from English Canada in 1888 and settled at Salem, Oregon. The local Methodist Willamette College, now University, was his alma mater. In 1891, he was agent for Elwood Steamship on the wharf.

In the 1910 federal census, Charles E., 40, is BIA Allotting Agent on the Blackfoot Reservation in Montana, having been naturalized in 1888 at the age of 18. In the 1930 federal census, Charles E., 60, and Ollie M., 47, have a son, Charles D., 13, daughter, Ruth E., 19, and a lodger Robert Henry, 31, born in Virginia of a father from Scotland and a mother from Ireland, working as an automobile salesman. Charles E. was born in English Canada, Ollie in Ohio of Ohio parents, Ruth in Arizona, and Charles D. in Ohio. Charles is listed as a special allotting agent for the U.S. government. Their home was worth $5000.

In the 1940 federal census, Charles E., 70, born in English Canada, is living in Salem and still listed as working as a supervisor for the Government Indian Bureau at a salary of $2700. His wife Ollie, 57, was born in Indiana [not Ohio], and son Charles D., 23, was born in Ohio and a cannery worker at $575. In the column for education, Charles has C-4 and the others H-4, presumably four years of college or high school. Their housekeeper is Mabel Robson, 32, born in Washington. Their home was worth $7000.

Charles died September 6, 1953, aged 83; his son Charles Dana and daughter Ruth, who was then married to Carl Shantz and living in Milwaukee, Oregon, fought each other in court over his will. His most valued possessions were his home place, an arrowhead collection, and an elk's head he bequeathed to the Salem Elk's Club.[2]

Summary

In sum, Roblin was a career civil servant who married late, had an over-indulged son and stolid daughter, and exemplified unusually high job dedication. Born a subject of the British Empire, he strangely carried on the colonial enterprise, augmented by careful notes in red pen, that later served to gain federal recognition.

Today, the Snohomish at Chimakum, including Bishops, lack federal recognition, and the first land claim cases became mute. But persistence was rewarded by the second land claims cases in the 1950s, though some tribes, like the Lummi, have forcefully refused any payment. By focusing on treaty promises and legalities, Roblin and Bishop helped the sentiments and identities of Western Washington Indiens find a most effective means to better their communities and gain the political clout that eventually became funded, and well funded, by tribal casinos. In sum, "As Harriette Shelton [Dover, daughter of Tulalip leader William Shelton] said, the Indians lost [that time], but at least there were a lot of meetings" that got everyone mobilized (Harmon 1999:187).

The greatest irony of all, moreover, is that revising this draft I was shocked to realize that Thomas Bishop died in 1923. That means he was not there for the native voting rights, nor the 1927 land claim depositions, yet so strong is his legacy that it long seemed to me that he was always there. Instead, it is his green ink on depositions and power of attorney for Roblin that best show his meticulous efforts, and their work for the greater good.

NOTES

[1] Roblin had investigated conditions on the Suiattle River in 1916 and done a census of these Sauks. Like those at Lake Sammamish, many families had taken out Indian homesteads but because <u>farming</u> was a requirement for continued ownership and these lands were in the national forest, where logging was a ready source of money, many of these homesteads were rejected for failure to comply with federal regulations. Forest rangers were especially cruel, destroying stored shingles, bolts, and lumber waiting in family yards for sale. After Dr. McChesney died suddenly at the start of the 1918 enrollment efforts, Roblin was called back to finish these tribal registers for the 1919 roll.

In between, Roblin reviewed the applications of "fish eating" Indiens for land at Quinault. As a result, the original of the 1919 Roblin Schedule and a carbon are filed in "11697-19-053 Taholah" in the central classified files of the Bureau of Indian Affairs (entry 121). The suffix 053 deals with issues of membership and enrollment.

[2] http://or.findacase.com/research/wfrmDocViewer.aspx/xq/fac.
19570515_0040106.OR.htm/qx

Long before I settled in the Northwest, my motto was "bloom where you are planted," encouraging me to seek place-based knowledge wherever I was in the Americas. In the Northwest, it has meant experiencing the entire coast from Alaska to California, the Plateau into the interior of Montana, and the Great Basin into Nevada. This wide overview contrasts with my understanding of other regions of Native North America, where I focus on integrating past reports and fieldwork with respect to a noteworthy tribe, territory, and rite.

Traditionally, for academics, the appeal of Native North America has been an arcane study mixing dazzling details with the search for order, pattern, themes, and structures (struckons). But there is also the dark side of diseases, depopulation, enslaving, and habitat destructions. Indeed, the Americas were not so much invaded as they were massively exploded, with bits widely scattered across time and space. Through study, especially wide review of literature and fieldnotes, we can restore pieces, such as with the article on "widower weirs" (see p. 135, this volume), but the enormity of the catastrophe still boggles the mind.

Throughout, while "marching to the beat of my own drum," certain subjects, themes, or topics have intrigued me enough, via synthesis of complex details and pattern recognition, to pursue them into print. While ensconced academics wait until grants pay their way, I have relied on jobs in the local community—as a teacher, researcher, heritage advisor, or, most recently, truth broker—to situate and direct my interest, as well as establish my trustworthy reliability to elders and tradition teachers.

Thus, my interest in the Northwest became place-based when I came from New Jersey, after a dissertation about New Mexico, to Washington state intending to continue my Puebloan research. Instead, I turned to the Tsimshian, a language isolate, and decided to unravel its fourfold Crests (Orca, Raven, Eagle, Wolf), having already been influenced by a new understanding of such systems in Australia as composed of "semi-moieties." This analogy proved true, complementing other work being done on the internal rankings within each Crest, as well as an intertribal–international understanding of these moieties among all the matrilineal nations of the North Coast.

Living in Seattle, WA, I was soon pulled into the magnetic orbit of Vi Hilbert, who kept us all fed, entertained, and busy working on translations, books, tapes, videos, and parties featuring her Lushootseed–Puget Salish language. Like others, I became her driver, thus immediately justifying my presence at a wide variety of traditional and private events around the Sound. I was also her escort to national honoring events in Washington, D.C.

Over time, my own focus became the complex regional rite last held in 1900 and variously called the Spirit Canoe, Recovery, and, most recently, Redeeming Rite. Interviewing an aged elder, who had run errands as a boy in preparation for the rite, enabled me to add a personal voice to a century of descriptions in print and notes. My first book set this rite in global comparative perspective, and my second placed it within the context of its own Lushootseed culture. Moreover, there is always more to learn. For instance, only years after his death, did I learn that this elder was also, as a young man, the patient at a final, less-known rite in 1908.

Indeed, in hindsight, I have better learned the virtues of luck, pluck, and loyalty. Luck got me into and out of intriguing situations, and pluck kept me going while I made sense of them, often years later. As a general rule, I get to know a person or community for five years before presuming to write about him, her, or them. In some cases, this writing makes good on an initial promise, as my *Tsimshian Culture* book, dedicated to the tribal school, summarizes decades of time and pages into one volume, and answers basic questions along the way, such as "Why Crest hats?" or "Why face masks?" For my research in other regions, the same type of question can be used for such persistent topics as "Why mounds?" Throughout, my loyalties intensified with other Americanists, while decreasing precipitously with an alienating anthropology.

Because Indiens thrive on differences, usually spiritually justified, I have learned to appreciate that I work by deduction much more often than by induction, setting me apart from most academics. Grasping the whole picture or final conclusion means more work writing out the baby steps that would lead anyone else, however hostile, to an understanding is both grueling and often frustrating.

Since my aim has been to understand native systems, especially in terms of native languages, I have developed conventions to make this easier in print. Since the words are seen, their meaning becomes obvious. My coinages, some transferred from other languages or countries, include Indien for the peoples of the Americas in contrast to those of India, Colvile (single L) for the native tribe at Kettle Falls in contrast to the Colvilles (double Ls) confederating a dozen neighboring tribes on that reservation, tysic for time ~ space ~ center by analogy to the deictic of linguistics. My increasing use of the tilde ~ meets a need to convey a sense of "same as, similar, and like" in contrast to the back stroke / used to convey "opposed to, opposite." Above all, I am willing to bend the English to better translate native terms, rather than bow to English priority ~ dominance.

Over four decades, I have watched as "hot shots" have flamed out and manipulative "king makers" became senile droolers. Fads have built careers, but death takes its toll without any lasting contribution. By grounding myself in deep data and middle range theory, topics long integral to Americanist research have received new insights and direction. Basic or core units have been established, such as the phoneme for languages, and the nodal nexus for bilateral kindreds, a kinship system that baffled Boas his entire career.

Persistent problems—such as matri-moieties, place-based Traditional Ecological Knowledge (TEK), and Native Cosmology vs. Western classroom suppression—have enhanced the understanding of human Culture and intellectual complexity. More recently, however, there have been taunts from the dark side, where tribal politics outweigh reason, justice, or truth. Decades of emersion in local communities, a mind favoring the nuances of kinship genealogies, and outrage at injustice has drawn me into conflicts over base rolls, membership, and constitutional requirements that were never taught in graduate school. Threats of harm and violence are rumored, but families take out their frustrations on each other rather than outsider academics. Tribes have suppressed basic information in government reports, ignoring libraries full of the same information. Wondering what to do, specifically and generally, the protection and sharing of basic information from a range of reliable elders becomes more paramount.

Yet it is tribal support and involvement that will grow the list of Traditional Cultural Places (TCPs) in Washington and the Northwest, where a rich body of fieldnotes, publications, and tribal traditions has maintained the integrity of these places and properties. Filling out the forms begins the process, but tribal clout pressuring bureaucrats carries them through. Support from church, civic, and business organizations also needs to be gained for Olympia, Washington and Washington, D.C., to take notice.

Above all, data must be digested and shared to have lasting value, and that has been the aim of *Northwest Anthropological Research Notes* (*NARN*) and now the *Journal of Northwest Anthropology* (*JONA*), for which we are all grateful. Assembling these articles into one place and making them available electronically through the web thereby enables them to circulate more widely in the life's blood enriching all of the cultures in the Pacific Northwest.

Appendix A—Locations of Source Documents for Natives in Puget Sound

One of my on-going ~ working lists is this preliminary inventory of names, places, and projects useful for research and cultural resource management in Seattle and native Puget Sound. They are being shared with the hope that others can and will add to them, as well as put them to use.

Appendix B—*Arky Epitaph* ~ Washington Archaeology to ±1975

Frequent frustration when seeking a chronology of local archaeological research compelled this listing of people, places, and projects (for others to expand) as *Arky Epitaph* ("memorial memory").

Appendix C—Bibliography of Jay Miller, Ph.D.

This is a listing of my various publications dealing with Native tribes and ideas all across North America, mostly in the Northeast and Southwest, with the Southeast on the increase.

Journal of Northwest Anthropology, Memoir 9:234–236 2014

Appendix A

LOCATIONS OF SOURCE
DOCUMENTS FOR NATIVES IN PUGET SOUND

ABSTRACT

Sources for the native peoples of the greater Seattle region are widely scattered. This on-going, open-ended, working list presents many of the best known sources in hopes that more obscure but equally vital locations can be added in the future.

Introduction

Washingtons occur on both coasts of the United States, with many of the earliest reliable records for the native peoples of the State linked to residents and archives of the City because they came west under federal auspices. In a continuing effort to locate the main reliable authors, early documents, and prime locations, this list is intended to grow with further input from future researchers. Because so many of these records are securely stored out of sight, those few locations with public shelves are clearly indicated by the phrase (look the books).

The Seattle Public Library

Pioneers File Seattle Room materials
Northwest Regional Shelves (see stacks ~ look the books)

Museum of History and Industry (MOHI), Seattle (archives at new location apart from museum)

Photo Archives
Denny Family Papers (Seattle founders), especially Lushootseed-speaking David (1832–1903)
Newspaper Files (P-I)
Lucile Saunders McDonald (1898–1992) *Times* features, local articles

University of Washington Special Collections (UW SC), Seattle
Isaac Stevens Papers (below, territorial governor, senator, Indian agent)
Edmond Meany Papers (1862–1935, early historian, biased materials)
Jerry Meeker Notebooks (Puyallup Elder, Developer)
Erna Gunther Papers (1896–1982, early anthropologist, museum director)
Melville Jacobs Papers (1902–1972, linguist, folklore, Oregon)
Hill Family (Nathan was local BIA agent at Holmes Harbor, 1850s)
Willoughby Family (Sarah, artist, Charles, Quinault Indian Agent)
Anthropology Department Records
Seattle Directories, Local Histories, Biography Files, Newspapers
John Peabody Harrington microfilms (1884–1961, early linguist)
Lushootseed Research Archives (Vi Hilbert's notes, texts by elders)

Ethnomusicology Archives, UW, Seattle

> Lushootseed Research Video and Sound Tape Archives
> Thom Hess recordings

Burke Museum, UW, Seattle

> Erna Gunther Papers (see above)
> Director's Files ~ car & boat use, correspondence
> Ronald Olson, typed Quinault stories
> Leon Metcalf (first tapes, reel to reel, in early 1950s of native speech)

Suquamish Archives and Museum (new facility)

> Interview Files

Filipino American National Historical Society, Seattle, WA

> Biography Files
> Indapino [Indian—Filipino] Records

National Archives and Records Administration (NARA), Sand Point, Seattle, WA

> Homestead Records, Homestead Plats, Homestead Tract Books
> Reservation Agency Records, Census Records
> Microfilms, M5 Washington Superintendency Records

Washington State Regional Archives, Bellevue

> King County Tax records (marked "I" for Indian)

Port Townsend, Jefferson County Historical Society

> Hill family records, Snoqualmie 1856 Census
> James Swan materials (his watercolors at Yale)

Tacoma Public Library

> Pioneer Files
> Newspaper index
> Open Shelves by Locale (see stack ~ look the books)
> Local Histories

Washington State Historical Society, Tacoma

> Edwin Eells Papers (Pioneer, Indian Agent)
> Photo Archives
> Ezra Meeker Papers (1830–1928, Pioneer, Hops King)

Washington State Library, Tumwater, WA

> Pioneer Files
> Newspaper Clipping Files
> Isaac Stevens Library (First Governor, Senator, Bureau of Indian Affairs Official, federal
>   grant to purchase books for first state library)
> George Gibbs Letters and Tribal Censuses, esp. Nez Perce Tribe

White River Valley Museum, Auburn, WA

>Arthur Ballard (1876–1962) (lost copy of "Listen My Nephew")
>Photo Archives
>Hops Farming Records

Bancroft Library, University of California, Berkeley

>T.T. Waterman notes
>Anthropology correspondence
>Arthur Ballard stories
>Erna Gunther Element Distribution manuscript (300pp)

American Philosophical Society, Philadelphia, PA

>Franz Boas (1858–1942) archive
>Herman Haeberlin (1891–1918) letters
>James Teit 1910 letters
>Ethel Aginsky (1910–1990) Puyallup linguistics (notebooks at Willits, CA)

National Anthropological Archives, Smithsonian, Washington, D.C.

>George Gibbs (1815–1873)—in the Northwest 1854–1859, native language word lists
>Herman Karl Haeberlin (1891–1918)—fieldwork 1916–1917
>Thomas Talbot Waterman (1885–1936)—in Seattle 1918–1920
>John Peabody Harrington (1884–1961) first anthropologist at the University of Washington in 1910; in the Northwest 1942

National Museum of the American Indian, Washington, D.C.

>T.T. Waterman notes and artifacts

American Museum of Natural History, New York

>Franz Boas (1858–1942), in Washington State 1890, 1927
>Herman Haeberlin (1891–1918), Tulalip 1916–1917, artifacts

Royal Anthropological Society Archives, London

>Marian Smith, Puget Sound, Sto:lo (microfilm at RBCM Victoria, Ottawa)

Journal of Northwest Anthropology, Memoir 9:237–245 2014

Appendix B

ARKY EPITAPH ~
WASHINGTON ARCHAEOLOGY TO ±1975

ABSTRACT

Working with Doc Daugherty and other pioneers of Washington anthropology, hearing their coming of age stories, and knowing that novices today are largely ignorant of these people, places, and events; I began what I first called a "winter count" of significant archaeological persons and events (mostly along the coast) to keep track of their names and dates. My intent was a major event for each year, like a Plains Indian's life story in personal pictographs. Soon, however, memorializing the names of these workers gained priority, with the subsequent change of title. Entries are in a short hand, with institutional abbreviations listed at the end, with locations indicated by @, movements or transfers by >, equivalents by ~, and = to link authors with their topics ~ report titles. Each entry begins with a date within a decade, followed by month /# number (if known), name(s), location(s), date of report, and incidental ~ interesting information. Question marks ? require more study for this working list in progress.

Proto-Arkies

1850s	George Gibbs = place names, sites (seeking possible mounds)
1850s	James Swan = Willapa Bay in 1857
1850s	John K. Lord = Ft Colville sketch of skulls & burials
1880s	Myron Eells = Hood Canal, Peninsula
1890s	James Wickersham = South Sound
1890s	William H. Thacker = San Juan Islands (archaeological sites, artifacts, published in *The American Archaeologist* in 1898)
1890s	Charles Hill-Tout = *Museum and Art Notes*, Vancouver; Merton L. Miller; H J Rust @ Coeur d'Alene
1891	George Howe, *The Antiquarian* 1891 Vols 1–3 (including Eels, Wickersham, Deans) @ Albany, Oregon. Cf. Nephew Carrol B Howe @ Klamath
1900–07	Jesup North Pacific, Harlan Smith (1898–1936) = Yakima 1910 (Boas @ AMNH NY)
1905>20s	Albert Reagan = outer Coast of Washington, entire length (south side) of the Strait of Juan de Fuca, and vicinity of Bellingham Bay
1912–26	Arthur G. Colley = San Juan Islands (in unpublished notes @ Burke UW)

Professionals

1901	A L Kroeber hired @ Berkeley, UCB students researching into the NW 1906 *US Antiquities Act*

1910   John Peabody Harrington @ UW summer school, local fieldwork

1913   AW Mangum and party = Soils Reconnaissance of Southwestern Washington

1920s   Dalles-Deschutes = Wm Strong, W Egbert Schenk, Julian Steward, 1930 [Judge Emory Strong F of Wm Duncan Strong]

1920s   Columbia River Archaeological Society, RT Congdon, MD, gives his relics to Chelan Historical Society

1920   *UW Publications in Anthropology* series started by TT Waterman

1920–21 FS Hall at WSM (now Burke) mid-Columbia burials @ Trinidad

1921   Leslie Spier to UW, Erna Gunther fills in for him, then hired on her own

1927–38 Harold J. Cundy sketched & plotted rock images

1929   12/5 Claude Schaeffer survey = Puyallup

1929   9/ – 63 6/30 Luther Cressman @ OU

1933   OU *Monographs, Studies in Anthropology* (series started 1926 ?); Rock Island 1st dam on the Columbia; Columbia River Archaeological Society moved 2 petroglyphed boulders to Wenatchee museum

1933–42 Grand Coulee Dam, survey in 39 due to Edith Dunning of Inland Empire Indian Relics Society engaging UW, pre-WSU, & Joel Ferris of Eastern Washington Historical Society Ball Mortuary hastily exhumed graves (filmed in color)

1934   Herbert Krieger (USNM DC) = Bonneville

1935   *Historic Sites Act*

1937   Bonneville Dam done

1938   Marian Smith begins study of Old Man House artifacts of Ernest Bertleson, published 1950

1938   Ethel Carlson survey of South Puget Sound

1939   Alex Krieger 1st MA @ OU

1939   Charles Borden (1905–78) UBC German Dept, BC Arky 45 > , Agnes Anderson Funds, *ABC* [Anthropology in British Columbia]

1939   Jay Perry = report in *El Palacio* (started 1913)

1939–40 Columbia Basin Archaeological Survey, Grand Coulee to BC (Lake Roosevelt); Dr. Phillip Drucker, Joseph Jablow, Arlo Ford, Alex Krieger (aided by elder Billy Andrews), Robert Stephenson, Allen Murphy, Kenneth Leatherman, workers from National Youth Administration, published by Donald Collier, Alfred Hudson, Arlo Ford (1942). June 1939 – September 1940

1945   Inter-Agency Archaeological Salvage Program, River Basin Survey (RBS), Frank H H Roberts of Bureau of American Ethnology (BAE), Smithsonian

1946   Lucille McDonald, *Seattle Times*, 40 feature articles over 25 years

1946–7 Friday Harbor Lab > Cattle Point (field school), survey = Byrd Helligas, Peter Kilburn, Robert Lane / crew 46 = Dorothy Anderson Birner, Richard Daugherty, Carle Graffunder, Mary Gormly, Roderick Hardies, Ellen Kohler, Nancy Imber, Donald Nyman, Frank Barnett (photos) / crew 47 = Ann & Robert (took photos) Booher (Ann later married Elmer Seikula) Paul Friedman, Jack & Winifred Harrison, Peter McLellan, Carroll Perry, Lucile Rehm, Patricia Woodruff (Wilson Memorial Archaeological Fund ?)

1947   RD Daugherty = outer Coast survey

1947–53 Columbia Basin Project, River Basin Surveys, mimeographed reports 47–53 > 6 years 40 surveys, 9 reports Philip Drucker @ OU, crews (from UCB UW OU SCW) Daugherty, Franklin Fenega, Douglas Osborne, Francis Riddle, Joel Shiner, Clarence Smith > 53 Park Service @ SF, Cal, Paul JF Schumacher

1947–53 Louis Caywood = Fts Vancouver, Okanogan, Clatsop, Spokane House

1947   Bill Ruddell = Straits?

1947   John (& Marcia) Winterhouse = survey S Puget Sound

1947   Lind Coulee IDed by George Beck @ CWC; Daugherty shifts crew from Moses Lake; RD & F Riddell at Potholes (O'Sullivan) for River Basin Survey

1948   Doug Osborne hired from NM & WWII as lab director of Smithsonian River Basin Survey (RBS) @ Burke Museum, joins UW 1950; PhD work = McNary for UCB Berkeley 51 PhD, also @ Chief Joe Dam

1948   May 8 NAC 1st @ Portland affiliate of AAA Western

1948   Robert Hudziak, Clarence Smith, Fred Pennoyer = Western Cascade foothills to Longview [Site forms for Cl-1, Cl-2, Cl-3, Cl-4], Peninsula

1948–50 Thomas Garth = Whitman Mission

1948~54 San Juans > Warren Caldwell, Richard Daugherty, Malcolm Forbes, Byrd Helligas, Robert & Barbara Lane, Ralph Turman, Donald Nyman, Wayne Suttles, Keith Thomson, and Peter Kilburn (killed as a Beirut hostage, nephew of Ann Gayton, wife 2 of Leslie Spier)

1949   Florence Howard (by canoe) = An Archaeological Site Survey of Southwestern Puget Sound

1949   WSU hired Doc > Lind Coulee 47 survey, excavation 51–2, his 53 UW PhD; 53 McGregor Cave

1950s   Arden King, publication outlets *APS*, *AAn*, *AAA*

1950s   Syntheses by Borden 54, by Osborne, Caldwell, Crabtree 56, by Chard 56

1950   Marian Smith typology; Carl Borden of UBC = Pt Roberts Whalen Site

1950–56 *ABC* # 1–5, *Memoirs* 1952–64, #1–5

1950   Doug Osborne (UBC PhD) joins UW; wife Carolyn for textiles @ Burke, start Seattle Young Archaeologists Society, with girls added to boys 1953; 1950 Cal Burroughs joins UW, ABD @ UCB, never finishes, friend of Osbornes; William Massey digs at Old Man House with Warren Snyder, John Mills,

1950   Camano Island = Burroughs drives around for rapid survey by Ralph Woodward, Nancy Meagher, Elmer Seikula, Norman Leerman, Dick Huber, Bill Bock, Bonnie Halloran

1950s   Chief Joseph Dam 52

1950s   Richard V Emmons = Nooksack Survey published in 52 ABC

1950   Priest Rapids by John M Campbell, reported by Joel Shiner

1951–52 Wakemap survey?

1951   Oregon Archaeological Society auctions off 5 foot squares to diggers; 52 published *Screenings*, Emory Strong active = *Stone Age on the Columbia River* 59

1951   Ft Spokan House = Louis Caywood, Roy Carlson found grave of Jocko Finley

1952   Herb Taylor to WWU; Luther Cressman = Dalles

1952   Cave survey = Alan Bryan, Earl Swanson, Don Tuohy

1953   UW (Doug & Carolyn Osborne) had two field schools: = Wakemap Mound (dug 52 by Joel Shiner) under Warren Caldwell, and = Vantage under Earl Swanson. Pam

Amoss @ Wakemap, where Osbornes improved the food. She recalls Bob Crabtree, Mark Hedin (rock art), Bill Pope (ROTC), Bob Butler (volunteer cook, goad), Roy and Maureen Carlson (married Sat, begin as chaperones on Monday because a coed camp), Peggy Copeland (Corley), Jean Patterson (who married Earl Swanson, met when the Vantage crew came down to visit at Wakemap). Pope had antique firearms with him, dating Pam. Lucy Steelman at hub of most UW activities. She did osteology for Carlson's MA write up of San Juan surveys, not the excavations. Osbornes arrived at Wakemap to find crew eating a freshly cooked porcupine, after their meager supper, and Carolyn insisted that food get better, and it did. Roy flaked a clear point from the bottom of a glass gallon jug and planted it in Butler's square, but he refused to believe it was a fake until shown the pile of flakes up on the hill where Roy knapped it. Years later, Butler and his wife double suicide when their health got worse. Roy barely missed a bite from a rattler while recording rock art, jumped away just in time when Maureen shouted a warning on hearing the rattles. Maureen, in an email [Thu, Jun 14, 2012, 05:09 PM], confirmed participants were Peggy Copeland, Pam Thorsen, Jean Patterson, Warren Caldwell, Bob Butler, Bill Pope, Roy and Maureen Carlson, and 2 high school boys, Jim Smith and Fritz Cornford (probably via Osborne's Seattle arky club).

1953   Luther Cressman and crew were digging across the Columbia River in Oregon.

1953   Vantage site must have included Schaake Village; Daugherty in Palouse

1953~54 Alan Bryan, Ralph Turman = N Puget Sound

1953~54 Alan Bryan, John Osmundson = Camano Island

1953   Marmes 53, 62, 63, 64, 65 (2 wks)

1954   Warren Caldwell = Okanogan *ABC* ; Herb Taylor on Lopez

1955   Bruce Stallard & Clayton Denman = coast 56 (7/8)

1955   Lower Columbia, Claude Warren and Frances Eng; Emory Strong in Vancouver vicinity; Borden at Marpole

1955   Washington State Parks survey begun @ Fort Simcoe = George Coales & Edward Larrabee

1955   Davidson Journal @ UW printed for 3 ½ years Osborne UW job offered in turn to Daugherty, Borden (pointed rejection), taken by Greengo, who blamed [victim] Osborne; Bob Theodoratos only grad OK thru transition

1955   *Method & Theory in Archaeology*

1955   WAS ~ *The Washington Archaeologist* 57 >

1950s   Earl Swanson = 56 Archeological Studies in the Vantage Region of the Columbia Plateau, Northwestern America. Douglas Osborne Fund for Plateau Anthropology Illustrators = Alix Gordon, Aylene Loughnan, Josephine Ravsten
        Crew 53 = RL Shalkop, Mike Griffin, Claude Warren, Harvey Harmon, Bill Rathbun, Gene Giles, Fred Giesa, Robert Crabtree, Bill Chambers
        Crew 54= Gene Giles, Helen Brannan, Verna Washburn, Bob Schoos, Sterling Lanier, Alan Reece, Alysn Tree, John Tyler, Grant Gauger

1956   Earl Swanson = Vantage for 1958 PhD UW

1956   *Federal Highway Aid Act*

1956   RSSCW

1957   Earl Swanson = Archaeological Survey of the Methow Valley, from Ft Okanogan before 1948 flood added 20 feet at mouth 1958–9 Crew = Mr & Mrs Claude Warren, Matt Hill, Christopher Hulse (S of Fred), John Rice, Earl's family. [Hulse later resigned from UW during 50s bloodbath, went to U Arizona, retired, driving to

Monterrey car rolled over and wife killed.]

1957   Earl Swanson to ISU; Ft Okanogan = Earl Swanson & Garland Grabert > 65; Herb Taylor & Angelo Anastasio = Semiahmoo

1957   Robert Greengo crew @ Priest Rapids ~ Wanapam Salvage

1957   Highway Salvage WSU Doc & Bruce Stallard > 58 Booklet *WSU Laboratory of Anthropology, Report of Investigations*, 57 Stallard; #s added 1962, redo # 1–19; Clayton Denman digs Toleak Point, 58 T. Stell Newman

1958–61 WSU = Sun Lakes = Doc, Osborne, Sprague, Steven Clinehens; Oscar L Mallory = Olympics WSU T Stell Newman, Stanley J Gwinn; Claude Warren, Alan Bryan, Donald Tuohy @ SW WA

1958   *Tebiwa* means "homeland" in Shoshone; BR Butler

1960s   Edward Larrabee, Susan Karda = @ Grand Coulee Survey

1960   Roderick Sprague = Sun Lakes

1960   Robert Greengo Spring Quarter Saturday field class; @ Olcott with Robert Kidd

1960s   early WAC = Fishtown, Beiderbost

1960s   Robert Greengo = Marymoor, Wenatchee

1960s   U Calgary > BC

1962   Charles Nelson = Vantage 69

1962   Doc [RDD] = The Intermontane Western Tradition > *AAn*; Earl Swanson = The Emergence of Plateau Culture; Earl Swanson ISU #10 = Point Typology.

1963, 65 Arky films; UW summer field school = Wells Dam

1963   Sonia Solland, Nancy Stenholm, Mary Ann Duncan = State Parks in western Washington 73 Sonia Solland, Mary Ann Duncan

1963   Mt Rainier = Allan Smith, Richard Daugherty, crew = Barbara Grater, Winston Moore, Roger Nance, Charles Nelson, David Rice

1963   South Puget Sound = R Greengo, Brian Holmes, Robert Free, Frank Tarver, D Keenleyside

1963–4 W Wa Geochronology = R Fryxell, V Steen, G Richmond, R Wilcox with USGS

1964   Palus Cemetery = Rick Sprague

1965   OSU hired Wilbur A Davis PSU hired Thomas M. Newman = Cascadia Cave

1965   Windust Harvey S. Rice (Pete); David Browman along Cowlitz

1966   Salvage UW = David Browman, Dave Munsell, Wm Dancey WSU = Barbara Grater, Charles R Nance, Monte R Kenaston IU = 65 R Sprague 66 John Combes @ Kettle Falls 68 Frank Leonardy

1966   *National Historic Preservation Act*

1966   Ft Vancouver NPS; Alex Krieger and Dave Munsell = survey WA highways

1966–79 Ozette

1967   Warren Caldwell = Hells Canyon arky Oscar Mallory

1967   CWC William Smith = survey of Kittitas County

1967   *NARN* Rick Sprague = NW Arky Biblio 90pp Alfred Bowers retires, Sprague > IU OU MNH Bulletin

1968   UW *Reports in Arky WAC Occasional Papers Syesis* starts

1968   David Chance = Oregon BLM report; Onat = Fishtown, Gerald Hedlund @ Green River

1969   WA State Archaeological Council; Garland Grabert @ WWC

1970   William Dancey = Yakima Firing Range; Tom Roll = Minard

1971   D Cole & M Southard = Columbia Gorge

1972   NPS Pacific NW office @ Seattle, Charles Bohanan > James W Thomson ? Bob Mierendorf; Ann Irwin & Ula Moody = Lind Coulee

1973   Glenn Greene & Henry Irwin = Lower Crab Creek; J Hoffman = Ft Vancouver

1974   Bryan Seymour SFU = Maple Beach (Whalen site); Office of Public Archaeology (OPA) @ UW 74–83 = Dave Munsell, Jerry Jerman, Tom Lorenz, Jim Chatters

1975   Gregory Cleveland = Horse Heaven BPA; Joseph Randolph & David G Rice UI; R Spear = Nooksack Valley

1979   *Archaeological Resources Protection Act*

1990   *Native American Graves Protection and Repartriation Act* (*NAGPRA*) CRM Cultural Resource Management firms blossom

Basic Backgrounds

Roy Carlson = Archeological Investigations in the San Juan Islands 54 UW: MA >> Arden King survey 46, 47, 48 / Carroll Burroughs field school 49, 51 Aden Treganza field school 50 (visiting prof from SF State, baby), 48 Cattle Point 49 SJ- 2 3 4 5 99 / 49 William Liston & Malcolm Forbes SJ-185, 186 / 50 AE Treganza SJ-25 West of English Camp SJ-24 / 50–51 Warren Caldwell SJ-3 / 51 Burroughs resurvey

Robert Herre Crabtree 1957 Two Burial Sites in Central Washington. UW: MA (last by Osborne, approved 13 June 1957) [Rabbit (burial) Island, Pot Holes near Trinidad, where FS Hall dug Oct 1920, revisit Oct 1921] 51 Initiative 171 Funds from RD Daugherty ?

Crews = 51 = Carlos Kaufeldt, Ralph Woodward, Eugene Dammel, Tom Miller, Paul Sellin, Boris Fine; 52 = Donald Tuohy, John Osmundson, Robert Kawauchi [became social worker SF], Ralph Turman, Elmer Seikula

Illustrators = Helmi Munz, Robert Ormsby, Alix Coron, Aylene Laughman

Brian Holmes 66 Schaake Site: A New Study UW MA

Appendix 1 Personnel = PI - Greengo, Field Dir - Claude Vaucher, Foreman - Brian Holmes, Karen Carlson, Randall Dinwiddie, Lucia Esthers, Robert Free, William Goebel, Jane Goforth, Suzanne Holmes, Elaine Inouye, Peggy Larson, Lynn Lundquist, John Mattson, Richard Pedersen, Robert Reed, Robin Ridington, Lynette Sanford, Sonja Solland, Nancy Stenholm, Margo Stevenson, Frank Tarver, Kathleen Toner, David Wyatt

Bibliography

Charles Borden 1975 Origins and Development of early Northwest Coast Culture to About 3000 B.C. National Museum of Man, Mercury Series, *Archaeological Survey of Canada*, 45.

Roy Carlson 1990 History of Research in Archaeology, *Northwest Coast*, Handbook of North American Indians 7, 107–115. Wayne Suttles, ed. DC: Smithsonian.

John M Campbell 1950 Report of an Archaeological Survey, Priest Rapids Reservoir, State of Washington. Burke

George Coale 1956 Archaeological Survey of Mt Sheep and Pleasant Valley Reservoirs. *Davidson Journal of Anthropology* I (II), 11–29, Summer. 9 Oct to 30 November 1955,

Donald Collier, Alfred Hudson, Arlo Ford 1942 Archaeology of the Upper Columbia Region. *University of Washington Publications in Anthropology*, 9 (1):1–178.

Luther Cressman 1977 *Prehistory of the Far West. Homes of Vanished Peoples.* Salt Lake City: University of Utah Press.

Richard Emmons 1952 An Archeological Survey in the Lower Nooksack River Valley *ABC*, 3: 49–56.

Robert Greengo 1986 The Prehistory of the Priest Rapids – Wanapum Region: A Summary. Seattle: Burke Museum Contributions in Anthropology and Natural History # 2, 1–22. ms. Prehistory of the Northwest Coast. 12/91

Florence Howard 1949 An Archaeological Survey of Southwestern Puget Sound. Office of Public Archaeology, UW, Seattle; WSU, Pullman

Robert Kidd 1964 A Synthesis of Western Washington Prehistory from the Perspective of Three Occupation Sites. UW MA.

Warren T Lee 1955 An Archaeological Survey of the Columbia Basin Project in Grant County, Washington. *Davidson Journal of Anthropology*, I (II):141–5 Winter 1955. [based on collection made 1938–54. Sites 45-GR-59>78 + 3 sites in Kittitas County]

Frank C. Leonhardy and David G. Rice
1970 A Proposed Culture Typology for the Lower Snake River Region, Southeastern Washington. *Northwest Anthropological Research Notes*, 4(1):1–29.

Charles Luttrell 2006 Archaeology for Young Diggers: Douglas and Carolyn Osborne, the Seattle Young Archaeologists' Society, and the Washington Archaeological Society. *Archaeology in Washington*, 12, 5–13.

AW Mangum and others 1913 Reconnaissance of Southwestern Washington, US Dept of Agriculture, Bureau of Soils, DC: US Government printing office.

Charles Nelson 1969 The Sunset Creek Site (45 KT 28) and Its Place in Plateau Prehistory. Pullman: *Washington State University, Laboratory of Anthropology, Report of Investigations*, 47.

Douglas Osborne 1967 Archaeological Tests in the Lower Grand Coulee, Washington. Pocatello: *Occasional Papers of the Idaho State University Museum*, 20:1–83.

Yvonne Peterson 1981 Indians of Washington State Dec, revised Oct 88. Reprinted Feb 89. July 89 130pp Olympia: Office of Public Instruction

David G. Rice
1964 Indian Utilization of the Cascade Mountain Range in South Central Washington. *The Washington Archaeologist*, 8(1):5–20.
1968 Archaeological Investigations in the Coulee Dam National Recreation Area, *Washington State University, Laboratory of Anthropology, Reports of Investigations*, 45:1–53.
1969 Archaeological Reconnaissance, Southcentral Cascades, Washington. *Washington Archaeological Society, Occasional Paper*, 2.

Joel Shiner 1959 An Appraisal of the Archaeological Resources of the Priest Rapids Reservoir RBS, *Tebiwa*, 2 (1), 69 # 2, Winter 1958–9 [John Campbell 50 survey]

Roderick "Rick" Sprague 1967 A Preliminary Bibliography of Washington Archaeology. *Washington State University, Laboratory of Anthropology, Report of Investigations*, 43 (with list of all 1–43). Also NARN 1 (1):1–88.
1973 The Pacific Northwest, 250–285, *The Development of North American Archaeology*. James Fitting, ed. NY: Anchor Books.

Earl Swanson 1958 Methow Survey NPS, *WAS* 3 (1), 1 1959; *Tebiwa*, 2 (1):72–82, 1958–9.
1962 First Conference of Western Archaeologists on Problems of Point Typology. Pocatello: *Occasional Papers of Idaho State College Museum*, #10.

Frank Tarver and Robert Free 1963 An Archaeological Survey of Southern Puget Sound. Ms. Office of Public Archaeology, UW, Seattle

Jack Thomson 19?? Preliminary Archaeological Survey of the Pilchuck River and South Fork of the Stillaguamish River. *WAS*, 5(6) Les Olcott brought in finds in 59

Claude Warren   1968   *The View from Wenas*: *A Study in Plateau Prehistory*. Pocatello: *Occasional Papers of the Idaho State University Museum*, 24:1–89.

John (Marcia) Winterhouse   1948   A Report of an Archaeological Survey of Lower Puget Sound. Seattle: UW Office of Public Archaeology.

Archaeology Programs

WSU Doc WARC
WWU 52 Herb Taylor, ?? Garland Grabert
CWU ? Wm C Smith 65
EWU ?
UW / Burke Osborne/Krieger/Greengo ?
OU Cressman
PSU
OSU ?
SCCC Onat,
SFU Carlson 1965, separate dept 1970

Who? Where? When?

Roy Carlson = San Juans MA UW 54
George & Marge Coale
John Combes = Spokan House
Gerry Galm
Thomas Garth = Walla Walla, Published his agreement with James Teit, doomed at UW
Garland Grabert = Okanogan
Glenn Hartmann =
Gerald Hedlund = Green River
Bryan Holmes = highways WSDOT
Donald Mitchell = Vancouver Island
Jay Perry 39 midColumbia @ NM
Harvey (Pete) Rice = Columbia
Tom Roll = Minard
Joel Shiner =
Warren Snyder = Ol' Man House WSU 56
Herbert Shippen = Natalie Burt
Robert Stephenson =
Donald Touhy =
Claude Warren =
Rick Sprague = historic arky at English Camp, z Ardyth Sprague, Derrick Whitmarsh

Davidson Journal of Anthropology

Davidson Journal of Anthropology 1 (1) Staff Editors = David Adams, James Garner, Robert Theodoratus

Production Managers = Grover Allred, Melvin Firestone, Felix Moos, Shirley Sylliaasen
Production Staff = James Alexander, George Coale, Marge Coale, Clayton Denman, Bea Garner, Mary Gormly, Mark Gumbiner, Joanne Hirabayashi, Saburo Katamoto, Beatrice

Miller, Fusa Moos, Ruby Morris, Lucy Steelman
Corresponding Secretary = Charles Taylor

Davidson Journal of Anthropology 2 (1) Staff

Editors = James Garner, Robert Theodoratus, Charles Taylor
Production Managers = Clayton Denman, Melvin Firestone, Felix Moos
Production Staff = Donna Lotz, Bruce Stallard
Corresponding Secretary = Mary Gormly
Cover Design = Del Nordquist

Abbreviations

AAA = *American Anthropologist*
AAn = *American Antiquity*
AAOJ = *American Antiquarian and Oriental Journal*
ACE = Army Corps of Engineers
BR = Bureau of Reclamation
CWSC = Central Washington State College > CWU
EP = *El Palacio*, NM
GRCC = Green River Community College
MCAS = Mid-Columbia Archaeological Society
NPS = National Park Service
OAS = Oregon Archaeological Society
OPA= Office of Public Archaeology, UW
RBS = River Basin Survey, Smithsonian
RSSCW = *Research Studies of State College of Washington*
SCCC = Seattle Central Community College
SCW = State College of Washington
Screenings = Portland 50s
Tebiwa = ("homeland") UI
UA = U of Arizona
UI = U of Idaho
UO = U of Oregon
USGS = United States Geological Survey
UW = University of Washington
WaDOT = Washington Department of Transportation
WARC = Washington Archaeological Research Center, WSU
WAS = Washington Archaeological Society @ Seattle & Pullman
WSC = Washington State College
WSP = Washington State Parks
WWSC = Western Washington State College > WWC > WWU

"Dig in the Dirt, Delve in the Soul"
Ray Bradbury, *Dandelion Wine*, 51.

Appendix C

BIBLIOGRAPHY OF JAY MILLER, PH.D.

Books / Ethnographies / Monographs

Introduction. 2012. In *Honne, Spirit of the Chehalis*: *The Indian Interpretation of the Origin of the People and Animals*, George Sanders, Author, and Katherine Van Winkle Palmer, editor. Bison Books Edition, University of Nebraska Press, Lincoln.

Richard "Doc" Daugherty's Ethnographic Notebooks: The Hoh Tribe in 1949. Jay Miller, ed. *Journal of Northwest Anthropology*, 44 (2):137–218. 2010.

Regaining Dr. Herman Haeberlin. *Early Anthropology and Museology in Puget Sound, 1916–17*. Lushootseed Press. 2005

Winds, Waterways, and Weirs. Ethnographic Study of the Central Link Light Rail Corridor. Seattle: Sound Transit, Contract Rta/Lr 69-00. Boas Project No 20005.D (Astrida Blukis Onat, PI). 2004.

Chehalis Area Traditions: A Summary of Thelma Adamson's 1927 Ethnographic Notes. *Northwest Anthropological Research Notes*, 33 (1), 1–72, Spring 1999.

Suquamish Traditions (With Warren Snyder). *Northwest Anthropological Research Notes*, 33 (1), 105–175, Spring 1999.

Lushootseed Culture and the Shamanic Odyssey: An Anchored Radiance. University of Nebraska Press, Lincoln. 1999.

The Tillamook of Oregon. Smithsonian Handbook of North American Indians, *Northwest*, Volume 7, 560–567. 1990. (with William Seaburg)

The Southwest Oregon Athapaskans. Smithsonian Handbook of North American Indians, *Northwest*, Volume 7, 580–588. 1990. (with William Seaburg)

Middle Columbia River Salishans. Smithsonian Handbook of North American Indians, *Plateau*, Volume 12, 253–270, 1998.

Tsimshian Culture: A Light Through the Ages. University of Nebraska Press, 1997, Paperback 2001.

Earthmaker. Tribal Stories from Native North America. Perigree Books, New York. 1992.

Mourning Dove, A Salishan Autobiography. Indian Lives Series. University of Nebraska Press, Lincoln. 1990. Paperback, 1994

Coyote Stories by Mourning Dove. Introduction, Notes. Bison Books, University of Nebraska Press, Lincoln. 1990.

The Tsimshian and Their Neighbors of the North Pacific Coast. Jay Miller and Carol Eastman, eds. University of Washington Press, Seattle. 1984.

Oral Literature. A Sourcebook. D'Arcy McNickle Center for the History of the American Indian, Occasional Papers in Curriculum Series # 13, 1992.

Shamanic Odyssey: A Comparative Study of the Lushootseed (Puget Salish) Journey to the Land of the Dead in Terms of Death, Power, and Cooperating Shamans in Native North America. Ballena Press Anthropological Papers 32, 1988.

Writings in Indian History, 1985–1990. Compiled by Jay Miller, Colin G. Calloway, and Richard Sattler. University of Oklahoma Press, Norman. 1995.

Articles

The Wooden Idols of Benavides. *Awanyu*, 2(2):42–44. 1974.

Kwulakan: The Delaware Side of Their Movement West. *Pennsylvania Archaeologist*, 45(4):45–46. 1975.

Addendum On Ethno-Taxonomic Congresses. *American Anthropologist*, 77(4):887. 1975.

The Cultural View of Delaware Clan Names as Contrasted with a Linguistic View. *Man in the Northeast*, 9:60–63. (cf. Nora Thompson Dean (63–65), Ives Goddard (65–67). 1975.

Delaware Alternative Classifications. *Anthropological Linguistics*, 17(9):434–444. 1975.

James Swan and Makah Cosmology: A Clarification. *Northwest Anthropological Research Notes*, 10(2):217–219. 1975.

The Delaware Doll Dance. *Man in the Northeast*, 12:80–84. 1976.

The Role of the Sea in North Pacific Indian Societies. *Sea Pen*, 5(4):16–18. 1976.

Delaware Anatomy: With Linguistic, Social, and Medical Aspects. *Anthropological Linguistics*, 19(4):144–166. 1977.

Delaware Terms For Playing Cards. *International Journal of American Linguistics*, 44(2):145–146. 1978.

A Personal Account of the Delaware Big House Rite. *Pennsylvania Archaeologist*, 48(1–2), 39–43. 1978. (with Nora Thompson Dean).

Moiety Birth. *Northwest Anthropological Research Notes*, 13(1):45–50. 1978.

A 'Struckon' Model of Delaware Culture and the Positioning of Mediators. *American Ethnologist*, 6(4):791–802. 1979.

A Structural Study of the Delaware Big House Rite. *Papers in Anthropology*, 21(2):107–133. 1980.

High-Minded High Gods in North America. *Anthropos*, 75:916–919. 1980.

The Matter of the (Thoughtful) Heart: Centrality, Focality, or Overlap. *Journal of Anthropological Research*, 36(3):338–342. 1980.

Tsimshian Moieties and Other Clarifications. *Northwest Anthropological Research Notes*, 16(2):148–164. 1981.

Moieties and Cultural Amnesia: Manipulation of Knowledge in A Pacific Northwest Coast Native Community. *Arctic Anthropology*, 18(1):23–32. 1981.

Numic Religion: An Overview of Power in the Great Basin of Native North America. *Anthropos*, 78:337–354. 1983.

Basin Religion and Theology: A Comparative Study of Power (Puha). *Journal of California and Great Basin Anthropology*, 5(1–2):66–86. 1983.

Salish Kinship: Why Decedence? *Proceedings of the 20th International Conference on Salish and Neighboring Languages*. August 15–17. Vancouver, BC. 1985.

An Overview of Northwest Coast Mythology. *Northwest Anthropological Research Notes*, 23(2), 125–141. 1989.

Delaware Masking. *Man in the Northeast*, 41:105–110. 1991.

Delaware Personhood. *Man in the Northeast*, 42:17–27. 1991.

Art, Attitude, and Appropriation. *American Woodturner*, 6(4):17. 1991.

Mourning Dove: Editing in All Directions To "Get Real." *SAIL (Studies in American Indian Literatures*, Series 2, 7(2):65–72. Summer 1995.

Changing Moons: A History of Caddo Religion. *Plains Anthropologist*, 41(157):243–259. 1996.

Old Religion Among the Delawares. *Ethnohistory*, 44(1):113–134. 1997.

Back To Basics: Chiefdoms in Puget Sound. *Ethnohistory*, 44(2):375–387. 1997.

Tsimshian Ethno-Ethnohistory: A "Real" Indigenous Chronology. *Ethnohistory*, 45(4):657–674. 1998.

Inflamed History: Violence Against Homesteading Indians in Washington Territory. *North Dakota Quarterly*, American Indian Issue, Summer/Fall, 67(3/4):162–173. 2000

Keres: Engendered Key to the Pueblo Puzzle. *Ethnohistory*, 48(3):495–514. Summer 2001.

Dr. Simon: A Snohomish Slave At Fort Nisqually and Puyallup. *Northwest Anthropological Research Notes*, 36 (2):145–54. 2002.

Dibble Cultivating Prairies to Beaches: The Real All Terrain Vehicle. *Journal of Northwest Anthropology*, 39(1):33–39. 2005.

Charlie Quintasket, Mourning Dove's Brother. *Journal of Northwest Anthropology*, 42(1):109–120. 2008.

Mourning Dove's Other Women *Northwest Anthropological Research Note Journal of Northwest Anthropology*, 42 (1):121–129. 2008.

Synopsis, Synthesis, Skimping, and Scholarship: A Case Example From Chehalis in the "Other" Washington. *Journal of Northwest Anthropology*, 43 (2):171–178. 2009.

Startup: Richard "Doc" Daugherty's 1947 Archaeological Survey of the Washington Coast. *Journal of Northwest Anthropology,* 44 (2):257–265. 2011.

First Nations Forts, Refuges, and War Lord Champions Around the Salish Sea. *Journal of Northwest Anthropology*, 45(1):71–87. 2011.

Lamprey "Eels" in the Greater Northwest: A Survey of Tribal Sources, Experiences, And Sciences. *Journal of Northwest Anthropology*, 46 (1):65–84. 2012.

Skookumchuck Shuffle ~ Shifting Athapaskan Swaals Into Oregon Klatskanis Before Taitnapam Sahaptins Cross The Cascades. *Journal of Northwest Anthropology,* 46(2):167–175. 2012.

Ross's Monumental *Spokan* Study: Grasping—Galloping—Graphics. *Journal of Northwest Anthropology*, 47(1):84–85. 2013.

Commentary

The Shell(Fish) Game: Rhetoric, Images, and (Dis)Illusions in Federal Court. *American Indian Culture and Research Journal*, 23(4):159–173, 1999. [Reprinted *Gathering Native Scholars: UCLA's Forty Years of American Indian Culture and Research 2009*].

Indien Personhood. *American Indian Culture and Research Journal,* 24(1):121–141. 2000.

Indien Personhood II: Baby in the Oven Sparks Being in the World [Ovens of Incarnation]. *American Indian Culture and Research Journal*, 24(3):155–160. 2000.

Instilling the Earth: Explaining Mounds. *American Indian Culture and Research Journal*, 25(3):161–177. 2001.

Indien Personhood III: Water Burial. *American Indian Culture and Research Journal*, 29(3). 2005.

Chapters

Delaware Language and Culture. *Papers of the 1978 Mid-America Linguistics Conference,* edited by Ralph Cooley, Melvin Barnes, and John Dunn, pp. 23–31. University of Oklahoma Press, Norman. 1979.

Ethnohistoric Section. Chief Joseph Dam, Ancestral Burial Relocation Survey, Rufus Woods Lake, Washington. *University of Idaho Anthropological Research Monograph Series,* 51: 9–41. Roderick Sprague and Jay Miller. 1979.

Tsimshian Religion in Historical Perspective: Shamans, Prophets, and Christ. *The Tsimshian and Their Neighbors*, edited by Jay Miller and Carol Eastman, pp. 137–147. 1984.

Feasting with the Southern Tsimshian. *The Tsimshian, Images of the Past, Views for the Present*, edited by Margaret Seguin, pp. 27–39. University of British Columbia Press, Vancouver. 1984.

Shamans and Power in Western North America: The Numic, Salish, and Keres. *Woman, Poet, Scientist: Essays in New World Anthropology Honoring Dr. Emma Louise Davis*, edited by Great Basin Foundation, pp. 56–66. Ballena Press Anthropological Paper 29. 1985.

Free Translations of "Fly," pp. 33–41, "Moose," pp. 145–49, Verse Translation of "Boil and Hammer," Appendix 1, pp.169–78, Text Data, Appendix 2, pp. 179–82, Bibliography, pp. 183–204. *Haboo, Native American Stories From Puget Sound*, translated and edited By Vi Hilbert. University of Washington Press, Seattle. 1985.

Viola Garfield. *Directory of Women Anthropologists. Biographical Dictionary*, edited by Ute Gacs, Aisha Khan, Jerrie Mcintyre, and Ruth Weinberg, pp. 109–114. Greenwood Press, Westport, CT. 1988.

Mourning Dove: The Author as Cultural Mediator. *Being and Becoming Indian: Biographical Studies of North American* Frontiers, edited by James Clifton, 160–182. The Dorsey Press, Chicago. 1989.

Land and Lifeway in the Chicago Area: Chicago and the Illinois – Miami, Indians of the Chicago Area, edited by Terry Straus, pp. 101–107. NAES College Publications. 1989.

Deified Mind Among the Keresan Pueblos. *General and Amerindian Ethnolinguistics*. Remembrance of Stanley Newman, edited by Mary Ritchie Key and Henry M. Koeningswald, pp. 151–156. *Contributions To the Sociology of Languages*, 55. Mouton De Gruyter Press, Berlin. 1989.

A Kinship of Spirit. *Society in the Americas in 1492*, pp. 305–337. Alfred Knopf, New York. 1992.

North Pacific Ethno–Astronomy: Tsimshian and Others. *Earth and Sky: Visions of the Cosmos in Native American Folklore*, edited by Claire Farrer and Ray Williamson, pp. 193–206. U of New Mexico Press, Albuquerque. 1992.

Society in America in 1492. *America in 1492*: Selected Lectures From the Quincentenary Program, the Newberry Library. D'Arcy McNickle Center For the History of the American Indian. Occasional Papers in Curriculum Series 15, edited by Harvey Markowitz, pp. 151–169. 1992.

Caring For Control: A Pivot of Salishan Language and Culture. *American Indian Linguistics and Ethnography in Honor of Laurence C. Thompson*. University of Montana, Occasional Papers in Linguistics, 10:237–239. 1993 (with Vi Hilbert)

Canadian Native Studies in the United States. *Northern Exposures. Scholarship on Canada in the United States*, edited by Karen Gould, Joseph Jockel and William Metcalfe, pp. 373–395. Chapter 16. The Association for Canadian Studies in the United States (Acsus). 1993.

Blending Worlds. *The Native Americans. An Illustrated History*, edited by Betty and Ian Ballantine, pp. 111–209. Turner Publishing. 1993.

Northern Worlds. *Through Indian Eyes*. Readers Digest Publishing. 1995.

Lushootseed Animal People: Mediation and Transformation From Myth to History. *Monsters, Tricksters, and Sacred Cows. Animal Tales and American Identities*, edited by A. James Arnold, New World Studies, pp. 138–156. University of Virginia Press, Charlottesville. 1996. (with Vi Taqᵂšəblu Hilbert).

Naming as Humanizing, *Strangers to Relatives, The Adoption and Naming of Anthropologists in Native North America*, edited by Sergei Kan, pp. 141–158. U of Nebraska Press, Lincoln. 2001.

That Salish Feeling..." *Studies in Salish Linguistics in Honor of M. Dale Kinkade*, edited by Donna B. Gerdts and Lisa Matthewson, pp. 197–210. University of Montana, *Occasional Papers in Linguistics*, No. 17. 2004. (Vi Hilbert first author).

Choice and Commitment: Black Indians Across North America. *Race, Roots, and Relations: Native and African Americans*, edited by Terry Strauss, pp. 413–419. #31. Albatross Press, Brooklyn, NY. 2005.

Fly: A Southern Lushootseed Epic, Told by Annie Daniels and Peter Heck. *Salish Myths and Legends, One People's Stories*, edited by M. Terry Thompson and Steven M Egesdal, pp. 78–83. 2008.

The Sailor Who Jumped Ship and Was Befriended By Skagits: A Lushootseed Historical Story. Told by Susie Sampson Peter, edited by Jay Miller and Vi Taqʷšəblu Hilbert. In *Salish Myths and Legends, One People's Stories*, edited by M. Terry Thompson and Steven M. Egesdal, pp. 277–286. 2008

Storied Arts: Lushootseed Gifting Across Time and Space (with Vi Taqʷšəblu Hilbert). In *S'abadeb – The Gifts. Pacific Coast Salish Art and Artists*, edited by Barbara Brotherton, pp. 6–17. University of Washington Press, Seattle. 2008.

The Sixties in the Pacific Northwest. In *Visions and Voices: American Indian Activism and the Civil Rights Movement*, edited by Kurt Peters and Terry Strauss, pp. 190–198. Albatross Press, Brooklyn, NY. 2009.

Entries

Native America in the Twentieth Century: An Encyclopedia (Garland Publishing). Delaware (pp. 169–70), Cultural Revitalization (pp. 156–158).

American National Biography, edited by John A Garraty and Mark C Carnes. (Oxford University Press, 1999). Teedyuskung 21, 425–426, Mourning Dove 15, 37–38.

The Encyclopedia of the American Indian (Houghton Mifflin): Colville Tribes, Delaware, Salishan Languages, Native American Family, Mourning Dove, Chief Seattle, Taboo, Rio Grande Pueblos.

Blackwell Companion To Native American History, edited by Neil Salisbury and Philip Deloria, Chapter 11 "Kinship, Family Kindreds, and Community." 2002, 2004.

Encyclopedia of Literature in Canada. (University of Toronto), edited by William New. Tsimshian Oral Literature. 2002.

Encyclopedia of American Indian Religious Traditions. NW Religious Leadership, NW Ritual and Ceremony, NW Spiritual and Ceremonial Practitioners, NW Winter Spirit Dances, NW Shamanic Odyssey (Spirit Canoe) Ceremony. 2004.

Encyclopedia of Appalachia, Center for Appalachian Studies and Services (CASS) at East Tennessee State University. Native Theatrical Traditions, 2005.

American Indian Places, edited by Frances H. Kennedy. (Houghton Mifflin). Schoenbrunn Village State Memorial, Ohio. 2008.

On Line

Library of Congress/Ameritech Digital/UW, American Indians of the Pacific Northwest http://Content.Lib.Washington.edu/Aipnw/

Encarta Encyclopedia 2000, Microsoft

Knowledge Bank, The Ohio State Library:
Keres Culture and Chaco Canyon. [Revised] http://kb.osu.edu/dspace/handle/1811/29276
Regaining Dr. Herman Haeberlin. Early Anthropology and Museology in Puget Sound, 1916–17. [Revised]. http://kb.osu.edu/dspace/handle/1811/29277

Keynotes

The Northwest Coast of What?' Conference On Northwest Coast Studies. Simon Fraser University and Canadian National Museum of Man. 12–16 May 1976.

Tsimshian Art, Bringing Light to the World. Native Arts Council, Seattle Art Museum, 14 June 2000.

Triumphs of Native Ohio: Success Strategies from the Civil Engineering of Monuments to the Social Engineering of International Alliances. AISES Region 6 Annual Conference. April 2006.

Editor at the D'Arcy McNickle Center

Meeting Ground, Biannual Newsletter of the D'Arcy McNickle Center for the History of the American Indian, Issues For 1988 (# 18, 19),1989 (# 20, 21), 1990 (# 22, 23), 1991 (# 24).

Annual Bibliography of Books and Articles in American Indian History (with Colin Calloway), 1987, Revised 1987, 1988.

Overcoming Economic Dependency, Papers and Comments From the First Newberry Conference On Themes in American Indian History. D'Arcy McNickle Center for the History of the American Indian, Occasional Papers in Curriculum Series #9. 233pp.

Proceedings of the 23rd International Conference on Salish and Neighboring Languages. 11–13 August 1988. University Of Oregon, Eugene. 200pp.

Teaching American Indian History: A Selection Of Course Outlines. D'Arcy McNickle Center for the History on the American Indian, Occasional Papers in Curriculum Series #11. 257pp.

The Struggle For Political Autonomy, Papers and Comments from the Second Newberry Conference On Themes in American Indian History, D'Arcy McNickle Center for the History of the American Indian, Occasional Papers in Curriculum Series # 11. 195pp.

Writings in Indian History, 1985–1990. Compiled By Jay Miller, Colin G. Calloway, and Richard Sattler. University Of Oklahoma Press, Norman. 1995.

Editor For Lushootseed Press

The Wisdom of Aunt Susie Sampson Peter, A Skagit Elder (Lushootseed~English) 1994

The Wisdom of Ruth Shelton, A Tulalip Elder (Lushootseed~English) 1995

The Wisdom of Isadore Tom, A Lummi Elder 1995

Hilbert, Vi, Jay Miller, and Zalmai Zahir 2001 *Puget Sound Geography ~ sdaʔdaʔ gʷəł dibəł ləšucid ʔacaciɬtalbixʷ*. A Draft Study of the Thomas Talbot Waterman Place Name Manuscript and Other Sources, Edited with Additional Material. (Lushootseed~English)

Regaining Dr. Herman Haeberlin. Early Anthropology and Museology in Puget Sound, 1916–17. With 4Culture, King County, Revised Yearly and Posted On Line at Ohio State Library Knowledge Bank.

Academic Advisor, Time-Life Books

The Spirit World
Keepers of the Totem
Entire Series, *North American Indians*, Specific Queries

Academic Advisor, Media

Huchuseda ~ Teachings From the Heart: Vi Hilbert (Video) KCTS ~ PBS & BBC ~ Cymru ~
    Wales TV
Teachings of the Tree People: Bruce Miller

Native Honors

On Request, or See Kan, ed. 2001 above.

Scholarly Reviews & Children's Books

On request, or @ Amazon.com.

REFERENCES CITED

Adair, John
1775   *History of the American Indians.* Edward and Charles Dilly, London. Reprinted, 2005, Kathryn Holland Braund, editor. University of Alabama Press, Tuscaloosa.

Adams, John
1973   *The Gitksan Potlatch.* Holt, Rinehart and Winston of Canada, Toronto, ON.

Adamson, Thelma
1927   Unarranged Sources of Chehalis Ethnography. Melville Jacobs Collection, University of Washington, Special Collections, Seattle. [See Miller 1999a].
1934   Folktales of the Coast Salish. *Memoirs of the American Folklore Society, 27.* New York.
2009   *Folk-Tales of the Coast Salish.* Introduction by William Seaburg and Laurel Sercombe. University of Nebraska Press, Lincoln. Originally printed in 1934.

Ames, Kenneth, and Herbert Maschner
1999   *Peoples of the Northwest Coast: Their Archaeology and Prehistory.* Thames and Hudson, London.

Amoss, Pamela
1978   *Coast Salish Spirit Dancing: The Survival of an Ancestral Religion.* University of Washington Press, Seattle.
1988   Erna Gunther (1896–1982). In *Women Anthropologists, A Biographical Dictionary,* edited by Ute Gacs, Aisha Khan, Jerrie McIntyre, and Ruth Weinberg, pp. 133–139. Greenwood Press, New York.
1990   The Indian Shaker Church. In *Handbook of North American Indians, Northwest Coast,* Vol. 7, edited by Wayne Suttles, pp. 633–639. Smithsonian Institution, Washington, D.C.

Andrade, M. J.
1931   Quileute Texts. *Columbia University Contributions to Anthropology,* 12. New York.

Angelbeck, William
2007   Conceptions of Coast Salish Warfare, or Coast Salish Pacifism Reconsidered: Archaeology, Ethnohistory, and Ethnography. In *Be of Good Mind. Essays on the Coast Salish,* edited by Bruce Granville Miller, pp. 260–283. UBC Press, Vancouver, B.C.
2009   They Recognize No Superior Chief: Power, Practice, Anarchism and Warfare in the Coast Salish Past. Doctoral dissertation, University of British Columbia.

Arnold, Laurie
2012   *Bartering with the Bones of Their Dead. The Colville Confederated Tribes and Termination.* University of Washington Press, Seattle.

Asher, Brad
1995   A Shaman-Killing Case on Puget Sound, 1873–1874. American Law and Salish Culture. *Pacific Northwest Quarterly,* 86 (1):17–24.
1999   *Beyond the Reservation. Indians, Settlers, and the Law in Washington Territory, 1853–1889.* University of Oklahoma Press, Norman.

Ballard, Arthur C.
1927   Some Tales of the Southern Puget Sound Salish. *University of Washington Publications in Anthropology,* 2:57–81. Seattle.

1929   Mythology of Southern Puget Sound. *University of Washington Publications in Anthropology,* 3(2):31–150. Seattle.

1950   Calendric Terms of the Southern Puget Sound Salish. *Southwestern Journal of Anthropology,* 6 (1):79–99.

1951   Deposition on Oral Examination of Arthur Condict Ballard. November 26, 27, 28. Testimony before the Indian Claims Commission of the United States, Docket 98. Carolyn Taylor, court reporter. 2 volumes.

1957   The Salmon-Weir on Green River in Western Washington. *Davidson Journal of Anthropology,* 3:37–53.

1999   *Mythology of Southern Puget Sound.* Edited by Kenneth (Greg) Watson. Snoqualmie Valley Historical Museum, North Bend, WA.

Barbeau, Marius

1917   Review of Franz Boas: Tsimshian Mythology. *American Anthropologist,* 19(4):548–563.

1928   *The Downfall of Temlaham.* MacMillan Company of Canada, Toronto.

1929   Totem Poles of the Gitksan, Upper Skeena River, British Columbia. *Canadian Geological Survey, Bulletin* 61, *Anthropological Series,* 12. Ottawa.

1950   Totem Poles. *National Museum of Canada, Bulletin 119; Anthropological Series, 30.* Ottawa.

1951   Tsimsyan Songs (with 75 song texts). The Tsimshian: Their Arts and Music, *Proceedings of the American Ethnological Society,* 18:97–157. J.J. Augustin, New York.

1961   Tsimsyan Myths. *National Museum of Canada, Bulletin 174; Anthropological Series, 51.* Ottawa.

1990   *Totem Poles II: According to Location.* Originally published in 1950. Canadian Museum of Civilization, Hull.

Barbeau, Marius, and William Beynon

1987a   *Tsimshian Narratives I: Tricksters, Shamans and Heroes,* edited by John J. Cove and George F. MacDonald. *Canadian Museum of Civilization, Mercury Series, Directorate Paper* 3.

1987b   *Tsimshian Narratives 2: Trade and Warfare.* Edited by John J. Cove and George F. MacDonald. *Canadian Museum of Civilization, Mercury Series, Directorate Paper* 3.

Barnard, Jeff

2011   NW Tribes Drive Effort to Save Primitive Fish. *Associated Press,* 2 August.

Barnett, Homer

1940   Field Notes: Three Volumes from Mathew Johnson, Port Simpson, and Hazelton. Special Collections, University of British Columbia Library, Vancouver, B.C.

1942   Applied Anthropology in 1860. *Applied Anthropology,* 1(3):19–32.

1955   The Coast Salish of British Columbia. *Studies in Anthropology* 4. University of Oregon Press, Eugene.

1957   *Indian Shakers, A Messianic Cult of the Pacific Northwest.* Southern Illinois University Press, Carbondale.

Bates, Dawn, Thom Hess, and Vi Hilbert

1994   *Lushootseed Dictionary.* University of Washington Press, Seattle.

Beamish, R.J.

1980   Adult Biology of the River Lamprey (*Lampetra ayresi*) and the Pacific Lamprey (*Lampetra tridentata*) from the Pacific Coast of Canada. *Canadian Journal of Fisheries and Aquatic Sciences*, 37:1906–1923.

Beavert, Virginia, and Sharon Hargus

2009   *Ichishkiin Sinwit ~ Yakama / Yakima Sahaptin Dictionary.* Heritage University and University of Washington Press, Toppenish and Seattle, WA.

Benedict, Ruth

1934   *Patterns of Culture.* Houghton Mifflin, Boston, MA.

Bent, A.C.

1919   Life Histories of Diving Birds. U.S. National Museum [USNM] #107.

1925   Life Histories of North American Wild Fowl. U.S. National Museum [USNM] #130, part 2.

1937   The Haleyt And All The Different Kinds Of Haleyt. Text from Mrs. Julia White and Mrs. R. Tate. Vol. 12, Text # 179, Aug-Sept. Reel 3. Microfilm of Beynon Manuscripts in Butler Library, Columbia University.

Best, Elsdon

1952   *The Maori As He Was.* Government Printer, Wellington.

Beynon, William

1927   Field Notes from James Robertson on the Southern Tsimshian. Beynon-Barbeau Tsimshian File. Centre for the Study of Canadian Folklore, National Museum of Man, Ottawa.

1937   Text 179. Microfilm. Interview with Julia White and Mrs. R. Tate, Reel 3, Volume 12, pp. 74–106. ("Haleyt of Legaix").

n.d   Re: Ligeek's pictograph. Microfilm. Reel 2:111–128.

Birket-Smith, Kaj and Frederica de Laguna

1938   *The Eyak Indians of the Copper River Delta, Alaska.* Copenhagen.

Bjerselius, R., W. Li, J.H. Teeter, J.G. Seelye, P.B. Johnsen, P.J. Maniak, G.C. Grant, C.N. Polkinghorne, and P.W. Sorensen

2000   Direct Behavioral Evidence that Unique Bile Acids Released by Larval Sea Lamprey (*Petromyzon marinus*) Function as a Migratory Pheromone. *Canadian Journal of Fisheries and Aquatic Sciences*, 57:557–569.

Blukis Onat, Astrida

1984   The Interaction of Kin, Class, Marriage, Property Ownership and Residences with Respect to Resource Locations among Coast Salish of the Puget Sound Lowland. *Northwest Anthropological Research Notes*, 18(1):86–96.

2002   Resource Cultivation on the Northwest Coast of North America. *Journal of Northwest Anthropology*, 36(2):125–144.

Boas, Franz

1894   Chinook Texts. *Bureau of American Ethnology, Bulletin* 20. Washington, D.C.

1896   The Growth of Indian Mythologies. *Journal of American Folklore,* 9:1–11.

1898a Introduction, to Traditions of the Thompson Indians of British Columbia. *Memoirs of the American Folklore Society,* 6:1–18.

1898b The Mythology of the Bella Coola Indians. *Memoirs of the American Museum of Natural History,* 2:25–127.

1901   Kathlamet Texts. *Bureau of American Ethnology, Bulletin* 26. Washington, D.C.

1902   Tsimshian Texts. *Bureau of American Ethnology, Bulletin* 27. Washington, D.C.

1905   Kwakiutl Texts. *Memoirs of the American Museum of Natural History*, 5:1–532.

1906   Kwakiutl Texts, New Series. *Memoirs of the American Museum of Natural History*, 1:41–269.

1910   Kwakiutl Tales. *Columbia University Contributions to Anthropology*, 2:1–495. New York.

1911   *Handbook of American Indian Languages*, Bulletin 40, part 1 (1911 – grammars of Hupa, Tlingit, Haida, Tsimshian, Kwakiutl, Chinook, Maidu, Fox, Datoka, Eskimo); part 2 (1922 – Takelma, Coos, Lower Umpqua, and Chuckchee); part 3 (1933 – Tonkawa, Quileute, Yuchi, Zuni, and Coeur d'Alene), part 4 (1941 – Tunica).

1912   Tsimshian Texts (New Series). *Publication of the American Ethnological Society*, 3:65–284.

1914   Mythology and Folk-Tales of the North American Indians. *Journal of American Folklore*, 27:374–410.

1915   *Anthropology in North America.* G.E. Stechert and Co, New York.

1916a   The Development of Folk-Tales and Myths. *Scientific Monthly*, 3:335–343.

1916b   Tsimshian Mythology. *Thirty-first Annual Report of the Bureau of American Ethnology*, 29–979.

1916c   Phonetic Transcription of Indian Languages: Report of Committee of American Anthropological Association. *Smithsonian Miscellaneous Collection*, 66(6):1–15.

1925   Contributions to the Ethnology of the Kwakiutl. *Columbia University Contributions to Anthropology*, 3:1–357. New York.

1927   Chehalis Fieldnotes. 14 notebooks. Ms., Boas Collection, American Philosophical Society Library, Philadelphia, PA.

1928   Bella Bella Texts. *Columbia University Contributions to Anthropology*, 5:1–291. New York.

1929   Metaphorical Expressions in the Language of the Kwakiutl Indians: Reprinted 1949 in *Race, Language, and Culture*, pp. 232–239. The Macmillan Co., New York.

1930   The Religion of the Kwakiutl Indians. *Columbia University Contributions to Anthropology*, 10:1–284. New York.

1932   Bella Bella Tales. *Memoirs of the American Folklore Society*, 25.

1935a   Kwakiutl Culture as Reflected in Mythology. *Memoirs of the American Folklore Society*, 28:1–190.

1935b   Kwakiutl Tales, New Series. *Columbia University Contributions to Anthropology*, 26(1):1–230. New York.

1943   Kwakiutl Tales, New Series. *Columbia University Contributions to Anthropology*, 26(2):1–228. New York.

1966   *Kwakiutl Ethnography.* Edited by Helen Codere. University of Chicago Press, Chicago, IL.

2002   *Indian Myths and Legends of the North Pacific Coast.* Edited by Randy Bouchard and Dorothy Kennedy, and translated by Dietrich Bertz. Talonbooks, Victoria, B.C. Originally titled: Indianishe Sagen von der Nord-Padifischen Küste Amerikas. Sonder-Abdruck aus den Verlandlungen der Berliner Gesellschaft fur Anthropologie, Ethnologie und Urgeschichte. Originally published in 1895. Verlag von A Asher, Berlin.

Boas, Franz and Pliny E. Goddard

1924   Vocabulary of an Athapaskan Dialect of the State of Washington. *International Journal of American Linguistics*, 3(1):39–45.

Bolt, Clarence

1992   *Thomas Crosby and the Tsimshian. Small Shoes for Feet Too Large.* University of British Columbia Press, Vancouver, B.C.

Boyd, Robert
1999   *The Coming of the Spirit of Pestilence. Introduced Infectious Diseases and Population Decline among Northwest Coast Indians, 1774–1874*. University of Washington Press, Seattle.
2011   *Cathlapotle and its Inhabitants: 1792–1860*. U.S. Fish and Wildlife Service, Cultural Resource Series # 5. Portland, OR.

Brightman, Robert
1993   *Grateful Prey. Rock Cree Human-Animal Relationships*. University of California Press, Berkeley.

Brock, Peggy
2011   *The Many Voyages of Arthur Wellington Clah. A Tsimshian Man on the Pacific Northwest Coast*. University of British Columbia Press, Vancouver, B.C.

Brotherton, Barbara, editor
2008   *S'abadeb ~ The Gifts. Pacific Coast Salish Art and Artists*. SAM and University of Washington Press, Seattle.

Bright, William, editor
2004   *Native American Placenames of the United States*. University of Oklahoma Press, Norman.

Brown, Larry, Shawn Chase, Matthew Mesa, Richard Beamish, and Peter Moyle, editors.
2009   *Biology, Management, and Conservation of Lampreys in North America*. American Fisheries Society Symposium 72, Bethesda, MD.

Bruseth, Nels
1977   *Indian Stories and Legends of the Stillaguamish, Sauks, and Allied Tribes*. Originally published 1926. Arlington Times Press, Arlington, WA.

Bryan, Alan
1963   An Archaeological Survey of Northern Puget Sound. *Occasional Papers of the Idaho State University Museum*, No. 11. Pocatello.

Carlson, Keith Thor, editor
1997   *You are Asked to Witness: The Sto:lō in Canada's Pacific Coast History*. Sto:lo Heritage Trust, Chilliwack, B.C.
2001   *A Sto:lō and Coast Salish Historical Atlas*. Douglas and McIntyre, Vancouver, B.C.

Carlson, Roy
1983   *Indian Art Traditions of the Northwest Coast*. Simon Fraser University, Archaeology Press, Burnaby, B.C.

Carpenter, Cecelia Svinth
1986   *Fort Nisqually. A Documented History of Indian and British Interaction*. Tahoma Research Service, Tacoma, WA.

Castillo, Bernal Diaz de
1568   *True History of the Conquest of New Spain*. [1632]

Chandhuri, Jean Hill, and Joytotpaul Chaudhuri
2001   *A Sacred Path: The Way of the Muscogee Creeks*. UCLA American Indian Studies Center, Los Angeles, CA.

Chowning, Ann
1962   Raven Myths in Northwestern North America and Northeastern Asia. *Arctic Anthropology*, 1(1):1–5.

Clark, Ella E.
1953   *Indian Legends of the Pacific Northwest.* University of California Press, Berkeley.

Clemens, Benjamin, Thomas Binder, Margaret Docker, Mary Moser, and Stacia Sower
2010   Similarities, Differences, and Unknowns in Biology and Management of Three Parasitic Lampreys of North America. *Fisheries*, 35(12):580–594.

Close, D. A., M. S. Fitzpatrick, and H. W. Li.
2002   The ecological and cultural importance of a species at risk of extinction, Pacific Lamprey. *Fisheries*, 27(7):19–25.

Close, David, Aaron Jackson, Brian Conner, and Hiram Li
2004   Traditional Ecological Knowledge of Pacific Lamprey (*Entosphenus tridentatus*) in Northeastern Oregon and Southwestern Washington from Indigenous Peoples of the Confederated Tribes of the Umatilla Reservation. *Journal of Northwest Anthropology*, 38(2):141–162.

Collins, June McCormick
1949   John Fornsby: The Personal Document of a Coast Salish Indian. In Indians of the Urban Northwest, edited by Marian Smith, pp. 287–341. *Columbia University Contributions to Anthropology*, 36. New York.
1950a   Growth of Class Distinctions and Political Authority among the Skagit Indians During the Contact Period. *American Anthropologist*, 52(3):331–342.
1950b   The Indian Shaker Church. *Southwestern Journal of Anthropology*, 6:399–411.
1952a   An Interpretation of Skagit Intragroup Conflict during Acculturation. *American Anthropologist*, 54:347–355.
1952b   The Mythological Basis for Attitudes toward Animals among Salish Indians. *Journal of American Folklore,* 65(258):353–359.
1966   Naming, Continuity, and Social Inheritance among the Coast Salish of Western Washington. *Papers of the Michigan Academy of Science, Arts, and Letters* 51: 425–436.
1974   *Valley of the Spirits, the Upper Skagit Indians of Western Washington.* University of Washington Press, Seattle.
1979   Multilineal Descent: A Coast Salish Strategy. In *Currents in Anthropology*, edited by Robert Hinshaw, pp 243–254. Mouton, The Hague.
1980   Report on the Use of the Skagit River, Including Village Locations by the Upper Skagit Indians. In *Cultural Resource Overview and Sample Survey of the Skagit Wild and Scenic River*, edited by Astrida Blukis Onat, Lee Bennett, and Jan Hollenbeck, 2:1–17. Study Area on the Mt. Baker-Snoqualmie National Forest, WA.

Connaway, John
2007   *Fishweirs ~ A World Perspective with Emphasis on the Fishweirs of Mississippi.* Mississippi Department of Archives and History, Archaeological Reports, 33. Jackson.

Coupland, Gary
1988   *Prehistoric Cultural Change at Kitselas Canyon.* Canadian Museum of Civilization, Ottawa.

Cove, John
1985   A Detailed Inventory of the Barbeau Northwest Coast Files. *Canadian Centre for Folk Culture Studies,* Paper 54. Ottawa.

Crum, Steven
1994   *The Road on Which We Came ~ Po'i pentun tammen. A History of the Western Shoshone.* University of Utah Press, Salt Lake City.

Crum, Beverly, Earl Crum, and Jon Dayley
2001   *Newe Hupia ~ Shoshoni Poetry Songs.* Utah State University Press, Logan.

Culin, Stewart
1903   Games of the North American Indians. Bureau of American Ethnology, AR 24, Washington, D.C.

Dauenhauer, Nora Marks and Richard Dauenhauer
1987   *Haa Shuka, Our Ancestors. Tlingit Oral Narratives.* University of Washington Press, Seattle.

Dean, Jonathan
1993   Rich Men, Big Powers, and Wastelands ~ The Tlingit-Tsimshian Border of the Northern Pacific Littoral, 1799 to 1867. Doctoral dissertation, University of Chicago. University Microfilm International, Ann Arbor, MI.
1994   Those Rascally Spakaloids: The Rise of Gispaxlot Hegemony at Fort Simpson, 1832 to 1840. *BC Studies*, 101:41–78.
n.d.   My Canoe Was Full of People—But It Capsized—& all the People Lost but Myself: The Rise and Fall of Legaic, 1840 to 1865.

de Laguna, Frederica
1972   *Under Mount Saint Elias.* Yakutat Tlingit. Smithsonian Press, Washington, D.C.

Densmore, Frances
1939   Nootka and Quileute Music. *Bureau of American Ethnology, Bulletin* 124. Washington, D.C.
1953   The Belief of the Indian in a Connection Between Song and the Supernatural. Bureau of American Ethnology, Bulletin 151:217–223, Washington, D.C.

Dickey, George, editor
1989   The Journal of Occurrences at Fort Nisqually, Commencing May 30, 1833, Ending September 27, 1859. Fort Nisqually Association.

Dobyns, Henry
1983   *Their Number Become Thinned. Native American Population Dynamics in Eastern North America.* University of Tennessee Press, Knoxville.

Donald, Leland, and Donald Mitchell
1974   Some Correlates of Local Group Rank among the Southern Kwakiutl. *Ethnology,* 14 (4):325–346.

Donald, Leland
1997   *Aboriginal Slavery on the Northwest Coast of North America.* University of California Press, Berkeley.

Dorsey, George
1897   The Geography of the Tsimshian Indians. *American Antiquarian*, 19(4):276–282.

Drucker, Philip
1940   Kwakuitl Dancing Societies. *Anthropological Records*, 2(6):201–230.
1950   Culture Element Distributions: XXVI Northwest Coast. *Anthropological Records,* 9(3):153–294.

Du Bois, Cora
2007   *The 1870 Ghost Dance.* Originally published in 1939. University of Nebraska Press, Lincoln.

Duff, Wilson
1952   The Upper Stalo Indians of the Fraser River of British Columbia. British Columbia Provincial Museum, *Anthropology in British Columbia*, Memoir 1. Victoria, B.C.
1959   Histories, Territories, and Laws of the Kitwankool. *Anthropology in British Columba*, Memoir 4. Victoria, B.C.
1961   Problems in the Interpretations of Marius Barbeau's Tsimshian Materials. Paper delivered at the 14th Annual Northwest Anthropological Conference, Vancouver, B.C.
1964   Contributions of Marius Barbeau to West Coast Ethnology. *Anthropologica*, 6(1):63–96.

Dunn, John
1978   A Practical Dictionary of the Coast Tsimshian Language. *National Museum of Man, Mercury Series, Canadian Ethnology Service, Paper 42*. Ottawa.
1979a   Inter-Ethnic Generation Skewing: Tsimshian, Tlingit, Haida. Paper delivered at the International Congress of Americanists, Vancouver, B.C.
1979b   Tsimshian Internal Relations Reconsidered: Southern Tsimshian. In *The Victoria Conference on Northwestern Languages*, edited by Barbara Efrat. *British Columbia Provincial Museum, Heritage Record*, 4:62–82. Victoria, B.C.
1979c   A Reference Grammar for The Coast Tsimshian Language. *Canada. National Museum of Man. Mercury Series. Ethnology Service Paper 55*. Ottawa.
1984   International Matri-Moieties: The North Maritime Province of the North Pacific Coast,. In *The Tsimshian. Images of the Past: Views for the Present*, edited by Margaret Sequin, pp. 99–109. UBC Press, Vancouver, B.C.
1988   Aesthetic Properties of a Coast Tsimshian Text Fragment. In *Proceedings of the 23rd International Conference on Salish and Neighboring Languages,* pp. 78–89.
1995   *Sm'algyax / A Reference Dictionary and Grammar for The Coast Tsimshian Language.* University of Washington Press for Sealaks Heritage Foundation, Seattle.

Eaton, Diane, and Sheila Urbanek
1995   *Paul Kane's Great Nor-West.* University of British Columbia Press, Vancouver, B.C.

Edel, May M.
1944   Stability in Tillamook Folklore. *Journal of American Folklore,* 57(224):116–127.

Ellis, Peter Berresford
1990   *The Celtic Empire: The First Millennium of Celtic History, 1000 BC–51 AD.* Carolina Academic Press, Durham, NC.

Elmendorf, William W.
1960   The Structure of Twana Culture. *Washington State University Research Studies,* 28(3), *Monographic Supplement,* 2. Pullman.

1961 Skokomish and Other Coast Salish Tales. *Washington State University Research Studies,* 29(1):1–37; 29(2):84–117; 29(3):119–150. Pullman.

1970 Skokomish Sorcery, Ethics, and Society. In Systems of North American Witchcraft and Sorcery, edited by Deward E. Walker, Jr., pp. 147–182. *Anthropological Monographs of the University of Idaho*, No. 1. Moscow.

1993 *Twana Narratives. Native Historical Accounts of a Coast Salish Culture.* University of Washington Press, Seattle.

Emmons, George

1991 *The Tlingit Indians.* Edited by Frederica de Laguna. University of Washington Press, Seattle.

Faris, James

1990 *Nightway. A History and a History of Documentation of a Navajo Ceremonial.* University of New Mexico Press, Albuquerque.

Farrand, Livingston

1902 Traditions of the Quinault Indians, with assistance by WS Kahnweiler. Memoirs of the American Museum of Natural History IV, *Publications of the Jesup North Pacific Expedition* III:77–132. New York.

Farrand, Livingston and Theresa Mayer

1919 Quileute Tales. *Journal of American Folklore,* 32(124):251–279.

Fienup-Riordan, Ann

1990 *Eskimo Essays. Yup'ik Lives and How We see Them.* Rutgers University Press, New Brunswick, NJ.

Fish, Jean Bedal, and Edith Bedal

2000 *Two Voices: A History of the Sauk and Suiattle People and Sauk Country Experiences.* Editorial assistance by Astrida R Blukis Onat. Self published.

Fowler, Don, and Catherine Fowler, editors

1971 *Anthropology of the Numa: John Wesley Powell's Manuscripts on the Numic Peoples of Western North America, 1868–1880.* Smithsonian Contributions to Anthropology 14, Washington, D.C.

Fowler, Don, and John Matley, eds.

1979 Material Culture of the Numa: John Wesley Powell Collection, 1867-1880. *Smithsonian Contributions to Anthropology,* 26, Washington, D.C.

Frachtenberg, Leo J.

1913 Coos Texts. *Columbia University Contributions to Anthropology,* 1:1–216. New York.

1914 Lower Umpqua Texts and Notes on the Kusan Dialect. *Columbia University Contributions to Anthropology,* 4:1–156. New York.

1915 Shasta and Athapascan Myths from Oregon, Collected by Livingston Farrand. *Journal of American Folklore,* 28(109):207–242.

1920 Alsea Texts and Myths. *Bureau of American Ethnology, Bulletin* 67:1–304.

Freelan, Stephan

2009 *The Salish Sea Map.* Map of the Salish Sea (Mer des Salish) and Surrounding Basin Website, <http://staff.wwu.edu/stefan/SalishSea.htm> (accessed February 11, 2011). Western Washington University.

Friederich, Steven
2010   Artifacts found at Hoquiam. *The Daily World*. Saturday, May 29.

Frykman, George A.
1998   *Seattle's Historian and Promoter, the Life of Edmond Stephen Meany*. Washington State University Press, Pullman.

Gacs, Ute, Aisha Khan, Jerrie McIntyre, and Ruth Weinberg.
1988   *Women Anthropologists. A Biographical Dictionary*. Greenwood Press, Westport, CT.

Gallatin, Albert
1836   A Synopsis of the Indian Tribes within the United States East of the Rocky Mountains and the British And Russian Possessions in North America. In *Archaeologia Americana: Transactions and Collections of the American Antiquarian Society*, 2:1–422. Cambridge.

Garfield, Viola E.
1939   Tsimshian Clan and Society. *University of Washington, Publications in Anthropology*, 7(3):167–340. Seattle.
1953   Contemporary Problems of Folklore Collecting and Study. *Anthropological Papers of the University of Alaska,* 1(2):25–37.
1961   *The Wolf and the Raven: Totem Poles of Southeastern Alaska.* University of Washington Press, Seattle.
1966   The Tsimshian and Their Neighbors. In *The Tsimshian and Their Arts*, by Viola E. Garfield and Paul S. Wingert, pp. 3–70. University of Washington Press, Seattle.

Garfield, Viola E. and Linn A. Forrest
1961   *The Wolf and the Raven: Totem Poles of Southeastern Alaska.* University of Washington Press, Seattle.

Garfield, Viola and Paul Wingert
1950   *The Tsimshian and Their Arts*. University of Washington Press, Seattle.

Gibbs, George
1855   *Report . . . to Captain Mc'Clellan on the Indian Tribes of the Territory of Washington. Pacific Railroad Report 1:402–436.* Reprinted Ye Galleon Press, Fairfield, WA, 1972. 33rd Congress, 2nd Session, Senate Executive Document 78.
1877   Tribes of Western Washington and Northwestern Oregon. Department of the Interior, U.S. Geographical and Geological Survey of the Rocky Mountain Region. *Contributions to North American Ethnology*, 1, Part II:157–360. Washington, D.C.
1970   Dictionary of the Niskwalli (Nisqually) Indian Language—Western Washington. Extract from 1877 *Contributions to North American Ethnology*, 1:285–361. Shorey, Seattle, WA.

Gitsegukla
1979   Gitsegukla History (*Anawkhl Gitsegukla*). By the Band Council.

Goggin, John, and William Sturtevant
1964   The Calusa: a stratified, nonagricultural society (with notes on sibling marriage), in *Explorations in Cultural Anthropology*; essays in honor of George Peter Murdock, edited by Ward Goodenough. McGraw-Hill Book Co., New York.

Golder, F.A.
1907   Tlingit Myths. *Journal of American Folklore,* 20(76):290–295.

Goodman, D.H., S.B. Reid, M.F. Docker, G.R. Haas, and A.P. Kinziger
2008   Mitochondrial DNA Evidence for High Levels of Gene Flow among Populations of a
        Widely Distributed Anadromous Lamprey *Entosphenus tridentatus* (Petromyzontidae).
        Journal of Fish Biology, 72:400–417.

Grumet, Robert
1975   Changes in Coast Tsimshian Redistributive Activities in the Fort Simpson Region of
        British Columbia, 1788–1862. *Ethnohistory*, 22(4):295–318.
1982   Managing the Fur Trade: The Coast Tsimshian to 1862. In *Affluence and Cultural
        Survival*, edited by Richard Salisbury and Elisabeth Tooker, pp. 26–39. 1981 Proceedings
        of the American Ethnological Society. West Publishing Co, St. Paul.

Gunther, Erna
1925   Klallam Folk Tales. *University of Washington Publications in Anthropology,* 1:113–169.
        Seattle.
1945   Ethnobotany of Western Washington. *University of Washington Publications in
        Anthropology,* 10(1). Seattle.

Haeberlin, Herman
1916–1917 Puget Salish, 42 Notebooks. National Anthropological Archives #2965, Washington,
        D.C.
1918   SbEtEtda'q: A Shamanic Performance of the Coast Salish. *American Anthropologist*,
        20(3):249–257.
1924   Mythology of Puget Sound. *Journal of American Folklore*, 37(143–144):371–438.

Haeberlin, Hermann, and Erna Gunther
1930   The Indians of Puget Sound. *University of Washington Publications in Anthropology*,
        4(1):1–84. Seattle.

Hajda, Yvonne
1990   Southwestern Coast Salish. In *Handbook of North American Indians, Northwest Coast*,
        edited by Wayne Suttles, pp. 503–517. Smithsonian Institution, Washington, D.C.

Hallowell, Irving
1963   American Indians, White and Black: The Phenomenon of Transculturation. *Current
        Anthropology*, 4(5):519–531.

Halpin, Marjorie
1973   The Tsimshian Crest System: A Study Based on Museum Specimens and the Marius
        Barbeau and William Beynon Field Notes. Doctoral dissertation, University of British
        Columbia, Vancouver, B.C.

1978   William Beynon, Tsimshian, 1888–1958. American Indian Intellectuals, edited by Margot
        Liberty. *Proceedings of the 1976 American Ethnological Society*. West Publishing Co., St.
        Paul, MN.
1994a   Critique of the Boasian Paradigm for Northwest Coast Art. *Culture* 14 (1):5–16.
1994b   The Structure of Tsimshian Totemism. A Critique of the Boasian Paradigm for Northwest
        Coast Art. *Culture*, 14(1):5–16.
n.d.   Masks as Metaphors of Anti-Structure. Manuscript.

Halpin, Marjorie, and Margaret Seguin
1990   Tsimshian Peoples: Southern Tsimshian, Coast Tsimshian, Nishga, and Gitksan. In *Handbook of North American Indians, Northwest Coast,* Vol. 7, edited by Wayne Suttles, 267–284. Smithsonian Institution, Washington, D.C.

Hardesty, M. W., and I. C. Potter
1971   *The Biology of Lampreys*, 4 Volumes. Academic Press, New York.

Harkin, Michael
1988   *Dialogues of History: Transformation and Change in Heiltsuk History, 1790–1920.* Doctoral dissertation, University of Chicago. University Microfilm International, Ann Arbor, MI.

Harmon, Alexandra
1995   *Different Kind of Indians. Negotiating the Meanings of Indian and Tribe in the Puget Sound Region, 1820s–1970s.* Doctoral dissertation, University of Washington, Seattle. I - 1-365, II - 366-741. University Microfilms International, Ann Arbor, MI.
1998   *Indians in the Making.* Ethnic Relations and Indian Identities around Puget Sound. American Crossroads Series. University of California Press, Berkeley.

Harper, J. Russell, editor
1971   *Paul Kane's Frontier.* University of Texas Press, Austin.

Harrington, John Peabody
1942   Chehalis Notes. Microfilm Reels 17, 18. National Anthropological Archives, Washington, D.C.
1981   The Papers of John Peabody Harrington in the Smithsonian Institution, 1907–1957. Edited by Elaine Mills. 30 reels. Krause International Publications, Millwood, New York.

Harris, Heather
1997   Remembering 10,000 Years of History: The Origins and Migrations of the Gitksan. In *At A Crossroads: Archaeology and First Peoples in Canada, edited by* George Nicholas and Thomas Andrews, pp. 190–196. Simon Fraser University Archaeology Press, Burnaby.

Harrison, John
1972   *The Chinese Empire*: *A Short History of China from Neolithic Times to the End of the Eighteenth Century.* A Harvest/HBJ Book, New York.

Heizer, Robert, and Theodora Kroeber, editors
1979   *Ishi the Last Yahi: A Documentary History.* University of California Press, Berkeley.

Helm, June, editor
1966   *Pioneers in American Anthropology*: *The Uses of Biography.* University of Washington Press, Seattle.

Hess, Thom, and Vi Hilbert
1976a *Lushootseed I, II.* Daybreak Star Press, United Indians of All Tribes Foundation for the University of Washington American Indian Studies Program, Seattle.
1976b Recording the Native Language. *Sound Heritage,* 4(3–4):39–42.
1977   How Daylight was Stolen (Lushootseed). Native American Text Series: *Northwest Coast Texts*, edited by Barry Carlson. International Journal of American Linguistics.

Hewitt, J. N. B.

1920　"A Constitutional League of Peace in the Stone Age of America: The League of the Iroquois and its Constitution." SI-AR (1918): 527-545.

Hickerson, Harold

1970　*The Chippewa and Their Neighbors: A Study in Ethnohistory*. Holt, Rinehart and Winston, New York.

Hilbert, Vi Taqʷšəblu

1974　On Transcribing the Metcalf Tapes. Proceedings of the 9th International Conference on Salish and Neighboring Languages. Vancouver, B.C.

1979　*Yehaw*. Lushootseed Literature in English. Seattle, WA

1980a　*Ways of the Lushootseed People: Ceremonies and Traditions of the Puget Sound Indians*. Daybreak Star Press, United Indians of All Tribes Foundation. Reissued 1991, Lushootseed Research. Seattle, WA.

1980b　*Huboo*. Oral Literature of the Lushooteed. Seattle, WA.

1983　Poking Fun in Lushootseed. *Proceedings of the 18th International Conference on Salish and Neighboring Languages*. Seattle, WA.

1985a　*Haboo: Native American Stories from Puget Sound*. University of Washington Press, Seattle.

1985b　Sharing Legends at Upper Skagit. Videotape. Lushootseed Research, Seattle.

1991a　To a Different Canoe: The Lasting Legacy of Lushootseed Heritage. In *A Time of Gathering: Native Heritage of Washington State*, edited by Robin Wright, pp. 254–258. University of Washington Press, Seattle.

1991b　When Chief Seattle Spoke. In *A Time of Gathering: Native Heritage of Washington State*, edited by Robin Wright, pp. 259–266. University of Washington Press, Seattle.

1992a　Art of the First People of the Lushootseed (Puget Sound). In *A Field Guide to Seattle's Public Art*, edited by Dian Shamash and Steven Huss, pp. 61–63. Seattle Arts Commission, Seattle, WA.

1992b　Coyote and Rock and Other Lushootseed Stories. Audiotape. Harper Collins, Parabola Storytime Series, New York.

1992c　*Loon and Deer Were Traveling: A Story of the Upper Skagit of Puget Sound*. Children's Press, Chicago, IL.

1993　*Lifting the Sky*. The Storyteller's Art Series, Cycling Frog Press.

Hilbert, Vi (Taqʷšəblu), and Jay Miller.

1994　*The Wisdom of Aunt Susie Sampson Peter, A Skagit Elder*. Lushootseed Press, Seattle, WA.

1996　Lushootseed Animal People: Mediation and Transformation from Myth to History (with Vi Taqʷšəblu Hilbert). In *Monsters, Tricksters, And Sacred Cows. Animal Tales and American Identities*, edited by A. James Arnold, pp. 138–156. New World Studies. University of Virginia Press, Charlottesville.

2004　That Salish Feeling…" (Vi Hilbert first author). In Studies In Salish Linguistics In Honor Of M. Dale Kinkade, edited by Donna B. Gerdts and Lisa Matthewson. *Occasional Papers in Linguistics,* 17:197–210. University of Montana, Missoula.

2008a　Fly: A Southern Lushootseed Epic, told by Annie Daniels and Peter Heck. In *Salish Myths and Legends, One People's Stories*, edited by M Terry Thompson and Steven M Egesdal, pp. 78–83. University of Nebraska Press, Lincoln.

2008b The Sailor Who Jumped Ship and Was Befriended by Skagits: A Lushootseed Historical Story. Told by Susie Sampson Peter, Jay Miller and Vi taqšəblu Hilbert. In *Salish Myths and Legends, One People's Stories*, edited by M Terry Thompson and Steven M Egesdal, pp. 277–286. University of Nebraska Press, Lincoln.

2009 Storied Arts: Lushootseed Gifting Across Time and Space. In *S'abadəb – The Gifts. Pacific Coast Salish Art and Artists*, edited by Barbara Brotherton, pp. 6–17. University of Washington Press, Seattle.

Hilbert, Vi Taqʷšəblu, Jay Miller, and Zalmai Zahir
2001 *Puget Sound Geography sdaʔda gʷəł dibəł əšucid ʔacaciłtalbixʷ: A Draft Study of the Thomas Talbot Waterman Place Name Manuscript and Other Sources*, edited with additional material. Lushootseed Press, Seattle.

Hilton, Susanne, and John Rath
1982 Objections to Franz Boas's Referring to Eating People in the Translation of the Kwakwala Terms baXwbakwalnuXwsiwe and hamats!a. *Working Papers of the 17th International Conference on Salish and Neighboring Languages*, 17: 98–106. 9–11 August. Portland State University, Portland, OR.

Hodge, Frederick, editor
1906 Handbook of American Indians North of Mexico. A–M. *Bureau of American Ethnology Bulletin*, 30, Volume I. Smithsonian Institution, Washington, D.C.

1910 Handbook of American Indians North of Mexico. N–Z. *Bureau of American Ethnology Bulletin*, 30, Volume II. Smithsonian Institution, Washington, D.C.

Hoffman, W. J.
1884 Selish Myths. *Bulletin of the Essex Institute,* 15. Salem, MA.

Hofman, Charles
1968 Frances Densmore and American Indian Music: A Memorial Volume. *Contributions from the Museum of the American Indian, Heye Foundation*, 23, New York.

Holder, Preston
1970 *The Hoe and the Horse on the Plains: A Study of Cultural Development among North American Indians.* University of Nebraska Press, Lincoln.

Honigmann, John
1976 *The Development of Anthropological Ideas.* The Dorsey Press, Homewood, IL.

Hunn, Eugene
1990 *Nch'i-Wana "The Big River." Mid-Columbia Indians and Their Land*, with James Selam and Family. University of Washington Press, Seattle.

Hunt, George
1906 The Rival Chiefs, a Kwakiutl Story, In *Anthropological Papers Written in Honor of Franz Boas*, pp. 108–136. G.E. Stechert and Co., New York.

Hymes, Dell
1953 Two Wasco Motifs. *Journal of American Folklore*, 66(259):69–70.

1965 Some North Pacific Coast Poems: A Problem in Anthropological Philology. *American Anthropologist*, 67:316–341.

1968 The 'Wife' Who 'Goes Out' Like a Man; Reinterpretation of a Clackamas Chinook Myth. *Social Science Information (Studies in Semiotics)*, 7(3):173–199.

1975a   Breakthrough into Performance. In *Folklore and Communication*, edited by Dan Ben-Amos and Kenneth Goldstein, pp. 11–74. The Hague.

1975b   Folklore's Nature and the Sun's Myth. *Journal of American Folklore*, 88:147–369.

1976   Louis Simpson's 'The Deserted Boy.' *Poetics*, 5:119–177.

1981   *"In Vain I Tried To Tell You." Essays in Native American Ethnopoetics*. University of Pennsylvania Press, Philadelphia.

1985   Language, Memory, and Selective Performance: Cultee's "Salmon Myth" as Twice Told to Boas. *Journal of American Folklore*, 98(390):391–434.

1987   Anthologies and Narrators. In *Recovering the Word: Essays on Native American Literature*, edited by Brian Swan and Arnold Krupat. University of California Press, Berkeley.

Inglis, Richard, and James Haggarty

1987   Cook to Jewitt: Three Decades of Change in Nootka Sound. "Le Castor Fait Tout." In *Selected Papers of the Fifth North American Fur Trade Conference, 1985*, edited by Bruce Trigger, Toby Morantz, Louise Dechene, pp. 193–222. Lake St. Louis Historical Society, Montreal.

Jacobs, Elizabeth Derr

1959   Nehalem Tillamook Tales. *University of Oregon Studies in Anthropology*, 5:1–216. Eugene.

Jacobs, Melville

1940   Coos Myth Texts. *University of Washington Publications in Anthropology*, 8 (2):127–259. Seattle.

1949   Kalapuya Texts. *University of Washington Publications in Anthropology*, 11:1–394. Seattle.

1952   Psychological Inferences from a Chinook Myth. *Journal of American Folklore*, 65(256):121–137.

1959a   A Few Observations on the World View of the Clackamas Chinook Indians. *Journal of American Folklore*, 68:283–289.

1959b   The Content and Style of an Oral Literature: Clackamas Chinook Myths and Tales. *Viking Fund Publications in Anthropology*, 26:1–285. New York.

1959c   Folklore. In Anthropology of Franz Boas. *American Anthropologist*, 61(5)[part 2]:119–138.

1960   *The People Are Coming Soon, An Analysis of Clackamas Chinook Myths and Tales*. University of Washington Press, Seattle.

1962   The Fate of Indian Oral Literature in Oregon. *Northwest Review*, 5:90–99.

1966   A Look Ahead In Oral Literature Research. *Journal of American Folklore*, 79:413–427.

1967   Our Knowledge of Pacific Northwest Indian Folklores. *Northwest Folklore*, 2(2):14–21.

1972   Areal Spread of Indian Oral Genre Features in the Northwest States. *Journal of the Folklore Institute*, 9(1):10–17.

n.d.   A Popular Account of Oral Literature in the Northwest States.

James, Justine E., Jr., with Leilani Chubby

2002   Quinault. In *Native Peoples of the Olympic Peninsula. Who We Are*, edited by Jacilee Wray, pp. 99–117. University of Oklahoma Press, Norman.

Jefferson, Thomas

1785   *Notes on the State of Virginia*. Privately published. Paris.

Jenness, Diamond
1935   The Saanich Indians of Vancouver Island. Canadian Ethnology Service Archives,
       # VII-G-8M, Ottawa.
1955   The Faith of a Coast Salish Indian. *Anthropology in British Columbia, Memoir* 3:1–92.
       Victoria, B.C.

Jennings, Katie
1995   HuchooSedah: Traditions of the Heart. KCTS ~ PBS ~ BBC ~ Cymru ~ Wales TV.

Jilek, Wolfgang
1982   *Indian Healing. Shamanic Ceremonialism in the Pacific Northwest Today.* Hancock House
       Publishers, Ltd., Surrey, B.C.

Judd, Neil
1967   *The Bureau of American Ethnology, A Partial History.* University of Oklahoma Press,
       Norman.

Kan, Sergei
1989   *Symbolic Immortality. The Tlingit Potlatch of the Nineteenth Century.* Smithsonian
       Institution Press, Washington, D.C.

Kane, Paul
1925   *Wanderings of an Artists among the Indians of North America, from Canada to
       Vancouver's Island and Oregon through the Hudson's Bay Company's Territory, and
       Back Again.* The Radisson Society of Canada, Toronto. Previously published in 1858.

Keddie, Grant
2006   *Aboriginal Defensive Sites: Part 1: Settlements for Unsettling Times, Part 2: Amateur
       Archaeology Begins, Part 3: Modern Archaeologists Collect Evidence, Part 4: Local Sites
       are Dated; Final Conclusions.*
       <http://www.royalbcmuseum.bc.ca/Content_Files/Files/AboriginalDefensiveSites
       articleOct2006.pdf> (Accessed February 2011)

Kelley, Klara Bonsack, and Harris Francis
1994   *Navajo Sacred Places.* Indiana University Press, Bloomington.

Kemp, P.S., T. Tsuzaki and M.L. Moser
2009   Linking Behaviour and Performance: Intermittent Locomotion in a Climbing Fish. *Journal
       of Zoology,* 277:171–178.

Kennedy, Dorothy
1993   Looking For The Tribe In The Wrong Places: An Examination of the Central Coast Salish
       Social Network. Master's thesis, University of Victoria.
2000   Treads to the Past: The Construction and Transformation of Kinship in the Coast Salish
       Social Network. Doctoral dissertation, Oxford University, Exeter College. University
       Microfilms International, Ann Arbor, MI.

Kennedy, Dorothy, and Randy Bouchard
1983   *Sliamon Life, Sliamon Lands.* Talon Books, Vancouver, B.C.

Kenyon, Susan
1980   The Kyuquot Way: A Study of a West Coast (Nootkan) Community. *National Museums of
       Canada, Mercury Series, Canadian Ethnology Service,* Paper 61.

Kinkade, Dale

1963a Phonology and Morphology of Upper Chehalis: I. *International Journal of American Linguistics,* 29(3):181–195.

1963b Phonology and Morphology of Upper Chehalis: II. *International Journal of American Linguistics,* 29(4):345–356.

1964a Phonology and Morphology of Upper Chehalis: III. *International Journal of American Linguistics,* 30(1): 32–61.

1964b Phonology and Morphology of Upper Chehalis: IV. *International Journal of American Linguistics,* 30(3):251–260.

1966 Vowel Alternation in Upper Chehalis. *International Journal of American Linguistics,* 32(4):343–349.

1967 Prefix-Suffix Constructions in Upper Chehalis. *Anthropological Linguistics,* 9(2):1–4.

1983 "Daughters of Fire:" Narrative Verse Analysis of an Upper Chehalis Folktale. *University of Oklahoma, Papers in Anthropology,* 24(2):267–278. Norman.

1987 "Bluejay and His Sister." *Recovering the Word: Essays on Native American Literature,* edited by Brian Swann and Arnold Krupat, pp. 255–296. University of California Press, Berkeley.

1991 Upper Chehalis Dictionary. *University of Montana Occasional Papers in Linguistics* 7, Missoula.

1992a Kinship Terminology in Upper Chehalis in a Historical Framework. *Anthropological Linguistics,* 34(1/4), 84–103.

1992b Translating Pentlatch. In *On the Translation of Native American Literatures,* edited by Brian Swann, pp.163–175. Smithsonian Institution Press, Washington, D.C.

Kraus, Michael

1990 Kwalhioqua and Clatskanie. In *Handbook of North American Indians, Northwest Coast,* edited by Wayne Suttles, pp. 530–532. Smithsonian Institution, Washington, D.C.

Krieger, Judith

1989 Aboriginal Coast Salish Food Resources: A Compilation of Sources. *Northwest Anthropological Research Notes,* 23(2):217–231.

Kroeber, Alfred

1919 Sinkyone Tales. *Journal of American Folklore,* 32(125):346–351.

1923 American Culture and the Northwest Coast. *American Anthropologist,* 25(1):1–20.

1925 Handbook of the Indian of California. *Bureau of American Ethnology Bulletin* 78, Washington, D.C.

1939 *Cultural and Natural Areas of Native North America.* University of California Press, Berkeley.

Laird, Carobeth

1975 *Encounter with an Angry God. Recollections of my Life with John Peabody Harrington.* Malki Museum Press, Banning, CA.

La Flesche, Francis

1963 *The Middle Five: Indian Schoolboys of the Omaha Tribe.* University of Wisconsin Press, Madison. [1900].

Lane, Robert, and Barabara Lane

1977 Indians and Fisheries of the Skagit River System. Mid-Project Report. Skagit Salmon Study.

LeClerc, Georges Louis (Compte de Buffon, 1707–1788)
1791   *Natural History*. Paris.

Lethbridge, Roger
1971   The Socialist Lamprey. In *The Biology of Lampreys*, edited by M.W. Hardesty and I.C. Potter, Volume 4:ix. Academic Press, New York.

Lewis, Robin Peterson
2009   Yurok and Karuk Traditional Ecological Knowledge: Insights into Pacific Lamprey Populations of the Lower Klamath Basin. In *Biology, Management, and Conservation of Lampreys in North America*, edited by Larry Brown, Shawn Chase, Matthew Mesa, Richard Beamish, and Peter Moyle, pp. 1–40. American Fisheries Society Symposium 72, Bethesda, MD.

Levi-Strauss, Claude
1967   The Story of Asdiwal, translated by Nicholas Mann, pp. 1–47 in "The Structural Study of Myth and Totemism," edited by Edmund Leach, pp. 1185. *ASA Monographs*, 5. London.
1969   *Tristes Tropiques*. Antheneum, New York.
1971   L'Homme Nu. *Mythologiques* 4. Plon, Paris.
1981   The Naked Man. Introduction to *The Science of Mythology*, Volume 4, translated by John and Doreen Weightman. Harper and Row, New York.
1982   *The Way of the Masks*. Sylvia Modelski, translation. University of Washington Press, Seattle.

Liljeblad, Sven
1962   The People Are Coming Soon: A Review Article. *Midwest Folklore,* 12(2):93–103.

Locke, John
1689   *Two Treatises of Government*.

Losey, Robert
2010   Animism as a Means of Exploring Archaeological Fishing Structures on Willapa Bay, Washington, USA. *Cambridge Archaeological Journal*, 20(1):17–32.

Lurie, Nancy Oestreich
1966   Women in Early American Anthropology. In *Pioneers in American Anthropology*, edited by June Helm, pp. 29–81. University of Washington Press, Seattle.

McAllister, Don and Edward Kott
1988   *On Lampreys and Fishes: A Memorial Anthology in Honor of Vadim D. Vladykov*. Kluwer Academic Publishers, Dordrecht.

McAtee, W.L.
1955   Folk Names of New England Birds. *The Bulletin of the Massachusetts Audubon Society,* Boston.

McClellan, Catharine
1963   Wealth Woman and Frogs among the Tagish Indians. *Anthropos,* 58:121–128.
1970   The Girl Who Married the Bear. *National Museums of Canada, Publication in Ethnology*, 2:1–58. Ottawa.

McDaniel, Nancy L.
2004   The Snohomish Tribe of Indians: Our Heritage, Our People, Volume 1, # 1. By the author, Chimakum.

MacDonald, George
1979   Kitwanga Fort National Historic Site, Skeena River, British Columbia. Historical Research and Analysis of the Structural Remains. Parks Canada, *Manuscript Report*, No. 341. Ottawa.
1984   The Epic of Ne<u>k</u>t: The Archaeology of Metaphor. In *The Tsimshian: Images of the Past: Views for the Present*, edited by Margaret Sequin. UBC Press, Vancouver, B.C.

MacDonald, George and John Cove
1987   Tsimshian Narratives. I: Trickster, Shamans and Heroes. II: Trade and Warfare. *Canadian Museum of Civilization, Mercury Series, Directorate Paper* 3. Ottawa.

McDonald, Lucile
1972   *Swan among the Indians. Life of James G Swan, 1818-1900.* Binfords & Mort, Portland, OR.

McIlwraith, Thomas
1948   *The Bella Coola Indians.* University of Toronto Press.

McNeary, Stephen
1976   Where Fire Came Down, Social and Economic Life of the Niska. Doctoral dissertation, Bryn Mawr College, PA. University Microfilms International, Ann Arbor, MI.

Maclachlan, Morag, editor
1998   *The Fort Langley Journals, 1827–30.* University of British Columbia Press, Vancouver, B.C.

Marsden, Susan
n.d.   Controlling the Flow of Furs: Northcoast Nations and the Maritime Fur Trade.

Marsden, Susan, and Robert Galois
1995   The Tsimshian, the Hudson's Bay Company, and the Geopolitics of the Northwest Coast Fur Trade, 1878–1840. *The Canadian Geographer*, 39(2):169–183.

Mason, Otis T
1894   *Women's Share in Primitive Culture.* New York.

Mathews, Darcy
2006   Burial Cairn Taxonomy and the Mortuary Landscape of Rocky Point, B.C. Master's Thesis, University of Victoria.

Matson, Emerson
1968   *Longhouse Legends.* Thomas Nelson and Sons, Camden, NJ.
1972   *Legends of the Great Chiefs.* Storypole Press, Tacoma, WA.

Matson, Richard, and Gary Coupland
1995   *The Prehistory of the Northwest Coast.* Academic Press, San Diego, CA.

Matson, R.G., and Martin Magne
2007   *Athapaskan Migrations: The Archaeology of Eagle Lake, British Columbia.* University of Arizona Press, Tucson.

Mattina, Anthony
1987   Colville-Okanagan Dictionary. *University of Montana, Occasional Papers in Linguistics*, 5. Missoula.

Maud, Ralph
1982   *A Guide to B.C. Indian Myth and Legend. A Short History of Myth-Collecting and a Survey of Published Texts*. Talonbooks, Vancouver, B.C.
1989   The Henry Tate-Franz Boas Collaboration on Tsimshian Mythology. *American Ethnologist*, 16(1):158–162.

Mauze, Marie, Michael Harkin, and Sergei Kan
2004   *Coming to Shore. Northwest Coast Ethnology, Traditions, and Visions*. University of Nebraska Press, Lincoln.

Meeker, Ezra
1980   *Pioneer Reminiscences of Puget Sound, and the Tragedy of Leschi*. The Printers, Everett, WA. Previously published in 1905.

Meilleur, Helen
1980   *A Pour of Rain: Stories from a West Coast Fort*. Sono Nis Press, Victoria, B.C.

Menzies, Archibald
1923   Menzies' Journal of Vancouver's Voyage, April to October, 1792. Edited by C.F. Newcombe. *Archives of British Columbia*, Memoir No. 5. Victoria, B.C.

Miles, George
2003   *James Swan, Cha-tic of the Northwest Coast*. Beinecke Rare Book and Manuscript Library, Yale University, New Haven, CT.

Miller, Jay
1975   Passing the Torch. Symposium 401: Of the Field ~ In the Field. 2–6 December. *American Anthropological Association 74th Annual Meeting*, San Francisco, CA.
1976   The Northwest Coast of What? Paper delivered at the Conference on Northwest Coast Studies, Simon Fraser University, Burnaby.
1978   Moiety Birth. *Northwest Anthropological Research Notes*, 13(1):45–50.
1979   Symbolic Insights Deriving from Recent Northwest Coast Research. Paper delivered at the International Congress of Americanists, Vancouver, B.C.
1980   The Matter of the (Thoughtful) Heart: Centrality, Focality, or Overlap? *Journal of Anthropological Research*, 36(3):338–342.
1981a   Moieties and Cultural Amnesia, an Example of the Manipulation of Knowledge in a Pacific Northwest Coast Native Community. *Arctic Anthropology*, 18(1):23–32.
1981b   Tsimshian Moieties and Other Clarifications. *Northwest Anthropological Research Notes*, 16(2):148–164.
1984a   Introduction. In *The Tsimshian and Their Neighbors of the North Pacific Coast*, edited by Jay Miller and Carol Eastman. University of Washington Press, Seattle.
1984b   Tsimshian Religion in Historical Perspective, In *The Tsimshian and Their Neighbors of the North Pacific Coast*, edited by Jay Miller and Carol Eastman, pp. 137–147. University of Washington Press, Seattle.
1984c   Feasting with the Southern Tsimshian. In The Epic of Nekt: The Archaeology of Metaphor. In *The Tsimshian: Images of the Past: Views for the Present*, edited by Margaret Sequin. pp. 27–39. UBC Press, Vancouver, B.C.
1985a   Art and Souls: The Puget Sound Salish Journey to the Land of the Dead. *5th National Native American Art Studies Association Conference*. Ann Arbor/ Detroit, MI, October 16–19.

1985b   *Haboo: Native American Stories from Puget Sound.* Free Translations of "Fly":33–41; "Moose":145–49; Verse Translation of "Boil and Hammer," Appendix 1:169–78; Text Data, Appendix 2:179–82; Bibliography:183–204. University of Washington Press, Seattle.

1985c   Salish Kinship: Why Decedence? In *Proceedings of the 20th International Conference on Salish and Neighboring Languages*, 15–17 August, pp. 213–222. University of British Columbia, Vancouver, B.C.

1988a   *Shamanic Odyssey: The Lushootseed Salish a Journey to the Land of the Dead.* Ballena Press, Menlo Park, CA.

1988b   Viola Edmundson Garfield (1899–1983). In *Women Anthropologists, a Biographical Dictionary*, edited by Ute Gacs, Aisha Khan, Jerrie McIntyre, and Ruth Weinberg, pp. 109–114. Greenwood Press, New York.

1989   An Overview of Northwest Coast Mythology. *Northwest Anthropological Research Notes*, 23(2):125–141.

1990   *Mourning Dove, A Salishan Autobiography.* Indian Lives Series. University of Nebraska Press, Lincoln. 1990.

1992a   Earthmaker. *Tribal Stories from Native North America.* Perigree Books, New York.

1992b   Native Healing in Puget Sound: Portrayals of Native American Health and Healing. *Caduceus*, 8(3):1–15.

1992c   North Pacific Ethnoastronomy. In *Earth and Sky. Visions of the Cosmos in Native American Folklore*, edited by Ray Williamson and Claire Farrer, pp. 193–206. University of New Mexico Press, Albuquerque.

1992d   Society in America in 1492. In America in 1492, edited by Harvey Markowitz, pp. 151–169. Newberry Library, D'Arcy McNickle Center for the History of the American Indian, *Occasional Papers in Curriculum*, 15. Chicago, IL.

1997a   Back to Basics: Chiefdoms in Puget Sound. *Ethnohistory*, 44(2):375–387.

1997b   *Tsimshian Culture: A Light through the Ages.* University Of Nebraska Press, Lincoln.

1998   Tsimshian Ethno-Ethnohistory: A "Real" Indigenous Chronology. *Ethnohistory*, 45(4):657–674.

1999a   Chehalis Area Traditions, a Summary of Thelma Adamson's 1927 Ethnographic Notes. *Northwest Anthropological Research Notes*, 33(1):1–72.

1999b   *Lushootseed Culture and the Shamanic Odyssey: An Anchored Radiance.* University of Nebraska Press, Lincoln.

1999c   Suquamish Traditions (With Warren Snyder). *Northwest Anthropological Research Notes*, 33(1):1051–1075.

2000   Inflamed History: Violence Against Homesteading Indians in Washington Territory. *North Dakota Quarterly*, 67(34):162–173.

2002   Tsimshian Oral Literature. In *Encyclopedia of Literature in Canada*, edited by William New, pp. 1139–1141. University of Toronto Press, Toronto.

2005a   Dibble Cultivating Prairies to Beaches: The Real All Terrain Vehicle. *Journal of Northwest Anthropology*, 39(1):33–39.

2005b   Regaining Dr Herman Haeberlin. Early Anthropology and Museology in Puget Sound, 1916–17. Lushootseed Press, Seattle, WA.

2010   The Hoh Tribe in 1949: Richard 'Doc" Daugherty's Ethnographic Notebooks. *Journal of Northwest Anthropology*, 44(2):137–217.

2011   First Nations Forts, Refuges, and War Lord Champions Around the Salish Sea. *Journal of Northwest Anthropology*, 45(1):71–87.

n.d.   Giving Public Notice: Shifts in Labor and Loyalty at Potlatches and Communal Events. Manuscript in possession of the author.

Miller, Jay, and Carol Eastman
1984   *The Tsimshian and Their Neighbors of the North Pacific Coast*. University of Washington Press, Seattle.

Miller, Jay, and Vi Taqʷšəblu Hilbert
1993   Caring for Control: A Pivot of Salishan Language and Culture. In American Indian Linguistics and Ethnography in Honor of Laurence C. Thompson, pp. 237–239. *University of Montana, Occasional Papers in Linguistics*, No. 10. Missoula.
1996   Lushootseed Animal People: Mediation and Transformation from Myth to History. In *Monsters, Tricksters, and Sacred Cows: Animal Tales and American Identities*, edited by A. James Arnold, pp. 138–156. University of Virginia Press, Charlottesville.
2004   "That Salish Feeling…" (Vi Hilbert first author). In Studies in Salish Linguistics in Honor of M. Dale Kinkade, edited by Donna B. Gerdts and Lisa Matthewson, pp. 197–210. *Occasional Papers in Linguistics* #17. University of Montana, Missoula.

Miller, Jay, and Carol Eastman
1984   *The Tsimshian and Their Neighbors of the North Pacific Coast*. University of Washington Press, Seattle.

Miller, Robert
1952   Situation and Sequence in the Study of Folklore. *Journal of American Folklore,* 65(255):29–48.

Mills, Antonia
1994   *Eagle Down Is Our Law: Witsuwit'en Law, Feasts, and Land Claims*. University of British Columbia Press, Vancouver, B.C.

Mitchell, Donald
1981   Sebassa's Men. In *The World Is As Sharp As A Knife, An Anthology in Honour of Wilson Duff*, edited by Donald Abbott, pp. 79–86. British Columbia Provincial Museum, Victoria, B.C.
1983   Tribes and Chiefdoms of the Northwest Coast: The Tsimshian Case. In *The Evolution of Maritime Cultures on the Northeast and Northwest Coasts of America*, edited by Ronald Nash, pp. 57–64. Department of Archaeology Publications 11. Simon Fraser University, Burnaby, B.C.

Mooney, James
1928   The Aboriginal Population of America North of Mexico. *Smithsonian Miscellaneous Collections*, 80 (7):1-20 (Pub 2955).

Morgan, Lewis Henry
1851   *The League of the Iroquois*. Sage and Brother, Rochester, New York.
1871   Systems of Consanguinity and Affinity of the Human Family. *Smithsonian Contributions to Knowledge*,17, Washington, D.C.
1877   *Ancient Society*. Holt, New York.

Moser, Mary L., D.A. Ogden, C. Peery
2006   Migration Behavior of Adult Pacific Lamprey in the Lower Columbia River and Evaluation of Bonneville Dam Modifications to Improve Passage, 2002. Report by National Marine Fisheries Service to the U.S. Army Corps of Engineers, Portland District, Seattle, Washington, Contract E96950021.

Moser, Mary L., D.A. Ogden, H.T. Pennington, W.R. Daigle, C. Peery
2010   Development of Passage Structures for Adult Pacific Lamprey at Bonneville Dam, 2006. Contract by National Marine Fisheries Service to the U.S. Army Corps of Engineers, Portland District, Seattle, Washington, Contract E96950021.

Moser, Mary L., M.L. Keefer, H.T. Pennington, D.A. Ogden, J.E. Simonson
2011   Development of Lamprey-Specific Fishways at a Hydropower Dam. *Fisheries Management and Ecology*, 18:190–200.

Moss, Madonna, and Jon Erlandson
1992   Forts, Refuge Rocks, and Defensive Sites: The Antiquity of Warfare along the North Pacific Coast of North America. *Arctic Anthropology*, 29 (2):73–90.

Murray, Peter
1985   *The Devil and Mr. Duncan. A History of the Two Metlakatlas.* Sono Nis Press, Victoria, B.C.

Nez Perce, Umatilla, Yakama, and Warm Springs Tribes
2008   Tribal Pacific Lamprey *(Lampetra tridentata)* Restoration Plan for the Columbia River Basin. May 15.

Nies, Judith
1996   *Native American History. A Chronology of a Culture's Vast Achievements and Their Links to World Events.* Ballantine Books, New York.

Norton, Helen
1979a   Evidence for Bracken as Food for Aboriginal Peoples of Western Washington. *Economic Botany*, 33(4):384–396.
1979b   The Association between Anthropogenic Prairies and Important Food Plants in Western Washington. *Northwest Anthropological Research Notes*, 3(2):175–200.
1985   *Women and Resources of the Northwest Coast: Documentation from the 18th and Early 19th Century.* Doctoral dissertation, University of Washington, Seattle. University Microfilms International, Ann Arbor, MI
1990a   An Inventory of Goods and Resources Marketed By Native Groups, Fort Nisqually, 1833–1849. *Northwest Anthropological Research Notes*, 24(1):1–20.
1990b   Fort Nisqually: A Little Known Historical Treasure. Index for 1833–1849. *Seattle Genealogical Society Bulletin*, 39(3):103–118.
1990c   Fort Nisqually: A Little Known Historical Treasure: Part Two. *Seattle Genealogical Society Bulletin*, 39(4):161–177.
1990d   Fort Nisqually Index Part Two. Index for 1849–1859. *Seattle Genealogical Society Bulletin*, 39(5):7–14.
1990–1991 Fort Nisqually Index Part Three – Settlers' Accounts of 1841–1879. *Seattle Genealogical Society Bulletin*, 39(3):59–67.
1991a   Index IV: Fort Nisqually Servants' Accounts 1836–1867. *Seattle Genealogical Society Bulletin*, 39(3):111–115.

1991b Fort Nisqually Index 5: Women and the Frontier—1840–1872. *Seattle Genealogical Society Bulletin*, 39(5):5–10.

n.d. Huntington Microfilm, (inventory of frames not filmed in proper page order).

Oberg, Kalervo
1973 *The Social Economy of the Tlingit Indians*. University of Washington Press, Seattle.

Olson, Ronald
1949 Haihais Field Notes. Bancroft Library, Berkeley.
1950 Black Market in Prerogatives among the Northern Kwakiutl. *Kroeber Anthropological Society Papers*, 1:78–80.
1954 Social Life of the Owikeno Kwakiutl. *Anthropological Records*, 14(3):213–260.
1955 Notes on the Bella Bella Kwakiutl. *Anthropological Records*, 14(5):315-348.

Ortiz, Alfonso
1969 *The Tewa World: Time, Space, Being, and Becoming in a Pueblo Society*. University of Chicago Press, Chicago, IL.

Palmer, Katherine Van Winkle
1925 *Honne ~ Spirit of the Chehalis. The Indian Interpretation of the Origin of the People and Animals*, narrated by George Saunders, pp. 66–99. Press of W.F. Humphrey, Geneva, NY.

Palmer, Katherine Van Winkle, and George Sanders
2012 *Honne, Spirit of the Chehalis*, edited and introduction by Jay Miller. Previously published in 1925. University of Nebraska Press, Bison Books Edition, Lincoln.

Parsons, Elsie Clews
1939 *Pueblo Indian Religion*. University of Chicago Press, Chicago, IL.

Perry, Richard
1991 *Western Apache Heritage: People of the Mountain Corridor*. University of Texas Press, Austin.

Phinney. Archie M.
1934 Nez Percé Texts. *Columbia University Contributions to Anthropology*, 25. New York.

Pierce, William
1933 *From Potlatch to Pulpit*, edited by J.P. Hicks. The Vancouver Bindery, Vancouver, B.C.

Powell, John Wesley
1880 *Introduction to the Study of Indian Languages, with Words, Phrases, and Sentences to be Collected*, 2nd Edition [of 1877]. Washington, D.C.

Prince Rupert School District 52 (Vonnie Hutchingson, Susan Marsden)
1992a *Na Amwaaltga Ts'msiyeen*: The Tsimshian, Trade, and the Northwest Coast Economy. Teachings of Our Grandfathers (*Suwilaay'msga Na Ga'niiyatgm*) 1.
1992b *Adawga Gant Wilaaytga Gyetga Suwildook*. Rituals of Respect and the Sea Otter Trade. Told by Henry Reeves. Teachings of Our Grandfathers (*Suwilaay'msga Na Ga'niiyatgm*) 2.
1992c *Saaban*. The Tsimshian and Europeans Meet. Told by Dorothy Brown. Teachings of Our Grandfathers (*Suwilaay'msga Na Ga'niiyatgm*) 3.
1992d *Fort Simpson, Fur Fort at Laxłgu'alaams*. The Teachings of Our Grandfathers (*Suwilaay'msga Na Ga'niiyatgm*) 4.
1992e *Ndeh Wuwaal Kuudeex A Spaga Laxyuubm Ts'msiyeen*. When the Aleuts Were on Tsimshian Territory. Teachings of Our Grandfathers (*Suwilaay'msga Na Ga'niiyatgm*) 5.

1992f   *Conflict at Gits'ilaasu*. Teachings of Our Grandfathers (*Suwilaay'msga Na Ga'niiyatgm*) 6.

1992g   *Na Maalsga Walps Nisɬgumiik*: The Story of the House of Nisɬgumiik. Teachings of Our Grandfathers (*Suwilaay'msga Na Ga'niiyatgm*) 7.

Puyallup Land Commission Report

1903   Seattle: Puyallup Agency Records. Record Group 75, National Archives and Records Administration, Seattle, WA.

Quimby, George

1970   James Swan among the Indians. *Pacific Northwest Quarterly*, 61(4):212–216.

Randall, Betty Uchitelle

1949   The Cinderella Theme in Northwest Coast Folklore. In *Indians of the Urban Northwest*, edited by Marian Smith, pp. 243–285. Columbia University Press, New York.

Ray, Verne

1937   The Historical Position of the Lower Chinook in the Native Culture of the Northwest. *Pacific Northwest Quarterly*, 28(4):363–372.

1938   Lower Chinook Ethnographic Notes. *University of Washington Publications in Anthropology*, 7 (2):29–165, Seattle.

1966   *Handbook of the Cowlitz Indians*. Northwest Copy Company, Seattle, WA.

Reagan, Albert B.

1935   Some Myths of the Hoh and Quillayote Indians. *Transactions of the Kansas Academy of Science, 38*. Topeka.

Reagan, Albert B. and L.V. Walters

1933   Tales From Hoh and Quilleute. *Journal of American Folklore, 46*(182):297–346.

Reinhardt, U.G., L. Eidietis, S.E. Friedl, and M.L. Moser

2008   Pacific lamprey climbing behavior. *Canadian Journal of Zoology*, 86:1264–1272.

Richardson, Allan, and Brent Galloway

2011   *Nooksack Place Names. Geography, Culture, and Language.* UBC Press, Vancouver, B.C.

Ridington, Robin

1978   Swan People: A Study of the Dunne-za Prophet Dance. *National Museum of Man, Mercury Series, Canadian Ethnology Service*, Paper 38. Ottawa.

Riley, Carroll

1955   The Story of Skalaxt, a Lummi Training Myth. *Davidson Journal of Anthropology,* 1(2):133–140. Reprinted in *Northwest Anthropological Research Notes,* 21:141–148.

Roberts, Natalie

1975   A History of the Swinomish Tribal Community. Doctoral dissertation, University of Washington. University Microfilm International, Ann Arbor, MI.

Robinson, Michael

1996   *Sea Otter Chiefs*. Bayeaux Arts, Calgary.

Roblin, Charles

1919   M1344. 5 microfilmed reels, Records Concerning Applications for Adoption by the Quinaielt Indians, 1910–1919, Report of Special Agent [Charles] Roblin; Dr. Otis O Benson, superintendent.

1926   1926 Letter to Tulalip Agency. M1243, Reel 1, Applications for Enrollment and Allotment, 10 May, RG 75.

Ross, John Alan
2011   *The Spokan Indians*. Michael J. Ross, Spokane, WA.

Ruby, Robert, and John A Brown
1993   *Indian Slavery in the Pacific Northwest*. Clark & Co, Spokane, WA.

Sahagun, Bernardino de
1579   *General History of the Things of New Spain, the Florentine Codex*. [1829, 1982]

Saint Clair, H.H. and L.J. Frachtenberg
1909   Traditions of the Coos Indians of Oregon. *Journal of American Folklore*, 22(83):29–41.

Sampson, Chief Martin
1938   *The Swinomish Totem Pole, Tribal Legends: Told to Rosalie Whitney*. Union Printing Company, Bellingham, WA.
1972   Indians of Skagit County. *Skagit County Historical Society Historical Series* 2, La Conner, WA.

Sapir, Edward
1909a   Wishram Texts. *Publications of the American Ethnological Society*, 2:1–314.
1909b   Takelma Texts. *University of Pennsylvania Museum: Anthropological Papers*, 2:1–267.
1915   A Sketch of the Social Organization of the Nass River Tribes. *Anthropological Series* 7, *Canadian Geological Survey Bulletin* 19. Ottawa.
1919   A Flood Legend of the Nootka Indians of Vancouver Island. *Journal of American Folklore*, 32(124):351–355.

Sapir, Edward and Morris Swadesh
1939   *Nootka Texts*. Linguistic Society of America, Philadelphia, PA.

Schaepe, David
2006   Rock Fortifications: Archaeological Insights into Precontact Warfare and Socio-Political Organization among the Stó:lō of the Lower Fraser River Canyon, B.C. *American Antiquity*, 71(4):671–705.

Schoenberg, Wilfred P., S. J.
1962   *A Chronicle of Catholic History in the Pacific Northwest 1743–1960*. Catholic Sentinel Printery for Gonzaga Preparatory School, Portland, OR.

Schoolcraft, Henry
1839   *Algic Researches*. Harper and Brothers, New York.
1844   *Oneonta: The Indian in His Wigwam*.
1851   *Historical and Statistical Information Respecting the History, Condition and Prospects of The Indian Tribes of the United States, Collected snd Prepared Under the Direction of the Bureau of Indian Affairs*. Washington, D.C.

Scott, William, and Edwin Crossman
1998   *Freshwater Fishes of Canada*. Galt House Publishers, Oakville, Ontario.

Seaburg, William
1982   Guide to Pacific Northwest Native American Materials in the Melville Jacobs Collection and in Other Archival Collections in the University of Washington Libraries. University of Washington Libraries, *Communications in Librarianship*, 2. Seattle.

1999   Whatever Happened to Thelma Adamson? A Footnote in the History of Northwest Anthropological Research. *Northwest Anthropological Research Notes,* 33(1):73–83.

Seaburg, William, and Pamela Amoss
2000   *Badger and Coyote Were Neighbors. Melville Jacobs on Northwest Indian Myths and Tales.* Oregon State University Press, Corvallis.

Seguin, Margaret, editor
1984   *The Tsimshian*: *Images of the Past, Views for the Present.* University of British Columbia Press, Vancouver, B.C.

Shaul, David
1982   Ave Maria in Piman. *International Journal of American Linguistics*, 48(1):87–88.

Sheehan, Bernard
1973   *Seeds of Extinction: Jeffersonian Philanthropy and the American Indian.* University of North Carolina Press, Chapel Hill.

Smith, Edgar
1947   Indian Tribal Cases Decided in the Court of Claims of the United States, Briefed and Compiled to 30 June 1947. General Accounting Office, Washington, D.C.

Smith, Marian
1935–1936 Original Fieldnotes, MSS 2794, Royal Anthropological Archives; Microfilm, British Columbia Archives, MSS 2689.
1940a The Puyallup-Nisqually. *Columbia University Contributions to Anthropology*, 32. New York.
1940b The Puyallup of Washington. *Acculturation in Seven American Indian Tribes*, Chapter 1, edited by Ralph Linton, pp. 3–36. D. Appleton-Century Co, New York.
1941   The Coast Salish of Puget Sound. *American Anthropologist*, 43:197–211.
1949   Indians of the Urban Northwest. *Columbia University Contributions to Anthropology*, 36. New York.

Smith, Ross and Virginia Butler
2008   Towards the Identification of Lampreys (*Lampetra* spp.) in Archaeological Contexts. *Journal of Northwest Anthropology*, 42(2):131–142.

Snyder, Sally
1950s Fieldnotes 1952–1954 from Swinomish and Skagit Elders, Boxes 108–111 within Melville Jacobs Collection, University of Washington, Special Collections, Allen Library. [Identified by box, file, page, and coded initials of source elder]
1964   *Skagit Society and Its Existential Basis: An Ethnofolkloristic Reconstruction.* Doctoral dissertation, University of Washington, Seattle. University Microfilms International, Ann Arbor, MI.
1975   Quest For the Sacred in Northern Puget Sound: An Interpretation of Potlatch. *Ethnology*, 14(2):149–161.
1980   Aboriginal Settlements in the Skagit Drainage System. In *Cultural Resource Overview and Sample Survey of the Skagit Wild and Scenic River*, edited by Astrida Blukis Onat, Lee Bennett, and Jan Hollenbeck, pp. 2:1–39. Study Area on the Mt. Baker-Snoqualmie National Forest, WA.
1981   Swinomish, Upper Skagit, & Sauk-Suiattle. In *Inventory of Native American Religious Use, Practices, Localities, and Resources*, edited by Astrida Blukis Onat and Jan Hollenbeck, pp. 213–308. Mt. Baker-Snoqualmie National Forest, Seattle, WA.

n.d.   Folktales of the Skagit. Copies at Lushootseed Research and University of Washington Archives. Seattle.

Snyder, Warren
1952   U.S. National Archives, Record Group 279, Suquamish, Docket No. 133 (June).
1968   Southern Puget Sound Salish: Texts, Place Names, and Dictionary. *Sacramento Anthropological Society*, Paper 9.

Sower, Stacia
2010   UNH Laboratory for Molecular, Biochemical Endocrinology and Neuroendocrinology. <http://www.unh.edu/biochemistry/sower/inthenews.html> (Accessed 10 January 2011).

Speck, Frank
1917   Game Totems among the Northern Algonkians. *American Anthropologist*, 19(1):9–18.

Spencer, Robert F.
1952   Native Myths and Modern Religion among the Klamath Indians. *Journal of American Folklore,* 65(257):217–226.

Spier, Leslie
1931   Historical Interpretation of Culture Traits: Franz Boas' Study of Tsimshian Mythology. In *Methods in Social Science, a Case Book,* edited by Stuart Rice, pp. 449–457. University of Chicago Press, IL.

Spier, Leslie and Edward Sapir
1930   Wishram Ethnography. *University of Washington Publications in Anthropology,* 3(3):151–300. Seattle.

Spindler, George and Louise
1957   American Indian Personality Types and Their Sociocultural Roots. *The Annals of the American Academy of Political and Social Science*: 147-156.

Spitzka, Edward Anthony
1903   A Study of the Brain of the Late Major J.W. Powell. *American Anthropologist* 5(4):583–643.

Stevenson, Ian
1975   The Belief and Cases Related to Reincarnation Among the Haida. *Journal of Anthropological Research*, 31(4):364–375.

Stewart, Hilary
1982   *Indian Fishing. Early Methods on the Northwest Coast.* University of Washington Press, Seattle.
1991   The Shed-Roof House. In *A Time of Gathering, Native Heritage of Washington State,* edited by Robin Wright, pp. 212–222. University of Washington Press, Seattle.

Suttles, Wayne
1951   Economic Life of the Coast Salish of Haro and Rosario Straits. Doctoral dissertation, University of Washington, Seattle. University Microfilms International, Ann Arbor, MI.
1987   *Coast Salish Essays.* University of Washington Press, Seattle.
1989   They Recognize No Superior Chief: The Strait of Juan de Fuca in the 1790s. In *Cultures de la Costa Noroesta de America,* edited by Jose Luis Peset, pp. 251–264. Turner, Madrid.
1990   *Handbook of American Indians, Northwest Coast,* Vol. 7, editor. Smithsonian Institution, Washington, D.C.

Suttles, Wayne, and William W. Elmendorf
1963   Linguistic Evidence for Salish Prehistory. In Symposium on Language and Culture, edited by Viola E. Garfield and Wallace Chafe, pp. 41–52. *Proceedings of the 1962 Annual Spring Meeting of the American Ethnological Society.* University of Washington Press, Seattle.

Swan, James G.
1855   20 July letter from James Swan at Shoalwater to George Gibbs at Steilacoom. National Anthropological Archives, Washington, D.C.
1870   The Indians of Cape Flattery, at the Entrance to the Strait of Fuca, Washington Territory. Smithsonian Contributions to Knowledge, Vol. 16. Washington, D.C.

Swanton, John R.
1905a   Contributions to the Ethnology of the Haida. *American Museum of Natural History, Jesup North Pacific Expedition*, 5(1):1–300. New York.
1905b   Haida Texts and Myths. *Bureau of American Ethnology, Bulletin 29.* Washington, D.C.
1905c   Types of Haida and Tlingit Myths. *American Anthropologist*, 7(1):94–103.
1908   Haida Texts. *Memoirs of the American Museum of Natural History*, 14:273–812. New York.
1909   Tlingit Myths and Texts. *Bureau of American Ethnology*, Bulletin 39. Washington, D.C.
1928   Social Organization and Social Usages of the Indians of the Creek Confederacy. *Bureau of American Ethnology*, Annual Report 42 for 1924–1925, pp. 31–472. Washington, D.C.

Tedlock, Dennis
1985   *Popul Vuh. The Mayan Book of the Dawn of Life.* Simon & Schuster Touchstone Books, New York.

Teit, James
1910   Letters to Franz Boas. Correspondence in Franz Boas files. American Philosophical Society, Philadelphia, PA.

Terres, John
1980   The Audubon Society Encyclopedia of North American Birds. Alfred Knopf, New York.

Theodoratus, Robert
1989   Loss, Transfer, and Reintroduction in the Use of Wild Plant Foods in the Upper Skagit Valley. *Northwest Anthropological Research Notes*, 23(1):35–52.

Thom, Brian
2005   Coast Salish Senses of Place: Dwelling, Meaning, Power, Property and Territory in the Coast Salish World. Doctoral Dissertation, McGill, Montreal.

Thompson, Judy
1990   *An Ethnographic, Historic, and Archaeological Study of Prehistorically Built Rock Structures Using the Columbia Plateau of Washington State as a Test Case.* Bureau of Land Management, Spokane, WA.

Thompson, M. Terry and Steven Egesdal
2008   *Salish Myths and Legends. One People's Stories.* University of Nebraska Press, Lincoln.

Thompson, Stith
1966   *Tales of the North American Indians.* University of Indiana Press, Bloomington.

Thwaites, Reuben Gold, editor
1897a Hurons: 1636. In *Jesuit Relations and Allied Documents. Travels and Explorations of the Jesuit Missionaries in New France 1610–1791*. Volume X:167–168. The Burrows Brothers, Cleveland, OH.
1897b Hurons and Three Rivers: 1639–1640. In *Jesuit Relations and Allied Documents. Travels and Explorations of the Jesuit Missionaries in New France 1610–1791*. Volume XVII:197–201. The Burrows Brothers, Cleveland, OH.

Tollefson, Kenneth
1992 The Political Survival of Landless Puget Sound Indians. *American Indian Quarterly*, Spring:213–235.
1996 In Defense of a Snoqualmie Political Chiefdom Model. *Ethnohistory*, 43(1):145–171.

Tolmie, William Fraser
1963 *The Journals of William Fraser Tolmie: Physician and Fur Trader*. Mitchell Press, Vancouver, B.C.

Tooker, Elisabeth
1964 *An Ethnography of the Huron Indians, 1615–1649*. Bureau of American Ethnology, Bulletin 190, Washington, D.C.

Trigger, Bruce
1969 *The Huron Farmers of the North*. Holt, Rinehart and Winston, New York.
1976 *Children of Aataentsic: A History of the Huron People to 1660*. McGill-Queen's University Press, Montreal.

Turner, Nancy
1975 Food Plants of British Columbia Indians, Part 1, Coastal Peoples. *British Columbia Provincial Museum, Handbook* 34. Victoria, B.C.

Tweddell, Colin
1950 The Snoqualmie-Duwamish Dialects of Puget Sound Salish. *University of Washington Publications in Anthropology*, 12. Seattle.
1974 A Historical and Ethnological Study of the Snohomish Indian People. In *Coast Salish and Western Washington Indians* V, pp. 475–694. Garland Publishing, New York.

Underhill, Ruth
1945 *Indians of the Pacific Northwest*. Department of the Interior, Bureau of Indian Affairs, Branch of Education, Washington, D.C.

Usher, Jean
1971 The Long Slumbering Offspring of Adam: The Evangelical Approach to the Tsimshian. *Anthropologica*, 13(1–2):37–61.
1974 William Duncan of Metlakatla, a Victorian Missionary in British Columbia. *National Museums of Canada, Publications in History*, 5. Ottawa.

Vance, Joseph A.
1957 The Geology of the Sauk River area in the Northern Cascades of Washington. Doctoral dissertation, University of Washington, Seattle. University Microfilm International, Ann Arbor, MI.

Velten, H.V.
1939 Two Southern Tlingit Tales. *International Journal of American Linguistics*, 10(2/3):65–74.

1944   Three Tlingit Stories. *International Journal of American Linguistics*, 10(4):168–180.

Veniaminov, Ivan
1984   Notes on Islands of the Unalaska District. In *Alaska History*, 27, edited by Richard Pierce, and translated by Lydia Black and R. H. Geoghegan. Elmer E. Rasmusen Library Translation Program, Fairbanks, AK.

Walls, Robert
1987   *Bibliography of Washington State Folklore and Folklife*. University of Washington Press, Seattle.

Warren, William Whipple
1855   *History of the Ojibways, Based Upon Tradition and Oral Statements*. Minnesota Historical Society, St Paul.

Waterman, Thomas T.
1914   The Explanatory Element in the Folk-Tales of the North American Indians. *Journal of American Folklore*, 27(103):1–54.
1922   The Geographical Names Used by the Indians of the Pacific Coast. *Geographical Review*, 12(2):175–194.
1924   The Shake Religion of Puget Sound. In *Smithsonian Institution Annual Report for 1922*, pp. 499–507. Washington, D.C.
1973   Notes on the Ethnology of the Indians of Puget Sound. Museum of the American Indian, Heye Foundation, *Indian Notes and Monographs, Miscellaneous Series*, No. 59. New York, New York.

Waterman, Thomas T., and Collaborators
1921   Native Houses of Western North America: Museum of the American Indian, Heye Foundation, *Indian Notes and Monographs, Miscellaneous Series*, No. 11. New York.

Waterman, Thomas T., and Geraldine Coffin
1920   Types of Canoes on Puget Sound. Museum of the American Indian, Heye Foundation, *Indian Notes and Monographs. Miscellaneous Series*, No. 4. New York, New York.

Waterman, Thomas T., and Ruth Greiner
1921   Indian Houses of Puget Sound. Museum of the American Indian, Heye Foundation, *Indian Notes and Monographs, Miscellaneous Series*, No. 5. New York.

Waterman, T.T., and Alfred E. Kroeber
1919   Selected Readings in Anthropology. *University of California Syllabus Series*, No. 101. Prepared for Department of Anthropology, University of California, Berkeley and Department of Sociology, University of Washington, Seattle.
1938   The Kepel Fish Dam. *University of California Publications in American Archaeology and Ethnology*, 35(6):49–80.

Wehr, Wesley
2000   Helmi, Letters from Elma. *Columbia*, 14(2):24–31.

Welch, Jeanne
1983   The Kwalhioqua in the Boisfort Valley of Southwestern Washington. In *Prehistoric Places on the Southern Northwest Coast*, edited by Robert Greengo, pp. 153–167. Thomas Burke Memorial Washington State Museum, Seattle.

Weltfish, Gene
1971   *The Lost Universe, the Way of Life of the Pawnee*. Ballantine Books, New York.

Wessen, Gary
2011   The Daugherty 1947 Washington Coast Site List. *Journal of Northwest Anthropology*, 45(1):123–127.

Wickersham, James
1892   *A Plea for the Puyallups*, by A. Boston Tillicum. Privately printed.
1896   Pueblos on the Northwest Coast. *American Antiquarian*, 18:21–24.
1898   Nisqually Mythology, Studies of the Washington Indians. *Overland Monthly*, 32:345–351.
1899   Notes on the Indians of Washington. *American Antiquarian*, 21:269–375.

Wilkes, Charles
1845   *Narrative of the United States Exploring Expedition during the Years 1838, 1839, 1840, 1841, 1842*. Five Volumes. Lea and Blanchard, Philadelphia.

Wike, Joyce
1941   Modern Spirit Dancing of Northern Puget Sound. Master's Thesis, University of Washington, Seattle.
1952   The Role of the Dead in Northwest Coast Culture. In *Indian Tribes of Aboriginal America*, edited by Sol Tax, pp. 97–103. Proceedings of the International Congress of Americanists.

Willoughby, Charles
1889   Indians of the Quinaielt Agency, Washington Territory. In *Smithsonian Institution Annual Report for 1886*, pp. 267–282. Facsilime Reproduction, 1969, Shorey Book Store, Seattle, WA.

Wilson, Roy
1998   *Legends of the Cowlitz Indian Tribe*. Cowlitz Tribe, Bremerton, WA.

Witherspoon, Gary
1977   *Language and Art in the Navajo Universe*. University of Michigan Press, Ann Arbor.

Wray, Jacilee, editor
2002   *Native Peoples of the Olympic Peninsula: Who We Are*. University of Oklahoma Press, Norman.

Yoder, Janet, editor
1992   *Writings about Vi Hilbert, by her Friends*. Lushootseed Press, Seattle.

Younkin, Alice
1980   *Timber Bowl Valley*. The author, Medford, OR.

Ziontz, Lenore
1986a   Erna Gunther and Social Activism: Profit and Loss for a State Museum. *Curator*, 19(4):307–316.
1986b   The State Museum Comes of Age. *Washington Trust for Historic Preservation Landmarks*, 4(1):4–10.

INDEX

289

290

Festschrift in Honor
of Max G. Pavesic

Contributors:

Kenneth M. Ames
Keo Boreson
Jerry R. Galm
Thomas J. Green
Dana Komen
Dan Meatte
Carolynne Merrell
Susanne Miller
Susan Pengilly
Ken Reid,
Lori K. Schiess
Robert Yohe

This volume is dedicated to Max G. Pavesic and honors his long years of service to the anthropology and archaeology of the Northern Great Basin and Columbia Plateau. Max's professional career spanned more than four decades and included teaching and research experiences in California, the Great Basin, the Pacific Northwest, Canada, and England. The nine chapters in this volume reflect Max's long interest in radiocarbon dating and cultural chronology, in prehistoric mortuary behavior on the Southern Plateau and northern Great Basin, in the region's rich rock art record, and in the variable role that different types of artifact caches played in prehistoric lifeways.

Available at Amazon.com   204 pages
Paperback: $17.99   Max G. Pavesic bibliography

Journal of Northwest Anthropology, Memoir 7

Action Anthropology and Sol Tax in 2012: The Final Word?

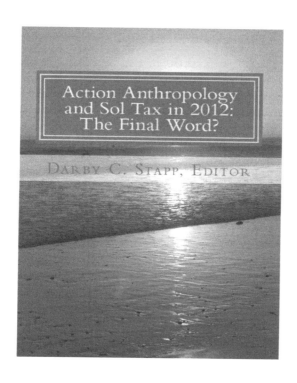

Contributors:

Joan Ablon
John H. Bodley
Marianna Tax Choldin
Douglas E. Foley
Susan Tax Freeman
Robert E. Hinshaw
Solomon H. Katz
Joshua Smith
Darby C. Stapp
Albert L. Wahrhaftig
Tim Wallace

Action Anthropology and Sol Tax are both important chapters in the development of contemporary anthropology and applied social science. Although unknown or forgotten by most, both continue to be revered and applied by a group of intellectual descendants who will not let die either the man or the approach to helping communities. In 2010 and 2011, former students, colleagues, the two Tax daughters—both academic professionals—and others came together to explore the relevance of Action Anthropology and Sol Tax to applied social science today. In reflecting on the history of the man and the intellectual tradition that he inspired, the authors document the many contributions made by Tax and his student-colleague cohorts. Using examples from contemporary applications, the contributors also demonstrate the present-day power of the ideas and approaches developed over the first 75 years.

Available at Amazon.com
Kindle Edition: $3.99
Paperback: $9.89

Journal of Northwest Anthropology, Memoir 8

Journal of Northwest Anthropology
Memoir Series

The *Journal of Northwest Anthropology* publishes occasional monographs and multi-author collections under the *Memoir* series. Those issued prior to 2005 appear as *Northwest Anthropological Research Notes Memoirs*. Authors interested in publishing through this series should contact the *Journal of Northwest Anthropology* ,<JONA@pocketinet.com>. The following are titles of the memoirs published to date:

Memoir 1 (1967)
An Examination of American Indian Reaction to Proposals of the Commissioner of Indian Affairs for General Legislation, 1967. Deward E. Walker, Jr.

Memoir 2 (1973)
Influences of the Hudson's Bay Company on the Native Cultures of the Colville District. David H. Chance

Memoir 3 (1976)
Quileute Dictionary. J.V. Powell and Fred Woodruff, Sr.

Memoir 4 (1978)
Flat Glass: Its Use as a Dating Tool for Nineteenth-Century Archaeological Sites in the Pacific Northwest and Elsewhere. Karl G. Roenke

Memoir 5 (1979)
A Bibliography of Idaho Archaeology, 1889–1976. Max G. Pavesic, Mark G. Plew, and Roderick Sprague

Memoir 6 (2002)
It's About Time (híiwes wiyéewts'etki), It's About Them (paamiláyk'ay), It's About Us (naamiláyk'ay): A Decade of Papers, 1988–1998. Michael S. Burney and Jeff Van Pelt, editors

Memoir 7 (2012)
Festschrift in Honor of Max G. Pavesic. Kenneth C. Reid and Jerry R. Galm, editors

Memoir 8 (2012)
Action Anthropology and Sol Tax in 2012: The Final Word? Darby C. Stapp, editor.

Memoir 9 (2014)
Rescues, Rants, and Researches: A Re-View of Jay Miller's Writings on Northwest Indien Cultures. Darby C. Stapp and Kara N. Powers, editors.

To purchase Memoirs 1 through 6, contact Coyote Press, P.O. Box 3377, Salinas, CA 93912. http://www.californiaprehistory.com. Memoirs 7, 8 and 9 available through Amazon.com.

Made in the USA
San Bernardino, CA
01 February 2014